T0328551

The Global Financial and Economic Crisis in the South

This book is a product of the CODESRIA South-South Programme.

The Global Financial and Economic Crisis in the South
Impact and Responses

Edited by

José Luis León-Manríquez
Theresa Moyo

Council for the Development of Social Science Research in Africa
DAKAR

© CODESRIA 2015

Council for the Development of Social Science Research in Africa

Avenue Cheikh Anta Diop, Angle Canal IV

BP 3304 Dakar, 18524, Senegal

Website : www.codesria.org

ISBN: 978-2-86978-637-0

All rights reserved. No part of this publication may be reproduced or transmitted in any form or by any means, electronic or mechanical, including photocopy, recording or any information storage or retrieval system without prior permission from CODESRIA.

Typesetting: Djibril Fall

Cover Design: Ibrahima Fofana

Distributed in Africa by CODESRIA

Distributed elsewhere by African Books Collective, Oxford, UK

Website: www.africanbookscollective.com

The Council for the Development of Social Science Research in Africa (CODESRIA) is an independent organisation whose principal objectives are to facilitate research, promote research-based publishing and create multiple forums geared towards the exchange of views and information among African researchers. All these are aimed at reducing the fragmentation of research in the continent through the creation of thematic research networks that cut across linguistic and regional boundaries.

CODESRIA publishes *Africa Development*, the longest standing Africa based social science journal; *Afrika Zamani*, a journal of history; the *African Sociological Review*, the *African Journal of International Affairs*, *Africa Review of Books* and the *Journal of Higher Education in Africa*. The Council also co-publishes the *Africa Media Review*; *Identity, Culture and Politics: An Afro-Asian Dialogue*; *The African Anthropologist*, *Journal of African Tranformation*, *Method(e)s: African Review of Social Sciences Methodology*, and the *Afro-Arab Selections for Social Sciences*. The results of its research and other activities are also disseminated through its Working Paper Series, Green Book Series, Monograph Series, Book Series, Policy Briefs and the CODESRIA Bulletin. Select CODESRIA publications are also accessible online at www.codesria.org.

CODESRIA would like to express its gratitude to the Swedish International Development Cooperation Agency (SIDA), the International Development Research Centre (IDRC), the Ford Foundation, the Carnegie Corporation of New York (CCNY), the Norwegian Agency for Development Cooperation (NORAD), the Danish Agency for International Development (DANIDA), the Netherlands Ministry of Foreign Affairs, the Rockefeller Foundation, the Open Society Foundations (OSFs), TrustAfrica, UNESCO, UN Women, the African Capacity Building Foundation (ACBF) and the Government of Senegal for supporting its research, training and publication programmes.

Table of Contents

Abbreviations

AAPSO	Afro-Asian People's Solidarity Organization
AfDB	African Development Bank
AFP	Armed Forces of the Philippines
AGP	Gabonese Press Agency
ALBA	Bolivarian Alternative for Latin America
AMIA	Mexican Automotive Industry Association
APDP	Automotive Production and Development Programme
APEC	Asia-Pacific Economic Cooperation
ARPU	Average Revenue Per User
ASEAN	Association of Southeast Asian Nations
BBC	British Broadcasting Corporation
BBEE	Black Based Economic Empowerment
BEAC	Banks of Central African States
BMV	Mexican Stock of Exchange
BOE	Bank of England
BOJ	Bank of Japan
BOK	Bank of Korea
BRICS	Brazil, Russia, India, China and South Africa
BSP	Central Bank of the *Philippines*
CARICOM	Caribbean Community
CAS	Central Asian States
CASE	Cairo and Alexandria Stock of Exchange
CASS	Chinese Academy of Social Sciences
CBN	Central Bank of Nigeria
CCP	Chinese Communist Party
CEA	United Nations Economic Commission for Africa
CED	Centre for Environment and Development
CEMAC	Economic and Monetary Community of Central Africa
CERAPE	Centre of Studies and Research on Economic Analysis and Policy
CGE	Computable General Equilibrium
CIA	Central Intelligence Agency, US
CIB	Congolese Industrial Bois

CMI	Chiang Mai Initiative
CMIM	Chiang Mai Initiative Multilateralization
CODESRIA	Council for the Development of Social Science Research in Africa
COMTRADE	United Nations Commodity Trade Statistics Database
COSATU	Congress of South African Trade Unions
CTCP	Clothing and Textile Competitiveness Programme
CUF	Cameroon Forest United
DRC	Democratic Republic of Congo
EBITDA	Earnings Before Interest, Taxes, Depreciation, and Amortization
ECB	European Central Bank
ECM	Error Correction Model
ECLAC	Economic Commission for Latin America and the Caribbean
ECOWAS	Economic Community of West African States
EESA	Emergency Economic Stabilization Act
EGG	Harvest Bonus and Operations Gabonese Timber
EPA	Economic Partnership Agreements
EVAT	Extended Value Added Tax
FAO	(UN) Food and Agriculture Organisation
FATA	Pakistan Federal Administered Tribal Areas
FCR	Frontier Crime Regulation
FDC	Forestry Data Centre
FDI	Foreign Direct Investment
FITA	Federally Administered Tribal Areas
FOB	Free On Board
FRG	Family Readiness Group
FSC	Forest Stewardship Council
FTA	Free Trade Agreement
G-20	Group of Twenty Finance Ministers and Central Bank Governors of major world economies
GDP	Gross Domestic Product
GFEC	Global Financial and Economic Crisis
GNP	Gross National Product
GSA	Global mobile Suppliers Association

GSMA	Global System for Mobile Association
IBRD	International Bank for Reconstruction and Development
IDC	Industrial Development Corporation
IFI	International Financial Institution
IFO	Forest Industry of Ouesso
IIFCL	India Infrastructure Finance Company Ltd
IMSS	Mexican Institute of Social Security
IMF	International Monetary Fund
IMU	Islamic Movement of Uzbekistan
IPAP	Industrial Policy Action Plans
ISI	Inter-Services Intelligence of Pakistan
ISR	Mexican Income Tax
IT	Information Technology
JSE	South African Johannesburg Stock Exchange
KIKO	Knock-in, Knock-out investments
KOSPI	Korean Stock Change
LAC	Latin America and the Caribbean
LDC	Least Developed Countries
M&A	Mergers and Acquisitions
MIDP	Motor Industry Development Programme
MILF	Moro Islamic Liberation Front
MNLF	Moro National Liberation Front
MPR	Monetary Policy Rate
MTN	South Africa-based multinational mobile telecommunications company
NAACAM	National Association of Automobile Component Manufacturers
NAAMSA	National Association of Automobile Manufacturers of South Africa
NAFINSA	Mexican Development Banking
NAFTA	North America Free Trade Agreement
NATO	North Atlantic Treaty Organisation
NBER	US National Bureau of Economic Research
NGO	Non-governmental organization
NIKKEI	Japanese Stock Market
NIPF	National Industrial Policy Framework

NSE	Nigerian Stock of Exchange
NUMSA	National Union of Metalworkers of South Africa
ODA	Official Development Assistant
OECD	Organisation of Economic Co-operation and Development
OEM	Original Equipment Manufacturers
OPEC	Organization of the Petroleum Exporting Countries
OSPAAAL	Organization of Solidarity with the People of Asia, Africa and Latin America
PEMEX	Mexican Oil Company
PFI	Private Finance Initiative
PGM	Platinum Group Metals
PPP	Public-Private Partnerships
PRC	People's Republic of China
RIO	Resign-Impeach-Oust process of President Joseph Estrada in the Philippines
ROK	Republic of Korea
SADC	Southern African Development Community
SEATO	South East Asian Treaty Organization
SEC	Securities and Exchange Commission
SIP	Strategic Industrial Projects
SME	Small and Medium Enterprises
SNBG	National Society of Gabon Wood
SOE	State-Owned Enterprises
STATSSA	Statistics South Africa
TCIDP	Textile and Clothing Industry Development Programme
TELMEX	Mexican Telephone Company
TFSA	Textile Federation of South Africa
TIA	Telecommunications Industry Association
TNC	Transnational Corporation
TUN	Tunisian Bourse
UK	United Kingdom
UN	United Nations
UNCTAD	United Nations Commission on Trade and Development
UNDP	United Nations Development Programme
UNECA	United Nations Economic Commission for Africa

UNICEF   United Nations Children's Fund
UNODC   United Nations Office on Drugs and Crimes
US   United States of America
VAT   Value Added Tax
WTO   World Trade Organization

Acknowledgements

This book is an outcome of the 'South-South Conference: The Global Financial and Economic Crisis and the South: Impact and Responses', which was held 17-18 May 2012 in Dakar, Senegal. The conference was jointly organized by the Asian Political and International Studies Association (APISA), the Latin American Council of Social Sciences (CLACSO) and the Council for the Development of Social Science Research in Africa (CODESRIA). The original papers presented at the conference have been thoroughly reviewed and updated in order to craft a comprehensive text on the effects of and responses to the global crisis in Africa, Asia and Latin America.

We are grateful to CODESRIA for its outstanding organization of the South-South Conference and for giving us a unique opportunity to co-edit this volume. In particular, Ebrima Sall, Executive Secretary, Carlos Cardoso, Head of Programme (Research), Alexander Bangirana (Head of Publications & Dissemination), and Sokhna Thiare (Bilingual Assistant). Your support and encouragement made the task that much easier.

To all of the colleagues who contributed chapters, this book would not have been possible without you. Thank you, everyone, for the cooperation and support. We learned a lot from you all; we deeply regret, however, that the Argentinean scholar Gastón Joaquín Beltrán, author of Chapter 2, passed away in 2013. Finally, we are grateful to an anonymous reviewer, whose comments have been very useful in improving the final version of the book.

Words are not enough to express the co-editors' mutual appreciation for the opportunity to work together. The healthy debate, e-dialogue and the intellectual engagement (and sometimes disagreement too), that always kept us focused and energized to push on, all contributed to the success of this work. Beyond rhetoric, we think this book is an epitome of the huge potentialities of South-South cooperation.

Theresa Moyo would like to thank her family that has been a pillar of strength. Special appreciation goes to her two daughters, Unesu and Atida-Melody for their unwavering support and confidence in her.

José Luis León-Manríquez would like to thank Carolina Mera, former coordinator of the International Relations Area at CLACSO, for her enthusiastic support to this project. He is also grateful to Eduardo Tzili, who provided helpful research assistance for the introductory chapter. Last, but certainly not the least, he is profoundly thankful to his wife Patricia González and his daughters, María and Ana Sofía, for their continuing love and understanding.

Our greatest hope is that this book will contribute significantly towards the agenda for rethinking development and the quest for alternative paradigms for a just, stable and equitable global political, economic and social system in which countries of the South have the space to chart their own destinies towards a better life for their peoples. A future where Africa, Asia and Latin America are emancipated from the shackles of hegemonic and anachronistic neoliberal dictates that have nothing more to offer other than crises, vulnerabilities and dependency.

Contributors

Terfa Williams Abraham is a Research Officer (Economist) at the Research Division of the National Institute for Legislative Studies, National Assembly, Abuja, Nigeria. His research fields are financial markets, public finance, climate change and development economics. An Associate Member of the Nigerian Economic Society (NES) and an individual member of the Council for the Development of Social Science Research in Africa (CODESRIA), he has participated in several internationally-funded conferences and workshops. His recent journal articles include: 'Testing the Relationship between Government Revenue and Expenditure: Evidence from Nigeria' (2012) and 'Impact of Public Expenditure on Climate Change in Nigeria: Lessons from South Africa' (2012).

Tanvir Aeijaz is Senior Assistant Professor in the Department of Political Science, Ramjas College, University of Delhi. He has been teaching development studies, public policy and governance to undergraduate and graduate students during the last 14 years. He is an adjunct faculty and associate fellow at the Centre for Multilevel Federalism (CMF) in the Institute of Social Sciences, New Delhi. Recently, he was awarded teacher's fellow at the Centre for Studies in Developing Societies (CSDS) for his work on public private partnership in the health care sector in India. He has been a visiting faculty member in the School of Development Studies for Post-graduate students at Ambedkar University, Delhi. He is joint secretary of the Delhi Chapter of the United Nations Educational, Scientific and Cultural Organization (UNESCO).

Gaston J. Beltrán passed away in October 2013 in Tolhuin, Argentina. He was a Professor at the University of Buenos Aires and Researcher for the National Council for Research in Science and Technology (CONICET). He held a PhD in Social Science from the University of Buenos Aires and was PhD candidate at the State University of New York (SUNY) at Stony Brook. He published several articles on such issues as business political action, economic elites and the role of economic experts. His areas of study included the problem of the limits of rationality in the decision-making processes, as well as the economic crisis and the spread of political economic ideas through the globe. He published, among other books, *Los intelectuales liberales. Poder tradicional y poder pragmático* and *¿Qué hacen los sociólogos?*

Horace G. Campbell holds a joint Professorship in the Department of African-American Studies and the Department of Political Science, Maxwell School, Syracuse University. He is a Special Invited Professor at Tsinghua University, Beijing. He has just published *Global NATO and the Catastrophic Failure in Libya* (Monthly Review Press, 2013). His previous book was *Barack Obama and 21st Century Politics: A Revolutionary Moment in the USA* (Pluto Press, 2010). He is also the author of *Reclaiming Zimbabwe: The Exhaustion of the Patriarchal Model of Liberation*, and *Pan Africanism, Pan Africanists and African Liberation in the 21st Century*. His most famous book, *Rasta and Resistance: from Marcus Garvey to Walter Rodney* is going through its eighth printing. He has published more than 40 journal articles and a dozen monographs as well as chapters in edited books.

Maxwell Chanakira is a telecommunications and management consultant who has worked in the academic and telecommunications sectors of SADC countries for over twenty years. He holds a doctorate in Organizational Leadership from Tshwane University of Technology, South Africa, and has presented and published over 20 papers on strategy issues in telecommunications, energy and development in Africa. He lectures on Strategy and Organisational Leadership at the Harare Institute of Technology, Zimbabwe. His research interests focus on strategy and leadership in private, public and multilateral organizations in Africa as they relate to telecommunications, energy and development.

José Luis León-Manríquez holds a PhD in Political Science from Columbia University, New York. His research interests include international relations and economic development in Latin America and East Asia. He was a member of the Mexican Foreign Service and Deputy Director of the Matías Romero Institute of Diplomatic Studies. He has been consultant for Asia-Pacific Economic Cooperation (APEC) and the United Nations Development Programme (UNDP). A worldwide lecturer, he is editor or author of nine books and more than 100 book chapters and journal articles. His newest edited book is *China Engages Latin America. Tracing the Trajectory*. Currently, he is a Professor in the Department of Politics and Culture of Universidad Autónoma Metropolitana (UAM), Mexico City.

Bertrand Mafouta is Director of Training and Communication and Researcher at the Centre for Studies and Research on Analysis and Economic Policy (CERAPE), a research centre based in Congo Brazzaville. He holds two Master's degrees in Human Resource Management and in International

Economic Relations. He works on issues of poverty, entrepreneurship, the timber industry and HIV/AIDS. He is member of research networks such as the African Economic Research Consortium (AERC), the Agence Universitaire de la Francophonie (AUF) and the International Development Research Centre (IDRC).

Theresa Moyo is a Senior Lecturer at the Turfloop Graduate School of Leadership, University of Limpopo where she lectures in Development Theory and Practice and Research Methodology. She holds a PhD degree in Economics and has 20 years' lecturing experience at university level (University of Limpopo and University of Zimbabwe). She has published widely in the areas of economic policy and development, particularly on issues of structural adjustment programmes, trade, industrialization and gender. She has edited a CODESRIA book on *Re-thinking Trade and Development In Africa*. She has also published several book chapters and journal articles. Over the last three years, she has been a trainer on the UNDP Gender and Economic Policy Management Initiative (GEPMI).

Pablo Alejandro Nacht is a PhD candidate at the Latin American School of Social Sciences (FLACSO) in Buenos Aires, Argentina. He got his Master's degree in International Economic Relations and his undergraduate degree in Political Science in the University of Buenos Aires. He is Reseacher at the Institute Studies of Historic, Economic, Social and Foreign Affairs (IDEHESI). His main research focus is on contemporary political, economic and defence relations of China with Latin America and Argentina. He has been visiting scholar in academic institutions in Norway, Germany, Cuba and the Dominican Republic.

Hidayet Siddikoglu was born in Afghanistan. He is a PhD student at the Graduate School for International Development and Cooperation, Hiroshima University, Japan. He holds a Master's degree in International Politics from Hiroshima University. He was director of Ipakyol, a privately-owned company based in Hiroshima, Japan. Between 2007 and 2009 he created, under Ipakyol, a project to support unemployed Afghan refugees by providing jobs, particularly to refugee women who were skilled carpet weavers.

Rolando Talampas teaches graduate Philippine and Asian Studies courses at the Asian Center, University of the Philippines at Diliman (UPD). He has written extensively on Philippines' trade union history, health issues and migration. He compiled and co-edited *Khutba on Disability and Inclusive Development* (2011) for an AusAid initiative in Muslim Philippines. He was research fellow of the Southeast Asian Studies Regional Exchange Program (SEASREP). He has presented papers at conferences in Europe, Southeast Asia and the United States. Rolando Talampas received his Bachelor's and Master's degrees in Asian Studies from UPD. Currently, he is working on his PhD dissertation. He is also engaged in UPD Asian Center's research projects on the Indonesian diaspora in southern Philippines and a comparative study of social health in Thailand, Vietnam and China.

List of Tables, Figures and Maps

PART I

BACKGROUND TO THE GLOBAL FINANCIAL
AND ECONOMIC CRISIS

1

The Global Financial and Economic Crisis: Origins, Effects and Responses in the Global South – An Overview

José Luis León-Manríquez

The Global Crisis: Four Reasons and Two Mechanisms of Transmission

Recent economic literature generally converges in the idea that there are four fundamental explanatory variables of the Global Finance and Economic Crisis (GFEC), also known as 'Great Recession'. The main independent variables of the crisis that officially started in 2008 were: a) scanty regulation of the financial system after the fall of the Bretton Woods monetary order in 1971; b) lack of information and conflict of interest because of incentives and excessive risk-taking and fraudulent behaviour, which in turn is a result of the failure of economic and financial models; c) presence of typical factors linked to financial crises, such as a credit boom and a real state bubble, especially in sub-prime mortgages and toxic credits; and d) 'spillover' or 'contagion effects' triggered by increasing interdependence in the global financial sphere (Roubini 2008: Stiglitz 2009, 2010; Acharya et al 2009).

Another consensus is that the crisis started in the US but was swiftly transmitted to the rest of the world via two main channels: international trade and the financial system. As noted by Eaton et al (2011), during 2008-2009 trade as a share of global GDP fell 30 per cent. This was due largely to the decline in demand for durable goods, which accounted for over 80 per cent of the global decline in trade relative to GDP in those years. Bagliano and Morana (2010) also highlight the importance of trade as a transmitter of the recession, particularly in durable goods' manufacturing and exporting. In analyzing a sample of 50 countries, the authors found that the US crisis had a significant impact in decreasing trade from Latin America and Southeast Asia.

Regarding financial contagion, Imbs (2010) argues that global financial integration reached a threshold that makes the system vulnerable to specific impacts. That reflects an interdependent banking system such that any local shock may have a global scope. One factor that made the Great Recession so deep and widespread was the very nature of international banking integration, which led to unprecedented transmission of financial instability. According to the OECD (2012), 'contagion through international banking occurs when banks in a given country respond to deteriorations in their balance sheet by reducing cross-border loans, including vis-à-vis clients in countries that are not directly exposed to the initial financial shock'. The role of spillover effects via the financial channel had also been extensively discussed well before the GFEC by Marxist economists such as Magdoff (1987).

The Great Recession in Historical Perspective: Implications and Future Scope

According to the International Labour Organization (ILO 2010), between 1970 and 2008 the world underwent 124 systemic banking crises, 208 currency crises, 63 sovereign debt crises, 42 twin crises, 10 triple crises and a global economic recession every ten years. In addition, the global economy experienced large shocks in commodity prices (two lofty impacts caused by increased oil prices in the 1970s, and the effects of rising food and energy prices in the early 2000s).

Given this evidence, a key question arises: what has made this crisis different from previous economic turmoil? To answer this question, it seems necessary to clarify the concepts of recession and depression. The limits between one and another are still imprecise, even for economists. While economic literature usually defines recession as two or more quarters of declining real GDP, there is no consensus on this point. For instance, the US National Bureau of Economic Research (NBER) usually supports the above definition, but sometimes includes other variables, such as the performance of real Gross Domestic Income (GDI).

Regarding depressions, the NBER does not identify them separately. Instead, the NBER business cycle chronology recognizes the dates of peaks and troughs in economic activity. Thus they refer to 'the period between a peak and a trough as a contraction or a recession, and the period between the trough and the peak as an expansion. The term depression is often used to refer to a particularly severe period of economic weakness' (NBER 2013).

On the basis of the above definitions, at least three specificities of the Great Recession deserve further discussion: 1) its depth and scope with respect to previous crises during the twentieth and twenty-first centuries, 2) its dynamic nature, which has affected different regions and countries in a successive and unequal fashion, and 3) the ability of the Global South to either evade or cushion the worst effects of the GFEC. Let us discuss briefly each of these three points, understanding that this is just a small appetizer within a much larger intellectual feast.

Regarding the first point, Imbs (2010) has conducted research that identifies patterns of synchrony of industrial production cycles with global crises since 1980. He finds a very negative variation in industrial output during this period after 2008. Imbs adds that the cyclic correlation is more pronounced for OECD countries than for emerging and developing economies. It is therefore possible to argue that despite recurring crises in the global economy in the last decades, the GFEC has been the first truly global recession since the end of World War II.

However, as shown in Figures 1.1 and 1.2, the scale of this crisis in terms of GDP growth has been significantly lower than the Great Depression but deeper that any other world crisis after 1945. Figure 1.1 shows clearly that the global economic recovery from 1929 was far from linear. In fact, the worst years were not 1929 and 1930, but those corresponding to the Second World War. As can be seen, the effects of the Great Depression prevailed for a decade and a half. It took a world war and a complex Fordist-Keynesian political and economic agreement to overcome the Great Depression. The new phase of growth and stability would last until the 1970s (Marglin and Shorr 1990).

There are many similarities between the Great Depression and the more recent Great Recession, albeit differences are superior. As Almunia et al (2009) emphasize, those two economic upheavals were originated in the United States and became global through financial and trade channels. Authors like Krotayev & Tsirel (2010) put forward an optimistic view, ensuring that the recent recession has not been as severe as the Great Depression. They understand the GFEC as a temporary fall between two peaks of the upswing in the 5th Kondratieff wave, and not as the starting point in the border of a K-wave, just as the 1929 Great Depression was. According to other scholars (Keohane & Nye 1989; Kindleberger & Aliber 2011: 15–18), bounded economic damage has to do with the changing nature of international political economy, which is extremely sensitive to market fluctuations, but still less vulnerable as a result of successive agreements to deal with international crises. The experiences of 1970, 1985, 1994, 1997 and 2001 have created a sort of a collective knowledge, very useful to deal with economic downturns.

Figure 1.1: Evolution of the World's GDP Annual Growth Rates
(per cent), 1871-2007

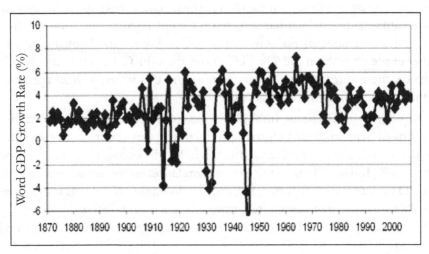

Source: Korotayev and Tsirel 2010: 6

Figure 1.2: Economic Performance in Selected Economies 1920-2011
GDP Growth (per cent)*

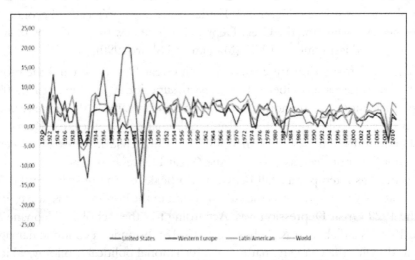

*   From 1920 to 2000, the data is in 1990 International Geary-Khamis million dollars.
    From 2000 to 2011, the data is in current US dollars.

Source: World Bank 2013; GGDC 2013

Yet the GFEC is far from over. Although there is not much talk of this, the current global crisis is still an open file. There is no guarantee that the Great Recession will not bring further economic decline in the coming years. This argument is based on Table 1.1 which shows that the global crisis has affected successively different geographical areas and countries. As the epicentre of the crisis, the US was harshly shaken in 2008 and 2009, when it experienced negative growth rates. The US economy resumed growth in the ensuing years, but a complete recovery is far from granted. After GDP growth of -4.3 per cent in 2009, in 2010 and 2011 the EU seemed to restart its sluggish but acceptable growth of recent decades. However, the onset of European sovereign debt crisis, that started in 2010, again brought the EU to negative growth in 2011. Consecutive 'crises within the crisis' have beleaguered countries like Greece, Ireland, Spain, Portugal and Cyprus. The recession is clearly reflected in high unemployment rates, which by February 2013 affected 17.5 per cent of the labour force in Portugal, 23.9 per cent in Spain and 26.4 per cent in Greece (Eurostat 2013).

China and India, two of the three Asian giants (the other being Japan, trapped in a resilient recession since the early 1990s), featured a remarkable performance during the initial phase of the GFEC in 2008 and 2009. The dynamic growth in China contributed to the global economic recovery in those critical years. Hence the PRC was considered a key player in the new global economic architecture (IMF 2009; Lin 2011). Beijing's initiative of trading in local currencies and discarding US dollars in its transactions with Russia, Japan and Brazil was seen by some as a promising sign of an impending reform to the international financial system.

China seemed to be gaining the ability to 'decouple' from the crises in the United States and EU, thus fulfilling a forecast made by The Economist (2006). This prediction addressed the changing balance of the global economy and the emergence of the PRC as an alternative engine of the world economy in the following terms:

> As America's housing boom threatens to turn into a bust, many forecasters expect household spending to stall. A few even worry that America could come perilously close to a recession in 2007. Previous American downturns have usually dragged the rest of the world economy down, too. Yet this time its fate will depend largely upon whether China and the other Asian economies can decouple from the slowing American locomotive.

This possibility appeared imminent until 2011. But as long as economic drought in the United States and the European Union remains, China's exports to these entities have begun to slow and will necessarily affect the PRC's. This reality is readily reckoned by Chinese policy makers. As very few things in China are random, the 12th Five-Year Plan 2011-15, approved in October

2010, foresees that China will reduce its double-digit economic growth to an average of 8 per cent per annum, will lower energy consumption by 16 per cent, and will foster domestic consumption. While nobody expects negative rates for the immediate future, falls in the range of 2-3 per cent in the Chinese GDP would undoubtedly help reduce global demand and raw material prices.

This brings us to the third and final portion of our appetizer. The afore mentioned Table 1.1. and Figure 1.3 show that, with the exception of Japan, Asia has recorded very high growth rates since 2008. Latin America, in turn, was much less affected than during the external debt crisis in 1982-1983 – let alone the Great Depression. While in 2009 the region recorded a growth rate of -1.5 per cent, large economies like Argentina and Brazil were above that average. Africa, meanwhile, did not experience an immediate drop, but falling demand in China and the Eurozone precipitated a slight negative growth in 2011.

Figure 1.3 : World Economic Performance in Selected Regions, 1950-2008 GDP Growth (per cent)*

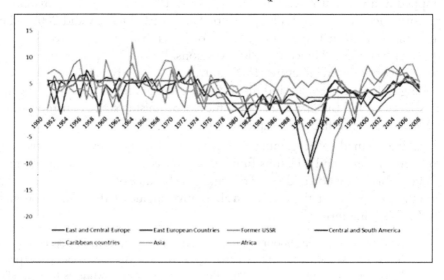

* In million 1990 International Geary-Khamis dollars

Source: GGDC (2013)

Table 1.1: World Economic Performance 2000-13

Selected regions and countries

	2000	2001	2002	2003	2004	2005	2006	2007	2008	2009	2010	2011	2012	2013*
United States	4.2	1.1	1.8	2.6	3.5	3.1	2.7	1.9	-0.4	-3.5	3.0	1.7	2.2	1.7
Asia+	5.9	5.5	5.9	8.1	8.3	9.2	9.8	10.6	6.2	7.4	9.2	7.4	5.4	4.8
East Asia & the Pacific	7.5	6.7	7.9	8.8	9.0	9.8	10.9	12.3	8.5	7.5	9.7	8.3	7.5	6.2
South Asia	4.2	4.4	3.8	7.3	7.6	8.7	8.7	9.0	3.9	7.4	8.6	6.5	3.3	3.3
China	8.4	8.3	9.1	10	10.1	11.3	12.7	14.2	9.6	9.2	10.4	9.3	7.7	7.9
Japan	2.3	0.4	0.3	1.7	2.4	1.3	1.7	2.2	-1.0	-5.5	4.4	-0.7	2.0	0.6
European Union	3.9	2.1	1.3	1.5	2.5	2.1	3.3	3.2	0.3	-4.3	2.2	1.5	-0.3	0.6
Eurozone	3.8	2.0	0.9	0.7	2.2	1.7	3.2	3.0	0.4	-4.4	2.1	1.5	-0.6	0.3
Latin America and the Caribbean	4.0	0.3	-0.4	2.1	6.1	5.0	5.8	6.0	4.3	-1.5	6.2	4.7	3.1	3.9
Africa	3.5	3.1	3.3	3.8	6.1	5.1	5.8	6.0	4.8	2.9	4.7	-0.7	5.7	4.7
Middle East and North Africa	3.4	2.6	3.3	3.5	6.2	4.7	5.5	5.9	4.7	3.6	4.2	-6	7.5	4.4
Sub-Saharan Africa	3.6	3.6	3.2	4.1	5.9	5.5	6.1	6.1	4.8	2.2	5.1	4.7	3.9	5

* Forecast. + Average of East Asia and the Pacific and South Asia ~ Average of North and Sub-Saharan Africa (includes the Middle East)

Source: World Bank (2013); European Commission (2012); DESA (2013)

The ability of many of the Global South economies to cushion the negative effects of the crisis in 2009 was due largely to the economic performance of China and India, whose growth was around 9.6 per cent and 5.7 per cent respectively. As has already been mentioned, China made a special contribution to the recovery of world trade in 2009-10, insofar as its imports grew 22 per cent. By contrast, US imports fell 16.5 per cent and European imports plummeted 14.5 per cent in the same *annus horribilis* (WTO 2010, 2011).

If the scenario of a substantial decline in Chinese growth finally materializes, it will affect, to varying degrees, those countries in Africa, Latin America and Southeast Asia that had benefited from the boom in commodity prices in the 2000s (León-Manríquez 2011). If the economies of the US and the EU do not resume substantial growth in the coming years, and if GDP in China and India falls further than official forecasts predict, one can expect a considerable impact on the Global South – that would lead to the possibility of a deepest and most synchronized phase of the GFEC. If that is indeed the case, the thesis of 'decoupling' will be discarded. Overwhelming global economic links will not allow any country or region to eschew the new crunch. Soon we will know how plausible this scenario is.

Keynes to the Rescue: Worldwide Responses to the Great Recession

> *The ideas of economists and political philosophers, both when they are right and when they are wrong, are more powerful than is commonly understood. Indeed the world is ruled by little else. Practical men, who believe themselves to be quite exempt from any intellectual influences, are usually the slaves of some defunct economist.*

John Maynard Keynes (2003 [1936])

For the sake of analytical simplicity, some economic publications characterized responses to the GFEC with phrases like 'we are all Keynesians now' (The Economist 2009). Yet, there was a division in the orthodox quarters between The Economist's almost Taoist acceptance of Keynes' rebirth and the reluctance of die-hard neoliberal economists to undertake any expansionary strategy to circumvent it. In an open letter to the then new US President Barack Obama (published in the New York Times on 28 January 2009 and financed by the libertarian Cato Institute), dozens of orthodox US economists, including some Nobel prizewinners, insisted on implementing the old recipes of Reaganomics and Thatcherism to overcome the crisis:

> Notwithstanding reports that all economists are now Keynesians and that we all support a big increase in the burden of government, we the undersigned do not believe that more government spending is a way to improve economic perfor-mance... To improve the economy, policymakers should focus on reforms that

remove impediments to work, saving, investment and production. Lower tax rates and a reduction in the burden of government are the best ways of using fiscal policy to boost growth.

The old separation of Cambridge versus Chicago reappeared. Who won this round in the North? What kind of anti-crisis policies were implemented in the Global South? To answer these questions, there is no better resource than reality itself. The International Labour Organization (ILO 2010) investigated the kind of policies implemented by different governments to mitigate the effects of the crisis. Unlike the 1980s and 1990s, Keynesian Cambridge won this time, as the bulk of economic strategies were countercyclical, designed to mitigate the effects of the unavoidable downturns of the capitalist system. However, the ILO found that mixed and even liberal policies were also implemented, although in a less ambitious fashion. Policy choices varied in different countries or regions depending on the GFEC's scope as well as the specific sectors affected by it.

Those countries that resorted to Keynesian countercyclical measures did so by implementing three kinds of actions: a) monetary bailouts and injections into the financial system aimed at re-establishing credit flows, b) interest rate cuts to stimulate investment and loans, and c) additional public expenditure to shore up aggregate demand. A sample of 20 low- and middle-income countries (ILO 2010) found that the most common policies were the support for small and medium enterprises (70 per cent of the countries did this), the reduction of interest rates (75 per cent), the implementation of deposit warranty schemes or other measures to protect the financial sector (75 per cent), and the increase of public investment in infrastructure (100 per cent). Such measures prevailed over the creation of public employment (20 per cent), support of migrant workers (30 per cent) or the provision of 'green jobs' (10 per cent). Tax cuts were also universally applied.

All in all, countercyclical policies were implemented in most countries. The US, epicentre of the crisis, undertook remarkable Keynesian measures. Perhaps more by necessity than by choice, the United States nationalized financial institutions like Fannie Mae and Freddie Mac, recapitalized banks and devoted significant resources to boost infrastructure, science, health, energy, education, training the workforceand protection to the most vulnerable social groups. Between 2008 and 2010 the amount of successive fiscal stimulus packages amounted to almost 5 per cent of GDP, despite Republican opposition and the open letters of neoliberal think-tanks'.

The G-20 and emerging countries also dressed in countercyclical clothes. As Paul Krugman (2010) wrote, Asia went Keynesian. Together with India and South Korea, the PRC was a quintessential example of aggressive fiscal policies. By late 2008 and early 2009, analysts were concerned that the plummeting demand from the US and EU would affect Chinese exports and growth. In March 2009 the World Bank forecast China's annual growth at 6.5 per cent, while Morgan Stanley estimated 5.5 per cent. Despite such 'gloomy' prognoses, China deployed a vigorous strategy, mostly based on the promotion of its huge internal market. Taking advantage of abundant reserves, China's policymakers designed a comprehensive stimulus package. The Chinese fiscal policy included both existing and new economic initiatives, rolling out massive infrastructure projects, tax breaks, green energy programmes, and the promotion of spending in the countryside. State-owned banks issued loans amounting to a stunning US\$ 660 billion just in the first three months of 2009. The stimulus strategies bore fruits promptly: by June 2009, IFI and consulting firms had raised their forecasts for the Chinese economy. At the end of the year, GDP grew 9.2 per cent, less than the 9.6 per cent of 2008, one of the highest growth rates in the world. In 2010 annual growth returned to double digits.

The worldwide heterodox responses to the GFEC have brought healthy consequences for economics as a discipline. In the 1970s and 1980s, this field began to be dominated by the theses of Hayek (1944), Friedman (1980), and other liberal and even libertarian thinkers such as Nozick (1974). Under the motto 'governs best who governs least', they claimed that the political modality more suited to economic prosperity was a minimal state. Such a state should only fulfil certain functions essential for growth: adjudication of justice, enforcement of private property rights, and provision of public goods. These assumptions, applied in the economic reforms in developing countries, were the backbone of the 10 points of the Washington Consensus, which included privatization, trade openness and de-regulation, among other measures of economic policy (Williamson 1990).

The Great Recession may not be the end of capitalism, but it certainly has affected neoliberal hegemony within economic theory. The late development economist Albert O. Hirschman (1981) coined the term 'monoeconomics' to criticize the belief that there is only one economics (just as there is only one chemistry), applicable to all countries and at all times. That very idea is now under stress. Fortunately for the social sciences, schools of economic thought that had been declared extinct by the neoclassical tsunami have gained new legitimacy. Not only has Keynesianism performed a vigorous comeback, but Marxism, neo-Marxism, dependency, development economics and structuralism are being seriously discussed again. An unexpected gift from the GFEC has been 'letting a hundred flowers bloom and a hundred schools of thought contend', as the Maoist dictum requested (not too successfully, however) in 1956.

Impacts and Responses in the Global South: Overview of this Book

What have been the consequences of the GFEC in the South? There is a large body of literature on the causes and responses to the global crisis in the North. Inasmuch as the crisis started in the US and later affected the EU, plenty of publications and conferences have been devoted to studying these actors. Economic agencies of the UN system have also published abundant analyses of the effects of the crisis in Africa, Asia and Latin America. There is also a generous amount of works on specific national cases, both in the North and South. Less attention, however, has been set on the comparative discussion of the effects of the crisis upon the Global South. This is precisely the main goal of this book.

The bulk of the chapters included herein examine the crisis, its effects and responses within the traditional chasm between neoliberals and Keynesians. Only a few works apply, implicitly or explicitly, Marxist approaches and dependency theories. As Theresa Moyo's concluding chapter contends, the empirical studies in this book show a significant heterogeneity in the Global South. Case studies include a diversity of developmental trajectories: the sample encompasses G-20 members, middle-income countries with high shares of manufacturing exports and outstanding penetration in the world market; economies based on the export of commodities, and post-war societies whose main source of income is development aid. In order to organize the discussion, and bearing in mind this diversity, the editors have chosen an approach predominantly based on geographic, political and social similarities.

The book is divided into five parts which, in turn, comprise a total of 13 chapters. After this introduction, the next three sections are devoted to analysing the impacts and responses to the global crisis in Latin America, Asia and Africa, respectively. The last part includes an overview of policy alternatives to the crisis, as well as a discussion of the main findings, lessons and proposals derived from reading the book. It should be noted that, like many other phenomena in the social sciences, the division of the world into continents and sub-continents is a construct. To that extent, it is unavoidable that the countries and regions studied here will feature very different characteristics. Yet, this diversity is also a source of the richness, as long as it entails a possibility of disciplinary and geographic cross-fertilization. This was the spirit of the South-South Conference and the publication of this book, both sponsored by CODESRIA. The following paragraphs explain, in some detail, the hypotheses, contents and main findings of each chapter.

The second part of the book is focused on discussing the GFEC and its scope in Latin America and the Caribbean. Starting the discussion, the late Gastón J. Beltran criticizes what he considers a fallacy of *secundum quid* or hasty generalization. Beltran argues that the Great Recession, far from being a process with the same roots and impacts throughout the global economic and financial system, was actually a crisis bred in the North with several implications for developing countries. After providing an operational concept of globalization, the author explores the political and economic effects of the economic recession in Latin America. In his multilevel analysis, Beltran identifies three different trajectories of the crisis in the region. According to him, Central America and Mexico suffered more the effects of the crisis than South American countries, due to overdependence on a faltering US economy. He also posits that state capacity seems to be an important instrument for dealing with the crisis.

In Chapter 3, José Luis León-Manríquez undertakes a comparative study of the diverging responses of Mexico and the Republic of Korea (ROK) to the GFEC. The two economies share such similarities as their rank in the world economy, parallel experiences in trade liberalization and a generous share of manufacturing exports. Their top technocrats attended the same graduate schools of economics in the US. These coincidences notwithstanding, the ROK and Mexico embarked on opposite responses and outcomes. While the former underwent a rapid recovery from the negative effects of the turmoil, the latter recorded its deepest economic decline since the Great Depression. According to the author, the diverging performances can be explained by two main factors: the coherence and drive of monetary and fiscal policies and the broader context of economic integration. Mexico's overdependence on the US market and half-hearted implementation of stimulus packages contrast with Korea's trade diversification in East Asia and vigorous fiscal policies.

Chapter 4 is the last chapter in the Latin American section. Written by Pablo Alejandro Nacht, its title is, 'The global crisis and the arrival of the Dragon in Latin America and the Caribbean'. Nacht frames the discussion of current Sino-Latin American relations in the global division of labour. The author argues that, although many Latin American countries (LAC) with nationalist or left-wing ideologies prefer the so-called 'Beijing Consensus' over the familiar 'Washington Consensus', LAC will barely benefit from a hypothetical consolidation of the first. Accordingly, the reemergence of China induces countries like Argentina, Brazil and Chile opting for neo-extractive economies based on commodity exports. For Mexico, the Central American countries, and the industrial sectors in South America, China's industrial clout means fierce competition in manufacturing of low and medium technological intensity. This asymmetry between the PRC and LAC makes it difficult to think about 'South-South' cooperation between both parties.

The third part of the book deals with the national and sectoral effects of the GFEC in some African countries. In Chapter 5, Terfa Williams Abraham analyses the degree of integration of African stock exchanges with those in the North and the South. Responding to the general survey question: 'Would the consequences of the 2007-2009 Global Financial Crisis be minor if the integration of African stock markets were tilted towards countries of the global South?', the author criticizes the lack of empirical evidence to measure the susceptibility of African countries to external shocks via stock markets. Abraham investigates the integration among stock exchanges in Nigeria, Tunisia, Egypt and South Africa with the United States, the United Kingdom and Japan. Contrary to the 'conventional wisdom' on the issue, Abraham finds that some countries would be better off integrating with the Global South, but some others would strengthen their economies by increasing integration with the Global North. Both possibilities would certainly entail a degree of vulnerability to external shocks.

In Chapter 6, Theresa Moyo takes the discussion away from the financial markets to the real economy. Her contribution scrutinizes the impacts of the GFEC on South Africa and its response to the crisis. In so far as South Africa is one of the most industrialized countries in Africa, Moyo studies three key manufacturing sectors: automobiles, textiles and mining. After a thorough statistical research, the author makes it evident that the recession affected all of the three sectors equally, in so far as they are closely linked to global production chains and markets. The author acknowledges that the South African government's response to the crisis was resolute and comprehensive. Gathered under the umbrella of a 'Framework Agreement', the wide panoply of responses included countercyclical fiscal and monetary policies as well as industrial and trade policies. Moyo ends her text with a set of recommendations for improving the South African economy; she strongly advocates increasing the technological intensity of exports.

In yet another comparative case study, Bertrand Mafouta's Chapter 7 assesses the effects of the GFEC on the timber industry of three African countries: Congo, Cameroon and Gabon. The author states that gold aside, the terms of trade of African commodities have been facing a major deterioration. Although China's purchases of Central African timber have been growing continuously since 1994, European countries still account for 60 per cent of these countries' wood exports. Hence, decreasing demand from the EU precipitated a crisis in Africa's timber industry. There were massive job losses, tropical plywood prices dropped 20 per cent at the end of 2008 and timber firms underwent serious financial troubles. Mafouta analyses the measures taken by African governments to offset the worst effects of the crisis. He posits that these measures may have been effective in the short term, but will be useless if demand of wood keeps on declining. The chapter closes with some recommendations aimed at enhancing this sector's productivity.

In Chapter 8, Maxwell Chanakira studies the influence of the Great Recession upon the African telecommunications industry. The general opinion that Africa would be 'decoupled' from the crisis, because of its limited integration to the global financial system, proved to be incorrect.

Chanakira contends that the telecommunications sector is an increasingly important sector of the continent's economy. The author explains the nature of the African crisis in an attempt to debunk it from general overviews; he finds that Africa's GDP suffered a 2 per cent drop in 2008. Then he illustrates the increasing importance of the telecommunications industry and conducts an investigation through the annual reports of five transnational telecommunications operators in Africa in order to evaluate the impacts of the GFEC. Chanakira concludes that the most harmful effects took place in 2009, suggesting a time lag between the effects of the global crisis in the advanced economies and Africa. Chanakira advocates further regulation and improved services in this sector.

The fourth part deals with the impacts of the global crisis in Central, South and Southeast Asia. In Chapter 9, Rolando Talampas expounds the experiences of the Philippines in the Asian crisis of 1997 and the recession of 2008. His hypothesis is that both economic and financial uncertainties have undermined Philippines' state capacities. As long as policymakers have not learned the lessons of recurring crises, he states that yet another crisis of even greater magnitude may hit his country. While the author acknowledges that the Philippines were able to overcome the worse effects of the Thai baht devaluation in 1997, the country's conditions deteriorated afterwards. Something similar happened in 2008. Despite the tax reforms and social policies pushed by President Gloria Arroyo in the 2000s, in the end the Philippine government relied too much on remittances from migrant labour. Talampas identifies 'roller coaster' cycles caused by the perverse interaction between economy and politics. The outcomes have been stagnant employment, bad income distribution and resilient inflation.

As argued above, the studies of the impacts of the recession focus primarily on developed countries and developing ones. Very few studies have dealt with GFEC effects on less developed states in a post-conflict situation. In Chapter 10, Hidayet Siddikoglu reviews three countries in South and Central Asia. Due to the US war on terror after 9/11, Afghanistan, Pakistan and Tajikistan acquired a central role in global security. These countries' political instability, extremist movements, poor governance, rampant drug-trafficking and enduring geopolitical tensions have been boosted by the global recession. Siddikoglu argues that, while other countries of the Global South have undergone economic turmoil as a result of decreasing exports or financial contagion from the North, this Asian 'triangle' has suffered from plummeting economic aid from the developed countries. This fact has undermined the limited gains that had been made in the construction of enhanced political governance and stronger economies.

Chapter 11, written by Tanvir Aeijaz, addresses a strategy that some countries have launched for streamlining the provision of social services, curbing fiscal crises and avoiding privatization. In Public-Private Partnerships (PPPs), the governments transfer part of their responsibility for the provision of public goods to private companies. As a case study, the author uses the emerging structure of PPPs in the public health system in India. He focuses on the potential clash between private initiative's primary goal of capital accumulation versus the distribution and efficient use of wealth pursued by the government. Aeijaz argues that PPPs may be useful if enough accountability is ensured. The author observes that India has been one of the least affected countries by growth deceleration, and adds that its fiscal package has been one of the largest, as a percentage of GDP, within the G-20. Despite such developments, Aeijaz argues, in its 11th Five-Year Plan (2007-12) India has pressed hard to push PPPs as the new face of development.

The book's closing section contains two articles on political and economic alternatives to the global crisis. In Chapter 12, Horace G. Campbell focuses on China's social transformations and their implications for global change. The author argues that, for decades, the West has been attempting to undermine any social progress in the South. The economic institutions of the Bretton Woods system have brought new forms of colonialism and imperialism. Campbell states that China, the Association of Southeast Asian Nations (ASEAN), the BRICS and the Bolivarian Alternative for Latin America (ALBA) are facing the same adverse attitude from the West. The author gives the example of China's relations with Africa, which have been labelled as 'new colonialism'. But in China and African quarters, Campbell argues, that relation is appreciated as a form of South-South cooperation that still represents the spirit of Bandung. Thus, Campbell is optimistic about the potential scope of the Bank of the South and the Chiang Mai Initiative.

In Chapter 13, Theresa Moyo recalls the original logic of the book and beefs up its main convergences, divergences and findings. Issues include the deep causes of the crisis and its effects on the different regions and economies of the Global South; the transmission channels of the GFEC to emerging and developing countries, and the implications of the crisis in terms of present and future strategies and policies in the South. Moyo identifies some common characteristics of the crisis. At the same time, she finds variations in the mechanisms of transmission, affected sectors and countries' responses. The explanatory factors of these differences have to do with the extent of integration with the US and Europe, the diversification and composition of exports, state strength to buffer external shocks, the shape of economies prior to the onset of the GCEC, and the diverging countries' economic policies. At the end of her chapter, Moyo recommends reducing the external vulnerability of the Global South, strengthening state capacity for running the economy and providing social services, and enhancing South-South cooperation.

References

Acharya, V.V., Philippon, T., Richardson, M., and Roubini, N., 2009, 'Prologue. A Bird's Eye View. The Financial Crisis of 2007-2009: Causes and Remedies', in V. V. Acharya and M. Richardson, eds, *Restoring Financial Stability. How to Repair a Failed System*, New York: NYU Stern School of Business and John Wiley & Sons. .

Ali, S., Dadush, U., and Falcao, L., 2009, Financial Transmission of the Crisis: What's the Lesson? Washington: Carnegie Endowment for International Peace. June 17. Available at http://carnegieendowment.org/2009/06/17/financial-transmission-of-crisis-what-s-lesson/ner.

Almunia, M., Bénétrix, A.S., Eichengreen, B., O'Rourke, K.H., and Rua, G., 2009, *From Great Depression to Great Credit Crisis: Similarities, Differences and Lessons*, NBER Working Paper No. 15524, National Bureau of Economic Research, November.

Bagliano, F.C., and Morana, C., 2010, *The Great Recession: US Dynamics and Spillovers to the World Economy*, ICER Working Papers – Applied Mathematics Series No. 34. International Centre for Economic Research.

DESA, 2013, World Economic Situation and Prospects 2013, United Nations: Development Policy and Analysis Division. Available at: http://www.un.org/en/development/desa/policy/wesp/index.shtml.

Eaton, J., Kortum, S., Neiman, B., and Romalis, J., 2011, *Trade and the Global Recession*. NBER Working Paper No. 16666, National Bureau of Economic Research, January.

European Commission, 2012, European Economic Forecast, Directorate-General for Economic and Financial Affairs, Commission Staff Working Document. Available: http://ec.europa.eu/economy_finance/publications/european_economy/2012/pdf/ee-2012-7_en.pdf.

Eurostat, 2013, *Unemployment Statistics*, European Commission Eurostat, February. Available at: http://epp.eurostat.ec.europa.eu/statistics_explained/index.php/Unemploy- ment_statistics.

Friedman, M. and Friedman, R., 1980, *Free to Choose. A Personal Statement*, New York: Harcourt Brace Jovanovich.

Hayek, F. A., 1944, *Road to Serfdom*, Chicago: University of Chicago Press.

Hirschman, A.O., 1981, *Essays in Trespassing: Economics to Politics and Beyond*, New York: Cambridge University Press.

ILO, 2010, *The Great Recession of 2008-2009: Causes, Consequences and Policy Responses*, Employment Working Paper No. 61, Geneva: International Labour Office.

Imbs, J., 2010, 'The First Global Recession in Decades', *IMF Economic Review* 58 (2).

IMF, 2009, 'China's Leadership Key in Global Economic Recovery and Reform, IMF Managing Director Dominique Strauss-Kahn Says', International Monetary Fund: Press Release. Available at: http://www.imf.org/external/np/sec/pr/2009/pr09408.htm.

Keynes, J. M., 2003 [1936], *The General Theory of Employment, Interest, and Money*, Adelaide: University of Adelaide Library Electronic Text Collection.

Kindleberger, C.P. and Aliber, R.Z., 2011, *Manias, Panics and Crashes. A History of Financial Crisis*, Sixth Edition, New York: Palgrave McMillan.

Keohane, R.O. and Nye, J. Jr., 1989, *Power and Interdependence. World Politics in Transition*, Little. Brown and Company.

Korotayev, A.V., and Tsirel, S.V., 2010, 'A Spectral Analysis of World GDP Dynamics: Kondratieff Waves, Kuznets Swings, Juglar and Kitchin Cycles in Global Economic Development, and the 2008-2009 Economic Crisis', *eJournal of Anthropological and Re- lated Sciences*, Institute for Mathematical Behavioral Sciences. University of California, Vol. 4.

Krugman, P., 2010, 'Keynes in Asia', *New York Times*, 24 July.

León-Manríquez, J. L., 2011, 'China's Relations with Mexico and Chile: Boom for Whom?', in J. L. León-Manríquez, and A. H. Hearn, eds, *China Engages Latin America. Tracing the Trajectory*, Boulder: Lynne Rienner Publishers.

Lin, J.Y., 2011, 'China and the Global Economy'. *Asia's Role in the Post-Crisis Glob- al Economy Conference*, World Bank: San Francisco Federal Reserve Bank. Paper for Remarks. Available at: http://siteresources.worldbank.org/DEC/Resourc- es/84797-1104785060319/598886-1104852366603/599473-1223731755312/ JustinLin-China_and_the_Global_Economy-SF-Fed-final.pdf.

Magdoff, Harry, 1987, *Stagnation and the Financial Explosion*, New York: Monthly Review Press.

Marglin, S.A. and Schor, J.B., 1990, *The Golden Age of Capitalism: Reinterpreting the Postwar Experience*, Oxford and New York: Oxford University Press.

NBER, 2013, 'The NBER's Business Cycle Dating Procedure: Frequently Asked Questions', National Bureau of Economic Research. Available at http://www.nber.org/cycles/reces- sions_faq.html.

Nozick, R., 1974, *Anarchy, State, and Utopia*, New York: Basic Books.

Reyes Guzmán, G. and Moslares García, C., 2010, 'La Unión Europea en Crisis: 2008-2009'. *Problemas del Desarrollo. Revista Latinoamericana de Economía* 41 (161).

Roubini, N., 2008, 'The Coming Financial Pandemic', *Foreign Policy*, Washington: Mar/Apr. Issue 65.

Stiglitz, J.E., 2009, *The Financial Crisis of 2007/2008 and Its Macroeconomic Consequences*, Working Paper, New York: Initiative for Policy Dialogue.

Stiglitz, J. E., 2010, 'Lessons from the Global Financial Crisis of 2008'. *Seoul National University, Seoul Journal of Economics*, 23 (3).

The Economist, 2006, 'The Alternative Engine', *The Economist*, 19 October.

The Economist, 2009, 'Keynesian Principles. This House Believes We Are All Keynes- ians now', *The Economist*, 10 March. Available at: www.economist.com/debate/days/ view/276.

Williamson, John, ed., 1990, *Latin American Adjustment: How Much Has Happened?*, Washington, DC: Institute for International Economics.

World Bank, 2013, GDP *Growth (Annual %)*. The World Bank Data. Available at: http://data.worldbank.org/indicator/NY.GDP.MKTP.KD.ZG

WTO, 2010, *World Trade Report 2010. Trade in Natural Resources*, World Trade Organization.Available at: http://www.wto.org/english/res_e/booksp_e/anrep_e/world_trade_report10_e.pdf.

WTO, 2011, *World Trade Report 2011. The WTO and Preferential Trade Agreements: From Coexistence to Coherence*, World Trade Organization. Available at: http://www.wto.org/english/ res_e/booksp_e/anrep_e/world_trade_report11_e.pdf

PART II

THE CRISIS IN LATIN AMERICA:
ORIGINS, RESPONSES, CONNECTIONS AND
COMPARISONS

2

The Financial Crisis, its Diverse Economic Effects and Responses from Latin America: A Global Crisis?

Gastón J. Beltrán

Introduction

This chapter was written in two different phases and with a focus on interconnected but also different goals. It was initially thought of as a cold description of the effects of the 2007-2008 financial crises on the Latin American region. The aim was to show how the crisis spread through the region, and also to identify its consequences as well as the responses of governments in the region. As an outcome of this first goal, I arrived at three main conclusions: a) in Latin American terms, the crisis was far from being 'the worst in history' as many analysts had put it; b) although negative effects could be traced in most cases, it was inaccurate to talk about a single crisis for the region as a whole; and c) it seemed that rather than being a *global* process it was a crisis which originated in the North but with heterogeneous effects over the Latin American region – and this diversity could be explained by the local characteristics of each country.

These three conclusions lead to a set of questions that, eventually, became the second goal of this text: to debate the actual *global* scope of the crisis and to open a discussion about what globalization means from a South-South perspective. The argument suggests that the specific form of the crisis and its impacts were different from what most analyses of the crisis produced in the North have predicted. First of all, the correlation between the crisis in the North and the crises in the South was (at least in some areas) less than expected: the crisis heavily affected some countries but had a weaker effect on others. Second, the responses to the crisis were not exactly the same throughout the region: compared to past crises, national governments showed greater room for making political decisions. The argument suggests also that this crisis was not, in essence, different from other financial crises that previously originated in the world capitalist system. However, the main and very important difference was that it started in the North and not in the South, as the typical 'crisis of globalization' of the 1990s did – including the Mexican crisis (or tequila, 1995), the Asian crisis (1997), the Brazilian crisis (or samba, 1999), and the Turkish and Argentina ones (2001-02).

What was striking about the 2007-08 crisis was the 'globality' of its categorization and that was, in my view, largely because it originated in the United States. Due to the dominance of the US and, indeed, the North in terms of global power relations, that characterization was promoted for obvious reasons. I argue that calling the crisis 'global' is not only inaccurate; it also moves the focus of who was primarily responsible for the crisis in a sort of 'Fuente Ovejuna' effect.[1]

In other words: while the Mexican, Brazilian, Turkish and Argentina crises were seen as the consequence of these countries' mistakes, the term 'global' seems to address no one but the system as a whole as the cause of the crisis and, in that way, it actually exonerates those who were fundamentally responsible.

In order to address the above issues, this chapter is divided into three parts. First, I will provide a general definition of the term 'globalization' because that will be useful to set the discussion around the scope of the crisis and the meaning of the term from a South-South perspective. I will also define the main characteristics of the financial crisis and its main effects over the Latin American region. In the second section, I will analyse how the crisis arrived in the region, identifying its effects in different sub-regions and countries; I shall argue that differences had to do with a set of economic and institutional variables as well as the political responses of key local actors. Finally, I will open a discussion on the meaning of globalization for the South and the consequences of thinking global processes exclusively as a North-South relationship.

Methodological Approach

This chapter is based on data from two different sources. Firstly, it is based on secondary data on the economic and political evolution of the Latin American countries between 2007 and 2011. Data are available at public statistics offices and international institutions such as the United Nations (UN), the International Monetary Fund (IMF), the Economic Commission for Latin America and the Caribbean (ECLAC), and the Organisation for Economic

Co-operation and Development (OECD). I used these data in order to create a typology which classified the countries of the region according to how the crisis affected them and how they responded to it.

The second source was based on in-depth interviews conducted between 2008 and 2011 in several countries of the region with experts (economics, sociologists and policy makers) with the aim of understanding the situation of the countries and the effects of the financial crisis both at the macro and micro level. Interviews were conducted in Argentina, Bolivia, Paraguay, Chile, Peru, Colombia, Dominican Republic, Ecuador, Venezuela and Costa Rica.

By combining quantitative and qualitative sources, this chapter seeks to show how, with the large and complex Latin American region, homogeneity and heterogeneity coexist.

Theoretical and Conceptual Framework

The chapter explores the thinking in three areas of conceptual debate:

a) the discussion on the scope and meaning of the crisis;

b) the meaning of globalization, its consequences and effects and, also, its connection with the current notion of crisis; and

c) the sociology of development, focusing on the problems of state formation, autonomy and capacity as well as the problem of political decision-making.

Sociology of crisis (Holton 1987) opens a set of relevant questions concerning the issues of this chapter: What is a crisis? How can we distinguish crisis from normality? What does crisis imply at the macro and micro levels? A crisis is a deep change in the structures of a given society. It may be economic, institutional, cultural, social or all of these together. Usually, a period of crisis implies that going back to the previous situation is not possible or is very complicated. A crisis, to this extent, changes the general situation of a society and opens a period of great uncertainty. Generally, it includes both an objective and a subjective dimension: on the one hand, it is possible to identify a set of indicators of the crisis; on the other hand, it is also explained by the way the population 'reads' the critical situation. In fact, as soon as the population interprets a condition as critical, new microeconomic strategies emerge, deepening even more the already existing situation. Finally, there is a critical question concerning what causes the crises and how countries respond to them. Although globalization theory tends to assume that both causes and responses may be explained by external forces, others suggest that internal factors are critical to explaining them. Gourevich (1986), for instance, argues that each country's responses to crisis depend on the characteristics of dominant sectors within this country, meaning the context and the type of coalitions created in this particular context.

The scope and meaning of globalization will be discussed in the next section. Globalization is considered in relation with the problem of crisis based on two assumptions: a) it implies a greater level of exchange and contact among countries increasing the possibility of global crises that are 'contagious'; b) processes (effects and its responses) exist that are greatly homogeneous – in the extreme, this implies that the crises may assume the same form in different places around the world. This second assumption will be discussed and questioned here.

Finally, the concepts connected with the sociology of development will be discussed in the last section. The argument presented here is that national states still matter and that decisions made by national governments have effects both in the way the global crisis affects local economies as well as the way local economies deal with its effects. In other words: globalization has homogenizing effects, but the level of transnational convergence is weaker than mainstream theory argues (Guillén 2001).

Literature Review

Castells (1996) argues that in the latter part of the twentieth century, a new economy emerged around the world. This new economy is characterized by three main features: a) productivity and competitiveness are a function of knowledge generation and information processing; b) firms and territories are organized in networks of production, management and distribution; c) the core economic activities are global – i.e. they have the capacity to work as a unit in real time on a planetary scale (Castells 2001: 52)

Castells defines globalization as a specific process taking place in a specific time, adding some precision to the more common definitions: a shorthand way of describing the spread and connectedness of production, communication and technologies across the world. That spread has involved the interlacing of economic and cultural activities. Although globalization, in the sense of increasing connectivity in economic and cultural life across the world, has been happening for centuries, the current situation is fundamentally different from what has happened before. The speed of communication and exchange, the complexity and size of the networks involved, and the sheer volume of trade, interaction and risks give what we now label as globalization a peculiar force (Smith and Doyle 2002).

Globalization has not been described only as increased interconnections, but also as the source of important political changes. According to this view, poorer, 'peripheral', countries became even more dependent on activities in 'central' economies where capital and technical expertise tend to be placed. There has also been a shift in power away from the nation state and toward multinational corporations (Beck 2004).

Economic globalization is measured in terms of international trade and foreign direct investment (FDI); political globalization is measured in terms of international organizations and international treaties and collaborations; and social globalization is measured in terms of telephone lines, personal travels, personal transfers of money, transnational families and the number of internet users. As Ortiz (2004) points out, it is necessary to distinguish between 'globalization' and 'worldlization'. According to him, what became globalized are the market and the technology, while the culture goes through a process of 'wordlization'. Due to this distinction, it is possible to differentiate a process that can be assumed as an economic and technological strategy for the expansion of corporations, from another that projects a net of ideas and representations through cultural industries. This second process appears in everyday life.

Although this distinction is important for a better understanding of the global processes, the most dynamic and visible aspect of globalization is the transformation of the financial system. In fact, the exchange of goods has reached only a fraction of the dynamism shown by the financial system due in part to the high levels of protectionism in the core countries.

This is one of the reasons why globalization is usually equated with financial globalization. From this point of view, globalization can be described as a process led by the developed countries and the bigger multinational corporations. From a financial viewpoint, two-thirds of the population became even more marginalized than in the past, as 71 per cent of the origin and 85 per cent of the destiny of financial flows is concentrated in the northern hemisphere (World Investment Report 2011).

The discussion about globalization frames the debate about the relationship among nations as well as North-South relations. The base of this debate is the increasing dependency among states and societies on a worldwide scale. This assumes that decisions and activities in one part of the planet have effects on societies far away from them. When talking about interconnection and its effects, most theories describe the processes taking place at the economic and financial level rather that in the cultural sphere. Thus, globalization is usually seen as the spread of capital, rules and values from the North to the South. Therefore, when globalization is thought of as a one-way process, the northern countries are usually thought of as the active ones while the southern countries are thought of as passive/receptive.

There is not, of course, agreement on this point. In fact, a good deal of the more interesting debates on globalization discusses the way globality and locality intersect. Giddens (1990: 64), for instance, has described globalization as 'the intensification of worldwide social relations which link distant localities in such a way that local happenings are shaped by events occurring many miles away *and vice versa*'. Interestingly, the *vice versa* side of globalization had captured much less attention than the worldwide effects of the interlink processes.

For this reason, analyses of globalization which primarily focus on assessing its effects on the developing world have tended to focus on identifying its threats to these economies. The literature distinguishes five negative consequences of globalization: a) unequal distribution of the advantages, b) incomplete globalization because only some factors (not including labour, for instance) became globalized; c) absence of coherence in macroeconomic policies in attending to local issues and demands; d) weakening of political institutions to regulate the processes and to discipline capital; and e) problems derived from financial globalization.[2]

Globalization represents a complex process of intensification of both the economic and cultural interlinks among nations. Economic globalization is critical for the Global South as it defines the types of relations that are established with the North. Globalization, however, does not need to be thought of as a one-way process but may include a more interactive and proactive set of relationships among nations.

In the next section, before opening a discussion on the conceptual and political consequences, I will discuss the main characteristics of the financial crisis of 2007 and 2008 and its effects on Latin America.

The Financial Crisis and its Effects on Latin America

The financial crisis that began in 2007 was produced by the interplay of valuation and liquidity problems in the United States banking system. The bursting of the US housing bubble caused the values of securities tied to US real estate pricing to plummet, damaging financial institutions globally. Problems regarding bank solvency, declines in credit availability and investors' confidence impacted on global stock markets, where securities suffered large losses during 2008 and 2009. Economies worldwide slowed during this period. Although there have been aftershocks, the financial crisis itself ended sometime between late-2008 and mid-2009.

The crisis was characterized as the worst since the early 1980s recession with negative 2009 growth for the US, the Eurozone and the UK. With a recession in the US and the increased savings rate of US consumers, growth elsewhere has been also affected: in 2009 the decline in GDP was -2.7 per cent in the US, -5.6 per cent in Germany, -6.2 per cent in Japan, -4 per cent in the UK and -6 per cent in Mexico (International Monetary Fund).

The effects of this crisis on Latin America are still being debated. However, when the current crisis and previous ones are compared, two conclusions can be extracted. First, the results as well as the responses were heterogeneous and there was not a single regional pattern that explains the crisis. Second, at least for some countries, the crisis was less severe than expected and the path to recovery was faster compared to past experiences such as the debt crisis in the 1980s and the financial crises of the late 1990s. From a Latin American perspective, the 2007-08 financial crisis produced a set of clearly negative consequences, but it was less drastic than what had been foreseen during 2007. What is more important: the crisis was not interpreted as such by the populations of many Latin American countries – in part, because the parameter for what a 'real' crisis means is higher in the region than in other regions of the world. In conclusion, the 'global' 2007-08 crisis had its more severe effects in the North, when it originated, and the way in which it spreads to the South depended on the type of relationships the southern countries previously had with the northern ones – i.e., Mexico and most Caribbean countries, more dependent on the US economy than those from the South, were more directly and deeply affected by the crisis (see León-Manríquez 2013).

Different Realities, Different Impacts: the Heterogeneity of the Crisis in Latin America

Looking at the Latin American countries and their different realities allows a better understanding of why the crisis did not hit the whole world with the same intensity. Although sharing a set of common features (their peripheral position, lack of industrial development, high degree of social inequality and the weakness of the financial system among others), there are very different realities within Latin America. Differences have to do with divergent historical developments, political dynamics and economic structure.

In the context of the crisis, a set of variables became critical in explaining the different effects, performance and responses that emerged throughout the region. The first variables are economic: the type of goods produced in each country, the level of diversification of the economy and the variety of market allocations for the exports were key during the process. The second set of variables is linked to the political dimension. They include the political orientation chosen by the governments, their options in terms of public policy and the capacity of each state to act autonomously. To this extent, both political decision-making and state capacity were critical in defining the type of responses. Generally speaking: the stronger the capacity to define autonomous responses, the greater the chances to escape from the negative effects of external threats. In fact, in the context of the crisis, more or less dynamic and aggressive responses implied different performances during and after the crisis. However, state capacity does not itself explain the political options: Mexico, for instance, is an example where the absence of state intervention was rather the result of an ideological-political orientation than the result of lack of state capacity.

Different performances show that the crisis did not have equal effects on the whole region. In fact, some countries were severely affected (for instance, in terms of domestic consumption and GDP growth). From these countries, some recovered very fast while others (such as Mexico and Costa Rica) took a longer period of time to get back to their pre-crisis condition. In other countries, on the other hand, the effects were less severe. In some cases, like in Colombia, the crisis was less severe because it hit gradually; in others (like Argentina, Chile and Peru) this was because both the price of primary goods and low dependence on the US market counterbalanced the negative effects.

Taken together, both economic and political variables explain the diversity of situations that can be traced throughout the region. At the same time, they show to what extent crises, and the possibilities of avoiding them, are the result of a complex combination of different factors.

Size of the economy and type of production: While some countries have benefited from their export position due to the rise in the prices of food (Argentina and Brazil), oil (Brazil, Bolivia, Mexico and Venezuela) and mining (Chile and Peru), others did not (ECLAC 2011). Clearly, producers of commodities with high international prices were in a better position. This position was fueled by the growing demand from Asia, which also explains why these countries diversified their markets in the last decade. The strongest global position of these diversified their markets in the last decade. The strongest global position of these countries, then, was more the result of an increase in the demand from China than the outcome of a national trade strategy. In any case, it was the turn towards Asia which produced the impulse of these economies and reduced their vulnerability in relation to the US market. While in 2000 China accounted for just one per cent of Latin America's exports, by 2010 it accounted for 8 per cent of exports. Also, Asia as a whole increased its participation from 3.5 to 15 per cent, becoming more important than Europe (and behind the US and the region) (ECLAC 2012). Therefore, mid-size countries like Peru, Chile or Argentina, were in a better position to face the crisis than a much bigger economy like Mexico.

The reality was very different in another set of countries of smaller size and located closer to the influence of the US economy. Particularly, those countries from the Caribbean and some from Central America were not producers of those primary goods that were boosted by the price rise. They were not oriented to the Asian markets and were highly dependent on the demand from the US economy.[3] As a result, their economies were more fragile and vulnerable not only to external shocks but, even more important, to the fluctuations of the US economy.

Thus, while the producers of primary goods from the South had benefited since 2000 from the increase in the value of the products they export, in Central America and the Caribbean the importance of these types of products decreased. Therefore, the performance of the sub-regions of Latin America was linked to the participation of primary and non-primary goods in the export baskets of each country. In South America, in the last decade, prices showed greater increase than exported volume. Conversely, in Central America and the Caribbean that were less favored by the increase of commodity prices, exports grew more in volume. If during the 1990s the dynamic of exports was defined by the increase in the volume, in the 2000s the incidence of prices was higher (ECLAC 2012).

Level of diversification of export allocation: Diversification of markets seems to be one of the recipes to avoid global crises. The more diversified the markets, the lower the risks of being affected by the negative performance of a key economic partner. In the case of Latin America, the region was historically highly dependent on United States politics and economy. Being the 'backyard' of the US meant having a constant dispute over political and economic autonomy. Due to some political processes inherent to the region and to the shift in the foreign policy of the US, there occurred a change in this situation in the last two decades. Part of this change had to do with the relative position of the Asian countries in the global economy, which became one of the main destinations for Latin American exports. Under these circumstances, some Latin American countries were able to diversify their markets. The Peruvian case is pertinent: after signing the Trade Promotion Agreement with the United States, their exports diversified equally among the US, European and the rest of the markets.

However, as the table shows, the level of autonomy regarding the US economy is not equal throughout the region. While the bigger countries from the South (particularly Brazil, but also Chile and Peru) have diversified their markets, the countries from the north of Latin America are still highly dependent on the United States economy – not only due to the smaller sizes of their economies, but also the geographical proximity to the US, like in the case of Mexico.

Figure 2.1: Exports by Region and Destination per cent of value
exported by destination)

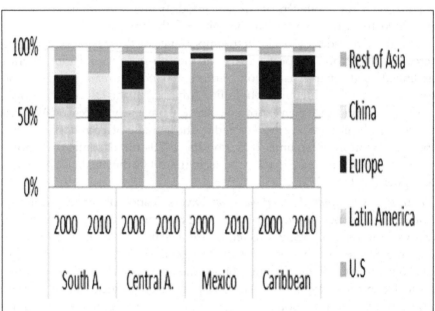

Source: ECLAC 2012

Mexico and the Caribbean, the two sub-regions more dependent on the
US, felt the crisis more deeply than the rest of the region. In the case of
Mexico, the country suffered a decline in its exports to the US and a drop
in remittances, and this ultimately had a negative effect on domestic demand
(León-Manríquez 2013). As León-Manríquez argues, since the signature of
NAFTA in – 1994, Mexico focused its exports on the United States market.
By 2009, this constituted around 80 per cent of the country's total exports.
Such level of concentration increased Mexico's vulnerability, which was even
worse since the crisis originated from its main trading partner.

A similar situation faced the Caribbean countries such as Dominican
Republic and, to a lesser extent, the Central American ones such as Costa Rica.
In the case of Costa Rica, the retraction of US demand implied a different
transmission process as compared to Mexico. In the case of the Dominican
Republic and other countries of this sub-region, remittances are among the
main economic resources and the drop in remittance flows affected not only
their economies as a whole, but also the domestic economies of families.

As a consequence, in Central America and the Caribbean, the effects of the US crisis were much more severe than in those countries that had diversified their markets. Depending on just one economy was critical for those countries that, at the same time, were not able to produce goods that would allow them to look for new markets when the crisis hit them.

Size of the economy, type of goods produced and level of diversification of the markets are three key economic variables. They are not always acting together, as there are countries which are highly dependent on the US but their economies are among the bigger and more sophisticated of the region (like Mexico); and others whose economies are smaller but have a more diversified export basket than others from the same size (like in the case of Uruguay). So, if each of these variables is taken separately, it would not explain the difference in performance; if they are taken together, they provide a better understanding of the differences.

The economic features of each country help to understand the diverse effects of the crisis. However, the *political* capacity of these countries is perhaps the most critical aspect that explains not only their fragility, but the type of responses they followed during and after the crisis. At the same time, the economic causes of the crisis show to what extent the crisis was not 'global' but originated in the US.

State capacity: State capacity can be decomposed into two broad dimensions. The first one is an intrinsic component, namely, the cohesiveness of the state as a strategic actor which can formulate and implement policy in a coherent fashion. The second is an extrinsic component, which is the state's ability to extract performance from private firms (Wade 1990; Chibber 2003). Both components were critical in allowing governments to take autonomous decisions. In the case of Latin America, the lack of state capacity has been a historic trait; this capacity was further reduced between the 1970s and 1990s. Although in the 2000s some countries made some efforts in order to reinforce the state's position, this political shift did not mean a higher level of institutionalization but the existence of more powerful governments. The change was limited, but it gave some countries more room for manueuvre when facing critical decisions. The difference can be found not in the institutional capacity but in the political strength of each country vis à vis their northern counterparts. During the crisis, those countries with more powerful states were able to use wider instruments of political economy than weaker states. Nevertheless, lack of state capacity is still a common feature that characterizes the whole region.

Orientation of public policies: Different conceptions on the orientation of public policies led to different responses to the crisis. Although there is wide agreement at the macroeconomic level (fiscal balance, surplus, savings, etc.)

differences emerged in the way governments define whether the state should intervene in the economy or not. In countries like Brazil and Argentina, state intervention was the core of the government agenda. In spite of the lack of state capacity and the weakness of political institutions, those governments defined instruments of political economy in order to regulate the markets and behaviours of the economic actors. During the crisis, some forms of state intervention were adopted in practically the whole region while some countries (Mexico, and to a lesser extent, Costa Rica and Peru) decided to follow more orthodox paths. Basically, those countries that decided to follow more interventionist strategies defined more dynamic responses to the crisis, expressed, among other indicators, in the levels of public spending.

The types of strategies followed by these countries are part of an on-going process of debate on the orthodox alternative and its consequences during the 1990s. As part of this debate, some countries like Argentina, Brazil and Venezuela led a shift in the region towards more Keynesian policies, while others like Mexico, Chile and Peru stayed closer to the orthodox view. The case of Mexico is interesting, because here the orthodox conception was so strongly rooted that even when facing the worst stage of the crisis, government officials decided to stay on this course without introducing important modifications – as was done in Chile, where the state played a leading role by injecting money from its reserves into the economy.

In terms of policies then, the region also shows great variety. There are at least three groups of countries: those that are critical of liberal orthodox policies and have moved towards a new type of Keynesianism; those that are 'orthodoxically' orthodox; and those that have applied a more flexible orthodox view on the economy.

The Crisis in the Latin American Countries

Taking both the economic and political variables into consideration, it is possible to say that Latin America shows at least two very different realities that explain the different levels of performance existing in the region. Then, Latin American countries can be grouped as follows:

a) *Those that belong to South America:* They have relatively diversified economies, numerous and relatively developed internal markets, and an export position that has improved in the last decade. Although they are still exporting mainly commodities, the destination of their sales has been diversified, reducing their dependency on the economy of the United States. Some of them have oriented their policies towards a stronger position of the state compared to the previous decade and, in most cases, they have reached a high level of political stability,

b) *A set of smaller countries, most of them located in Central America and the Caribbean:* With some exceptions (like Costa Rica) the production is not diversified and neither are their markets: they have the United States practically as the only destination of their exports. Also, they do not produce the type of primary goods (energy, mining and food) that have shown a greater increase in prices during the last decade. Finally, the fact that a high percentage of families in these countries live on remittances increases their dependence on the United States. In these countries, the states generally have lower capacity of intervention and have not developed regulatory policies.

c) *Mexico is a hybrid case:* It is, on the one hand, one of the biggest economies of Latin America. It has a highly diversified basket of export products and is a big producer of oil, one of the goods that explain the growth of the region in the last ten years. However, at the same time, Mexico's exports are concentrated in the US and hence it shares the same vulnerabilities as the much smaller economies of the Central America and Caribbean sub-region.

To make this distinction is important as the crisis was much more severe in the second set of countries (plus Mexico) than in the first. This was not only because of the size of their economies but also due to a set of locally defined variables: the type of state and the type of intervention, the availability of regulatory policies and the responses of local actors. Differences among countries help to explain the extent to which the 'global' scope of the crisis is not equal under any circumstances, but dependent on a set of critical local characteristics of each nation.

In fact, the more severe effects of the crisis were evident in the countries closer to the US. The effects were deeper in the second semester of 2008 and the first of 2009, producing a drastic reduction in GDP. The cut in exports to the US, the impact of declining tourism, and the reduction in remittances were among the main causes of the fall. In countries like El Salvador, Honduras and Guatemala, the level of activity was sustained during this period through public expenditure, though state intervention was confined to injecting money into the market in order to maintain the level of consumption.

Most countries were hit by the crisis in 2009 and then showed some degree of recovery in the next years. However, the impact of the crisis and the rhythm of the recovery vary among them.

Table 2.1: GDP Year-to-Year Variation (2007-11)

South America	2007	2008	2009	2010	2011
Argentina	8.7	6.8	0.9	9.2	8.9
Uruguay	6.5	7.2	2.4	8.9	5.7
Peru	8.9	9.8	0.9	8.8	6.9
Chile	4.6	3.7	–1.0	6.1	6.0
Colombia	6.9	3.5	1.7	4.0	5.9
Ecuador	2.2	6.4	1.0	3.3	8.0
Brazil	6.1	5.2	–0.3	7.5	2.7
Bolivia (Plurinational State of)	4.6	6.1	3.4	4.1	5.2
Paraguay	5.4	6.4	–4.0	13.1	4.4
Venezuela (Bolivarian Republic of)	8.8	5.3	–3.2	–1.5	4.2
República Dominicana	8,5	5,3	3,5	7,8	4,5

Source: Cepalstat

Considering the sub-regions defined above, the South American countries were the least affected during the period. In average, they grew 4.9 per cent annually between 2007 and 2011. Although in some cases (like Brazil, Paraguay, Colombia and Uruguay) they did not return to the rhythm of growth previous to the crisis, by 2010 these economies were again growing. Within this sub-region Venezuela is an outlier, with a worse performance than its neighbours: between 2007 and 2011 it grew 13.5 per cent or 2.7 per cent annually.

Table 2.2: GDP Year-to-Year Variation (2007-11)

Central America	2007	2008	2009	2010	2011
El Salvador	3.8	1.3	–3.1	1.4	1.5
Nicaragua	5.0	2.9	–1.4	3.1	5.1
Honduras	6.2	4.2	–2.1	2.8	3.6
Guatemala	6.3	3.3	0.5	2.9	3.9
Panama	12.1	10.1	3.9	7.5	10.8

Source: Cepalstat

According to their economic performance, the second group is the one of the Central American countries. This sub-region grew 3.8 per cent annually during the period. In general, the sub-region was more affected by the crisis in 2009 than the previous group of countries. Similarly to them, however, all returned to growth by 2010, although the rhythm was much more modest. Within this group there is also an outlier: Panama. During the same period, this country grew at an average rate of 8.9 per cent more than doubling the sub-region's mean. Without Panama, the sub-region just grew 2.6 per cent on average per year.

Table 2.3: GDP Year-to-Year Variation (2007-11)

Mexico	2007	2008	2009	2010	2011
	3.4	1.2	–6.0	5.6	3.9

Source: Cepalstat

The third case is the one of Mexico that shows poor performance during the period: it only grew 1.6 per cent on average every year. Mexico shows one of the most drastic drops in terms of GDP during 2009 (only surpassed by Bahamas, a very small economy compared with the Mexican, one of the biggest in Latin America). Mexico was severely affected also in 2008, a year that showed practically no negative effects within the southern countries.

Table 2.4: GDP Year-to-Year Variation (2007-11)

The Caribbean	2007	2008	2009	2010	2011
Antigua and Barbuda	96	0.0	–11.9	–7.9	–5.0
Bahamas	1.4	–2.3	–4.9	0.2	1.6
Barbados	1.7	0.1	–3.7	0.2	0.4
Belize	1.3	3.6	0.0	2.7	2.3
Dominican Republic	8.5	5.3	3.5	7.8	4.5
Haiti	3.3	0.8	2.9	–5.4	5.6
Cuba	7.3	4.1	1.4	2.4	2.7
Jamaica	1.4	–0.8	–3.5	–1.5	1.3
Trinidad and Tobago	4.6	2.3	–3.0	0.0	–1.4

Source: Cepalstat

Finally, the sub-region with the worst economic performance was the Caribbean. Taken as whole, the region grew only 0.9 per cent per year. Within the sub-region, the negative effects of the crisis emerged as early as 2008 and continued to affect some countries like Jamaica, Antigua or Haiti until 2010. Even by 2011, countries like Antigua and Trinidad and Tobago were still decreasing without signs of recovering. The outlier of this sub-region is the Dominican Republic, with a much better performance than the average of the region. It grew, between 2007 and 2011 at an average rate of 4.5 per cent. Without considering the Dominican Republic the average rate of growth of the sub-region is practically inexistent: 0.3 per cent annually.

Besides the macro effects of the crisis, the situation was perceived very differently in each region. In the case of the Caribbean and Central America, the increase in the unemployment rates heightened the sense of instability and uncertainty. This was fuelled by the problems originating in the US economy. Negative expectations then impacted on consumption strategies, thus affecting domestic demand and deepening further the effects of the external shock.

Within the South American countries, the situation was different. In fact, thanks to the previous performance of these countries and to the continuity in the high prices of commodities, the crisis was, at least between 2007 and 2008 imperceptible for the population. During this period, most governments injected money into the economy in order to keep consumption going. Infrastructure investment (like in the case of Bolivia) and consumption credits (like in Argentina and Chile) kept the domestic economies dynamic.

One consequence of these policies was inflation. Inflation emerged as an important problem for Argentina and Venezuela, where the rates are between 25 and 30 per cent. In other countries inflation is also an issue, but less worrisome: in Uruguay and Paraguay the inflation rate is between 6 and 10 per cent. At the other extreme, the rest of Latin American, Central American and the Caribbean sub-regions show very low inflation rates – below 5 per cent. Another problem, fuelled by the crisis was the high level of households debt, like in Chile (where 6 million people are not able to repay their debts) and Argentina (where credit for consumption has being one of the main means to acquire products).

The Answers to the Crisis

The answers to the crisis were different in the Latin American countries regarding two dimensions: state capacity and the political orientation of economic policies. Some countries showed greater levels of state intervention and regulation than others. Also, the option adopted in each case had more to do with the political orientation of the governments than to the structural characteristics of the countries. State intervention was the option chosen by Argentina and Brazil, but also by El Salvador and Costa Rica. On the other hand, other 'big' countries like Mexico opted for more orthodox solutions while traditional liberal ones like Chile gave to the state a more active role.

Most countries kept the same level of public expenditure or even increased it. The overall trend all over Latin America between 2007 and 2009 was the use of the public expenditure as a means to counterbalance the effects of the external situation. With a few exceptions counter-cyclical measures were undertaken, even in cases like Chile and Peru. As León-Manríquez (2013) argues, Mexico was an exception as it remained in its orthodox position even in the middle of the crisis. Interestingly, in most countries (with the exception of Venezuela and Argentina) there was also, and simultaneously, a wide acceptance of some of the more important predicaments of orthodox economics: fiscal balance and inflation control.

Political orientation and state capacity worked together to define the type of state intervention. In most countries it was assumed that the state needed be a tool to minimize the effects of the crisis and/or to restore the economic balance. However, success on such intervention depended on the capacity of the state to make the intervention effective. As state capacities in the region had been weakened during the 1980s and 1990s, in many countries the institutional instruments for intervention were not available or were not as efficient as was needed. Then, there was not only a problem of political decision-making but also of counting on the adequate instruments to produce positive intervention. In other words: one of the lessons of the crisis is that if state intervention is needed to face global crises and external shocks, the countries from the region need to reinforce state institutions and tools in order to be able to intervene appropriately.

Figure 2.2: Total Public Expenditure Year-to-Year Variations

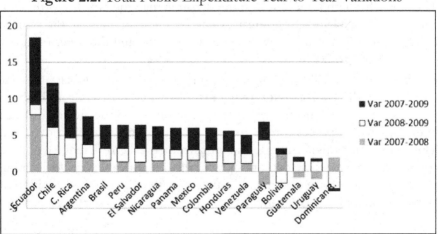

Source: Cepalstat

The diverse spectrum of situations identified in the Latin American region shows diverging degrees of vulnerability under different conditions. This opens a set of questions regarding the policies applied in the years previous to the crisis as well as during and after 2007 and 2008. It also opens a set of questions regarding the room some nations have in order to create adequate responses to external threats. In economic terms, the type of goods produced and the diversification of the export markets seem to be the key. In political terms, the development of stronger state capacities and the type of political decisions are also critical. Political responses have to do not only with internal strategies, but also with coordination among countries. The collaboration between the South economies emerged in this context as one of the best answers for a crisis originated in the North, showing that the South-South relations are not only important politically but also in terms of economic perspectives.

The current situation of the global economy indicates that this collaboration will be even more important in the near future. By 2012, and after five trimesters without economic growth, the crisis is deepening in the Eurozone (Cepal 2008). At the same time, the Eurozone crisis is affecting the economies of the US and China. In this context, world trade is de-accelerating: according to the WTO, global volume will grow at a rate of 3.7 per cent, compared to the 5.1 per cent of the last decade. Together with the crisis of the Eurozone, in 2012 the US showed a very low growth rate and high levels of vulnerability.

In this context, it is expected that for the next decade the global economy will have two speeds: the emergent economies will duplicate the expansion of the industrialized ones. The UN projects a low rate of growth (2.5 per cent) for the North between 2013 and 2020. For the South, the UN projects a rate of 5.6 per cent, and the IMF and the OECD are even more optimistic. Then, South-South trade will be more dynamic than the North-North trade. This is to be explained, to a great extent, by the continuity of the primary goods cycle influenced by the demand from China and the other emergent economies (Cepal 2008).

This process, finally, leads to debate on the meaning of globalization and its effects on the Global South. In the first place, questions concern both the scope of the homogenizing effects of globalization and the diverging effects in the South of a process originated in the North. The crisis was not equally 'global' for all nations and its effects were asymmetrical in different regions and countries – in fact, some countries practically did not experience deleterious effects stemming form the crisis. It is time now to return to the definition of globalization and discuss its implications for South-South relations.

Crisis and Globalization

In Latin America, the effects of the financial crisis were not homogeneous. The crisis, in fact, arrived in each country via very different paths, depending on a set of economic and political variables. This diversity on how the crisis reached each country opens the room for a debate on the meaning and scope of the processes of globalization: to what extent are global processes actually global? What are its limits? How do the processes of homogenization work? How do the mechanisms of re-localization work?

These questions can be set within the debates on the way global processes spread throughout the world. As part of this debate, some authors have analyzed globalization, stressing convergence (meaning: homogeneity) over the differences (heterogeneity). These authors usually look at the increasing similarities among national societies (Strange 1996; Dicken 1998; Slaugther 2000; Geschiere and Nyamnjoh 2001). According to this view, globalization is an isomorphic process that affects institutions, behaviours and organizations that become more and more similar (Di Maggio and Powell 1991; Schofer, Ramirez and Meyer 2000).

From this viewpoint, both political and economic dynamics need to be understood by looking at their global scope. For this reason, they call for an epistemological turn in social sciences, as its objects of research should not be the nations taken in isolation but the world as a whole (Wallerstein 1979; Robertson 2000; Beck 2004). According to them, both the economics and the culture of the global scene should be analysed as being connected to the general structural and action features of the global system.

Although not always on an explicit basis, these views usually share the assumption that globalization is mainly about North-North or North-South relations. For those who analyse these global processes as the extension and reproduction of a system of domination (Hardt and Negri 2009; Wallerstein 1979), the peripheral societies are the receptors of patterns generated in the North and spread to the South. The perspective that focuses on the mechanisms of isomorphism goes in the same direction: each type of isomorphism (normative, mimetic and coactive) implies a kind of power relationship and the extension of some legitimized models from some countries to others.[4] This view has impregnated most political and economic analysis produced from Latin America, where globalization is usually seen as synonymous with neoliberalization.

Economic globalization, stability and the peace of millions of people depend on the United States. It is the US that has promoted and supported the neoliberal ideas that serve its particular interests and privileges. Dressing up its ideology as science, neoliberalism pretended to discover how to solve the evils of capitalism. Globalization is at the service of the big multinationals because it allows them to increase their gains (Isaza 2004).

This critical view on globalization is by no means false. It shows the logic of international power and domination of states and corporations. However, it is a simplistic view because it only pays attention at one side of a much more complex process of globalization, meaning the whole set of macro and micro dynamics implied as well as the active role of the 'subordinate' countries in this process. What these visions criticize is the notion of globalization promoted by multilateral organizations such as the IMF, the World Bank and the World Trade Organization. In these views, globalization is in fact equated to economic globalization and to the spread and imposition of liberalizing policies.

In the case of South-South trade, a clear expansionist tendency can be observed, although the regional scope is limited. It is evident that South-South trade encloses a potential dynamism that can make the highest benefits more efficiently with new liberalization policies. This conclusion should neither detour our focus from the need to adopt new policies in order to liberalize North-South trade, nor should we underestimate the importance of creating the appropriate normative environment that would facilitate this trade. Commercial regional agreements have multiplied in the last ten years. The consequences of these agreements may be both positive and negative. The consequences are positive when the agreements contribute to narrowing the relations among regions, when new opportunities for trade are created, and when they imply that more countries are able to access to these markets. The consequences are negative when the agreements discriminate excessively against third parties and frustrate the achievement of multilateral goals. Governments should compose themselves in order to firmly promote the multilateral goals and ensure that those agreements will serve to support the WTO system and not to compete with it (WTO 2003).

The view on globalization supported by the WTO leaves no doubts: globalization should be a patterned process in which all countries must adopt the same type of trade agreements. Those governments that sign their own agreements with particular partners going against the free-trade logic are seen as promoters of discrimination. As well as providing the most critical perspectives on globalization, this view understands the global processes as a one-way track from the North to the South that results in the acceptance by the later of the rules defined by the former.

But this view is not monolithic among the theorists of globalization. Robertson (1995, 2000), for instance, argues that globalization is best understood as indicating the problem of the form in terms of which the world becomes united, but by no means integrated in naïve functionalist mode. Other authors have shown, in the same line, that globalization does not necessary mean convergence or, that a globalized world does not mean a homogeneous world (Guillén 2001; Fourcade-Gourinchas 2001; Fourcade-Gourinchas and Babb 2002; Dezalay and Garth 2002). Some of them have stressed that globalization implies both, and simultaneously, homogenization and heterogenization (Mann 1997; Helvacioglu 2000; Ortiz 2004).

To this extent, Ortiz (2004) argues that the features commonly associated with globalization do not imply complete homogeneity. In fact, he adds, when looking at its effects on the different domains of modern life, pattern should be distinguished from standard. He suggests that every society has a given pattern of social organization; this pattern, however, does not necessary mean that every unit of that society would be standardized. The same principle works for societies in the process of globalization. For Ortiz, there is no conceptual opposition between the common and the diverse.

From looking at the effects of the financial crisis in Latin America, it seems evident that global processes do not reproduce identically in each society. Rather than this, the way they reach each country should be explained, taking into account mechanisms of re-localization shaped by the characteristics of each locality and the decisions made by local governments and economic actors. Re-localization implies that global trends are re-defined and re-introduced by the *structurant structures* of each society (Ortiz 2004).

When looking at globalization from a South-South perspective, the idea of re-localization goes beyond the notion of 'resistance'. It implies a more dynamic and active position of the Global South. It implies a much more complex approach to globalization, assuming that global processes are at the end produced both at the centre *and* the periphery. Globalization, then, is not only a process of domination but also a process of creation that opens new room for thinking the political dynamics of the South. Globalization, as a general process of increasing the inter-links among societies is a tool that may facilitate the integration of the Global South.

While the scope and power of multinationals appear to have grown significantly, neither they, nor individual national governments, have all the control over macro-economic forces that they would like. Globalization also brings the possibility of more fluid and durable exchanges among countries from the South and facilitates the dialogues among cultures. It also opens the chance for diversifying the export markets for peripheral economies. And it opens the possibility for some economic actors to develop based on a global strategy even without great investment in economic capital – like in the case of the creative industries.

Policy Implications

According to the experience of the countries of Latin America during the crisis two types of implications may be identified.

Externally, it is clear that the countries from the South need to diversify the destination of their exports. Having a unique partner increases the level of vulnerability and links the capacity to recovery to the performance of that partner. Also, as the emerging economies are growing – and they are expected to grow at a faster rate than the industrialized ones – the focus should be on this area for the next decade. This includes, of course, China and India, but efforts may be made in enforcing South-South trade also with other regions and countries. The internal agenda of innovation and competitiveness should have the goal of increasing the link with these regions.

Internally, as state intervention seems to be an important instrument for dealing with the crisis, the countries from the South need to reinforce state instruments and tools in order to be able to produce more effective interventions. In Latin America, as well as in other regions from the South, there is a lack of state capacity that limits the ability to intervene in contexts of crisis.

Even more important than this, there is a need for an epistemological review in the way South governments define their position in relation with the North. The 2007-09 crisis opened an opportunity to redefine the symbolic relations between the South and the North. If there is a causal link, as Stiglitz suggests, between globalization and bad policymaking, there is now a chance to redefine the rules that govern globalization. These rules should be designed so as to guarantee social justice, while considering the needs of different countries and regions in the world.

Conclusion

The characteristics assumed by the financial crisis of 2007-08 in Latin America led to two conclusions: a) the effects of the global crisis were highly heterogeneous; b) the crisis was less deep in Latin America than other crises of the past. These conclusions led also to a set of questions regarding the scope of the crisis and the meaning of globalization for the Global South.

In the first place, it questions to what extent, in comparison to the region's history, this crisis was actually a crisis for the Latin American countries. Although there were some negative effects, they were apparently less severe than those that had been brought about by other crises in the past. Most countries were able to recover in the short term. The crisis that emerged in the North and then spread to the South seems to have had less severe consequences than previous crises. In the second place, it questions to what extent the crisis should be considered global or, to be more precise, it must be considered as another crisis of the capitalist system originated in one region with negative effects in the others. What is the difference between this crisis and those that originated in Asia, Russia, Mexico or Brazil in the 1990s? Perhaps most important is that the crisis started in the North; besides that, there seems to be no difference with the other crises.

The third question regards the way in which the crisis spread from the North to the South. Its effects were not homogeneous, meaning that the crisis left some room open for autonomous responses. This connects directly with the isomorphism versus lack of convergence debate. The characteristics of the crisis in different countries showed that there is no unique way of spreading from the North to the South, opening space for debate about the meaning of globalization and possible answers to global challenges that might be conceptualized and thought about within the South.

As for the solutions, the experience of the crisis shows some lights and shadows. Among the lights, the existence of some room for diverse responses allows us to think about the need for and importance of greater autonomy and to re-conceptualize globalization not just as a North-South relationship, but also as having South-South and South-North implications. The crisis made clear that many countries from the South are still highly vulnerable to external crisis and that their institutional tools are not strong enough to provide successful answers to crises. This leads to the second limitation, which is the lack of coordination and solidarity among the South countries when confronting the crisis. In fact, most answers were just at the national levels; there were just a few answers coordinated at a regional level. In other words, if the potential for greater autonomy emerges as a positive conclusion from how the crisis affected each country, lack of coordination remains one of the main flaws of the region as a whole.

Notes

1. *Fuenteovejuna* is a play by the Spanish writer Lope de Vega. The play is based upon an actual historical incident that took place in the village of Fuenteovejuna, Spain, in 1476. A commander, Fernán Gómez de Guzmán, mistreated the villagers, who banded together and killed him. When a magistrate sent by the king arrived at the village to investigate who had killed the commander, the villagers responded only by saying 'Fuenteovejuna did it.'
2. The crises of the 1990s have been called 'crises of globalization' due to its causes: 1) de-regulation of the bank system and its internationalization; 2) financial volatility producing an acceleration in the income and exit of financial investments; 3) the high risk of contagion; 4) its long term effects on the real economy. In terms of the

developing countries, the crisis came mostly from abroad via external shocks that rebounded in the domestic market. As León-Manríquez argues in this book for the cases of Mexico and South Korea, these shocks were transmitted through the external sectors and the financial market.

3. In the case of the other countries they not only produce high prices commodities, but they are also big players in the international markets. That is the case of Argentina and Brazil with soy and other grains, Chile with cooper, Mexico and Venezuela with oil, Peru with gold, etc. This gives them an additional privileged position in the global markets.

4. DiMaggio and Powell (1991) identify three mechanisms through which institutional isomorphic change occurs: 1) coercive isomorphism that stems from political influence and the problem of legitimacy; 2) mimetic isomorphism resulting from standard responses to uncertainty; 3) normative isomorphism, associated with professionalization.

References

Beck, U., 1992, *Risk Society*, London: Sage.

Beck, U., 1999, *What Iis Globalization?*, Cambridge: Polity Press.

Beck, U., 2004, *Poder y contrapoder en la era global. La nueva economía política mundial*, Barcelona and Buenos Aires-México: Paidós.

Castells, M., 1996, *The Rise of the Networked Society*, Oxford: Blackwell.

Castells, M., 2001, 'Information Technology and Global Capitalism', in W. Hutton and A. Giddens, On the *Edge. Living with Global Capitalism*, London: Vintage.

CEPALSTAT [on-line database from ECLAC], available at http://websie.eclac.cl/sis-gen/Consul- taIntegrada.asp/.

Chibber, V., 2003, *Locked in Place. State-building and Late Industrialization in India*, Princeton: Princeton University Press.

Dezalay, Y. and Garth, B. 2002, *The Internationalization of Palace Wars. Lawyers, Economists, and the Contest to Transform Latin America States*, Chicago, IL: University of Chicago Press.

Dicken, P., 1998, *Global Shift: Transforming the Economic World*, Chicago: Paul Chapman Publishing.

DiMaggio, P. and Powell, W. 1991, 'The Iron Cage Tevisited: Institutional Isomorphism and Collective Rationality in Organizational fields', in DiMaggio and Powell, *The New Institutionalism in Organizational Analysis*, Chicago, IL: University of Chicago Press.

ECLAC, 2011, *Panorama de la inserción internacional de América Latina y el Caribe. La región en la década de las economías emergentes*, Santiago de Chile: UN Publications.

ECLAC, 2012a, *La India y América Latina y el Caribe: Oportunidades y desafíos en sus relaciones comerciales y de inversión*, Santiago de Chile: UN Publications.

ECLAC, 2012b, *Panorama de la inserción internacional de América Latina y el Caribe. Crisis duradera en el centro y nuevas oportunidades para las economías en desarrollo*, Santiago de Chile: UN Publications.

Fourcade-Gourinchas, M. and Babb, S. 2002, 'The Rebirth of the Liberal Creed: Paths to Neo-liberalism in Four Countries', *American Journal of Sociology* 108 (3): 533–79.

Fourcade-Gourinchas, M., 2001, *The National Trajectories of Economic Knowledge: Discipline and Profession in the United States*, Great Britain and France, Massachusetts: Dissertation, Harvard University.

Geschiere, P. and Nyamnjoh, F. 2001, 'Capitalism and Autochthony: The Seesaw of Mobility and Belonging', in J. Comaroff, and J. L. Comaroff, *Millenial Capitalism and the Culture of Neoliberalism*, Durham and London: Duke University Press.

Giddens, A., 1990, *The Consequences of Modernity*, Stanford: Stanford University Press.

Gonzalez, I., 2010, *Indicadores del Sector Público: Gasto Público en América Latina*, Santiago de Chile: CEPAL-ILPES.

Gourevitch, P., 1986, *Politics in Hard Times. Comparative Responses to International Crises*, Ithaca and London: Cornell University Press.

Guillén, M., 2001, *The Limits of Convergence. Globalization and Organizational Change in Argentina, South Korea, and Spain*, Princeton and Oxford: Princeton University Press.

Hardt M. and A. Negri, 2009, *Commonwealth*, Harvard: Belknap Press of Harvard University Press.

Helvacioglu, B., 2000, 'Globalization In the Neighborhood. From the Nation-state to the the Bilkent Center', *International Sociology* 15 (2).

Holton, R., 1987, 'The Idea of Crisis In Modern Society', *British Journal of Sociology* 38 (4): 502–20.

IMF, 2012, *Perspectivas de la economía mundial*, Washington, DC: IMF. IMF, on-line database [World Economic Outlook].

Isaza, F., 2002, 'América Latina frente a la globalización', Bogotá: *Apuntes del Cenes* 22 (34).

León-Manríquez, J. L., 2013, 'All Keynesian Now? Mexico and South Korea's Diverging Responses to the Global Crisis', this volume.

Mann, M., 1997, 'Has Globalization Ended in the Rise and Rise of the Nation-state?', *Review of International Political Economy* 4 (3).

Meyer, J., 2000, 'Globalization. Sources and Effects on National States and Societies', *International Sociology*, Vol. 15(2).

OECD, 'OECDStat'. http://stats.oecd.org/Index.aspx.

OECD, 2005, *Measuring Globalization: OECD Handbook on Economic Globalization Indicators*, Paris: OECD Publishing.

OECD, 2012, *Economic Outlook*, Paris: OECD.

Ortiz, R., 2004, *Mundialización y Cultura*, Bogota: Convenio Andrés Bello. Featherstone et al., eds, Global Modernities, London: Sage.

Robertson, R., 2000, 'Glocalizacion: tiempo espacio y homogeneidad-heterogeneidad', *Zona abierta* 92-93: 213–41.

Schofer, E., Ramirez, F. and J. Meyer, 2000, 'The Effects of Science on National Economic Development, 1970 to 1990', *American Sociological Review* 65: 866–87.

Sen, A., 2002, 'How to Judge Globalization', *American Prospect Online*. Available online at http://www. prospect.org/print/V13/1/sen-a.html.

Slaugther, A.M., 2000, 'Governing the Global Economy through Government Networks', in Bayers, M., ed., *The Role of Law in International Politics*, Oxford: Oxford University Press.

Smith, M. K. and Doyle M., 2002, 'Globalization', *The Encyclopedia of Informal Education*. Available online at: www. infed.org/biblio/globalization.htm.

Strange, S., 1996, *The Retreat of the State: The Difusion of Power in World Economy*, Cambridge: Cambridge University Press.

United Nations, 2012, *World Economic Situation and Prospects as of Mid-2012*, New York,

United Nations, 2012, *World Investment Report 2012: Towards a New Generation of Investment-Policies* (UNCTAD/WIR/2012), Gineber: UN Pubications.

Wade, R., 1990, *Governing the Market,* Princeton and Oxford: Princeton University Press.

Wallerstein, I., 1979, The Capitalist *World-economy, Cambridge*: Cambridge University Press. WTO, 2003, *Informe sobre el Comercio Mundial*. Washington, DC: World Trade Organization.

3

All Keynesian Now?
Mexico and South Korea's Diverging
Responses to the Global Crisis

José Luis León-Manríquez

Introduction

As argued in the introductory chapter, the 'Great Recession' originated in the North in 2007-08. Over a few months, the crisis was transmitted to the rest of the world by either foreign trade or the financial markets. Despite some similarities that will be discussed later, both Mexico and the Republic of Korea (henceforth South Korea or ROK), were affected, but in different ways. Forecasts issued by the International Monetary Fund (IMF) and the Organisation for Economic Development and Co-operation (OECD) in late 2008 and early 2009 foresaw a moderate decline of GDP in both countries by the end of the latest year. Yet, Mexico's GDP plummeted to -6.5 per cent, while the ROK could preserve a modest growth of 0.2 per cent.

This chapter's thesis is that the dissimilar economic performances of the ROK and Mexico during the global crisis can be explained by two main factors. The first has to do with different degrees of development and support of the domestic market as a means of economic recovery. While Mexico was unable to move away from the economic orthodoxy prevailing since the 1980s, South Korea quickly implemented countercyclical, Keynesian-style measures. The second factor is linked to the broader contexts of economic integration – namely the North America Free Trade Agreement (NAFTA) and East Asia. Despite plunging imports from the United Sates, the Chinese and Asian markets remained very active for Korean exports. Mexican exports to the US were quite stressed by declining demand, but Mexico did not have a China-like resource to offset the negative impacts of the crisis in North America. From this viewpoint, regional integration becomes a factor that either hinders or facilitates economic recovery.

In order to understand the global crisis, its adverse effects upon the ROK and Mexico, these countries' economic policies to face the emergency and the role of their regional trade, the first part of the chapter puts forward some variables and explains the methodological approach for comparing the South Korean and Mexican economies. The second section deals with the mechanisms of transmission of the global crisis to both countries; special attention is put on the contagion which was through the real economy (mostly foreign trade) and the financial sector. The third section delves into Mexico's and the ROK's internal strategies for dealing with the global crisis. The discussion stresses the role of monetary and fiscal policies in economic recovery. The fourth part analyses how formal or informal integration affected economic performance during the global slump. While Mexican concentration on the NAFTA and the US market amplified the scope of the crisis, South Korea managed to buffer the most deleterious effects of the crisis thanks to increasing diversification of its foreign trade. The East Asian and Chinese cards made it possible for the ROK to offset the externally-transmitted effects of the crisis.

Why South Korea and Mexico? Theoretical Bases and Methodological Sources for a Cross-country Comparison

In fashionable terms, South Korea and Mexico can be classified as 'emerging countries'. They are two manufacturing-export economies of similar size, with parallel experiences of trade liberalization, privatization and productive restructuring in the 1980s and the 1990s. In terms of GDP, they rank as the fourteenth (Mexico) and the fifteenth (South Korea) economies in the world (World Bank 2011). Both of them belong to the Group of 20 (G-20), a consultation mechanism that brings together developed and emerging economies.

Yet, as Table 3.1 shows, both countries are hyper-dependent on their exports' access to big markets. In the Mexican case, getting into the U.S. market has always been vital. The ROK featu res a more diversified export market, but is still quite dependent on sales to such lofty economies as China, the US, the European Union (EU) and Japan. Trade to GDP ratio and financial internationalization are very high in both cases, which means that Mexico and the ROK are fairly vulnerable to external shocks.

There are still meaningful differences between the ROK and Mexico. Table 3.1 illustrates some of them. The main divergences have to do with GDP per capita and income distribution. In 1970, Mexico's GDP was double that of

South Korea. By 2011, ROK's GDP almost doubled Mexico's. Secondly, in 2010 Gini index in Mexico was .47, which depicted quite an uneven income distribution, very widespread in Latin America. By contrast, South Korea's Gini amounted to .31, which basically meant an even middle-class society.

Table 3. 1: South Korea and Mexico, Basic Indicators, 2011

Indicator	South Korea	Mexico
Population (thousands, 2011)	49,779	114,793
GDP (million current US$, 2011)	1,116,247	1,155,316
Current account balance (million US$, 2011)	26,505	- 9,031
Trade per capita (US$, 2009-2011)	21,575	5,525
Trade to GDP ratio (2009-2011)	108.0	61.2
Rank in the world economy measured by GDP (2011)	15	14
Rank in world exports (2011)	7	16
Rank in world imports (2011)	9	16
GDP per capita (US$, Atlas Method, 2011)	9,420	20,870
Gini Index (circa 2010)	.31	.47

Source: WTO 2012; World Bank 2012; OECD 2012.

With regard to methodology, the study is based on an extensive review and analysis of cross-country secondary data. In order to ensure the comparability of both countries' indicators, it was necessary to get cross-country databases. Among those sources, financial databases such as Bloomberg and Yahoo Finance have been useful to compare the evolution of the stocks.of exchange. Broader economic data have been sourced from such databases as World Economic Outlook of the International Monetary Fund (IMF), the World Development Indicators of the World Bank, the economic surveys elaborated by the Organisation for Economic Co-operation and Development (OECD), and countries' trade profiles of the World Trade Organization (WTO). I have also reviewed thoroughly information and databases elaborated by the central banks of Mexico and the ROK. A review of written media in both countries has been very helpful in tracing public statements of key economic officers as well as short-term economic analyses.

The Global Crisis and its Contagion to Mexico and South Korea

In the recent past, both Mexico and the ROK went through important economic crises. Figure 3.1 illustrates the economic evolution of both countries during the last two decades. Mexico had a deep crisis in 1995, while South Korea was seriously affected by the Asian crisis in 1997-98. This similarity notwithstanding, there are still some key differences between Mexico and the ROK with regard to economic growth. While South Korea's growth amounted to 5.6 per cent per annum between 1990 and 2000, Mexico just recorded 2.7 per cent growth. Despite being economies of about the same size, South Korea features an ascendant trajectory, while Mexico has been more or less stagnant during the last two decades.

Figure 3.1: Mexico and Korea: GDP Growth, 1990-2021
(percentage)

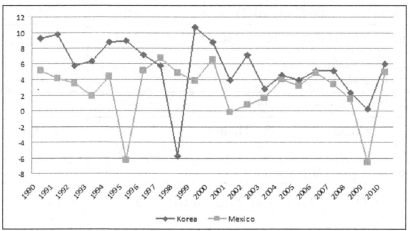

Source: IMF 2010

In 2008, the crisis for Mexico and South Korea came mostly from abroad, via external shocks that had lofty impacts upon the domestic markets. The main channels of transmission of the external shocks were foreign trade and the financial markets. In October, the ROK and Mexico were facing the global crisis in a similar situation, characterized by a rapid devaluation of their currencies against the dollar, falling exports, and deteriorating indicators in their stocks of exchange (KOSPI and BMV, respectively). For both countries, forecasts by the IMF and the OECD foresaw a moderate decline of GDP by the end of 2009. Yet, at the end of that period, Mexico's GDP recorded -6.5 per cent, while the ROK could maintain modest growth of 0.2 per cent.

Let me begin with the case of Mexico. The crisis was triggered by decreasing imports from the US, Mexico's main trade partner. Since late 2007, US imports from Mexico had been faltering, and the external sector came under serious stress. In 2006 the deficit in current account balance was US$ 6.1 billion. In 2007, red ink amounted to US$ 11.2 billion, but in 2008 the deficit reached US$ 17.4 billion (Secretaría de Economía 2011).

In the first semester of 2009, many external factors affected Mexican economic performance. Non-oil exports fell 24.3 per cent; oil exports plummeted almost 50 per cent; international tourism decreased 17 per cent, and remittances from Mexicans abroad diminished 11 per cent. To make things worse, Mexican currency underwent a more than 50 per cent devaluation, moving from 9.98 per US dollar in early August 2008, to 15.21 in early March 2009 (Banxico 2009). This was, at the same time, an outcome and a reason for financial panic.

Figure 3.2 depicts the nervousness of the Mexican Stock of Exchange (Bolsa Mexicana de Valores (BMV)), whose main index underwent a sustained fall after May 2008. While BMV recorded 31,975 points on 2 May 2008, it fell to 17,752 on 2 February 2009. After that, BMV started a recovery, but its level of May 2008 was reached in December 2009. In this sense, it can be argued that, at least initially, the financial channel was more sensitive to the crisis than the real economy.

The crisis in South Korea also came from abroad. Some domestic problems aggravated it though. The housing bubble of 2005-06 provoked a sharp increase in household credit, which moved from 40 per cent of GDP in 1997 to 73 per cent in late 2008. As the economic crisis deepened, non-performing loans of banks soared, further complicating the situation of financial institutions (Park 2009). In the few weeks running from September to October 2008, South Korea's economic prospects eroded quickly. Different forecasts predicted that the ROK would be one of the most affected Asian economies during the ensuing year. The South Korean scenarios passed from dim grey in September 2008 to deep black in early 2009. In April, the IMF (2009) predicted a 4 per cent contraction of South Korean GDP.

The situation got even more complicated by the rapid deterioration of some key indicators. For example, the won depreciated by 50 per cent between early 2008 and the first quarter of 2009. Foreign direct investment suffered a sharp decline. In the first semester of 2008, FDI balance in South Korea turned negative for the first time since 1980. According to the Bank of Korea (henceforth BOK), foreign investors withdrew a total of US$ 886 million during that period (Fackler 2008).In the financial realm, the Korea Composite Stock Price Index 100 (Kospi-100), the main indicator of the South Korean stock exchange, underwent free fall (see Figure 3.3). From a historic high of more than 2000 points in October 2007, Kospi-100 began a clear downward trajectory, only interrupted between March and May 2008. Since the latter month, Kospi-100 plummeted to a low of 946.45 points on 27 October 2008. Between October 2007 and November 2009, the stock index had lost almost half its value. Kospi-100 would only reach 2000 points again in December 2010 (Bloomberg 2011).

Figure 3.2: Monthly Evolution of the Mexican Stock of Exchange (BMV), June 2007-December 2010

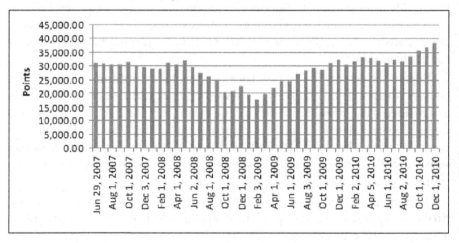

Source: Yahoo Finance 2012

Despite its healthy indicators (at least in appearance) and its bulky international reserves, between October 2008 and March 2009, the ROK's economy experienced strong speculative attacks. The ultimate reasons for such remarkable nervousness have been subject to diverging interpretations. Salient among them are the stagnation of domestic demand, the perception that financial sector reform and the regulation regime of the *chaebol* after the 1997 crisis had proven inadequate, the continued militancy of unions, and the credit cards crunch in 2002-03 (Park 2009).

Figure 3.3: Monthly Evolution of the KOSPI Index,
June 2007-December 2010

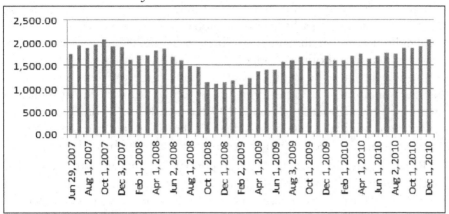

Source: Bloomberg 2011

Whatever the reasons, financial panic and speculative attacks provoked a lofty capital flight in portfolio investment. The stampede of capital was exacerbated by previous changes in the legal framework: the deregulation of capital account transactions, implemented in 2008, allowed greater mobility of resources, mostly in foreign bonds. ROK's international reserves lost more than US$ 60 billion during 2008. As mentioned, both financial institutions and companies in the manufacturing sector had been incurring heavy foreign debt. The banks' debt climbed from US$ 83.4 billion in 2005 to US$ 194 billion in late 2007. In turn, foreign debt of public and private firms (led by shipbuilders) increased from US$ 88.9 billion to US$ 134.8 billion in the same period. Thus, in late 2008, short-term foreign liabilities amounted to 97 per cent of Korea's foreign reserves (Park 2009).

The Role of Internal Markets, Monetary and Fiscal Policies

For Mexico, the period 2008-10 brought significant negative consequences. Those problems were exacerbated by the Mexican government's handling of the crisis based on orthodox, restrictive policies inherited from the 1980s. Given the close relation of Mexico with the US economic cycles, the echoes of the crisis were felt since early 2008, long before Lehman's Brothers bankruptcy in September. Initially, the Mexican government downplayed the crisis, arguing that it had started overseas and its national impacts would be limited. In February 2008, Minister of Finance Agustín Carstens distinguished the crisis from previous downturns, stating that Mexico would only have 'a slight cold, and not pneumonia as before' *(El Universal 2008).*

This relaxed attitude was embodied in the handling of monetary policy during 2008. In the first semester, the reference rate stayed at 7.5 per cent; it rose to 7.75 per cent in June, 8 per cent in July, and 8.25 per cent in August; and in spite of the official start of the global crisis in September, the central bank did not fix any reduction of the interest rate in 2008. In the first half of 2009, monetary authorities changed their mind and set a lower interest rate strategy. In January, the Bank of Mexico reduced the reference rate to 7.75 per cent; in April, to 6.75 per cent, and in July to 4.5 per cent. It remained unchanged throughout 2009 and 2010 (Banxico 2013). In other words, the central bank's initial reaction was sluggish, but it started a more proactive monetary policy by reducing interest rates to nearly half by mid-2009.

Regarding fiscal policy, the Mexican government initially had a somewhat quicker reaction. Before explaining the specific measures adopted, it is worth noting that in the last three decades, policymakers have been extremely reluctant to use fiscal policy as a means of economic incentive. The roots of this mistrust about the usefulness of fiscal policy have to do with the bulky deficits in the late 1970s and the early 1980s (in 1982 fiscal deficit rose to 17 per cent of GDP), which partially explains the crisis in 1982 and the ensuing change of economic model. This fear has been so engrained amongst incumbent economists in Mexico that in April 2006 the Congress approved a new budgetary law (*Ley Federal Presupuestal y de Responsabilidad Hacendaria*). The main goal of this law was to institutionalize, in its articles 17 and 18, a policy of 'zero fiscal deficit', preventing the left from wining Mexico's presidential elections in July 2006.

While economic balances are generally desirable, the above provision became a straitjacket for critical times, as was certainly the case in 2008-10. This caveat helped in understanding the design of Mexican fiscal policy during the global crisis. Between March 2008 and January 2009, the government issued three stimulus packages to deal with the effects of the Great Recession (Villagómez and Navarro 2010). As early as 3 March 2008, the Mexican government announced a programme to support economic growth and employment (*Programa de Apoyo a la Economía y el Empleo*). This programme provided provisional discounts on taxes to personal income, some reductions in specific services provided by the public sector, and scanty resources to reduce unemployment. The month before, President Felipe Calderón had announced the creation of a National Infrastructure Fund with an initial US$ 4 billion endowment, adding the possibility of reaching US$ 27 billion in the subsequent four years (SHCP 2008).

To add credibility to his response, in October 2008 President Calderón announced the second stimulus package. Among other measures, the package foresaw the enlargement and more efficient exercise of public spending; the construction of a new refinery for the state oil company Petróleos Mexicanos (PEMEX), worth US$ 1.2 billion; the launch of a special programme to support small and medium enterprises; and further steps on the road of deregulation and trade liberalization (Presidencia de la República 2008). Realizing that these measures could imply a change in the limits of fiscal policy, the government had to make an addition to the articles 17 and 18 of the 2006 budgetary law. The main change was that PEMEX's massive investment would not be included in the calculation of fiscal balance.

In January 2009, the Mexican government launched its third stimulus package, called 'National Agreement to Support Family Economy and Employment' (*Acuerdo Nacional a favor de la Economía Familiar y el Empleo*). The main measures were a reduction of the cost of gas for domestic use, the freeze of electricity and fuel prices, and credit disbursements of some US$ 150 million for industries hit by financial restrictions. Modest additional sources were granted to the Infrastructure Fund. With these measures, the Mexican government expected GDP to increase an extra one per cent, and to reduce inflation by one percentage point. The President's stimulus measures, as well as some international forecasts on the Mexican economy, seemed to validate the 'slight cold' thesis. By then, both the Bank of Mexico and some international consultancy firms forecast that Mexican GDP would plummet to zero per cent by the end of the year. In the ensuing months, however, these favourable expectations were virtually shattered.

Mexico suffered a collapse of oil prices, a sharp decline of its exports to the US, a drop in remittances from US-based Mexican workers, and a substantial contraction of domestic demand. To add fuel to the fire, in April 2009 H1N1 flu broke out, thus freezing the economy for several weeks. The service sector (restaurants, entertainment, tourism, retail trade) was particularly affected. In March 2009 the World Bank had forecast GDP decline of -2 per cent, but following the outbreak of H1N1 flu downgraded its prediction to -6 per cent. The IMF forecast, released in July, was even worse: -7.3 per cent for 2009.

As the crisis moved forward in 2009, the Mexican government spoke less about stimulus packages and more about its protracted fiscal crisis. From a structural viewpoint, it is true that one of Mexico's most anguishing problems is the low ratio of taxes in relation to GDP, which is only 10 per cent. Based on that argument, the emphasis of fiscal policy moved from increasing expenditure to budgetary cuts and tax collection. Mexican technocrats argued that there would be a fiscal gap of US$ 25 billion by the end of 2009 if fiscal discipline was not restored quickly. In May 28, the government started a first wave of budgetary cuts, which were deepened in July; this reduction amounted to 0.7 per cent of Mexican GDP (Villagómez and Navarro 2010).

In October 2009 the President proposed and the Congress approved an increase to Value Added Tax (VAT), which rose from 15 per cent to 16 per cent; in turn, Income Tax (ISR) grew from 28 to 30 per cent. This idiosyncratic, pro-cyclical recipe was crowned with generous under-expenditure in 2009 and 2010. In the end, GDP growth was -6.5 per cent for 2009: the worst annual regression since 1932. The decline was one of the most pronounced in Latin America, though in 2010 Mexico grew 4.5 per cent (IMF 2010). Social indicators clearly reflected the poor economic performance: in October 2009, President Calderón reckoned that of Mexico's 106 million people, the number in poverty soared from 14 to 20 million (La Crónica de Hoy 2009). Unemployment climbed from 4.6 per cent of the economically active population in January to 6.41 per cent in September 2009. This was the highest unemployment rate in 14 years (Lange 2009).

Why did Mexico undergo this economic cataclysm? Despite the government's early indications of an assertive response, orthodoxy prevailed. Unlike South Korea, which drew on its reserves and implemented a bold fiscal policy to alleviate the crisis, the Mexican government decided that it was more important to keep inflation under control and the fiscal deficit close to zero. Global crisis notwithstanding, the main goal of the Mexican decision makers was, as has been since the 1980s, to achieve a low inflation rate (less than 3 per cent), even if that meant lower growth. Facing the possibility that federal government could enlarge its funds for fiscal policy in 2009, the Bank of Mexico expressed its concern that 'the implemented policies of monetary and fiscal stimulus to support economic recovery could result in inflationary pressures in the future, if there are no measures to reverse them in a timely way' (Banxico 2009).

Under the imperative of lowering inflation, Mexico's reserves, which in July 2008 approached US$ 87 billion, remained virtually intact during the crisis. If some funds were taken from these reserves, it was to prevent further devaluation of the Mexican peso against the dollar. Between March and June 2009, the Bank of Mexico implemented daily auctions of dollars without a minimum price for US$ 100 billion, and sales with a fixed price for US$ 300 billion a day. In the first half of 2009, these auctions amounted to US$ 11.7 billion (Banxico 2009). This measure in the foreign currency market helped controlling currency volatility and the depreciation of the Mexican peso.

Contrary to the implicit consensus on application of Keynesian countercyclical policy responses, Mexico opted for procyclical fiscal measures. Instead of implementing a comprehensive stimulus package, Mexico underwent massive cuts in public spending and decreed new tax hikes. The result was a deepening of the crisis. When it came to measures to support consumers and businesses, performance was less than ordinary. In addition, the stimulus packages and the construction of new infrastructure were implemented half-heartedly, if at all. Let us take, for instance, the construction of the oil refinery foreseen in the October 2008 stimulus package. The government took seven months just to decide the refinery's location, which was announced in April 2009. Once decided, in June 2010 the Minister of Energy announced that the bid for the refinery would take place in 2012, and the facility would start working by 2015 (*La Jornada* 2010).

Given this excess of prudence, one is led to think that the new refinery will be ready for the next global crisis. The awkward handling of the Mexican crisis was not lost in international economic analyses. In November 2009, Joseph Stiglitz, Nobel prize-winner in economics in 2001, said Mexico's performance in handling the crisis had been among the worst in the world; by contrast, such countries as Australia and Brazil implemented strong government actions to effectively deal with the crisis. Stiglitz added that Mexico did not finance SMEs to engage in international trade and did not 'invest in technology, education and infrastructure – a fact that would stimulate development and growth of the economy in the short and long terms' (*El Universal* 2009a). He also predicted that tax increases would be inimical to economic growth. Finally, he warned that instead of waiting for a speedy economic recovery of the US, Mexico should consider other strategic alternatives for its own revitalization. In response, Ernesto Cordero, Minister of Social Development (later appointed by President Felipe Calderón as Minister of Finance) declared: 'I believe that Stiglitz does not know in detail the countercyclical policies implemented by the Mexican government; he does not know the reality of Mexican public finances. I think he should read a little more about Mexico' (*El Universal* 2009b).

Not everyone applauded economic policy within Mexico. The gloomiest warning of economic decay did not come from the leftist political parties, but from Carlos Slim, the owner of telecom giant Teléfonos de México (Telmex) – and incidentally the world's richest man. In February 2009, in a Conference organized by the Mexican Congress, Slim stated:

> Washington Consensus may have many virtues, but we have suffered its effects for so many years...There have been excesses by the IMF, technocrats, scholars, dogmatists, and ideologists... There is no doubt that Mexican GDP will drop, it is going to be negative, due to falling oil prices and diminishing exports. Thus, we must take care of the internal market, support SMEs, and adopt technology... Unemployment will rise as we have never seen in our personal lives, and companies small, medium and large will go bankrupt. There will be lots of empty stores and real estate unsold. I do not want to announce a catastrophe, but we have to prepare and prevent it now, instead of crying later...It is noteworthy how economic dogmas still stand, after 26 years of failure (Slim 2009).

Predictably, Slim's words sparked a heated reaction from defensive policymakers in the Calderón administration. The Minister of Labor, Javier Lozano, criticized the excessive prices charged by Telmex, the phone company owned by Slim. Lozano challenged Slim 'not to fire a single person, to maintain the purchasing power of workers, and to continue investing in Mexico'. In turn, Juan Molinar, director of the Mexican Institute for Social Security (IMSS), stated: 'Mr. Carlos (Slim) could help us very much by making much more competitive telecommunications sector in Mexico. It would be a direct benefit not only for households but also for businesses'. Finally, President Calderón said: 'We all have something to contribute to get ahead of the crisis, but even more those who have received so much from this great nation... The thing is not to see who makes the more pessimistic prognosis or who is able to instill more fear among the Mexicans, but what everyone, from his trench, his responsibility and his capacity for action, can do for Mexico' (*CNN-Expansión* 2009; Milenio 2009).

Despite international turmoil, by mid-2008, no disaster loomed in the economic horizon of South Korea. By September 2008 it seemed that the ROK would not substantially be affected by a global crisis that had been triggered by subprime mortgages in the US At that time, IMF forecast that South Korea would reach a positive growth rate of around 2 per cent by the end of 2009. The beast, however, lurked just around the corner. The source of the new South Korean crisis was mostly external and was transmitted to the ROK via two main mechanisms. The first was the financial sector crisis, which was preceded by massive contracting of foreign loans by South Korean firms in 2007-08. The second means had to do with decreasing exports to some relevant markets, such as the US.

What was the South Korean answer to this challenge? It is valid to argue that the government attempted a textbook Keynesian response, structured around a rapid expansion of public spending. The main elements of the anti-crisis policy were a sharp monetary policy; a comprehensive fiscal policy aimed at rescuing firms, investing in infrastructure, and avoiding massive job losses; and the acceleration of efforts to diversify exports. On the one hand, the South Korean case highlights how fast international turmoil can affect a given economy; on the other hand, it illustrates how the state's responses can either deepen or hinder the most deleterious effects of systemic turmoil.

The use of monetary policy to curtail the crisis was reflected in a substantial interest rate drop. To stimulate the economy, the monetary authority reacted swiftly by enacting a rapid decline in interest rates since September 2008. As the crisis deepened, this indicator reached new low levels: it fell below 5 per cent in October and less than 4 per cent in December. In March 2009 the interest rate had reached a floor of 1.77 per cent. Then, the interest rate started to increase again, albeit in a quite discreet fashion. Even in view of blatant signs of economic recovery, the interest rate in December 2010 was 2.5 per cent, still half its level in August 2008. In fact, in light of low inflation, the interest rate became negative in early 2009, thus providing a strong incentive for credit and investment. Needless to say, for indebted business and individuals, the reduction in interest payments was more than welcome news. The second element of the South Korean response to the crisis was a more expansionary fiscal policy, reflected in a substantial increase in public expenditure and the creation of a number of mechanisms to stimulate domestic demand. In late October 2008, President Lee Myung-bak instructed his economic team to increase public expenditure and implement tax cuts aimed at preventing the spread of financial crisis from negatively affecting the real economy. The same statement was made in December, when the president asked his economic team to support any public project that could be implemented immediately. At the same time, the National Assembly approved a generous budget of US$ 207 billion for 2009, which in real terms meant an increase of 10.6 per cent over 2008 (Xinhua 2008).

Fearing that the multiplier effect pursued via the large budget could not be accomplished, on 24 April 2009, the Minister of Finance and Strategy, Yoon Jeung-hyun, proposed to the National Assembly a supplementary amount of US$ 20.7 billion. The approval of these additional funds rounded up the largest South Korean budget in history. Of the additional resources, about US$ 12 billion would be invested in economic recovery programmes, subsidies to the poorest families, employment support, job training, financing of small and medium enterprises (SMEs), revitalization of regional governments, and incentives for research and development. The remaining US$8 billion would be used to offset the shortfall in tax revenues caused by both declining economic activity and tax cuts enacted in 2008. Minister Yoon said the additional budget growth would hit 1.5 percentage points of GDP and would lead to the creation of more than half a million jobs.

Given its impact on economic recovery, it is worth analysing stimulus measures at the sector level. A key activity in the expansion of public expenditure was construction, which accounts for almost 20 per cent of the ROK economy. In October 2008, the government announced it would spend US$ 3.8 billion to buy land and houses still unsold because of 'toxic' credits. South Korea's economic leaders also reduced some regulations on mortgages and eased the restrictions previously imposed on real estate transactions in some expensive urban zones. As a measure to curb speculation in areas such as southern Seoul, in 2006 the government had established some controls over bank lending and real estate transactions (Lowe-Lee 2008).

SMEs also seized considerable attention from South Korean economic planners, as they accounted for 90 per cent of employment in the services sector, and got half of loans from commercial banks. SMEs were experiencing an extreme liquidity shortage, since banks increased restrictions on lending standards as a response to the global crisis. The government offered guarantees for loans to SMEs and invested US$ 3.6 billion to rescue them. Meanwhile, the BOKdecided to raise the ceiling for loans at preferential interest rates that banks could grant to these firms. Small and medium businesses facing losses from so-called 'knock-in, knock-out' investments (KIKO), were given the option to either extend their due dates or get extra loans (Lowe-Lee 2008; OECD 2010).

One the most favoured sectors for expansionary policies was the ambitious project to position South Korea as a global model of environment-friendly growth. Taking advantage of the critical moments of 2009, the ROK launched a comprehensive five-year plan called 'National Strategy for Green Growth', soon known as the 'Green Growth Strategy'. In July that year, President Lee Myung-Bak announced that, between 2009 and 2013, South Korea would invest US$ 84 billion in this project, equivalent to 2 per cent of GDP in each of those years. The strategy includes measures for mitigating climate change, creating new engines of economic growth, and improving the quality of life of the South the Korean population.

Specifically, the plan includes 600 projects of different scales. The plan aims at transforming the ROK, by 2020, into one of the world's seven most energy-efficient countries, creating – at the same time – between 1.6 and 1.8 million new jobs. It is noteworthy that, lacking fossil fuels, South Korea is a net importer of oil and the fourth largest country in terms of energy intensity among the OECD members (Jones and Yoo 2010). As can be seen in Figure 4, oil imports from the Middle East account for the bulk of ROK's imports, thus reducing somehow the competitive edge of the ROK.

In no time, South Korea experienced a rapid recovery from the negative effects of the 2008 crisis. The ROK surprised friends and foes when, in the first quarter of 2009, it recorded a positive growth of 0.1 per cent and continued to show positive figures in the subsequent quarters. Against the IMF and Economist Intelligence Unit's forecasts, South Korea managed to avoid negative growth. Its GDP grew 0.2 per cent in 2009 and closed at 5.8 per cent in 2010. For 2011, it was expected to grow between 5 and 6.0 per cent. Fiscal stimulus created 300,000 temporary positions, thus curbing unemployment and helping to revive domestic consumption (OECD 2010). With this V-shaped recovery, Korea was recognized as the fastest country to surmount the crisis within the OECD.

In sum, South Korea's sharp recovery was closely linked to the vigour of monetary and fiscal policies. How large were, in comparative terms, economic stimulus packages in the ROK and Mexico? According to a study of the IMF, the percentage of GDP funnelled into fiscal stimulus in the Group of 20 (G-20) differed widely between 2008 and 2010.

Figure 3.4: Korea: Current Account per Selected Regions, 1998-2009

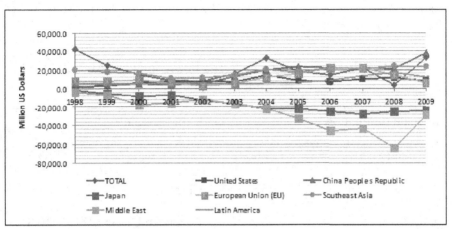

Source: BOK 2012

Saudi Arabia devoted 9.2 per cent of its GDP to its economic rescue. After the Saudis, the G-20 members which channelled most resources to the recovery were South Korea, with 6.2 per cent of GDP; China, with 6.1 per cent, and Australia, with 4.6 per cent. In Latin America the proportion of stimulus packages was much more modest. In the case of Mexico the figure was an accumulated 1.5 per cent of GDP in 2008-10. In Brazil, given its centre-left government, one may have thought that the fiscal stimulus package would be higher, but it only amounted to 1.4 per cent of GDP. In the United States, discretionary stimulus package rose to 4.9 per cent of GDP, in line with that country's importance for the world economy (Krugman 2010).

Diversification Versus Concentration: The Role of International Integration and Trade

Let me now analyse the role of foreign trade and regional integration as a means to deal with economic crisis. To what extent do trade links, either formal or informal, provoke or hinder global crisis? In the case of Mexico, regional integration was not an asset during such a crisis. One prominent shortcoming, entrenched since the establishment of NAFTA in 1994, is Mexico's single-minded focus on the US market. Table 3.2 shows that Mexico channels almost four-fifths of its exports to the US. Granted that many countries would sigh with relief to have Mexico's geographic position, combined with its almost unrestrained access to the world's biggest market. Indeed, since NAFTA came into force, Mexico's share of the US market has been climbing in absolute terms, reaching 12.2 per cent by mid-2010. Together with China, Mexico has gained penetration in the US; in contrast, other traditional US trade partners (Canada, Germany, Japan and the United Kingdom) have been losing market shares *(The Economist 2010)*.

Table 3.2: Mexico's Foreign Trade by Geographic Area, 2011
(per cent of total trade)

By main destination		By main origin	
1. United States	78.7	1. United States	49.8
2. European Union (27)	5.5	2. China	14.9
3. Canada	3.1	3. European Union (27)	10.8
4. China	1.7	4. Japan	4.7

Source: WTO 2012

Yet the advantages of over-concentration of Mexican exports to the US are its very disadvantages. Too much concentration in one market breeds vulnerability. The double-edged sword of Mexican trade with the US can be seen in Figure 3.5, which portrays the Mexican dependence on the US economy. For a long time, but even more so after NAFTA, the Mexican economy became a resonating chamber of the US economic cycles. When the US grows, Mexico rumbles. But, as the old saying goes, when the US sneezes, Mexico gets pneumonia.

A relevant case in point is the automobile industry, the Mexican champion of exports in the manufacturing sector (see Figure 3.6). Mexican automobile industry has gained high penetration in the US market, especially in the subsector of compact and sub-compact vehicles. But the crisis in the United States brought down the demand for cars, for as long as consumers were more concerned about solving their real estate problems than getting new cars. Immediately, US imports of cars made in Mexico underwent a free fall. According to data from the Mexican Automotive Industry Association (AMIA 2011), between 2008 and 2009 exports on Mexican cars to the US almost halved.

Figure 3.5: GDP Percentage Changes, Mexico
and the US 1980-2010

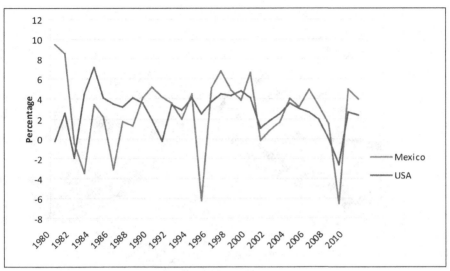

Source: IMF 2010

Given the negligible diversification of that industry's exports, as well as the reticent countercyclical measures implemented by the government, the Mexican automobile industry underwent a crisis within the bigger crisis. Unemployment skyrocketed and GDP plummeted in the northern Mexican states, where most of automobile assemblers are located. Those states were the most affected during the Great Recession (BBVA Research 2011). Once the US economy returned to growth, Mexican automobile exports boomed again in 2010, surpassing their levels prior to the crisis. Carmakers announced new investments of US\$ 4.4 billion over the next four years, and the market share of Mexican-made cars north of the border hit a historic level: by January 2011, 14 out of every 100 vehicles sold in the US were made in Mexico (Ilif 2011).

A further problem is that Mexican enthusiasm for the free market has not been accompanied by strategic industrial or trade policies, but rather by a reliance on reducing tariffs and signing FTAs, 12 of which have been established with 44 countries (including such juicy markets as the US, the European Union and Japan). Nevertheless, Mexico's network of FTAs has not been too useful in diversifying exports (see again Table 3.2). Although the agreement with the EU took into effect in 2000, a higher percentage of Mexican exports were sent to Europe in 1990. Despite the FTA with Japan, which was initiated in 2005, exports to Asia have been declining. Exports to Latin America represent the same percentage than in 1990.

Figure 3.6: Mexico – Percentage Distribution of 10 Main Exports, 2009

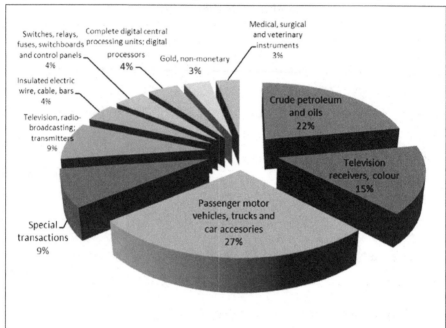

Source: ECLAC 2012

In the early 1990s, some of the initial expectations on NAFTA were that Mexico could become a major magnet for investment and exports to third markets. However, provisions on rules of origin included in most FTAs state that products must originate predominantly in Mexico. Overwhelming reliance on inputs imported from the US hinders tariff-free access to these products from other countries *(The Economist 2010)*.

A diversification strategy can only succeed if supported by effective industrial policy aimed at generating exports, rewarding productive actors, and incentivizing the diversification of Mexico's trade basket. Yet in contrast to many East Asian countries, the expressions 'diversification' and 'industrial policy', have become almost taboo in the discourse of Mexican economic officials. Mexico's development banking, led by the Nacional Financiera (NAFINSA), appears to be heading towards extinction; commercial banking does not support large industrial and exporting projects; investments in applied research and development by Mexican firms are virtually nil; and subsidies to production in the secondary sector have long exhibited levels below the average in OECD member countries (Clavijo and Valdivieso 1994).

The increasing concern about the lack of an industrial policy in Mexico is evident in the transformed ideas of Jaime Serra Puche, Minister of Trade and Industrial Development in the right-wing government of Carlos Salinas de Gortari (1988-94). An enthusiastic advocate of free trade, Serra Puche was the Mexican negotiator-in-chief of NAFTA. During his ministerial tenure, he was an unambiguous critic of industrial policies, and even declared, much to Mexican manufacturers' chagrin, that 'the best industrial policy is the one that does not exist'. Yet in June 2010, Serra Puche stated that Mexican exports have a scanty multiplier effect on gross domestic product (1.8 times their value compared to 2.3 in Brazil and 3.3 times in the US), due to the extreme concentration of markets for Mexican exports and the low level of domestic inputs added to those goods. Notably, he argued that the inadequate support of Mexican development banks to the export sector has eroded the country's chances of finding new external markets (Milenio 2010; *The Economist 2010*).

Is my argument a not-so-disguised anti-NAFTA manifesto? Not really. It is just a reminder of the vulnerability that excessive trade dependence can produce. It is worth remembering about Albert Hirschman's old warning about asymmetrical gains that derive from too much concentration on a single partner:

> A given volume of trade between countries A and B may be much more important for B than for A. A simple quantitative reflection of this asymmetry is present in the frequent case where as small, poor country (B) carries on a large portion of its trade with a large, rich country. In that case imports of A from B could well represent 80 percent of B's total exports while accounting for no more than 3 percent of A's total imports (Hirschman 1980).

In the case of South Korea, foreign trade and regional integration were at least as relevant as in the Mexican case. In the last quarter of 2008, there was a sharp drop in ROK's exports, especially to key markets like the US. In November 2008, South Korean exports shrank 19 per cent vis à vis the same month in 2007; in December, they fell 18 per cent (Park 2009). Figure 3.7 traces the behaviour of declining South Korean exports to the US and China. The high bill that South Korea still had to pay at that time through high energy prices and raw materials put the external sector under stress. Between May and September 2008, the ROK underwent a US$ -7 billion current account balance. By the end of the year, though, the current account was positive, reaffirming a sustained trend since 1998.

Figure 3.7: Korea: Short-term Evolution of Exports to USA
and China January 2008-January 2011

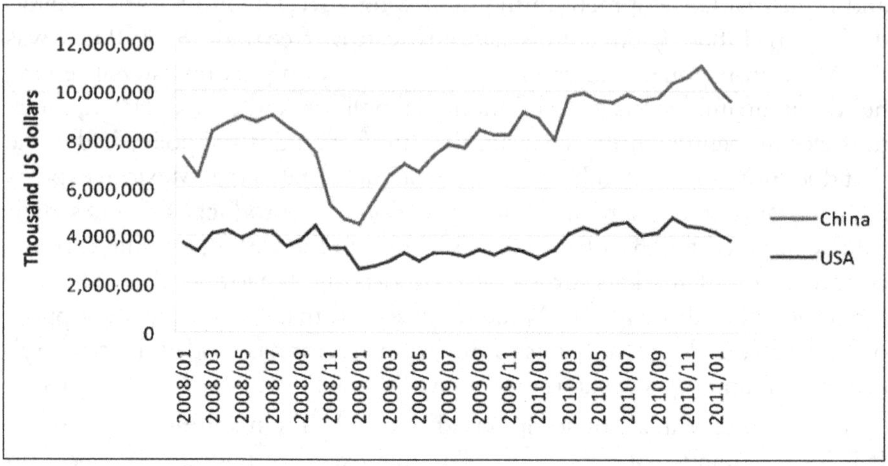

Source: BOK 2012

One key element that explains the rapid recovery of the South Korean economy is the diversification of its exports destinations. As can be seen in Table 3.3, China is the largest trading partner of the ROK. Until 2003, the US held that position. Between 2003 and 2008 South Korean exports to the US remained in the order of US$ 45 billion per annum; because of the global downturn, they fell below US$ 40 billionin 2009. Despite declining imports from the US, South Korea and other Asian countries were not decisively affected during the 2008-09 crisis. ROK's trade with emerging countries in general, and East Asia in particular, worked as a buffer. If in 2000, 49 per cent of South Korea's exports were bound for East Asia by 2008, the proportion had risen to 60 per cent. While it is true that ROK's exports to Japan have dropped in relative terms, China has more than compensated for such a decrease.

Moreover, ROK's exports are increasingly concentrating on the Chinese market. ROK's exports to China have skyrocketed since 1990. In relative terms, exports to China moved from 2.1 per cent of South Korean total exports in 1990 to 10.7 per cent in 2000, to almost 24 per cent in 2009 (ECLAC 2012). In absolute terms, exports to China rose from US$ 18.3 billion in 2001 to US$ 63 billon in 2005. By 2008, the amount had climbed to US$ 93.4 billion. The crisis brought down South Korean exports to China to US$ 89.3 billion in 2009. And ROK's imports from China fell even more, giving the ROK a bilateral current account surplus of US$ 37.8 billion.

Table 3.3: Republic of Korea's Foreign Trade by Geographic Area, 2011
(*per cent of total trade*)

By main destination		By main origin	
1. China	24.2	1. China	16.5
2. United States	10.2	2. Japan	13.0
3. European Union (27)	10.1	3. European Union (27)	9.0
4. Japan	7.1	4. United States	8.5
5. Hong Kong, China	5.6	5. Saudi Arabia	7.1

Source: WTO 2012

The virtual absence of crisis in China allowed South Korea to cope with the worst effects of shrinking US imports. According to Figure 3.8, during 2008 South Korean exports to both China and the US had been faltering. Yet in January 2009, the ROK's exports to China began an astounding recovery, while exports to the US remained stagnant. There is, at least, a close correlation between the resumption of Chinese demand and the unexpected recovery of South Korean economy since the first quarter of 2009. The diversification of South Korea's foreign trade and its reliance on Asian markets in the most critical moments was complemented by an exchange paradox: however anguishing it might have been, the sharp devaluation of the won assisted the increasing competitiveness of ROK's exports.

The diversification and 'asianization' of foreign trade was extremely useful for the ROK at the height of the global crisis. Apart from China, countries like India and Russia, and regions like Southeast Asia and Central Asia, have turned into major recipients of South Korean exports, thereby mitigating the impact of the falling US market (see Figure 3.9). As I mentioned above, Asia implemented generous economic stimulus packages, and has led the international economic recovery. This process has been a blessing for the ROK, insofar as the bulk of its exports are now directed to one of the world economy's main engines of growth. For South Korean business, ensuring a constant demand from different Asian sub-regions was particularly useful, inasmuch as their exports could keep running.

Figure 3.8: Korea: Short-term Evolution of Exports to USA and China, June 2008–June 2009

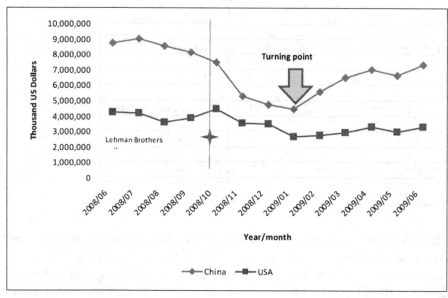

Source: BOK 2012

Figure 3.9: Korea: evolution of exports to eelected markets 1990-2010

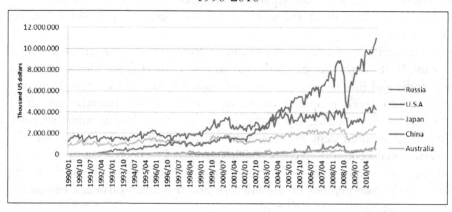

Source: BOK 2012

While trade diversification in the ROK has been progressing since the mid-1990s, during the global crisis the South Korean government insisted on seeking new alternatives to skew any negative impacts from economic dependence. In October 2008, President Lee asked his ministers to redouble their efforts to strengthen coordination in inte rnational economic policies and to conclude bilateral and multilateral FTAs under negotiation (Xinhua 2008).

These directions bore fruits quickly. In 30 October, the BOK was able to establish – as did the central banks of Brazil, Singapore and Mexico – a line of US$ 30 billion for a foreign exchange swap with the US Federal Reserve. This measure helped to appease, in the short term, further exchange rate pressures on the won. In December, the BOK ironed out similar agreements with Japan (US$ 20 billion) and China (US$ 26 billion) to stabilize currency markets in East Asia. To improve the anti-crisis coordination of the three largest economies in the region, on 13 December the leaders of China, Japan and South Korea held a trilateral summit in Fukuoka, Japan. Meaningfully enough, this meeting was the first of its kind outside the ASEAN plus 3 negotiations.

Conclusion and Recommendations

While globalization affected Mexico, South Korea and many more countries around the world, it did not breed the same type of responses everywhere. In so far as Mexico and the ROK are quite open economies, the Great Recession affected them via financial turmoil and decreasing exports to the US. Both countries implemented monetary policies aimed at reducing interest rates.

The differences in Mexico and South Korea's responses to the crisis have to do with two variables. The first is the degree of diversification of foreign trade. While Mexico features an overwhelming concentration of exports in the North American market, the ROK has been able to increasingly rely on East Asian markets, especially China; fortunately for South Korea, that region managed to offset the most adverse effects of the global crisis. It is true that ROK's exports are increasingly concentrated on China. Nevertheless, the Chinese share in South Korean exports is far from the sheer asymmetry (80 per cent of exports to a single country) that Hirschman proposes as a measure of dependency.

A second key variable to understand how both countries dealt with global hardship is the pace and scope of fiscal policies. Both from quantitative and qualitative viewpoints, South Korea crafted a much more dynamic response to global crisis than Mexico. While public spending in Mexico was sluggish in order to avoid inflation, the ROK designed a massive public budget for 2009. While South Korea cut taxes, Mexican policymakers increased them in the midst of a sinking GDP.

It is worth ascertaining, even if briefly, the reasons for this diverging response to the Great Recession. At least two explanatory variables could be further discussed in future research: 1) the resilience of the developmental state in the ROK, despite the neoliberal reforms that started in the early 1980s and were deepened after the Asian crisis in 1997-98; and 2) South Korean nationalism, that has been an enduring trait of ROK's developmental experience.

This chapter has been focused on the analysis of positive policies rather than on normative perspectives. Nevertheless, the comparative study of Mexico and South Korea's responses to the global crisis in 2008-10 draws some lessons that could be the basis for recommendations with further deductive scope. Let me sketch some:

1. Capitalism is vulnerable to periodic systemic crises. So far there is no a better invention than Keynesian, countercyclical policies to face the worst effects of the crises. In South Korea, as well as in most of the countries included in this book, economic recovery from the Great Recession has been closely linked to the assertiveness and generosity of discretionary packages. One should not ignore, however, the economic distortions that the massive injection of public funds in the economy can breed. Keynes (1981) foresaw state intervention as a temporary expedient to avoid the most deleterious effects of post-war depression. Once the economic cycle gets into an upward trajectory, it is advisable to implement a more orthodox economic policy and restore private demand. That is precisely what the ROK, China, Australia and other East Asian countries have been doing since 2011.

2. There is an important debate on the accuracy of neoliberal policies to improve economic efficiency in the Global South. While some countries (especially in Latin America) may claim some success in stabilizing the fiscal deficit, curbing inflation, promoting exports and putting in order other key economic variables after protracted periods of shakiness, to apply the Washington Consensus during systemic crises does not seem to be a sound strategy. In the Mexican case, the enduring faithfulness of policymakers to liberalism deepened the most injurious effects of the global shocks in 2008-09. The lesson here is that key decision-makers should avoid ideological approaches during the crisis. South Korean economists, educated in the same US graduate schools as Mexican top officers, showed quite a pragmatic attitude during the Great Recession.

3. Monetary and fiscal policies can be equally efficient to deal with economic crises. The South Korean case illustrates how, in the midst of economic problems, a low interest rate can be a boon for business in trouble. Fiscal policies via stimulus packages are also a powerful tool for reinvigorating the economy. There is, however, a hint on the use of these two policies. The Mexican case shows that a sluggish reduction of interest rates can be deleterious to the economy. In turn, fiscal policies lose strength if they are half-heartedly implemented, if the resources they get are insufficient or, even worse, if countries raise taxes in the middle of the economic crunch.

References

AMIA, 2011, 'Estadísticas. Exportación por región'. Asociación Mexicana de la Industria Automotriz. www.amia.com.mx/expr.html.

Banxico, 2009, *Política monetaria. Informe sobre el primer semestre de 2009*, Mexico City: Banco de México, September.

Banxico, 2013, 'Tasas de interés representativas 2008-2013'. Available online at : http://www.banxico.org.mx/SieInternet/consultarDirectorioInternetAction.do?accion=consultarCuadroAnalitico&idCuadro=CA51&sector=18&locale=es.

BBVA Research, 2011, México. Situación regional sectorial, Mexico City: BBVA Bank, January.

Bloomberg, 2011, 'Interactive Chart, Korea Kospi 100 Index, 5 Years (2006-2011)', *Bloomberg*. http://www.bloomberg.com/apps/quote?ticker=KOSPI100:IND#chart.

BOK, 2012, 'Economic Statistics System', Seoul: Bank of Korea. Available online at http://ecos.bok.or.kr/flex/EasySearch_e.jsp.

Clavijo, F. and Valdivieso, S., 1994, 'La política industrial de México, 1988-1994', in F. Clavijo and J. I. Casar, eds, *La industria mexicana en el mercado mundial: elementos para una política industrial*, Mexico City: Fondo de Cultura Económica.

CNN-Expansión, 2009, 'Slim vs Calderón, ¿huele a pelea?', CNN-Expansión.com. Availalble online at: http://www.cnnexpansion.com/negocios/2009/02/10/slim-vs-calderon-huele-a- pelea), 11 February.

Dent, C.M. and Dosch, J., eds, 2012, The Asia-Pacific, *Regionalism and the Global System*, Cheltenham (UK) and Northampton, MA: Edward Elgar and World University Network (WUN).

ECLAC, 2012, 'Database of the Division of International Trade and Integration', Economic Comission for Latin America and the Caribbean-Comisión Económica para América Latina y el Caribe. www.cepal.org/comercio/SIGCI.

El Universal, 2008, 'México tendrá catarrito por crisis en EU: Carstens', *El Universal*, Finance Section, 8 February.

El Universal, 2009a, 'México no supo manejar la crisis: Stiglitz', *El Universal*, 19 November.

El Universal, 2009b, 'Cordero pide a Stiglitz leer sobre México', *El Universal*, 19 November.

Fackler, M., 2008, 'South Koreans Reliving Nightmare of Last Financial Crisis', *New York Times*. http://www.nytimes.com/2008/10/24/business/worldbusiness/24iht-24won.17217405.html, 24 October.

Hirschman, A.O., 1980 [1945], *National Power and the Structure of Foreign Trade*, Berkeley and Los Angeles: University of California Press.

Ilif, L., 2011, 'Mexico Auto Exports Gobbling Up More US Market Share', *Wall Street-Journal*. Available online at http://online.wsj.com/article/BT-CO-20110209-715864.html, 9 February.

IMF, 2009, *World Economic Outlook: Crisis and Recovery*, Washington, DC: International Monetary Fund, April.

IMF, 2010, *World Economic Outlook: Rebalancing Growth*, Washington, DC: International Monetary Fund, October.

Jones, R. S. and Yoo, B.S., 2010, *Korea's Green Growth Strategy: Mitigating Climate Change and Developing New Growth Engines*, OECD Economics Department Working Papers, No. 798, 28 July.

Keynes, J.M., 1981, *The Collected Writings of John Maynard Keynes*, Vol. 20, London and New York: Royal Economic Society.

Krugman, P., 2010, 'Keynes in Asia', *New York Times*, 24 July.

La Crónica de Hoy, 2009, 'Admite Calderón: hay 6 millones más de pobres desde que estalló la crisis', *La Crónica de Hoy*, 3 October.

La Jornada, 2010, 'La refinería Bicentenario va, afirma Georgina Kessel', *La Jornada,* 24 June.

Lange, J., 2009, 'Mexico Unemployment Rate Hits 14-yr High in Sept', Reuters,. http://www.reuters.com/article/2009/10/21/mexico-economy-jobs-idUSN2150760420091021, 21 October.

Lowe-Lee, F., 2008, 'Korea Feels Wall Street Crisis... and Reacts', Korea Insight, 4 November.

Milenio, 2009, 'Calderón pide 'aportar, no atemorizar', Milenio. Available at http://www.milenio. com/node/165682, 20 February.

Milenio, 2010, 'Poco impacto de exportaciones mexicanas en PIB nacional: Serra Puche', *Milenio Diario*. Available at www.milenio.com/node/457836, 4 June.

OECD, 2010, OECD *Economic Surveys: Korea. Organisation for Economic Co-operation and Development,* Paris: OECD, June.

OECD, 2012, 'OECD Stat. Income distribution – Inequality'. Paris: OECD. Availalble at: http://stats.oecd.org/Index.aspx?DataSetCode=INEQUALITY.

Park, Y.C., 2009, Global Economic Recession and East Asia: How Has Korea Managed the Crisis and what Has it Learned? Working Paper num. 409, Seoul: Institute for Monetary and Economic Research, The Bank of Korea, November.

Presidencia de la República, 2008, 'Mensaje del Presidente Felipe Calderón sobre el programa para impulsar el crecimiento y el empleo', *Presidencia de la República*. Available online at www. presidencia.gob.mx/prensa/?contenido=39279.

Secretaría de Economía, 2011, 'Balanza Comercial de México con el Mundo', Secretaría de Economía. http://200.77.231.38/sic_php/pages/estadisticas/mexicojun2011/TTbc_e.html.

SHCP, 2008, 'El Gobierno federal anuncia el lanzamiento del Fondo Nacional de Infraestructura'. Secretaría de Hacienda y Crédito Público'. Available online at: http://www.indetec.gob.mx/   cpff/politica/opiniones/Fondo%20Nacional%20de%20Infraestructura%202007-2012.pdf.

Slim, C., 2009, 'Foro: México ante la crisis. ¿Qué hacer para crecer? Ponencia del Ingeniero Carlos Slim'. Available online at: http://www.carlosslim.com/preg_resp_videoslim_foro_mexi- co_crisis.html, 9 February.

The Economist, 2009, 'Keynesian Principles. This House Believes We Are All Keynesians Now', *The Economist*. www.economist.com/debate/days/view/276.

The Economist, 2010, 'Mexico's Economy. Bringing NAFTA Back Home', *The Economist*, 28 October.

Villagómez, A. and Navarro, L. 2010, Política fiscal contracíclica en México durante la crisis reciente: un análisis preliminar. Documentos de Trabajo del CIDE, No. 475, Mexico City: CIDE, March.

World Bank, 2011, World Development Indicators Database 2011, Washington, DC: World Bank.

WTO, 2012, 'Trade Profiles Korea, Mexico', World Trade Organisation. http://stat.wto.org/. CountryProfile/WSDBCountryPFView.aspx?Language=E&Country=KR,MX.

Xinhua, 2008, 'Corea del Sur reducirá impuestos para evitar que crisis financiera afecte a la economía real', Xinhua Press Agency. Available online at: http://www.spanish.xinhuanet.com/spanish/2008-10/26/content_748381.htm), 26 October.

4

The Global Crisis and the Arrival of the People's Republic of China in Latin America and the Caribbean

Pablo Alejandro Nacht

Introduction

A couple of processes are of crucial importance to assess the rise of the People's Republic of China (henceforth PRC) and its impacts on Latin America and the Caribbean (LAC). On the one hand, the PRC has become a major purchaser of Latin American commodities; on the other, Chinese goods are competing (whether in local, regional or world markets) with Latin American manufactured goods. If one aims at understanding the complexity of the phenomenon and the players involved, it is important to bear in mind that rising commodity prices (of which the PRC is a major consumer) have negative impacts on Central American nations that are net importers as well. Another deleterious effect has to do with the fact that agricultural and mining activities feature characteristics of a neo-extractive model. This model is embodied in Chinese investments in mining and raw materials in LAC.

This chapter's main hypothesis states that, in the midst of the global economic crisis it has become very clear that the renewed links between LAC and the PRC are strongly related to the interests of both the PRC and the dominant economic sectors within LAC. Within the main hypothesis, it is necessary to point out some secondary hypotheses that are the backbone of this piece of research:

1. In the context of economic slowdown in Europe and the US, the PRC is presented as a powerful engine for Latin America, because of

its demand for commodities. Nevertheless, the global economic crisis makes evident the asymmetric relationship between LAC and the PRC.

2. This dependent relationship is based on a type of agricultural and mining exploitation under a neo-extractive model that favours the interests of big exporters and fuels a subordinate and dependent relation with the PRC.

3. Moreover, Latin American nations with some industrial development and *maquila* systems see their interests collide with Chinese products due to intense competiton and industrial relocation.

4. Depending on the socioeconomic structure of each Latin American nation, there are complexities and tensions (latent and manifest) between agro-mineral exporters (who have PRC as a major buyer) and the industrial local sector whose production is threatened by Chinese manufactures.

5. Despite the PRC´s image spread by some journalists and scholars as a benevolent player and strategic partner for the region, the relationship has acquired some characteristics of North-South or center-periphery linkages.

The starting point of this chapter is a brief description of the global economic crisis sthat tarted in 2008 which, in turn, is linked to the erosion of US power worldwide. Secondly, the text reviews the PRC's international position and then analyses how it overlaps with Latin America and the Caribbean region. The third part discusses some features of the asymmetrical relation between the PRC and Latin America, while the fourth section analyses Chinese foreign direct investment (FDI) in LAC, mostly oriented to infrastructure and extractive activities. The fifth section of the chapter puts into question the extent to which Sino-Latin America exchanges qualify as a 'South-South' relation. The sixth part debates on the so-called 'Beijing Consensus' and its true scope as a cooperative stance devoid of conditionalities. The final sections wrap up the argument, positing that the economic relation between the PRC and LAC reinforces the new international division of labour in the Global South. Altrough some nations may have reached a degree of autonomy from the United States or the European Union, 'balancing' on the PRC may still have high economic costs for them.

The United States, the Periphery and the Crisis: The PRC in the Eye of the Storm

Since 1980, the world has undergone more than one hundred global economic crises (Stiglitz 2008), and some analysts have equated the Great Recession with the crisis that occurred in the 1930s. However, the United States is still the first world power, a position which needs massive resources. Yet as Arrighi points out (2007:203), the centrality of the United States in 1970 was unchallenged in terms of the international economy. By contrast, the crises that started in 2000 and 2008 may be affecting the role of the US as the paramount economic actor, giving way to the emergence of other economic powers.

In this situation, the PRC has created tremendous internal conditions – exceptionally competitive wages, high savings, economies of scale, a disciplined labour force, among others – that have facilitated its active participation in the globalization process and overcoming the global economic crisis. The opening of the PRC and its integration into international value chains of a lower but increasing technological basis has been provoking a relocation of these manufacturing processes from other parts of the globe, to the East Asian giant. This process involves not only the core countries, but the very peripheral ones that must compete with the PRC in this new scenario.

The preliminary outcomes of the Great Recession show that there is no longer a single global economic engine. The PRC and India are beginning to bear their own weight in the global economy. These two countries have a large domestic market to rely on, due to their huge population. Forty per cent of Chinese GDP depends on exports, while 60 per cent relies on domestic consumption. The assets placed in the United States account for 8 per cent of the PRC's gross domestic product. These data mean that if the US keeps on reducing its consumption and growth, the PRC will still have a very important domestic market to face the economic crisis. Not surprisingly, the PRC is becoming a centre in the world's economic actions such as free trade agreements and in its recognition as a market economy (Moneta 2008).

In 2007, the PRC was already the third largest global importer (ECLAC 2010). By February 2006 it had overtaken Japan (US$ 850 billion) as the main creditor of the US, with US$ 853 billion. Despite the downward trend in the current account deficit of the US, the PRC has become the main source of US red ink. In 2010, 65 per cent of the US$ 470 billion deficit stemmed from its trade with the PRC.

In the period 1980-2008 the Asian power grew at an average annual rate of 9.9 per cent. The PRC thus has become the second largest GDP after the US, measured by purchasing power parity (PPP), and the third after the United States and Japan, measured in current dollars (ECLAC 2012:23).

Chinese FDI has begun to compete with the West not only in Asia, its area of natural influence, but also in Africa and Latin America (Kurlantzick 2009). Figure 4.1 reflects the relevance of PRC as a partner for Africa and LAC. These regions' exports to the PRC jumped from less than one per cent in 1990 to more than 7 per cent in 2009.

Figure 4.1: China's Imports from Africa and Latin America, 1990 and 2009 *(as per cent of total imports)*

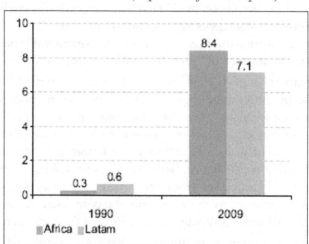

Source: COMTRADE (2010) and García-Herrero and Nigrinis (2010)

Figure 4.2 shows that Chinese products have successfully penetrated these new markets, in pursuit of the objective of sustaining China's large surplus with all countries or regions. While LAC accounted for only 0.4 per cent of Chinese exports in 1990, it skyrocketed to 8.7 per cent two decades later.

Chinese Strategy in Latin America and the Caribbean

A key aspect for understanding the PRC strategy for Latin America and the Caribbean is the diversification of risk to ensure access to natural resources, with the prior establishment of what Chinese political leadership calls 'strategic policy'. This view is anchored in the PRC's resource-seeking logic in commodities such as oil, iron ore, fisheries, forestry and strategic minerals (Cesarín 2004: 21–22). In this manoeuvre, the quest for strategic natural resources is combined with investment in extractive activities and infrastructure for transporting these materials.

LAC is presented by the PRC as an important area of political stability, peace and non-conflict scenarios. Not least if we consider other places such as the Middle East and Africa. Some scholars (Cesarín 2010), also highlight the place played by Chinese communities in Latin American countries, forming true 'business communities' that foster a meaningful link between the PRC and the recipient country.

Figure 4.2: China's Exports to Africa and Latin America 1990 and 2009
(as per cent of total exports)

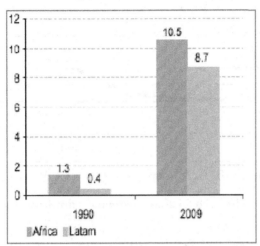

Source: COMTRADE (2010) and García-Herrero and Nigrinis (2010)

Chinese diplomacy in LAC has focused on commodity producers like Brazil, Argentina, Venezuela, Chile and Peru. Free Trade Agreements have been negotiated and enforced with Chile and Peru, while all of these countries have granted China the status of 'market economy' within the World Trade Organisation (WTO) (Laufer 2010). In turn, México became a key country, albeit not the only one, as the PRC's products importer.

Some analyses foresee that LAC's Chinese imports will soon displace those from the classic Latin American trading partners – i.e., the US and the European Union. As for Latin America exports, the Economic Commision for Latin America and the Caribbean (ECLAC 2011:16) has issued the following forecast:

> If the current rate of growth in demand for our products in the United States, the European Union and the rest of the world is sustained and the PRC's demand grows only half the rate recorded in this decade, that country would overtake the European Union in 2014 and would become the second largest market for exports from the region (ECLAC 2011:16).

Between 1990 and 2008 total trade (imports plus exports) between the PRC and LAC (excluding Mexico) grew 64 times. LAC exports to the PRC multiplied by 36, while imports grew 127 times. These data can be seen in Figure 4.3, which also depicts the recurrent LAC deficit with the Asian giant. If we include Mexico in the figure, the deficit in the region would go from US$ 16.8 billion to US$ 49.4 billion per annum (Freitas Barbosa 2011:277).

Figure 4.3: Trade Balance China-Latin America, 1990-2008 (US$ million)

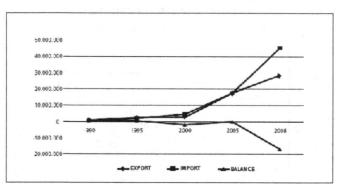

Source: Freitas Barbosa (2011:278) on the basis of ECLAC

Note: Mexico is not included in so far as its huge imports may have distorting effects in the overall data.

According to Freitas Barbosa (2011:281), although a trade deficit with Latin America is not a problem *per se*, it may still indicate a structural trend in the type of international integration of the PRC with Latin America and the Caribbean.

An Asymmetric Relationship

The PRC has acquired a remarkable role as a business partner of LAC in a relatively short period of time. This trend has changed the morphology of Latin American international economic relations. This break-neck process makes it imperative for the region to rethink its international integration with such a dynamic partner. Stallings (2009: 311) emphasizes that:

> The fear in South America is that the subregion might become sucked into the old model of progress of the 19th century, when it exported raw materials and imported manufactured goods. This type of exports has shown to have several disadvantages throughout the decades. Prices of commodities have generally been volatile and some analysts say it is likely to have a long-term price fall versus industrial goods. In terms of labor, the production of some raw materials requires unskilled labor, which is something Latin America has tried to refrain from using. In cases where high technology is used, the use of labor is kept to a minimum.

The increasing presence of the PRC in LAC economic relations is shown in Table 4.1. In 14 out of the 17 countries included, the PRC increased its participation as importer and became one of the top five export destinations for Argentina, Chile, Brazil, Costa Rica, Peru, Venezuela and Uruguay. As a source of imports for the region, the PRC jumped from a rather marginal location in 2000 among the top five in 16 of the 17 countries (the exception is Honduras, which ranks in sixth place).

Although several Latin American nations are 'big players' in the global market of agricultural and mining commodities such as copper (Chile) or soy (Brazil and Argentina), the PRC has structural power as the main world importer of a large number of basic products. Thus Sevares (2011:36) states that 'in 1990 the PRC reached 5 per cent of global consumption of commodities; today is the main consumer of aluminum, copper, tin, zinc and soy, and the second largest consumer of sugar and oil'. Needless to say, the effect of Chinese demand in the price of commodities exported by Latin America has been quite positive (Jenkins 2011). High prices notwithstanding, there is a global oligopsony that limits the LAC's room for manoeuvre.

Figure 4.4 corroborates the pattern of Sino-Latin American trade links. Accordingly, over 90 of PRC's imports from Latin America and the Caribbean is made of either primary products or manufactures based on natural resources. Commenting on this situation, ECLAC (2011:22) states:

> The growing demand from China has been a factor in the return of raw materials in the regional export structure. This is what allows us to speak of a tendency to reprimarisation in the export sector in the region in recent years.

Moreover, the PRC has turned to countries of ASEAN (Association of South East Asian Nations) for natural resource-based manufactures. The PRC also turned to Africa for oil and other commodities. This stategy has provoked a clear competition between these regions, which challenges LAC in terms of increasing value added in raw materials (Phillips 2009:107). Besides, several authors have warned that the region is at the risk of contracting the Dutch disease.[1]

Table 4.1: LAC. Ranking of China in Trade by Value, 2000-09

	Export		Import	
	2000	2009	2000	2009
Argentina	6	4	4	3
Bolivia (Plurinational State of)	18	11	7	4
Brazil	12	1	11	2
Chile	5	1	4	2
Colombia	36	6	9	2
Costa Rica	30	2	15	3
Ecuador	18	16	10	3
El Salvador	49	36	23	4
Guatemala	43	25	19	3
Honduras	54	11	21	6
Mexico	19	7	7	2
Nicaragua	35	27	20	4

Source: (ECLAC 2011), on the basis of United Nations, Database Trade Statistics Database (COMTRADE)

Between 2007 and 2009, and according to ECLAC, Argentina had 92 per cent of its exports concentrated in five products (soybeans, soybean oil, crude oil, other cattle, meat and offal), Bolivia 75.9 per cent (tin and alloys, tin concentrate, crude oil, non-coniferous wood, precious metals ore); Brazil 82.2 per cent (iron concentrate, soybeans, crude oil, iron pellets, chemical wood pulp).[2] Chile 92. 3 per cent (copper, copper concentrate, chemical wood pulp, iron concentrate, flour inedible), Honduras 92.7 per cent (zinc concentrate, lead concentrate, other non-ferrous scrap, shirts of all kinds, other wastes plastics), Venezuela 98.2 per cent (crude oil, iron ore concentrate, spongy ferrous products, artificial fibres for spinning, other non-ferrous scrap), Ecuador 98.4 per cent (crude oil, other non-ferrous scrap, non-wood conifers, inedible meals, other plastic waste), Guatemala 94.8 per cent (sugar, zinc non-wood conifers, inedible meals, other plastic waste), Guatemala 94.8 per cent (sugar, zinc concentrate, other plastic wastes, other non-ferrous scrap, waste polymers) and the Caribbean Community (CARICOM) 69 per cent (monohydric alcohols, alumina, non-coniferous wood, other non-ferrous scrap, liquefied natural gas). The only country with a smaller concentration in top five goods to PRC was Mexico, with 37 per cent.

Figure 4.4: LAC structure of exports by technological intensity and main destination, 2009 (per cent of total)

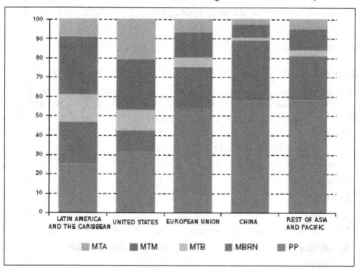

Source: ECLAC 2011, on the basis of COMTRADE

Note: Data for Antigua and Barbuda, Cuba, and Haiti are not available. The categories correspond to PP: primary products MBRN: Manufactures based on natural resources, MTB: low technology manufactures, MTM: Manufacturing technology media, MTA: high technology manufactures.

Chinese Investment

A new PRC policy to LAC has been deployed since the 1990s. The PRC's increased purchase of commodities from this region has been matched with foreign direct investment (FDI) in infrastructure projects related to the extraction and transport of raw materials (León-Manríquez 2006:35). Plenty of these projects were completed in the 2000s by new bodies created for that purpose. The Argentinean Centre for International Economics (CEI 2011:2) has found that through the creation of the China Investment Corporation in March 2007, China aimed at investing abroad a percentage of its lofty international reserves, estimated at U$S 2.73 trillion, under the model of 'sovereign fund'. The objective of this institution is to acquire strategic assets in selected world locations under the slogan of 'investment manager', responsible for long-term administration of assets entrusted.

This action is framed within the 'go out policy' of the PRC's state-owned enterprises (SOEs), aimed at setting profitable investments abroad and ensuring the supply of sensitive products for Chinese development (Zhang 2010:54). The PRC's FDI in Latin America rose from about US$ 916 million at the beginning of the century, reaching to US$ 50 billion by 2008. In 2007-08 FDI investment in LAC underwent an annual growth of 130 per cent. At the same time, global FDI fell by 14 per cent due to the global crisis (CEI 2011:3).

This broader framework makes it easier to understand Chinese FDI for modernizing some Latin American ports on the Pacific Ocean (Ensenada, Callao, Iquique, Manta and Buenaventura), those with access to the rivers but located in the Atlantic Coast (Timbúes in Rosario, Argentina), or huge investment projects with high environmental impact as the bi-oceanic corridors Manta-Manaos, Ilo and Paita in northern Peru. Projects that would link Iquique in northern Chile, with São Paulo in southern Brazil are under consideration. Another investment project is the Belgrano Cargo Railway, which would connect central and northern Argentina to Bolivia and the port of Iquique in Chile (Laufer 2010:5).

However impressive the new Chinese FDI wave in LAC may seem, it is worth noting that 95.9 per cent of it has been channeled to such tax havens as the Cayman Islands and the British Virgin Islands. After these, Brazil (0.7 per cent), Peru (0.7 per cent) and Argentina (0.5 per cent) account for the biggest shares of Chinese FDI in the region. ECLAC estimates that over 90 per cent of the PRC's 'productive' FDI in LAC has led to the extraction of natural resources, primarily oil and mining industries.

Trade agreements and diplomatic negotiations often respond to this type of commercial relationship, which benefits Latin American commodity exporters, but relegates to a subordinate position the domestic industrial sector, especially in Central America and Mexico.

This process is highly complex and entails an irony. While several Latin American governments, especially the Southern Cone, craft discourses with images of 'national and popular' autonomy as well as heterodox economic policies and neo-Keynesian strategies in defence of the domestic industry, their close relations with the PRC benefit the traditional agricultural and mining-export sectors. This new configuration opens the door for the so-called 'neo-extractivism', founded mainly on the exploitation of natural resources such as soybeans, minerals and crude oil (Gudynas 2009:220).

A South-South Relationship?

According to its own rhetoric, the PRC is a developing nation and member of the 'Global South'. Therefore, the PRC should be able to establish strong South-South relations. Yet, as Bolinaga (2007:12) notes:

> The per capita economic indicators are often used on the discursive level by (Chinese) central government as an instrument to reduce the economic weight of China and emphasize the 'South-South' idea, so that China retains its leadership within developing countries.

Obviously, this is not a relationship between equals. The PRC is in a superb position to exert influence over LAC through different channels. Coercion is not only used by the PRC, but also by Latin American export elites at the domestic level. Nicola Phillips (2009:101) warns:

> The celebration of the export opportunities provided by the emergence of China consequently has something of a strange ring to it, in that most of the–long-established anxiety about this form of dependence on raw materials appears curiously to have disappeared from the contemporary discourse. Yet, given what we know from both theory and past experience, the new strategy that is crystallizing around the Chinese demand for raw materials is without question inauspicious for the region's economies.

The PRC's emerging hegemony,[3] a mixture of consensus and coercion coordinated with local LAC elites, encompass the economic benefits of the relationship with the PRC and Latin America's agreement of not interfering in PRC's domestic issues such as human rights or the Taiwan problem. To provide greater certainty and less distrust of political leaders in Latin America and the Caribbean (along with a signal of transparency for skeptical US analysts), the PRC published on 5 November 2008, the first document aimed specifically at the Latin American region.[4] The 'Document on China policy toward Latin America and the Caribbean' was published on Xinhua News Agency website in both Spanish and Mandarin (Xinhua 2008).

Beijing Consensus Instead of Washington Consensus?

The Chinese approach to the underdeveloped countries has been labelled by some scholars as the 'Beijing Consensus', in opposition to the well-known 'Washington Consensus' that prevailed during the late 1980s and all through the 1990s. Several scholars have placed high expectations on this new 'Beijing Consensus. In the words of Zhang (2010:58):

> China is also promoting the appeal of its model of development. For example, China has recently started to launch the so-called Beijing Consensus as an alternative to the Washington Consensus, the latter of which promotes democracy and capitalism to the developing world. China claims that its economic miracle, amid political stability, is an alternative to the Western model. Although to date, and as can be observed on the current networks linking China with Latin America and the Caribbean, little seems to bring back important gains other than just profit margins to Latin American export elites, and a certain degree of autonomy to governments seeking to take some distance from the US and the European Union.

In turn, Detlef Nolte (2006:20) has noted that:

> There is fear in some Latin American countries to take advantage of the 'China card' for a more independent position from the United States. The presence of China in the Western Hemisphere is seen as emblematic of the erosion of US power and its geopolitical position.

However, there is a risky scenario should the LAC take greater distance from the United States and the European Union and looks for 'shelter' in a new 'South-South cooperation' with the PRC. The PRC is certainly a rising power seeking an important place in the world order; it is also expected to become an important provider of the world's public goods (Kappel 2011:3). Nonetheless, the PRC is not a revisionist power. Chinese officials constantly wield a rhetoric of 'peaceful rise' and low profile leadership. The regime denies explicitly any intention of developing a hegemonic foreign policy (Rocha Pino 2006:701; Noesselt 2012). Rather that attempting a radical transformation of the current world order, the PRC is legitimising the core of that very order and taking advantage of its benefits (Tokatlian 2009:79; Hirst 2009:123; Feng 2009:332; Cornejo and García Navarro 2010:81). Given these points it is very likely that, even if the Asian giant becomes a provider of public goods, LAC will find little room for redefining a new pattern of international economic integration.

What can be argued is that the Chinese reform process has become an important complement to the interests of transnational capital, which has moved a considerable part of their production processes into the PRC. This nation was integrated successfully into neoliberal globalization, but does not require (as the core nations did) the full-fledged liberalization of the markets where it operates. Chinese manufactured products can circumvent domestic protectionist barriers due to dumping prices and low production costs.

The PRC's behaviour may be interpreted by some as 'benign' by the absence of explicit demands for liberalization (Breslin 2010b:9). In the same fashion, this attitude could be seen as the empirical evidence that the Beijing Consensus[5] is friendlier and less forcible than its Washington counterpart. The truth is that the PRC's entry into the WTO in 2001 and the ensuing visit by then President Hu Jintao to several Latin American countries in 2004, followed the neoliberal logic of liberalization arrangements 'without obvious demands'. LAC's recognition of the PRC as a market economy was negotiated bilaterally with Brazil, Argentina, Chile, Venezuela and Peru, among others. By granting the PRC the status of a market economy, these and other states hinder their room for manœuvre for defending their industrial sectors, as long as dumping investigations should as a reference take domestic prices in the PRC and not those of a third country. The Protocol of PRC's Accession to WTO allowed 'market economy' recognition on a sectoral basis. While Canada proceeded this way, most of Latin American countries granted full recognition, thus exposing all of productive sectors to Chinese competition.

The PRC has realized that it is necessary to avoid anti-dumping measures by LAC governments in order to continue exporting its manufactures into Latin American markets. Thus, pressures from local industrialists in such countries as Brazil and Argentina barely find a way into national governments and then trade panels at WTO. Conversely, dumping complaints could be 'dangerous' to the interests of Latin American commodity exporters, to the extent that the PRC could slow their purchases, in retaliation for hypothetic anti-dumping measures pushed by Latin American industrialists. The Chinese government realized very soon after joining WTO that the way to stop or at least hinder the implementation of trade complaints was to be recognized as a market economy, replacing the 'transition economy' label.[6] The latter classification did not allow taking PRC's domestic prices as a yardstick in the evaluation of dumping practices.

The Chinese strategy did not only benefit its interests. It also opened a door for wider opportunities to the agricultural-mineral LAC exporters, while affecting industries linked to the domestic market. To further analyse the effects of the PRC in the region, we turn to a comprehensive approach to the global capitalist development process. This analysis can show better the risks of too much reliance on the PRC as an economic partner of Latin America.

The PRC and LAC in the New International Division of Labour

Since the 1980s the world has been witnessing a new configuration in the international division of labour. The new arrangement is detaching from the previous structure, based on the exchange of primary products from the periphery for manufactured goods in central countries. Nowadays, production requires different proportions of capital and labour, with the option of de-localizing different parts of the processes where producers can maximize earnings (Arceo 2005:32). Borrowing the description of Giovanni Arrighi (1997:187) in the current international division of labour, the centre undertakes the brain activities of transnational capital while the periphery is the 'locus of the muscles and nerves.'

Under this new scheme, international trade is no longer complementary but eminently competitive. Disputes arise not only within the centre-periphery relationship, but within the periphery itself, in order to accomplish a portion of the production process that multinationals decide to outsource. In practice, this means a race for implementing the recommendations of neoliberal international financial institutions (IFIs).

In different parts of the world, openness to trade and financial flows is leading to the loss of more complex manufacturing, leaving only room to primary or very low-tech production. The nations that liberalize their markets and are integrated with international production networks via the *maquila* processes (Central America and Mexico) can reduce unemployment without curbing poverty. This can be done by such factors as lower costs of labour, a privileged geographic location and a certain level of infrastructure.

Those nations with some level of industrial development protected by tariffs or regional agreements (like MERCOSUR) and abundant natural resource endowments, must face foreign competition that eroded the domestic industry. That is why industrial lobby takes place for anti-dumping or exchange rate devaluation, while primary exporting sectors pressure the government to keep an appreciated exchange rate, which creates great opportunities to dump their products abroad. The global economic crisis and the emergence of the PRC must be framed under this division of labour. Accordingly, Nicola Phillips (2009:117) explains:

> The story of the emergence of China, as such, is not one of a single national economy but, rather, one of a particular phase in global capital accumulation driven by mobile transnational capital. Transnational capital has 'landed' in China as a result of a particular set of factor endowments (…) facilitated by internal economic reforms undertaken by the Chinese government since the late 1970s. Therefore, it is misleading to talk about the emergence of China; rather, we are witnessing the consolidation of a particular phase in the evolution of global production and value chains, driven by strategies of transnational capital, within the territorial boundaries of the Chinese economy.

The PRC gains benefits from the neoliberal globalization in a large assembly world. Exporting manufactured goods requires large amounts of raw materials for PRC's internal development process; both processes feature a strong control from the central government (Duménil and Levy 2011:5). The other side of the insertion in neoliberal globalization has to do with Latin America and the Caribbean. The main thesis of Nicola Phillips (2009:101) is that:

> We are witnessing a contraction of existing and potential development spaces for Latin America and the Caribbean of an order that prompts a set of serious questions about the basis on which the region's economies can pursue their effective insertion into the global production and value chains and transnational division of labour.

Hence it seems wrong to think of the relationship between LAC and the PRC in terms of a 'threat to Mexico and Central America' and an 'opportunity-benefit to South America'.

Conclusion: Geopolitical Considerations of the Current Crisis

Previous sections of this chapter have dealt with two levels of analysis of great sensitivity: one is internal and the other external. The internal is linked to the commoditization process of a neo-extractive model which, on its way, threatens food sovereignty and the safeguarding of natural resources and native populations. The key fact is that this model of exploitation is highly concentrated in a few economic actors –most of them transnationalized. Both the national governments and agricultural and mineral exporters are engaged in dependent associations which reduce countries' degrees of autonomy.

The external risk derives from the fact that the PRC is a big purchaser of commodities exported by Latin America's Southern Cone countries. At the same time, it is a leading challenger for several of them at the global level. Although some Latin American nations are 'big players' in the world market, the PRC's oligopsony power hinders the range of negotiation for LAC nations.

An additional consideration, derived from the pattern of exports from the Southern Cone, is the real fragility which is exposed, both by the vicissitudes of good and bad harvests (in the case of agricultural products), as the volatility and the feasible long-term deterioration of terms of trade. Keep in mind that much of the export sector is based on an array of static comparative advantages, which is exacerbated by Chinese partner's demand. This is due to the pattern of trade where the income elasticity of imports is higher than the income elasticity of commodities in the Chinese market (Musacchio and Robert 2006:22).

The other side of this great benefit and opportunity with regard to the commodity-exporting sectors is the competition faced by either endogenous industry or the *maquila*'s sector. This is especially important in Central America and Mexico whose products are displaced in markets like the US and even in their domestic markets. Also noteworthy is the competition suffered by the industrial nations of the Southern Cone, such as Brazil and Argentina, where governments have granted the PRC market economy status. This move has meant, in practice, a clear benefit for Latin American commodity exporters and a stressful issue for national industries.

Under this situation, national governments are not neutral arbiters between exporters and industrial or *maquila* sectors, but actors in a complex and contradictory setting. Governments' finances are benefiting from increasing duties on the commodities exported to the PRC. These resources facilitate the implementation of social programmes and counter-cyclical economic policies. As long as social welfare improves, civil society eschews a deep discussion of the neo-extractive model and its relationship with the PRC, thus maintaining a certain degree of domestic consensus.

The other side of the coin is the need to protect domestic industries in order to increase the level of economic activity and avoid the loss of jobs. Under pressure from domestic industries, governments have tried to institute major anti-dumping measures against Chinese goods, but lobbying from commodity exporting domestic industries can neutralize the leverage of industrial sectors. As discussed above, commodity exporters fear retaliatory actions by the PRC. An example of this fear was confirmed in 2010 when the PRC stopped purchasing Argentinean soybean oil for several months.

From a geopolitical viewpoint, it is tempting to argue that many nations in the region may have found in the PRC a partner to rely on in order to counterbalance the power of the United States and the European Union. This possibility, however, should not lead to the hasty conclusion that the region stands to gain from the relationship with the PRC. It must be understood that the cost of this national government's 'political autonomy' has its counterpart in a deterioration of the industrial fabric, choked-off by the advance of Chinese goods in both local and third country markets. The consolidation of a neo-extractive model is matched by the possibility of the Dutch disease in exporting commodities countries.

To sum up, the current global financial and economic crisis has reinforced the discussion of the options for boosting Latin America's autonomy by means of the Chinese card. Yet more rigorous research is necessary to avoid falling into hasty or incomplete conclusions. This task is even more important as Sino-Latin American relations feature multiple levels of analysis in which the essence of phenomena is frequently coated with a different appearance. Such an intellectual task is not easy business but it still needs to be done if authentic national and regional independence is to be shaped. LAC should avoid any dependent and peripheral relation and look for alternatives that enhance its societies' welfare. The Great Recession should become an opportunity to rethink Latin America's internal but also external relations with new and old partner-allies. Furthermore, the South as a whole should be able to make and reflect their own strategic interests, design methods for breaking loose from all forms of dependency and establish new relations on the basis of integration, mutual benefit and equality.

Notes

1. This is an economic situation where the large increase in commodity prices pushes up currency appreciation, with a negative impact on the competitiveness of the industrial exporters. It takes that name from the symptoms suffered by the Netherlands in the 1970s due to the large increase in oil prices.
2. Sevares (2011:42) observes: 'Brazil registered a marked primarization of its exports, since the share of primary commodities in their exports increased from 24% to 44% between 2001 and 2010, while that of manufactured goods fell from 62% to 42%.'
3. In this discussion I adhere to the concept of hegemony that is retrieved by Cox, Arrighi and Wallerstein in a neo-Gramscian approach. Here consensus and coercion are separated analytically, but in practice they are part of the same phenomenon. Giovanni Arrighi (2007: 149) defines hegemony as 'the additional power that holds a group by virtue of its ability to lead society in a direction that not only serves the interests of the dominant group but also perceived by subordinate groups as functional to a more general interest'.
4. Oviedo (2009:14) concludes that 'The document does not add anything new to the policy toward the region, at least from the public level, but has the virtue of being a systematisation of various policies and positions that China has reiterated to each of the countries and now presented in terms of region. Its content insists on considering the region as homogeneous, stating a general policy, without understanding the peculiarities of each state. It would be similar to that Latin American states per se establish policies to Asia without distinguishing between its different parts. That is, treat China like Japan and Korea, India or Israel, Iraq or Russia'. For an analysis of the document see Oviedo (2009). For an analysis from the Chinese perspective see Xu (2008).
5. Some authors emphasize that the concept of Beijing Consensus was a creation of U.S. analyst Joshua Cooper Ramo (2004). According to Dauderstädt and Stetten (2005;-9), Cooper Ramo 'sees China emerging as a powerful alternative to the American role model and calls this the "Beijing Consensus". Where Washington has argued in favour of market orthodoxy and a lean state, Beijing is promoting a pragmatic approach to capitalism matched by the so-called developmental state. This approach fits very well with many Southern countries, if the many delegations from developing countries recently visiting the PRC are any guide. What remains to be seen, however, is how proactively the PRC will play the Beijing Consensus card.
6. Diana Tussie (2006:13) states that 'The Protocol provides that each WTO member countries can use the condition of economy is not a market for a period of 15 years, until 2017. A comparison of prices (low) the export of China and the "normal values" determined from surrogate countries, results in obtaining a higher dumping margin than it is to apply the charges in force in China'.

References

Arceo, E., 2005, 'El impacto de la globalización en la periferia y las nuevas y viejas formas de la dependencia en América Latina.' In CENDES *Journal* (22) N° 60, Available online at: 25/06/2010: http://www.cendes-ucv.edu.ve/pdfs/Arceo%2025-61.pdf.

Arrighi, G., 2007, *Adam Smith in Beijing. Lineages of the Twenty-first Century*, London: Verso.

Bolinaga, L., 2007, 'La *expansión del sistema político chino* como *motor* de su *ascenso* en la *estructura* de *poder internacional* (1989-2001)', Observatorio de la *política china*, Dec. 26.

Breslin, S., 2010a, 'Government-Industry Relations in China: A Review of the Art of the State', *East Asian Capitalism: Diversity Change and Continuity*, London: London School of Economics and Nottingham University.

Breslin, S., 2010b, 'China Engages Asia: The Soft Notion of China's 'Soft Power'', *Ethos Journal*, No. 8, August,.

Centro de Economía Internacional, Digital, 2011, 'La inversión china en el extranjero: a la búsqueda de recursos escasos.', in *Notas del CEI*, no. 18, March, Buenos Aires. Available online at: http://www.cei.gov.ar/userfiles/NotadelCEI18.pdf.

Cesarín, S., 2004, 'China, Boom…, Not Bomb', Conference at Bolsa de Comercio de Buenos Aires, 27 May, Buenos Aires.

Cornejo, R. and Navarro García, A., 2010, 'China y América Latina: recursos, mercados y poder global', *Nueva Sociedad* 228, July/August, Buenos Aires.

Domínguez, J., 2006, 'China's Relations With Latin America: Shared Gains, Asymmetric Hopes', in *Inter-American Dialogue Working Paper*, June.

Duménil, G. and Lévy, D., 2011:5, 'The Crisis of Neoliberalism as a Stepwise Process', in *EconomiX*, PSE: Paris. Available online at: http://www.jourdan.ens.fr/levy/ biblioa. htm.

ECLAC, 2007, *El Panorama de la inserción internacional de América Latina y el Caribe 2006 y proyecciones* 2007, Santiago de Chile: Naciones Unidas.

ECLAC, 2011, *La República Popular China y América Latina y el Caribe. Hacia una nueva fase en el vínculo económico y comercial*, Santiago de Chile: United Nations, June.

ECLAC, 2012, *China y América Latina y el Caribe. Hacia una relación económica y comercial estratégica*, March, Santiago de Chile: Naciones Unidas.

Feng, H., 2009, 'Is China a Revisionist Power?', in *Chinese Journal of International Politics*. Available from: http://cjip.oxfordjournals.org/con- tent/2/3/313.full.pdf

Freitas Barbosa, A., 2011, 'China e América Latina na Nova Divisão Internacional do Trabalho', *A na nova configuração global: impactos políticos e económicos*, R.P. Ferreira Leão and E.Costa Pinto, eds, Luciana Acioly. Brasília: Ipea.

Furtado, C., 2000, *Introdução ao desenvolvimento: Enfoque Histórico-estrutural*, 3. Paz e Rio de Janeiro: Terra, Rio de Janeiro.

García-Herrero, A. and Nigrinis, M., 2010, China's Partnership with Africa and Latin America: Going Beyond Common Wisdom, Cross-Country Emerging Markets *Analysist Economic Watch*, BBVA, 30 December, Available online at: www.asia.udp.cl/ Informes/2011/101217_EM%20Watch_China_Africa_Latam_EN.pdf.

Gudynas, E., 2008, 'Un análisis preliminar de las transformaciones recientes en la agricultura Latinoamericana', *Economía Crítica y Desarrollo* 3 (5), Chile.

Gudynas, E., 2009, 'Diez tesis urgentes sobre el nuevo extractivismo. Contextos y demandas bajo el progresismo sudamericano actual', in *Extractivismo, política y sociedad* (many authors), Quito: CAAP (Centro Andino Acción Popular) and CLAES.

Jenkins, R., 2008, *China's Global Growth and Latin American Exports*, En United Nations University-World Institute for Development Economics Research, Research Paper No. 2008/104, November, Helsinki.

Jenkins, R., 2011, 'El efecto en los precios de los productos básicos y en el valor de las exportaciones de América Latina', in CEPAL Journal 103 (4) Available online at: www.eclac.cl/publicaciones/xml/0/43080/rve103Jenkins.pdf.

Kurlantzick, J., 2009, 'La influencia creciente de China en el sudeste asiático', Paz, G. and Roett, R., eds, *La presencia de China en el hemisferio occidental, Consecuencias para América Latina y Estados Unidos*, Buenos Aires: Ed. del Zorzal.

Kuwayama, M. and Durán Lima, J., 2003, 'La calidad de la inserción internacional de América Latina y el Caribe en el comercio mundial, CEPAL, *Serie comercio internacional* nro 26, Santiago de Chile, May.

Laufer, R., 2010, 'Presente y perspectivas de la 'asociación estratégica' China–América Latina. Persistencia de una matriz histórica de relaciones internacionales', in XXII *Economic History Conference. Argentina Economic History Association*, Universidad Nacional de Rio Cuarto, 21 -24 September, Río Cuarto.

León-Manríquez, J.L, 2006, 'China-América Latina: una relación económica diferenciada' in *El desafío chino. Nueva Sociedad 203 Journal*, May/June, Buenos Aires.

Li, Mingjiang, 2009, 'China Debates Soft Power' in *Chinese Journal of International Poli- tics*. Available at: http://cjip.oxfordjournals.org/content/2/2/287.full.pdf.

McKinnon, R.,1993, 'The Rules of the Game: International Money in Historical Perspective'. *En Journal of Economic Literature* vol. XXXI, March.

Musacchio, A. and Robert, V., 2006, 'Opciones de inserción internacional y desarrollo económico y social en la Argentina del siglo XXI: rupturas y continuidades después de la devaluación', in J. Neffa, and H. Cordone, eds, *Escenarios de salida de crisis y estrategias alternativas de desarrollo para Argentina*. CEIL-PIETTE, Center for Labor Studies and Research, Technology Program, Economic Research on Labor and Employment, CONICET, Buenos Aires. Available online at: http://bibliotecavirtual. clacso. org.ar/ar/libros/argentina/ceil/escen.pdf.

Musacchio, A.; Fiszbein, M. and Braude, H. 2004, 'La expansión comercial con Asia ¿Una estrategia novedosa o parches para el viejo modelo?', in research project Ubacyt E-030 y E-038. Informe Económico IMA N° XXVI, Buenos Aires, November/ December 2004.

Noesselt, N., 2012, Interview with Nele Noesselt, 17/01/201 at GIGA-ILAS, Hamburgo.

Nolte, D., 2006, 'Potencias regionales en la política internacional: conceptos y enfoques de análisis', in GIGA *working paper* N° 30, October. GIGA Research Programme: Dynamics of Violence and Security Cooperation. Available online at: http://www.giga-hamburg.de/dl/download.php?d=/content/publikationen/pdf/wp30_nolte. Pdf.

Oliva, C., 2009, 'China y América Latina. Las posibilidades de un desarrollo armónico, in Res Diplomática (RD)', *Instituto del Servicio Exterior de la Nación Journal*, Segunda Época, No. 3, China e India, Buenos Aires.

Oviedo, E., 2005, 'Crisis del Multilateralismo y auge de la diplomacia bilateral en la relación Mercosur-China', in VI Meeting of the Study of Latin America and the Caribbean on Asia-Pacific Network (REDEALAP-BID), 12-13 October, Buenos Aires. Available online at: www.iadb.org/intal/aplicaciones/uploads/ponencias/Foro_REDEALAP_2005_16_Oviedo.pdf.

Phillips, N., 2009, 'Coping with China'. In *Which Way Latin America? Hemispheric Politics meets Globalization*, Andrew F. Cooper, and J, Heine, eds, Tokyo: United Nations University Press.

Stallings, B., 2009, 'El triángulo entre Estados Unidos, China y América Latina', in Paz, G. and Roett, R., eds, *La presencia de China en el hemisferio occidental. Consecuencias para América Latina y Estados Unidos*, Buenos Aires: Ed. del Zorzal.

Stiglitz, J., 2008, 'Crisis financiera - El desplome: sin producción, sin ideas nuevas, ¿en qué se basa nuestra economía?', in *Realidad Económica Journal*, September. Available: http://www.iade.org.ar/modules/noticias/article.php?storyid=2624.

Stiglitz, J., 2002, *El Malestar en la Globalización*, Buenos Aires: Ed. Taurus.

Tokatlian, G., 2009, 'Una mirada desde América Latina'. In Guadalupe Paz and Riordan Roett eds, *La presencia de China en el hemisferio occidental. Consecuencias para América Latina y Estados Unidos*, Buenos Aires: Ed. del Zorzal.

Tussie, D., 2006, 'La Organización Mundial de Comercio: ¿cuál es la gravitación de sus re- stricciones y exigencias?' in *Plan Fenix*, Working paper, Available at: http:// www. econ.uba.ar/planfenix/docnews/II/Condicionalidades%20de%20la%20 OMC/Tussie.pdf.

Xinhua, 2008, 'Paper on China's policy toward Latin America and the Caribbean'. Available at http://www.spanish.xinhuanet.com/spanish/2008-11/05/content_755432. htm.

Xu, S., 2008, 'Guía para promover aún más las relaciones sino-latinoamericanas y sino-caribeñas, Acerca del Documento del Gobierno Chino sobre América Latina y el Caribe'. Available: http://ilas.cass.cn/manager/jeditor/UploadFile/200915152646443. Pdf.

Zhang, B., 2010, 'Chinese Foreign Policy in Transition: Trends and Implications', in *Journal of Current Chinese Affairs* 39 (2): 39–68. Hamburg: GIGA, Hamburg.

PART III

THE GLOBAL CRISIS IN AFRICA:
PROFILES AND RESPONSES FROM COUNTRIES AND
ECONOMIC SECTORS

5

African Stock Exchanges: Does Integration with the Global South Reduce Susceptibility to Financial Crises?

Terfa Williams Abraham

Introduction

The 2008 global financial crisis, which started in 2007 with the housing market crash in the United States of America, had consequences for emerging and developing economies. While emerging stock markets in Africa were affected by the impact of the crisis, Asian stock markets were not spared. This situation further fueled debates on rethinking Africa's integration with the West (the global North) while it expanded the frontiers on the benefits that could accrue to countries of the global South if they were better integrated (e.g. Amin 2011, 2012). Prior to 2008, there were some doubts about whether African countries would not be affected by the crisis. As events unfolded, it became clear that Africa was not spared from the adverse impact of the global financial crisis as economic growth plummeted and Africa's largest economy, South Africa, got into recession for the first time since 1992 (IMF 2009). Within this period, however, China and Japan recorded mixed performance in their economy, while countries like Mexico and South Korea though with similar economic structures, responded differently depending on their exposure to the economies of the US and UK (see Park 2009).

As the West struggled with the financial crisis, they implemented policies that aimed at cushioning its impact (Amin 2011). The effectiveness of the policies, however, is questionable as it led to huge national debt that threw the Eurozone in crisis, kept the US on the verge of a fiscal cliff, while African countries (despite policy measures taken to cushion the impact of the crisis), have continued to deal with asset management issues in the banking sector, issues of forbearance in the capital market and increasing need for external borrowing to invest in critical infrastructure, stimulate growth and create employment. While studies (e.g. Ariyo and Fawowe 2009; Ackah et al 2009; Amin 2011, 2012) have debated normatively on whether the susceptibility of African countries to external shocks would reduce if integration with the global South is deepened or not, empirical evidence on the subject matter is lacking. The benefit of such empirical evidence is that it provides estimates on the extent to which countries were affected by the global financial crisis and how the degree of susceptibility would change if integration patterns were tilted towards the global South. Such evidence would be useful not only for country-specific policies on whether or not to maintain the path of globalization and in what pattern, but also for regional blocs like ECOWAS, for instance, to consider collaborative efforts with the MERCOSUR region and Africa to further consider possibilities of increased economic ties with Asia and Latin America or not. The aim of this chapter, therefore, is to examine the direction and degree of susceptibility of African stock markets with the US/UK and for African stock markets with Asia. Some reflections on how stock markets aid the spread of financial crises and lessons from China's experience during the 2008 global financial crisis are also provided.

This chapter is arranged into six sections. Section one presents the introduction, problem statement and objectives of the chapter. Section two discusses the theoretical and empirical literature. In section three, the research methodology is presented while the results from analysis of data are discussed in section four. Section five presents some reflections on how stock markets aid the spread of financial crises and lessons deduced for the global South from China's experience during the 2008 global financial. Lastly, section six presents the summary and conclusion of the chapter.

Literature Review

Debates on the benefits of globalization and capitalism have been the subject matter of many authors such as Samir Amin and Joseph Stiglitz in the last three decades. While advocates of capitalism argue that the market is self-correcting and financial crisis only represents a normal attribute of the market system, opponents on the other hand, have continued to see each episode of the financial crisis emanating from the West as a sign of the collapse of capitalism and as an anchor for a paradigm shift in favour of stronger integration among countries of the global South (see, for instance, Amin 2011, 2012; O'Neill 2011). From these debates, a simple question comes to mind: would the integration of economies in the global South reduce their susceptibility in times of financial crisis to external shocks? Although this question can be examined by an overview of historical trend on every episode of financial crises across countries, the focus on the 2008 financial crisis in the present chapter offers the choice of examining whether countries integrated with the global North or global South were affected by the crisis and to what extent their degree of susceptibility would vary on integration with the global North or South. One framework of carrying out such estimation in econometrics is via cointegration analysis (see Johnston and Dinardo 1997).

According to Engle and Granger (1987), the close linkage between cointegration and the error correction model stems from the Granger representation theorem which states that two or more integrated time series that are cointegrated have an error correction representation. On the reverse side, two or more time series that are error-correcting are, likewise, cointegrated. While there are several methods of estimating cointegration, the Engle and Granger approach is appraised for its simplicity (see Greene 1997, for instance) especially if the variables are first difference stationary. Stock market indices exhibit such a characteristic; hence the Engle and Granger approach is suitable. Engle and Granger (1987) provided the following definition of cointegration:

The components of the vector $X_t = (x_{1t}, x_{2t}, ..., x_{nt})$ are said to be integrated of order d, b, denoted by $Xt \sim CI\ (d,b)$ if

a) all components are integrated of order d. $X \sim I(d)$

(b) there exists a vector $ß = (ß_1, ß_2, ß_3, ... ß_n)$ such that the linear combination $ß = (ß_1 x_{1t} + ß_2 x_{2t} + ß_3 x_{3t} + ... + ß_n)$ is integrated of order (d-b) where b>0. The vector $ß$ is called the cointegrating vector.

There are several important points in this definition. Firstly, cointegration refers to a linear combination of nonstationary variables. Secondly, all variables must be integrated of the same order. However, this is only true for a two-variable case, if these two variables are integrated at different orders of integration, then these two series cannot possibly be cointegrated. However, it is possible to have a mixture of different order series when there are three or more series under construction in which various subsets may be cointegrated. Thirdly, if Xt has n components, there may be as many as *n-1* linearly independent cointegrating vectors. If X_t contains only two variables, there can be at most only one independent cointegrating vector.

Series that are cointegrated are related over time. Any non-stationary series that are cointegrated may diverge in the short run, but they must be linked together in the long run. Therefore, cointegration implies that there must be Granger causality in at least one direction – at least one of the variables may be used to forecast the other. Furthermore, it has been proved by Granger (1981) and Engle and Granger (1987) that if a set of series is cointegrated, there always exists a generating mechanism called *error correction model* that restricts the long-run behaviour of the endogenous variables to converge to their cointegrating relationship while allowing a wide range of short-run dynamics. Therefore, the cointegrated variables can be thought of as being generated by an error-correction model which can be used to measure the short and long-run relationship connecting two or more variables.

Empirical Review: Stock Markets and the Global Financial Crisis

In examining the impact of the 2008 financial crisis on developing countries, Dirk (2008) argued that the crisis affected private capital flows (Foreign Direct Investment), portfolio flows and international lending, official development assistance and remittances to developing countries. Trade openness was identified as the major channel through which developing countries contracted the crisis. Openness to trade made countries more vulnerable to downturns but also to upturns. Furthermore, that openness to financial markets increases the risk of financial contagion; at the same time, it could increase productivity and innovation in the long term.

The AU and ECA (2009) in their report noted that the global financial and economic crisis exposed the weaknesses in the functioning of the global economy and had led to calls for reforming the international financial architecture. On stock markets, the report noted that the crisis increased stock market volatility and also led to wealth loss in major stock exchanges in Africa. In the same vein, Ackah et al (2009) argued that spikes in global food and crude oil prices in the 2007-08 period also aggravated the impact of the global financial crisis and increased current account deficits in developing countries such as Ghana.

Using descriptive data from 2007-09, Ariyo and Fawowe (2009) analysed the implications of the global financial crisis on policy response measures. They argued that the transmission channels of the financial crisis to the Nigerian economy were through capital flows, trade and financial markets' channels, while fiscal and monetary policy were deduced to have the potential of cushioning the impact of the crisis on the Nigerian economy.

A general gap observed from the literature is that they examine the impact of the crisis on developing countries and concentrate on identifying the transmission channel, impact dimension and what should be done to cushion the impact of the crisis. By so doing, the trade link or exposure that developing countries have with developed countries went unquestioned. Considering how the degree of exposure of developing countries would vary if they were not integrated with developed economies and knowing what the degree of exposure would be if the integration were different, would provide useful insight for policy on financial markets and globalization in Africa.

Research Methodology

To achieve the objective of this chapter, stock market data were collected from August 2007 to April 2009. The data are stock price data collected for the stock market exchanges of Nigeria, Tunisia, Egypt and South Africa. Data was also collected for the United States and the United Kingdom for the West and Japan for Asia. The choice of these stock markets was informed by the works of Magnusson and Wydick (2004) and Marashdeh (2005). Their study listed Tunisia, Nigeria, South Africa and Egypt as some of Africa's biggest exchanges. On the other hand, the choice of the US and the UK was due to their linkage with the global financial crisis while Japan was chosen due to the size of its stock market in ASEAN + 3.

To estimate the degree of susceptibility of African stock exchanges vis à vis the US/UK or with Asia (proxied by Japan), the error correction model was used to measure the short and long-run cointegrating relationship. The size of their adjusted R-square represents the size of the extent of susceptibility. The model is presented below.

$$\Delta NSE_t = a_0 + \Delta a_1 USUK_t + a_2 \Delta RES1_{t-1} + U_{t1} \qquad (3.1.1)$$

$$\Delta CASE_t = b_0 + \Delta b_1 USUK_t + b \Delta RES2_{t-1} + U_{t2} \qquad (3.2.1)$$

$$\Delta TUN_t = c_0 + \Delta c_1 USUK_t + c_2 \Delta RES3_{t-1} + U_{t3} \qquad (3.3.1)$$

$$\Delta JSE_t = d_0 + \Delta d_1 USUK_t + d_2 \Delta RES4_{t-1} + U_{t4} \qquad (3.4.1)$$

Where NSE is the Nigerian stock market, TUN is the Tunisian bourse, JSE is the South African Johannesburg stock exchange, CASE is the Cairo and Alexandria stock exchange (now referred to as the EGX index), and NIKKEI represents the Japanese stock market. The US/UK markets are used as the independent variable because of the link other stock markets have with them. The coefficients $\Delta a_1 US/UK$,..., $\Delta d_1 US/UK$ in the equations measure the short-run relationship connecting the markets, while $\Delta a_2 RES1_{t-1}$,..., $\Delta d_2 RES4_{t-1}$, measure their long-run cointegrating relationship and has a negative *a priori* expectation sign. The estimated adjusted R-square from the model is used to measure the rate of susceptibility of African stock markets with the US/UK during the global financial crisis.

The Japanese stock market (NIKKEI) is then substituted with the US/UK stock markets to ascertain the extent of susceptibility African stock markets have if integrated with Asia. The *a priori* expectation is that the measure of exposure would be lower for Africa when integrated with Asia than with US/UK. The model is specified as below:

$$\Delta NSE_t = a_0 + \Delta a_1 NIKKEI_t + a_2 \Delta RES11_{t-1} + U_{t1} \qquad (3.1.2)$$
$$\Delta CASE_t = b_0 + \Delta b_1 NIKKEI_t + b_2 \Delta RES22_{t-1} + U_{t2} \qquad (3.2.2)$$
$$\Delta TUN_t = c_0 + \Delta c_1 NIKKEI_t + c_2 \Delta RES33_{t-1} + U_{t3} \qquad (3.3.3)$$
$$\Delta JSE_t = d_0 + \Delta d_1 NIKKEI_t + d_2 \Delta RES44_{t-1} + U_{t4} \qquad (3.4.4)$$

Where NSE is the Nigerian stock market, CASE is the Cairo and Alexandria stock exchange (now referred to as the EGX index), TUN is the Tunisian bourse, JSE is the South African Johannesburg stock exchange, and NIKKEI represents the Japanese/Asia stock market. The coefficients $\Delta a_1 NIKKEI$..., $\Delta d_1 NIKKEI$ in the equations measure the short-run relationship connecting the markets, while $\Delta a_2 RES11_{t-1}$,..., $\Delta d_2 RES44_{t-4}$, measure the long-run cointegrating relationships and, likewise, has a negative *a priori* expectation sign. The estimated adjusted R-square from the model is as well used to measure the extent of susceptibility that African stock markets had with Asia during the 2007-09 global financial crisis.

A historic approach was adopted to reflect on how stock markets aid the spread of financial crisis and lessons deduced for the global South from China's experience during the 2008 global financial crisis.

Results and Discussions

The time series data collected for the study were tested for stationarity and were all found to be non-stationary at levels, which is a requirement for estimating the two-step error correction model. The respective line graphs of the stock markets are presented in Figures 5.1 and 5.2. The trend shows that, all the African stock markets (except for Tunisia), as well as those of the US, UK and Japan, witnessed a downward trend within the study period.

Using Eviews econometric software, equations 3.1.1 to 3.4.4 are estimated and summarized in Table 5.1. The detailed Eviews output are presented in Annex 1. Below is a summary table showing their major finding.

For equation 3.1.1, the short-run relationship between the Nigerian stock exchange (NSE) and the US/UK stock market is positive but not significant. This implies that positive movement in the US/UK stock market could have a positive influence on the NSE while a negative movement in the US/UK was also likely to drag the NSE downwards. But this reaction is not likely to hold for all cases since the relationship is not statistically significant. In the long run, however, shocks from the US/UK will spill into the NSE with a susceptibility level of 1.6 per cent.

Figure 5.1: Nigerian All Share Index, South Africa, Tunisia and Egypt: closing Stock Price Index-10 December 2007 to 3 April 2009

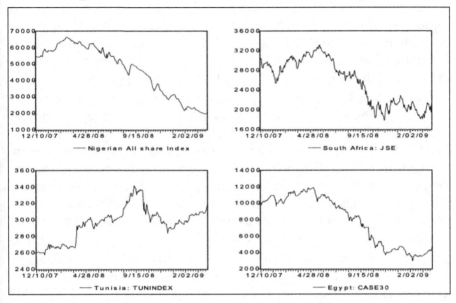

Figure 5.2: Nigerian All Share Index, FTSE 100, DOW JONES and NIKKE 1225: Closing Stock Price Index: 10 December 2007 to 3 April 2009

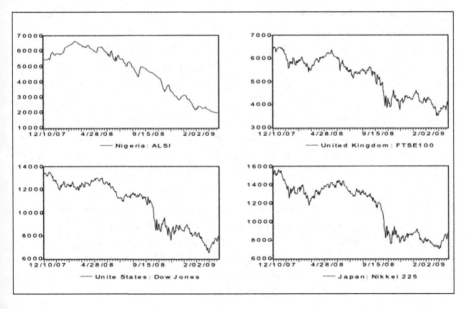

For equation 3.2.1, the short-run relationship between the Egyptian bourse (EGX) and the US/UK is positive and significant. This implies that positive adjustment in the US/UK stock market would affect the EGX positively, and negative adjustment, negatively. In this case, the reaction is likely to hold since the relationship is statistically significant. The long-run coefficient was also significant. This implies that shocks (positive or negative) from the US/UK will spill into the EGX with a susceptibility level of 8.7 per cent.

For equation 3.3.1, the short-run relationship between the Tunisian stock exchange (TUN) and the US/UK stock market is positive and significant implying that positive movements in the US/UK stock market would affect the TUN positively and negative movement, negatively. The degree of susceptibility of the TUN to such shocks would be 3.5 per cent and was likely to occur in the short run. Hence, the TUN would correct itself quickly restricting the impact of the shock on the short run only since the long-run relationship between the TUN and the US/UK stock market is not significant.

Estimated equation 3.4.1 shows that the South African stock exchange (JSE) has a significant and positive short-run relationship with the US/UK which is also sustained in the long run. The implication is that short-run shocks from the US/UK affecting the JSE are sustained in the long run and the JSE was found to be susceptible to the US/UK stock markets by 33.1 per cent.

In summary, Nigeria is the least integrated stock market to the US/UK. Therefore, the poor performance of its stock market within the period can rather be attributable to domestic factors than to shocks that emanated from the 2008 global financial crisis. South Africa on the other hand was the most susceptible.

Comparing Part (A) of Table 5.1 to Part (B) of it reveals something interesting for African stock markets in relation to those in the US/UK and Asia (using Japan as a case study). Though equation 3.1.2 for Nigeria is not significant, it suggests that Nigeria's susceptibility to global financial shocks is lower when integrated with Japan (at 0.4 per cent) than when integrated with the US/UK (at 1.6 per cent). For Egypt, however, the susceptibility rate is higher with Japan than with the US/UK, implying that further integration of Egypt's stock market would be more beneficial with the US/UK than with Asia (Japan). The same is the case for the Tunisian stock exchange in estimated equation 3.3.3. Its susceptibility rate is lower with the US/UK than when linked with Japan. The Tunisian stock exchange did not have a significant long-run relationship with either the US/UK or Japan. This explains why the market seemed to maintain an upward surge within the crisis period. For South Africa, however, its susceptibility rate is lower when integrated with Japan (18.3 per cent) that with the US/UK (33.1 per cent).

Table 5.1: Summary of error Correction Model for African Stock Markets with the US/UK and Japan

(A) Estimated Error correction models for African stock markets with the US/UK

S/N	Estimated Equations	African Stock Markets	Short-run relationship with the US/UK	Long-run cointegrating relationship with US/UK	Susceptible to Contagion from the US/UK Markets	Model Significance (f-statistic)
1	(3.1.1)	Nigeria	(+) but N.S	Significant at 5% level	1.6%	Yes
2	(3.2.1)	Egypt	(+) and Significant	Significant at 5%	8.7%	Yes
3	(3.3.1)	Tunisia	(+) and Significant	N.S	3.5%	Yes
4	(3.4.1)	S/Africa	(+) and Significant	Significant at 5%	33.1%	Yes

(B) Estimated Error Correction Models for African Stock Markets with Japan

S/N	Estimated Equations	African Stock Markets	Short-run relationship with Japan	Long-run cointegrating relationship Japan	Susceptible to Contagion from Japan Markets	Model Significance (f-statistic)
1	(3.1.2)	Nigeria	(-) but N.S	Significant at 10% level	0.4%	No
2	(3.2.2)	Egypt	(+) and Significant	N.S	11.9%	Yes
3	(3.3.3)	Tunisia	(+) and Significant	N.S	6.4%	Yes
4	(3.4.4)	S/Africa	(+) and Significant	Significant at 10% level	18.3%	Yes

Source: researcher's estimation

Note: N.S = Not significant statistically, (+) means positive, (-) implies negative.

The analysis so establishes that African stock markets were interlinked with those of the US/UK and, hence, were susceptible (though at varying degrees) to the impact of the global financial crisis. As will be discussed in the next section, it would however seem that there is no straight answer to whether integration with the global South would be more beneficial for Africa than with countries of the global North. The evidence is clearly country-specific and what is good for the goose may not be good for the gander.

Reflections on Countries of the Global South and Lessons from the Financial Crisis

Countries of the South are emerging economies. Coined in 1981 by Antoine W. Van Agtmael of the World Bank, an emerging market economy (EME) refers to an economy with low-to-middle per capita income (Kehl 2007). Countries in this category are considered emerging because of their commitment to development by implementing a wide range of reforms. Therefore, small economies (like Nigeria) and big ones (like China) can be labelled as emerging. EMEs are characterized as transitionally moving from a closed economy to an open market economy while building accountability within the system. Embarking on an economic reform programme to achieve higher economic performance is also a characteristic of emerging economies. Other characteristics include reforms to attract foreign investors and to reduce the desire for local investors to engage in capital flight, as well as to increase local and foreign investment (portfolio and direct) in general. Investment growth in an emerging country signals injection of foreign currency into direct and portfolio investment sectors of the local economy. For foreign investors therefore, an EME serves as an outlet for new sources of revenue. If the reform measures for such countries are not tightened, this would lead to capital flight and profit plough-backs. When these investors withdraw their funds in times of uncertainty in the international market, it leads to financial and economic crisis for the local economy. Although it is argued that emerging countries would benefit in the long run from liberalization policies as openness is likely to increase production, raise GDP and help emerging countries catch up with the economies of developed countries, it is also argued that market liberalization serves as an avenue for developed countries to exploit resources from emerging economies.

For instance, before 1985, the operation of the Nigerian stock exchange, founded in 1960 as the Lagos stock exchange, was weak. Its operation improved in 1977 within the major commercial cities of the country and, subsequently, strengthened with the implementation of the Structural Adjustment Programme (SAP) in 1986. During this period, the value of the Nigerian naira in relation to the dollar had depreciated significantly. By 1985, the Nigerian naira exchanged for a US dollar at 0.8938. By 1986, however, it exchanged by 2.0206. With the intent of addressing demand and supply constraints, currency devaluation policies have been implemented at different times in Nigeria. By 1999, the naira exchanged for 92.6934 to the US dollar. By 2008, the naira exchanged for the US dollar at 118.5669 and for 148.9017 by 2009 and around 155 naira by 2012. Despite several reforms to revamp the Nigerian stock market since the 2008 global financial crisis, its index has remained lower than the pre-2008 level. By March 2008, the Nigerian stock exchange index stood at 63,016.56 points and declined by almost 70 per cent by March 2009 to 19,803.60 points. Four years on, in May 2013, the Nigerian stock exchange is yet to attain its pre-2008 level as its index averaged 36,326.75 points in May 2013.

Based on the assessment conducted by the Ministerial Conference on Financial Crisis in 2008, Nigeria's financial sector had been in receipt of US$ 15.73 billion in portfolio flows as at 2007 (see Oteh 2010 and Sanusi 2011). With the 2008 global financial crisis, however, foreign investors withdrew holdings from the capital market in Nigeria. The withdrawals of portfolio holdings increased the volatility of stock prices across the Nigerian stock market. While some analysts have argued that sharp practices within domestic stock markets also contributed to steepening the depth of the impact of the financial crisis in Nigeria, the capitalist nature of stock markets which makes them vulnerable to exploitation by private interests, was the root cause of the 2008 global financial crisis, as has been the case since 1929. Hence, while this section argues that certain patterns of integration could offer lesser susceptibility for African stock exchanges, the solution itself can be considered as part of short-term measures to find less vulnerable paths to pursue. For sustainability and long-term focus, however, the debate transcends what patterns of integration offer lesser susceptibility to how to reconstruct the financial architecture of countries of the global South to focus on production, industry and real sector development.

To countries of the global South, the unclear impact of the global financial crisis on China offers some lessons to be learnt. While China faces its own unique challenges like all countries of the world, understanding the impact of the 2008 global financial crisis on China provides its own unique set of lessons for countries of the global South. China's economy is heavily dependent on international trade and investment flows. In 2007, China overtook the United States to become the world's second largest merchandise exporter after the European Union (EU). China's net exports contributed to one-third of its GDP growth in 2007 as its exports of goods and services (as a share of GDP) rose from 9.1 per cent in 1985 to 37.8 per cent in 2008 (Morrison 2009). The Chinese government estimates that the foreign trade sector employs more than

80 million people, of whom 28 million work in foreign-invested enterprises. Foreign direct investment (FDI) flows to China have been a major factor behind its productivity gains and rapid economic growth. FDI flows to China in 2007 totaled US$ 75 billion, making it the largest FDI recipient among emerging economies and the third largest overall, after the EU and the United States. Therefore, the transmission mechanism of the 2008 global financial crisis on China should ordinarily be through its export sector and industries that depended on FDI flows. However, China's exposure to the 2008 global financial crisis was curtailed, depending on how one looks at it.

On the one hand, China places numerous restrictions on capital flows, particularly outflows, so that it can maintain its managed float currency policy. These restrictions limited the ability of Chinese citizens and many firms to invest their savings overseas, but rather, compelled them to invest their savings domestically (such as in banks, the stock markets, real estate, and business ventures). Thus, the exposure of Chinese private sector firms and individual Chinese investors to the sub-prime US mortgages was small. On the other hand, if China held troubled sub-prime mortgage-backed securities, they would likely have been included in the corporate securities category which would have been invested in real estate. Yet, these holdings in China were a relatively a small share of China's total US security holdings and hence would have constituted a lesser risk (Morrison 2009). Thus, while the debate remains as to the extent to which China was affected by the 2008 global financial crisis, the strengthening of its economy around domestic investment and production made it less vulnerable to the crisis. While China was to a lesser extent exposed to the financial crisis, this was not the case for most countries of the global South. These were largely exposed to the vagaries of the crisis due to their high openness to the economies of the US and UK in direct and portfolio trade, and because their economies were largely monolithic and characterized by weak domestic investment and a low industrial base.

Summary and Conclusion

The impact of the 2007-09 global financial crises had consequences for African countries. But would the consequence be any less if the integration of African stock markets were tilted towards countries of the global South? The evidence provided in this paper suggests that some African countries would be better off integrated with the global South while others would be better off furthering their integration with the global North. Countries that would integrate both ways, however, would be likely to reduce susceptibility from external shocks. For instance, comparing the benefits on integrating with the West (the global North) or with the global South, it was found that the (South) African stock exchange (at 33.1 per cent) was more susceptible to external shock from the US/UK while the Nigerian stock market (at 1.6 per cent) was the least susceptible. When integrated with Japan, it was found that South Africa's susceptibility reduced from 33.1 to 18.3 but increased from 0.4 to 1.6 per cent for Nigeria. This finding implies that further integration of Nigeria with Asia would not be as beneficial as it would for South Africa. It also means that, while the decline witnessed in the South African stock exchange can be attributed to the global financial crisis, domestic factors, rather than the global financial crisis, were responsible for the decline in the performance of the Nigerian stock exchange. For Tunisia and Egypt, however, the extent of susceptibility to shocks was lower with the US/UK (at 3.5 and 8.7 per cent respectively) compared to when integrated with Asia (at 6.4 and 11.9 per cent respectively). Similarly, the deduction from this is that though the integration with the global North might have contributed to the negative spread of the global financial crisis to some countries in the global South (e.g. Nigeria and South Africa), it brought about some benefits to others in the global South as well (e.g. Egypt). Hence, the benefit for Egypt's integration with the global South could be explored while the direction of benefit for Tunisia is not clear.

In conclusion, while this chapter argues that a certain pattern of integration could offer lesser susceptibility for African stock exchanges, this solution itself can be considered as part of broader short-term policy measures to addressing vulnerability due to stock market integration. For sustainability and long-term policy measures, however, the debate would ordinarily transcend what pattern of integration offers lesser susceptibility and concern itself with reconstructing the financial architecture of countries of the global South by focusing on production, industry and real sector development.

References

Ackah, C.G, Aryeetey, E. B.-D. and Aryeetay, E., 2009, 'Global Financial Crisis Discussion Series: Ghana', A study coordinated by the Overseas Development Institute (ODI) London and supported by the UK Department for International Development (DFID) and the Dutch Ministry of Foreign Affairs.

Akyuz, Y., 2009, 'Policy Response to the Global Financial crisis: Key Issues for Developing Countries', paper published online by South Centre publishers, Switzerland (May). Available at: http://www.southcentre.org

Amin, S., 2012, 'The South Challenges Globalization'. *Pambazuka* News, Issue 580, 5 April. Available online at: http://pambazuka.org/en/category/features/81307

Amin, S., 2011, *Ending the Crisis of Capitalism or Ending Capitalism?*, Oxford: Pambazuka Press.

Ariyo, A and Fowowe, B., 2009, 'The Global Financial Crisis: Implications and Policy Issues for the Nigerian Economy', paper presented at the Nigerian Economic Society (NES) 50th Annual Conference, 28-30 September at Nicon Luxury Hotel, Abuja

AU and ECA, 2009, 'The Global Financial Crisis: Impact, Responses and Way Forward', Paper presented at the Meeting of the Committee of Experts of the 2nd Joint Annual Meetings of the African Union (AU) Conference of Ministers of Economy and Finance and Economic Commission for Africa (ECA) Conference of Ministers of Finance, Planning and Economic Development Cairo, Egypt, 2-5 June.

Dirk, W.V., 2008, 'Effects of the Global Financial Crisis on Developing Countries and Emerging Markets: Policy Responses to the Crisis', paper presented at the IN-WENT/DIE/BMZ conference in Berlin, December.

Engle, R.F., and Granger, C.W.J., 1987, 'Cointegration and Error Correction Representation, Estimation and Testing', *Econometrica* (March): 255–76.

Granger, C.W.J., 1981, 'Some Properties of Time Series Data and Their Use in Econometric Model Specification', *Journal of Econometrics* 16: 121–30.

Greene, W.H., 1997, '*Econometric Analysis*, 3rd edn, New York: Prentice Hall.

Johnston, J and Dinardo, J., 1997, *Econometric Methods*, New York: McGraw Hill Publishers.

Karolyi, G.A., Stulz, R.M., 1996, 'Why Do Markets Move Together? An Investigation of U.S-Japan Stock Return Comovements', *Journal of Finance* 51(3): 951–86.

Kehl, J.R (2007), 'Emerging Markets in Africa', *African Journal of Political Science and International Relations* 1 (1): 1–8.

Magnusson, M.A and Wydick, B., 2004, 'How Efficient Are Africa's Emerging Stock Mar- ket?', paper published in the African Capital Markets Forum (ACMF) contempo- rary issues vol. II (eds Mensah, S. and T. Moss).

Marashdeh, H., 2005, 'Stock Market Integration in the MENA Region: An Application of the ARDL Bounds Testing Approach'. Faculty of Commerce-Economics working paper, university of Wollongong: http://ro.uow.edu.au/commwkpapers/133.

Morrison, W.M., 2009, 'China and the Global Financial Crisis: Implications for the United States' Congressional Research Service (CRS), Washington DC.

O'Neill, J., 2011, *The Growth Map: Economic Opportunity in the BRICs and Beyond*, London: Penguin Books.

Oteh, A., 2010, 'The Global Financial Crisis and Financial Reform in Nigeria: A Capital Market Perspective', paper by the Director-General, Securities & Exchange Commission, Nigeria.

Park, Y.C., 2009, 'Global Economic Recession and East Asia: How Has Korea Managed the Crisis and What Has it Learned?' Working Paper 409, Seoul, Institute for Monetary and Economic Research, The Bank of Korea, November, pp. 11–13.

Sanusi, S.L., 2011, 'The Impact of the Global Financial Crisis on the Nigerian Capital Market and the Reforms', Paper presented by the Governor of the Central Bank of Nigeria at the 7th Annual Pearl Awards and Public Lecture Held at the Muson Centre, 27 May Lagos, Nigeria.

Tella, S., 2008, 'The Global Economic Crisis, Global Stock Market and the Nigerian Stock Market: Issues and Challenges', Paper presented at the 2008 Annual Get- together of the University of Benin Alumni Association, Ondo State Branch at Akure, 1 November.

Veronesi, P., 1999, 'Stock Market Overreaction to Bad News in Good Times: A Rational Expectations Equilibrium Model', *Review of Financial Studies* 12: 975–1007.

Annexes: Estimated Results for Equations 3.1.1 to 3.4.1, and 3.1.2 to 3.4.4

Table 5.2: Error correction model of the Nigerian stock exchange
with the US/UK

Dependent Variable: D(NSE)

Method: Least Squares

Sample (adjusted): 12/11/2007 3/04/2009

Included observations: 322 after adjusting endpoints

Variable	Coefficient	Std. Error	t-Statistic	Prob.
C	-96.21703	34.12462	-2.819578	0.0051
D(USUK)	0.332820	0.248962	1.336831	0.1822
RES1(-1)	-0.015864	0.006489	-2.444836	0.0150
R-squared	0.021885	Mean dependent var		-101.0146
Adjusted R-squared	0.015752	S.D. dependent var		613.8324
S.E. of regression	608.9785	Akaike info criterion		15.67072
Sum squared resid	1.18E+08	Schwarz criterion		15.70588
Log likelihood	-2519.985	F-statistic		3.568740
Durbin-Watson stat	1.213671	Prob(F-statistic)		0.029322

Source: Eviews Output, researcher's estimation

Table 5.3: Error Correction Model for Egyptian Stock Exchange
with the US/UK

Dependent Variable: D(CASE)

Method: Least Squares

Sample (adjusted): 12/11/2007 3/04/2009

Included observations: 322 after adjusting endpoints

Variable	Coefficient	Std. Error	t-Statistic	Prob.
C	-15.34515	9.292807	-1.651293	0.0997

D(USUK)	0.340666	0.067867	5.019578	0.0000
RES4(-1)	-0.038220	0.011575	-3.302028	0.0011

R-squared	0.092860	Mean dependent var	-20.09745
Adjusted R-squared	0.087173	S.D. dependent var	173.5812
S.E. of regression	165.8430	Akaike info criterion	13.06923
Sum squared resid	8773742.	Schwarz criterion	13.10440
Log likelihood	-2101.147	F-statistic	16.32731
Durbin-Watson stat	1.875695	Prob(F-statistic)	0.000000

Source: Eviews Output, Researcher's Estimation

Table 5.4: Error correction model of Tunisian stock exchange with the US/UK

Dependent Variable: D(TUN)

Method: Least Squares

Sample (adjusted): 12/11/2007 3/04/2009

Included observations: 322 after adjusting endpoints

Variable	Coefficient	Std. Error	t-Statistic	Prob.
C	1.895653	1.332923	1.422177	0.1560
D(USUK)	0.033629	0.009707	3.464435	0.0006
RES2(-1)	-0.006543	0.007178	-0.911480	0.3627

R-squared	0.040643	Mean dependent var	1.412019
Adjusted R-squared	0.034628	S.D. dependent var	24.21061
S.E. of regression	23.78774	Akaike info criterion	9.185490
Sum squared resid	180508.2	Schwarz criterion	9.220657
Log likelihood	-1475.864	F-statistic	6.757172
Durbin-Watson stat	1.870330	Prob(F-statistic)	0.001336

Source: Eviews Output, researcher's estimation

Table 5.5: Error correction model of South African stock exchange with US/UK

Dependent Variable: D(JSE)

Method: Least Squares

Sample (adjusted): 12/11/2007 3/04/2009

Included observations: 322 after adjusting endpoints

Variable	Coefficient	Std. Error	t-Statistic	Prob.
C	-6.053208	23.51797	-0.257387	0.7970
D(USUK)	2.127111	0.170642	12.46533	0.0000
RES3(-1)	-0.043490	0.015828	-2.747565	0.0063
R-squared	0.335551	Mean dependent var		-36.43882
Adjusted R-squared	0.331385	S.D. dependent var		513.3046
S.E. of regression	419.7235	Akaike info criterion		14.92634
Sum squared resid	56197534	Schwarz criterion		14.96151
Log likelihood	-2400.141	F-statistic		80.54835
Durbin-Watson stat	2.153188	Prob(F-statistic)		0.000000

Source: Eviews Output, researcher's estimation

Table 5.6: Error correction model of the Nigerian stock exchange with Japan

Dependent Variable: D(NSE)

Method: Least Squares

Sample (adjusted): 12/11/2007 3/04/2009

Included observations: 322 after adjusting endpoints

Variable	Coefficient	Std. Error	t-Statistic	Prob.
C	-101.8623	34.27122	-2.972239	0.0032
D(NIKKEI)	-0.040701	0.128695	-0.316256	0.7520
RES11(-1)	-0.010129	0.005532	-1.831156	0.0680
R-squared	0.011158	Mean dependent var		-101.0146
Adjusted R-squared	0.004958	S.D. dependent var		613.8324

S.E. of regression	612.3087	Akaike info criterion	15.68162
Sum squared resid	1.20E+08	Schwarz criterion	15.71679
Log likelihood	-2521.741	F-statistic	1.799787
Durbin-Watson stat	1.235813	Prob(F-statistic)	0.167009

Source: Eviews Output, Researcher's Estimation

Table 5.7: Error Correction model of Egyptian stock exchange
with Japan

Dependent Variable: D(CASE)

Method: Least Squares

Sample(adjusted): 12/11/2007 3/04/2009

Included observations: 322 after adjusting endpoints

Variable	Coefficient	Std. Error	t-Statistic	Prob.
C	-14.35707	9.117680	-1.574641	0.1163
D(NIKKEI)	0.232672	0.034497	6.744641	0.0000
RES44(-1)	-0.010015	0.009239	-1.084025	0.2792
R-squared	0.124808	Mean dependent var		-20.09745
Adjusted R-squared	0.119321	S.D. dependent var		173.5812
S.E. of regression	162.8965	Akaike info criterion		13.03338
Sum squared resid	8464748.	Schwarz criterion		13.06855
Log likelihood	-2095.374	F-statistic		22.74564
Durbin-Watson stat	1.853469	Prob(F-statistic)		0.000000

Source: Eviews Output, researcher's estimation

Table 5.8: Error Correction model of the Tunisian stock exchange with Japan

Dependent Variable: D(TUN)

Method: Least Squares

Sample (adjusted): 12/11/2007 3/04/2009

Included observations: 322 after adjusting endpoints

Variable	Coefficient	Std. Error	t-Statistic	Prob.
C	1.979744	1.311287	1.509772	0.1321
D(NIKKEI)	0.022983	0.004917	4.674171	0.0000
RES22(-1)	-0.006885	0.006843	-1.006251	0.3151
R-squared	0.069352	Mean dependent var		1.412019
Adjusted R-squared	0.063517	S.D. dependent var		24.21061
S.E. of regression	23.42910	Akaike info criterion		9.155108
Sum squared resid	175106.4	Schwarz criterion		9.190275
Log likelihood	-1470.972	F-statistic		11.88599
Durbin-Watson stat	1.884122	Prob(F-statistic)		0.000011

Source: Eviews Output, researcher's estimation

Table 5.9: Error correction model of South African stock exchange with Japan

Dependent Variable: D(JSE)

Method: Least Squares

Sample (adjusted): 12/11/2007 3/04/2009

Included observations: 322 after adjusting endpoints

Variable	Coefficient	Std. Error	t-Statistic	Prob.
C	-15.49737	25.97354	-0.596660	0.5512
D(NIKKEI)	0.846608	0.098580	8.588007	0.0000
RES33(-1)	-0.027543	0.015934	-1.728538	0.0849
R-squared	0.187899	Mean dependent var		-36.43882

Adjusted R-squared	0.182807	S.D. dependent var	513.3046
S.E. of regression	464.0207	Akaike info criterion	15.12701
Sum squared resid	68685553	Schwarz criterion	15.16218
Log likelihood	-2432.448	F-statistic	36.90412
Durbin-Watson stat	2.079122	Prob(F-statistic)	0.000000

Source: Eviews Output, researcher's estimation

6

Global Economic Crisis and South Africa's Manufacturing Industry: The Case of the Automotive, Textile and Clothing, and Mining Industries

Theresa Moyo

Introduction: The Global Financial and Economic Crisis

The most recent global financial and economic crisis (hereafter referred to as 'the crisis') which started around September 2008 has raised many questions about globalization and its effects on countries of the South. In an era where the ideology of free markets, trade liberalization and integration of the economies of developing countries to the global system is being promoted through trade, foreign direct investment and capital flows, among other mechanism, the crisis has renewed debates around the role of markets versus state intervention in the economy. The impact of the crisis on South Africa presents important lessons for many countries in the South for a number of reasons. Although it is classified as a middle-income country and is now part of the BRICS group (the others being Brazil, Russia, India and China), South Africa was adversely affected by the crisis. A study of the automobile, textile, clothing and mining industries provides some evidence to support this. This chapter explains why and how these sectors were affected and what the response of the government was. It also recommends strategies which could reduce the country's vulnerability to similar shocks in future.

The origins and causes of the global financial and economic crisis have been well documented. Evidence from several sources shows that the crisis started around September 2008 when the United States housing market bubble burst and sparked off one of the most severe global recessions since the Great

Depression of the 1930s. Bad loans in the mortgage market led to a credit squeeze and loss of consumer confidence. Values of stocks and domestic currencies plunged. Global growth was predicted to fall as a result. Zemsky (1998), Chari and Kehoe (2004), Alan (1999) and the African Development Bank (2009b) present this explanation. Aggregate demand by both consumers and firms declined and this affected developing countries through slumping exports and commodity prices.

The vulnerability of South Africa to the crisis has to be understood within a historical and political context. During the apartheid era, multinational companies, mainly from the United States, Britain, Germany and Japan, among others, invested in the country particularly in sectors such as mining, manufacturing and agriculture. Foreign direct investment was the cornerstone of the country's growth. Apartheid policies of racial discrimination against blacks created one of the most unequal societies in the world where the economy was largely owned and controlled by whites. The Native Land Act of 1913 dispossessed millions of blacks of their land. Discriminatory legislation on access to land, education, health services, housing and labour markets excluded the majority black population from the economy. Democratic transition was achieved in 1994. The government embarked on many programmes which aimed to rectify historical injustices and inequity, for example, the Reconstruction and Development Programme (RDP) of 1994, the Growth, Employment and Redistribution (GEAR) Programme, the Accelerated and Shared Growth Initiative of South Africa (AsgiSA), and more recently, the National Development Plan. Under GEAR, the government adopted market-friendly policies as a strategy to stimulate economic growth. It promoted export-oriented strategies and adopted trade liberalization. The country's ratio of trade in goods and services to GDP is more than 60 per cent. The country is also a major commodity exporter, particularly of minerals such as diamonds, platinum, iron ore and gold, to name but a few.

South Africa has one of Africa's largest automobile assembly and manufacturing industries, a sector which is dominated by MNCs which are based in the United States, Europe, Japan and Germany. As evidence shows, the automobile industry in Europe and the United States was one of the hardest hit by the global crisis as consumer demand for some durable goods declined. Since South Africa's automotive industry mainly exports to these same markets, it was bound to be affected. The country is also a major exporter of cotton and clothing and textile products. South Africa became a member of the World Trade Organisation (WTO) in 1994 and, since then, has liberalized its trade by reducing tariffs and removing other barriers to trade. Whereas this has contributed to a larger role for trade, it has also increased the vulnerability of the country to the dynamic changes and fluctuations in global trade, investment and economic activity in general. Because South Africa is also closely integrated with the Southern African Development Community (SADC), as well as other African countries, the negative impact of the crisis on South Africa also affected most of those countries.

The pace of change and transformation has been slow and the present government has acknowledged that. Although the government has legislation for land redistribution, land restitution and land tenure reforms, statistics show that only 30 per cent of the target for land redistribution had been achieved by 2010 (Department of Land Affairs and Rural Development 2010). The government has also tried to implement the Broad-Black Based Economic Empowerment (BBBEE) policy which aimed to increase economic ownership and participation by blacks. Progress on this has been slow as well. What does all this mean in relation to the global crisis? When the crisis hit, companies responded to the falling external demand by retrenching workers. As a result, thousands of workers in the three sectors under discussion, who had no access to land or the required skills to access labour markets and other opportunities for survival, found themselves with no alternatives. Thus the vulnerability of the economy arose not just because of its integration with global markets, but also because of patterns of racially-based inequality and social exclusion.

The choice of the three sectors here is informed by a number of considerations. These sectors are all significant contributors to GDP, job creation and poverty reduction, exports and earnings. The automotive sector is a major employer. Half of the automotive industry is located in one of South Africa's poorer provinces, the Eastern Cape and it is a major employer of the population there. The automotive components' manufacturing sector also has potential for participation of small and medium-sized enterprises (SMEs) in the manufacturing sector since their capital outlays and technological capabilities are much lower than thiose of vehicle manufacturers and assemblers. It also provides an opportunity for blacks to enter into the automotive industry which historically has been dominated by foreign capital and white businesses. The clothing and textile sector is labour-intensive (particularly in terms of low-skilled labour), is situated close to rural areas and so it is significant for rural development. It is also a major employer of women and, in that way, contributes to women's empowerment. The industry was once heavily protected through a tariff wall but since the liberalization of the economy, it has been severely affected. The textile and clothing industry is also known to be uncompetitive due to high wage costs, low skills and a lack of new technology. Productivity is lower than that of competitors in advanced and emerging economies and therefore the liberalization of the sector came at a time when it was least prepared for external competition. Since 2007, it has been struggling to compete against cheap imports from China, Malaysia and Singapore. The sector has suffered from widespread job losses and factory closures. Wooley (2009) refers to it as an industry which is 'in terminal decline'.

Mining companies are a major employer of unskilled labour from rural communities. The automotive and mining industries are also highly integrated into the global trading and financial system through the role of foreign investment, participation of multinational companies, their exports into advanced and emerging markets, imports of inputs and finished products, technology and skills transfer. In addition, the dominance of commodity production and exports in the case of the mining, textile and clothing industries makes these sectors particularly vulnerable to external crises. So it is relevant to examine the impact of the global financial and economic crises by studying how these sectors performed during the period 2008 to 2011.

The main objectives of the chapter are:

a. To review the impact of the global financial and economic crisis on the automotive, mining, and textile and clothing industries in South Africa;

b. To review and assess critically, the response of the public sector to the crisis.

The chapter postulates the hypothesis that the global financial and economic crisis had an adverse impact on South Africa's automotive, textile and clothing and mining sectors. It also argues that although the government's response was timely, it was not adequate to deal with the nature of the problem, which was deeply rooted in structural factors facing the industry.

Theoretical Framework

In order to understand the impact of the global economic and financial crisis on a country, one has to examine the economic policy in post-apartheid South Africa because this has determined the nature and extent of the country's integration into the world economy.

Greenberg (2004) aptly considers the South African economy in terms of what he refers to as the 'the post-apartheid developmental model' :

> The post-apartheid developmental model is situated in a context of a decades-long global restructuring of economic and political systems, driven by state managers, multilateral global institutions and profit-based economic elites. From an ideological point of view, the Project of restructuring is committed to opening up commodity and financial markets to increased competition (liberalisation and deregulation); the ceding to profit making organisations of potentially profitable economic activities formerly carried out by the state (deregulation and privatisation); and the use of the state to facilitate these goals. Given the integrated nature of the world economy, peripheral countries are compelled to follow the lead of core countries. Restructuring initiated by capital in the core capitalist economies

in response to overaccumulation and recession found fertile ground in South Africa too, where the apartheid growth path was also reaching structural limits. The economy was skewed towards the production and consumption of luxury goods for a narrow White domestic market. It relied on artificially cheap wages for the majority, thus preventing Fordist mass consumption that drove the expansions of the capitalist core economies from the Second World War. The result was overaccumulation and 'trapped capital', with limited potential growth in domestic effective demand for commodities.

Due to its integration into the global economy, South Africa was affected by the crisis in terms of its exports, imports, financial flows, production volumes and employment. The degree of openness as reflected in the tariff structure also gives an indication of vulnerability (Avery and Zemsky 1998; Chari and Kehoe 2004). This is reflected by, among other things, the country's ratio of trade in goods and services to Gross Domestic Product (GDP) being more than 60 per cent (Department of Trade and Industry 2009). Held et al (1999) speak of the dynamic nature of markets in the context of liberalization. When market conditions change, the actors and players in the system make some real adjustments and reposition, and restructure their operations in order to adapt and adjust to those changing market conditions. The crisis led to a fall in demand in the US and Europe. Because of the integration of emerging economies into the world system through their exports, imports and foreign direct investment flows, they were also negatively affected by the crisis as their exports into the US and Europe collapsed. Part of their re-adjustment or adaptation included diversion of their exports to developing country destinations like South Africa. Because South Africa had already started to remove tariff barriers, the flood of cheap imports could not be halted.

UNCTAD (2011) observes that:

> The global environment for African industrialization is also changing in several significant respects and efforts to promote industrialization in the twenty-first century must also take account of this new environment. First, multilateral trade rules as well as bilateral and regional trade agreements are shrinking the policy space available for promoting industrial development in African countries that are not classified as Least Developed Countries (LDCs).

South Africa was constrained in terms of using trade policy as a result of the situation which UNCTAD is describing. UNCTAD also gives as examples, first, the rules of the World Trade Organization (WTO) which prohibit the use of industrial policy instruments such as quotas and local content requirements. It also cites the use of export subsidies which has also been banned, except for the LDCs. The policy space has also been limited because South Africa, like a number of other African countries, has signed Economic Partnership Agreements (EPAs) with the European Union. African countries are under increasing pressure to abandon the use of tariffs as a measure of protection. As indicated in subsequent sections of this chapter, these issues also were constraints with regard to South Africa's public responses to the crisis.

Consequently, as UNCTAD emphasizes,

> African industrialization is taking place in an environment in which the use of some industrial policy instruments applied by the developed and emerging economies are either banned or regulated.

UNCTAD also notes that the global environment in which manufacturing production takes place has also changed in the sense that firms are increasingly facing stiff competition in global export markets due to the reduction in tariff and non-tariff barriers to trade in industrial products coupled with the significant decrease in transport costs and improvements in information and communication technology. For African countries, the new environment is challenging because of the rise and growing role of large developing countries such as China, India and Brazil in labour-intensive manufactures (Kaplinsky 2007).

Part of the challenge that South Africa has faced in some sectors, especially textiles and clothing, is the stiff competition from cheaper producers who found easy entry into the economy as the country liberalized prior to the crisis.

In short, the impact of the crisis on the three sectors is analysed within the context of an economy which has liberalized under the WTO rules and has become integrated into the world economy. As a higher-cost producer compared to external competitors, it was bound to be affected by global changes.

Methodological Approach

A desk study was conducted using secondary data from sources such as the National Association of Automobile Manufacturers of South Africa (NAAMSA), the National Association of Automobile Component Manufacturers (NAACAM), the Chamber of Mines-South Africa, the Textile Federation of South Africa (TFSA) and Statistics South Africa (STATSSA). Although. I would have liked to carry out a survey of the industries under study, this was not feasible within the short space of time available for preparation of the chapter. The findings presented in the chapter may not be comprehensive but, nonetheless, do present some evidence of how the crisis affected the three sectors, and also a critical review of the response of the public sector.

Overview of the Automotive, Mining, and Textile and Clothing Industries

The Automotive Industry

The automotive industry is regarded as a strategic sector for the South African economy and is the largest and leading manufacturing sector. Consequently, the government has identified the industry as a key growth sector, with the aim of increasing vehicle production to 1.2 million units by 2020, while significantly increasing local content at the same time. The country is the leading producer of automobiles in Africa, producing over 75 per cent of the total vehicles on the continent. (NAAMSA 2010). All of the major vehicle makers are represented in South Africa, as well as eight of the world's top ten auto component manufacturers and three of the four largest tyre manufacturers. Many of the major multinational companies use South Africa to source components and assemble vehicles for both the local and overseas markets.

The South African automotive industry consists of the manufacture, distribution, servicing and maintenance of motor vehicles and contributes significantly to the economy. The industry is largely located in two provinces, the Eastern Cape and Gauteng. Because these are coastal areas, the industry is able to take advantage of the low production costs, coupled with access to new markets as a result of trade agreements with the European Union and the Southern African Development Community free trade area.

The sector accounts for about 10 per cent of South Africa's manufacturing exports. According to data by the National Association of Automobile Manufacturers (NAAMSA 2011), annual production in 2007 was 535,000 vehicles. The sector contributes about 7.5 per cent of the country's gross domestic product (GDP) and employs around 36,000 people.

The country exports vehicles to more than seventy countries, mainly Japan (around 29 per cent of the value of total exports), Australia (20 per cent), the UK (12 per cent) and the US (11 per cent). African export destinations include Algeria, Zimbabwe and Nigeria.

Despite the government's BBBEE policy, transformation of the sector in terms of broadening participation to historically disadvantaged individuals (HDIs) (mainly black) has been so slow that ownership and control has largely remained unchanged. Thus the sector is still dominated by subsidiaries of MNCs. German companies such as Mercedes-Benz South Africa and Volkswagen South Africa, General Motors (GM), Ford from the United States and the Japanese Toyota South Africa are among the top car manufacturers or assemblers (NAAMSA 2011). The sector has been growing rapidly since 2003 but experienced some decline at the onset of the global crisis in 2008. The automotive industry is located in economically depressed industrial towns (Botshabelo, Phuthaditjhaba, Isithebe, Newcastle, Ladysmith, Atlantis, Worcester, Mogwase, Babalegi, Dimbaza) and major cities (Cape Town, Durban, Johannesburg, East London, Port Elizabeth, Pietermaritzburg) ((Department of Trade and Industry 2009a)

According to NAAMSA (2011), the auto industry was established in the 1920s and over time grew largely under protectionist policies of successive governments. Since South Africa became a member of the WTO in 1994, there has been a policy shift from import substitution to export promotion. State support to the sector has been extensive under the Motor Industry Development Programme (MIDP) which was started in 1994. The MIDP aimed to make the sector more competitive and also to assist it in increasing exports. The sector has been gradually liberalized through massive reduction of tariffs. For example, tariffs have been reduced from high protection levels of 65 to 36 per cent and duty-free allowances have been introduced. When the global crisis struck, South Africa was already in the process of liberalizing the sector. This is what contributed to its vulnerability because it has even been acknowledged by the government that the country's industry was not competitive globally largely due to high labour costs, low productivity and lack or shortage of skilled labour used in the industries.

Textile and Clothing Industry

The textile and clothing industry in South Africa includes sub-sectors such as fibre production, spinning, weaving, knitting, non-wovens, carpet production, fabric coating. The industry consists of around 300 manufacturers, based mainly in Kwa-Zulu-Natal, the Western Cape, the Eastern Cape and Gauteng. A few companies also operate in the Free State and Mpumalanga.

The liberalization of the economy which accelerated in 1994 when South Africa became a member of the WTO has had some negative impacts on the sector. Through the government's seven-year tariff phase down for textiles and clothing, introduced in 1995 by September 1999 duties had been substantially reduced so that the country was ahead of its WTO commitments. Removal or reduction of tariffs has led to a flood of cheap imports and the competition has led to the closure of a number of companies and some cutting down of production. Exports have also been adversely affected through the discontinuation of export incentives.

As a result of the changing market environment both domestically as well as globally, there have been major changes in ownership in a sector which was once dominated by multinational companies as the industry has braced itself for the challenges and opportunities of globalization.

Mining Industry

South Africa is one of the world's and Africa's most important mining countries in terms of the variety and quantity of minerals produced. According to Leon (2012), the centrality of mining to South Africa's economy is illustrated by the fact that nearly 60 per cent of the country's export revenue is attributable to mining, mineral and secondary beneficiated products. In 2010, Leon also indicates its mineral resources were approximately R 17.5 trillion –some of the largest in the world. Further, South Africa is also estimated to possess 89 per cent of the world's platinum group metal reserves and 13 per cent of its gold. The country also possesses significant quantities of chrome, vanadium and manganese.

Mining is also a major contributor to GDP, employment and export earnings. It is a major employer of both domestic and foreign labour. Migrant labour still plays an integral role in the mining industry, with labour being sourced from Lesotho, Mozambique, Botswana and Zimbabwe. The gold industry remains the largest employer, responsible for more than 50 per cent of total employment. The industry is predominantly foreign-owned and also white-controlled although there are efforts to transform under the Broad - Black Based Economic Empowerment (BBBEE) initiative of the government.

The Chamber of Mines of South Africa is the largest industry body which represents the mining sector. The country's mineral industry can be broken down into five broad categories – gold, PGM, diamonds, coal and vanadium. In 2010, there were forty-one mining companies in the country. South Africa is among the top ten global mining countries in the world, as measured by GDP. It has the largest mining companies, in terms of market capitalization. Some of the major mining companies operating in the country include the following:

1. Platinum Mining (Anglo Platinum Limited, Impala Platinum Limited, Lonmin Platinum Limited, Northam Platinum Limited, Royal Bafokeng Platinum, Xstrata Alloys of South Africa).

2. Gold mining (Anglo Gold Ashanti Limited, Harmony Gold Mining Company Limited, Goldfields)

3. Diamond mining (De Beers Consolidated Mining, Namakawa Diamonds)

4. Coal mining (BHP Billiton)

5. Chrome mining (Anglo American Corporation, Rio Tinto)

6. Others include base metal/minerals exploration companies (for example, Mvelaphanda Resources, Richards Bay Minerals, and African Rainbow Minerals Limited).

Most of the companies are subsidiaries of multinational companies. This again reflects the country's historical legacy where ownership and control of mining assets was and is still predominantly in the hands of export-oriented private foreign capital.

Literature Review

A number of studies have been conducted on the impact of the global and financial crisis on South Africa.

The United Nations Economic Commission for Africa (UNECA 2009a) argues that the global financial and economic crisis presents significant challenges for African countries. It has also exposed weaknesses in the functioning of the global economy and has led to calls for the reform of the international financial architecture. The crisis represents a serious setback for Africa because it is taking place at a time when the region is making progress in economic performance and management. Since 2000, the African region has had an average growth rate of real output of above 5 per cent and inflation has declined to single digits. The Commission argues that the global financial and economic crisis threatens to reverse these gains in economic performance and management. (UNECA 2008).

Studies by the African Development Bank (2009a, 2009b), the United Nations Economic Commission for Africa (UNECA 2009) and the International Monetary Fund (2009) all concur that the global financial and economic crisis had an adverse impact on most African economies and also that South Africa was among those worst affected because of its relatively larger share of exports to Northern countries as compared to the rest of Africa.

Using a Computable General Equilibrium (CGE) Model, Chitiga et al argue that the crisis affected South Africa, albeit with a lag. It was affected through a sharp decline in demand for its export products, the fall in the prices of some key export commodities and also through a fall in foreign investment. They also note that this was the first time in 17 years that the country was experiencing a recession of such a magnitude. Their study also indicates that economic growth also fell to its lowest level in five years, and the GDP dropped 1.5 per cent in six months to March 2009.

The study also predicted that declining export prices and export volumes would lead to a fall in government revenue. In the mining sector, the study observed that there was a decline in several commodity prices from 2008. Platinum Group Metals (PGM) were particularly hard hit, with prices falling by 60 per cent. Coal prices were reported to have fallen by 30 per cent and those for copper by 50 per cent. Gold prices, however, increased from US$

895/ounce in 2008 to US$ 916/ounce in 2009. A report by the Business Monitor International (2010) indicated that gold production declined over the period 2008 to 2009 not because of the crisis but rather, due to power shortages and also due to labour unrest. Wad (2010) writes that generally, the crisis did not impact automotive markets in developing countries severely, except for automotive exporting countries like Mexico, Thailand and South Africa. The impact was felt through declining production and export sales.

Chitiga et al (2010) predicted that the crisis would lead to unemployment, increasing it by as much as 10 per cent. Their study also highlighted the difficulty for most African countries, to finance rescue packages for industry. They also cited the limited fiscal space and international reserves of most African countries and explained that these were likely to constrain their capacity to respond both in a timely manner as well as adequately.

The literature also abounds with information on possible future strategies to respond to similar crises. They recommend a more flexible approach to macroeconomic policy such as adoption of countercyclical policies in times of crisis.

Kasekende et al (2010) emphasize the importance of a long-term approach. In that context, policies should focus on key structural reforms such as enhancing competition in the financial sector, vulnerable segments of the population. They also advocate the streamlining of labour market regulations, developing financial markets and strengthening governance, in order to improve domestic fundamentals, promoting private sector development and enhancing economic diversification. Equally important, they emphasize that reforms must accompanied by measures to protect vulnerable groups in the population. Essentially this means that governments have to allocate adequate resources into safety nets and, of course, create opportunities for new employment. In relation to South Africa, the authors welcomed the stance of the government of South African in adopting a countercyclical fiscal stimulus of R 787 billion for public investment during 2010-12. They also supported the decision of the South African Reserve Bank to ease monetary policy between December 2008 and October 2009, by cutting the policy rate by up to 500 basis points.

Wad's study (2010) reviews how the companies responded and indicates that most of them did what any company in crisis typically would do, for example, temporary downsizing, cost reductions, retraining, consolidation, innovation. Governments responded also by launching traditional stimuli packages (cash-for-clunkers, tax reductions on smaller and/or cleaner cars and so on). Strategic initiatives were taken to improve the competitiveness of the domestic industry. Strategies consisted of consolidation and liberalization, on the one hand, and those aimed to transform it from a brown industry to a 'greener' industry on the other hand. They included tightening environmental regulations, fuel efficiency and emission standards.

He recommends that in addition to traditional countercyclical measures, there is a need to mobilize key stakeholders so as to develop and implement strategies to increase productivity and innovation.

According to the UNECA (2009), many African countries have taken several steps to mitigate the impact of the financial crisis on their economies, including interest rate reductions, recapitalization of financial institutions, increasing liquidity to banks and firms, fiscal stimulus packages, trade policy changes, and regulatory reforms. The measures adopted differ from country to country, depending on available fiscal space as well as the degree of vulnerability to the crisis.

However, the author was not able to find a comprehensive study which focused particularly on the three sectors.

Presentation and Interpretation of Findings: Impact of the Crisis on the Three Sectors

Automotive Industry

Table 6.1 presents data on vehicle sales and exports from the automotive industry over the period 2006-10. Data for 2011-12 were not available.

As Table 6.1 shows, the global crisis contributed to the decline of the automotive industry in terms of vehicle production, sales, exports and imports. Total domestic production declined by 30 per cent over the 2008 to 2009 period but improved in 2010. Localsales of domestically produced vehicles also declined by 25 per cent over the same period. Exports fell from 195,670 units in 2008 to 128,602 in 2009, a 34 per cent decline. Total car imports also declined by 23 per cent in the same period. A similar pattern is observed in respect of light commercial vehicle production, sales and exports, which all declined in 2008 to 2009, but improved in 2010. While from a technical point of view, it may not be correct to infer that the decline in performance over the 2008-09 period was solely due to the global crisis, based on what industry players themselves said (notably NAAMSA, Chamber of Mines, NAACAM and others), there is a basis for concluding that, indeed, the crisis contributed to the poor performance over that period.

Table 6.2 shows that the global production of vehicles declined over 2008 and 2009. South Africa's share of global production also fell during that period, from 0.79 in 2008 to 0.6 in 2009.

Table 6.1: Automotive Industry Vehicl Sales 2006 10 and exports 2000-10

	2007	Per cent change 2006/2007	2008	Per cent change 2007/2008	2009	Per cent change 2008/2009	2010	Per cent change 2009/2010
Domestically produced								
Local sales	169558	-21.2	125454	-26.0	194379	-24.8	113740	20.5
Exports (CBU)	106460	-10.7	195670	83.8	128602	-34.3	181654	41.3
Total domestic production	276018	-17.5	321124	16.3	222981	-30.6	295394	32.5
CBU Imports								
NAAMSA	214873	899.4	169610	-21.1	130326	-23.2	165341	26.9
Non-NAAMSA	50222	-8.3	134198	-31.9	33424	-2.3	58049	73.7
Total car imports	265095	27.5	265095	-0.4	203808	-23	223390	
Total local car market	434653	-9.7	329262	-24.2	258129	-21.6	337130	30.6
Light Commercials								
Domestically produced								
local sales	156626	-1.8	118641	-24.3	85663	-27.8	96823	13
Exports	64127	6.6	87314	36.2	45514	-47.9	56950	25.1
Total domestic production	220753	0.5	205955	-6.7	131177	-36.3	153773	17.2
CBU imports	34592	27.2	40647	17.5	24459	-39.8	27796	13.6
NAAMSA	13168	1.2	10178	-22.7	8037	-21.0	9121	13.5
Non-NAAMSA members								

Source: NAAMSA Statistics 2011 (NAAMSA is an industry body for automobile manufacturers)

Table 6.2: Global South African Vehicle Production 2005-10

	2005	2006	Per cent change 2005/2006	2007	Per cent change 2006/2007	2008	Per cent change 2007/2008	2009	Per cent change 2008/2009	2010	Per cent change 2009/2010
Global vehicle production (millions)	66.49	69.33	4.27	73.1	5.44	70.53	-3.52	61.79	-12.39	77.86	-26.01
SA vehicle production	0.53	0.59		0.54		0.56	0.37		0.47		—
SA share of global production	0.79	0.85		0.73		0.79		0.6		0.6	

Source: NAAMSA Statistics 2010

Table 6.3 shows more details on the performance of the automotive industry over the period of the crisis. A number of observations can be made:

- Capital expenditure by Original Equipment Manufacturers (OEMs) declined by 25 per cent between 2008 and 2009 but increased significantly in 2010.

- The total number of units of vehicles produced fell from 562,965 in 2008 to 373,923 in 2009.

- There was a decline in total vehicle sales from 533,387 (2008) to 395,222 in 2009.

- The total number of vehicles exported fell from 284,211 in 2008 to 174,947 units in 2009 but increased to 239,465 in 2010.

- Productivity per employee fell from 18 to 13.2 over the 2008 to 2009 period as production falls.

- The contribution of the auto sector to GDP declined from 7.3 in 2008 to 5.9 in 2009 but picked up in 2010 when it rose to 6.5 per cent.

- The number of export destinations fell from 135 in 2008 to 125 in 2009, again a reflection of the fall in exports.

As Table 6.4 shows, South Africa's intra-regional trade is mostly with countries in Asia (share of total trade is on average 65 per cent), followed by a few countries in Latin America (for example, Brazil, Argentina and Mexico). Trade with the rest of Africa has the least share, averaging 16.5 per cent between 2008 and 2010. Some of the factors which explain this smaller share are the poor trade infrastructure in Africa, the high cost of doing business and lower incomes on average for most African countries since they fall in the low-income group. This means that demand could be much less than from the other trading partners in Asia and Latin America, most of which fall in the middle-income group of countries.

Table 6.5 also shows a decline of 10.5 per cent over 2008-09 in terms of total motor trade sales.

Table 6.6 presents performance in terms of capacity utilization in the motor manufacturing industry over the period 2007 to 2010. It is evident that, across all types of vehicles, there is a decrease in capacity utilization in 2009 but that this improved in 2010. Light commercial, medium and heavy commercial vehicles declined by over 20 per cent in 2009.

Table 6.3: Performance of South Africa's Automotive Industry 1995-10

Activity	1995	2008	2009	2010
Capital expenditure by OEMs (in Rand)	841 m	3,289.9 b	2,467b	4b
Export value (vehicles and components)	4.2b	94.2b	61b	75b
Total vehicles exported (units)	15,764	284211	174947	239465
Productivity (average no of vehicles produced per employee)	10	18	13.2	16.6
Automotive industry contribution to GDP(percent)	6.5	7.3	5.9	6.5
No of passenger car derivatives	356	1914	1842	1914
Export destinations for vehicles and components above R 1 m per annum	62	135	125	125
Total vehicles produced (units)	389392	562965	373923	472049
Total new vehicle sales (units)	399967	533387	395222	492907
No of model platforms	42	18	17	15
Models with production volumes 40 000 units or more	0	3	4	4

Source: National Association of Automobile Manufacturers of South Africa Statistics 2010

Average Rand/US$ exchange rates were as follows: 1995: R 3/US$; 2008 R 6.5/US$; 2010: R7/US$.

Table 6.4: South Africa's Intra-regional Trade 2005-10

Region	2005	2006	2007	2008	2009
Brazil (Latin America)	46.4	46.1	43.3	44	43.1
Russia-Commonent States	13.3	13.9	16.4	14.7	15.5
India (Asia)	30.3	31.3	31.7	33.1	29.6
China (Asia)	55.9	54	53	49.5	49.2
Argentina					
America	52.5	49.1	47.1	46.7	47.8
Mexico-America	93	92.5	95	93.2	94.6
Indonesia					
Asia	68.3	68.4	64.4	64.9	65.5
Thailand (Asia)	58.3	55.7	60.1	60.2	61.3
South Africa					
Africa	15.3	14.6	14.8	17	16

Source: Department of Trade and Industry Statistics. South Africa

Table 6.5: Total Motor Trade Sales (R million)

	2007	2008	2009	2010	2011
Total sales (Rm)		358,777	321,034	369,815	421,214
Per cent change in sales	9.4	4	-10.5	15.2	13.9

Source: Statistics South Africa (2012). Motor Trade Sales Average Exchange rates: 2006: R 5/US$; 2007 R6/US$; 2008: R6.5/USD.

Note: Sales include new vehicle sales, used vehicle sales, workshop income and income from exports.

Table 6.6: Motor Vehicle Manufacturing Capacity Utilization Levels 2007-10

	2007	Per cent	2008	Per cent change	2009	Per cent change	2010	% per cent change
Cars	67.7	-15.5	68.3	0.89	59.4	-13.03	77.1	29.8
Light commercials	82.7	-5.81	73.9	-10.64	56.5	-23.55	68.4	21.06
Medium commercial	91.7	-6.33	89.9	-1.96	64.6	-28.14	77.2	19.56
Heavy commercial	95.3	0.21	87.6	-8.08	66.1	-24.56	77.5	17.25

Source: NAAMSA Statistics 2011

Clearly, the overall picture in terms of performance of the automotive industry over 2008 and 2009 is that there was a decline in terms of production volumes, export and sales in general, capacity utilization and employment. Most, if not all, of this decline was attributed to the crisis, at least as confirmed by NAAMSA, the government and trade unions.

The Textile and Clothing Industry

Like the other two industries, the textile and clothing sector suffered from retrenchments due to falling global demand. Due to a decrease in demand in the largest markets including the US, Europe and Japan, there was a fall in demand for textile and clothing products. As companies cut down production, overcapacity resulted and led to downward pressures on prices around the world.

Large producers including China have turned to other export markets such as South Africa with products being sold to local retailers at unrealistic price. Preliminary January 2009 trade statistics from the South African Revenue Service showed a 44 per cent increase in the value of clothing and textile imports into South Africa, compared with January 2008.

According to the Department of Trade and Industry, clothing and textile exports decreased by 9 per cent from January 2008 to January 2009, compared with a 15 per cent increase from January 2007 to January 2008.The result is that South Africa's clothing and textile trade deficit increased by 65 per cent to R 16 billion. Local demand also declined. A number of textile and clothing companies are reported to have closed down. Some retrenched workers and this increased unemployment.Evidence from the South Africa Labour Research Institute indicates that the past six years have already seen industry employment falling by 69,000 or 39 per cent. The main cause of these job losses has been the continued high levels of cheap imports, both legal and illegal. Since 2007, the economy saw a decrease in the level of job losses. This was mainly as a result of the protection offered to a large part of the industry by the introduction of quotas on 31 products from China. However, with the end of the quotas and the arrival of the economic crisis, tens of thousands more jobs may be lost. The Institute also reported that the period January and February 2009 had already seen 2,200 people losing their jobs in the industry. Many clothing and textile companies were reported to be facing serious problems. Already, March 2009 had seen the final closure of SANS Fibres, one of the most technologically advanced plants in Africa with the loss of 1,500 jobs in only one year. It also reported that the three largest and most prominent clothing groups had all reported that they were experiencing severe difficulties. Retrenchments had started in some of the firms and more retrenchments were expected.

From the available evidence, it appears that the textile and clothing industry was also adversely affected by the crisis largely through retrenchments as companies had to deal with falling demand levels both domestically as well as internationally.

Mining Industry

From the available evidence, the mining sector was adversely affected by the crisis largely in the form of declining commodity prices, mineral sales and employment. Reports by the Chamber Mines in South Africa (2010) indicated that most commodity prices fell in 2009 and were clearly attributed to the crisis. Mineral sales fell by 10.6 per cent. These were driven by the fall in sales of manganese (down by 67.8 per cent), platinum group metals (down 36.7 per cent), and coal (down 9.8 per cent). The Chamber also reported that while total primary mineral export sales fell by 19.7 per cent to R 176 billion in 2009, they still accounted for 31.7 per cent of South Africa's total merchandise exports.Mining companies responded to the crisis by reducing supply and closing uneconomic production. According to a report by the Business Monitor International (2010), the combined effects of the global economic crisis, plummeting commodity prices and an earlier power crisis continue to impact on the South African mining sector. The downturn has prompted many mining companies to scale back operations, cut proposed exploration and development projects, and lay off workers.

The report also provided evidence of major closures which took place in the chromium and manganese sectors. There were reports of falling gold production by 14 per cent in 2008, largely caused by labour unrest and power shortages. It reported a crash in platinum prices from 2008 into 2009, resulting in falling production levels. The effects were not the same across all minerals. Iron ore producers were among the few in the sector who benefited from an upsurge in demand from China.

Table 6.7 shows that whereas gold prices increased over 2007-09, the prices of PGMs, namely, platinum, palladium and rhodium, all declined. This was due to a fall in external demand for the metals.

Table 6.7: Commodity Prices per Ounce ($)

	2007	2008	2009
Gold	697	895	916
Platinum	1304	1772	998
Palladium	353	393	196
Rhodium	6113	7550	3250
Oil	72.7	111.2	78.3

Source: Chitiga et al (2010)

Thus, evidence shows that the mining sector was also adversely affected by the crisis. As explained in the description of the sector earlier, since PGMs are a major mineral export for South Africa, the fall in prices was also bound to have a negative impact on exports and employment.

Table 6.8 shows declining mineral sales. These were largely attributed to falling prices and external demand.

Table 6.8: Total Sales 2006-12

2008	2009	2010	2011
300,714,5	241,364,6	300,685,6	370,841,6
34	-19.7	24.6	23.3

Source: StatsSA (2012). Mining Production and Sales

Note: R/USD Exchange rates were on average R6.7/US$ in 2011 and US$ 8/US$ in 2012 and R9.4/US$ in 2013.

In terms of mineral sales, it is noted that there was a decline of 19.7 per cent from 2008 to 2009. This improved in 2010. Employment in the mining and quarrying industry experienced a decline of 5.8 per cent over the period 2008 to 2011. In terms of the actual number of employees, 30,000 lost their jobs. Table 6.9 shows the decline in employment in the sector.

Policy Responses and Implications

The public sector response to the crisis is contained in the government's document, 'Framework for South Africa's Response to the International Economic Crisis' (commonly referred to as the 'Framework Agreement'). The Framework identified the clothing and textile industry as a vulnerable sector and recommended inclusion of the sector for rescue package. The Framework Agreement introduced a number of measures to support the auto and textile and clothing industries.

The policy response consisted of different policy packages. These were in the form of the following set of policies:

Countercyclical Fiscal and Monetary Policies

Countercyclical fiscal policy refers to those macroeconomic policies which seek to stimulate aggregate demand by increasing public expenditure when an economy is in recession and by decreasing it when there is inflation. They are founded in the Keynesian tradition which advocates that contrary to classical and neo-classical theory, markets are unstable and to restore stability may require interventions by the state in the form of countercyclical policies. Countercyclical monetary policy refers to the use of expansionary or easy monetary policy with the aim of stimulating aggregate demand and also inducing positive supply-side responses. A central bank can reduce interest rates or buy open market securities in order to increase liquidity in the economy.

As discussed in the literature review, these policies have been strongly recommended by Kasekende et al (2010, Wad (2010) and the AfDB (2009b), among others. UNECA (2009) emphazises the point:

> In the short run, African countries should pursue expansionary countercyclical fiscal and monetary policies to finance investment and infrastructure, education and health as a way to recover from the economic downturn. It also advised that a large proportion of the projects in the package should focus on labour-intensive projects, such as rural roads and water projects.

South Africa's public sector response to the crisis was informed by the government's serious concern about the adverse impact of the crisis on the automotive, textile and clothing and mining sectors. As indicated above, all these three sectors were losing jobs especially over the period 2008 to 2009 and investor and consumer confidence was being eroded. Government was particularly keen to save the textile and clothing industry which appears to have been the worst affected as reflected in the number of company closures and job losses experienced in that sector. It was also keen to save the textile and clothing sector because of the labour-intensive nature of its employment.

Examples of fiscal measures implemented by the South African government in order to deal with the effects of the global crisis are as follows.

Public Infrastructure Investment Programme

The government introduced a R 789 billion (approximately US$ 100 billion) public infrastructure investment programme which was designed to improve road and rail networks, public transport, port operations, dams, water and sanitation infrastructure, housing construction including low-income housing and publicly-owned rental stock, information and communication technology and energy generation capacity. No period was specified, the whole intention was to protect as well as create new jobs. It also included education and health infrastructure. Such a massive programme was also expected to create thousands of additional decent work opportunities (DTI 2009).

Table 6.9: Employment in the Mining and Quarrying Industry 2008

		Number of employees		Change in number of employees		Per cent Change in number of employees
Dec	2008	518000	2008	12000	2008	2.4
Dec	2009	488000	2009	-30000	2009	-5.8
Dec	2010	504000	2010	16000	2010	3.3
Dec	2011	518000	2011	14000	2011	2.8

Source: StatsSA 2012 Quarterly Employment Statistics (QES)

Thus, evidence shows that the mining sector was also adversely affected by the crisis.

The Public Infrastructure Investment Programme was welcomed by all parties, government, labour and business. It is still ongoing and has been acknowledged as a success already. For example, it is expanding energy, transport and social infrastructure. The Medupi power station construction currently employs many thousands of workers. Stadium construction programmes have been a significant stimulus in five localities with total spending of R14,6 bn. The improvements in public transport that include the rapid bus transport system have also contributed positively to employment. There is increasing local procurement and supplier development by SOEs associated with the infrastructure programme.

The Expanded Public Works programme aspect of the infrastructure programme was rolled out at the end of the second quarter of 2010. It was estimated that 223,568 work opportunities had been created. Of course, without knowing the exact target envisaged by the whole programme, it is difficult to judge success but at least the programme had started to yield results in terms of work opportunities.

Although the infrastructure programme was widely accepted by government and business as well as labour, represented by the Congress of South African Trade Unions (COSATU), some groups were critical of the bailout package. For example, the National Union of Metalworkers of South Africa (NUMSA), criticized the programme as being too capital-intensive, focusing on construction of 'fancy airports', stadia, ports and highways and not investing more significantly in low-cost housing which will benefit millions of South Africans who have no shelter. The potential to create new job opportunities was therefore likely to be limited. The union was also critical that the programme was too pro-corporate, and particularly of MNCs; and that the government was bowing unnecessarily to pressure from big business who really should not be bailed out because they could have set aside reserves to cater for crisis situations. The union also felt that the programme was also likely to be ecologically damaging (politicsweb 2012).

Training Layoff Scheme for Workers in Affected Industries

The government allocated R 2.1million towards a National Jobs Fund for the purpose of retraining workers who had been retrenched. The funds would be sourced from the National Skills Fund and the Unemployment Insurance Fund. It was reported that by end of 2009, 4,492 jobs had been saved already (Department of Trade and Industry 2009). No data is available to show progress since then.

The Tax Incentives

In 2010, the government introduced a new tax incentive programme to raise the productivity of the manufacturing sector. A total of R17.5 billion was provided for in tax incentives. The new incentive programme replaced the Strategic Industrial Projects (SIP) programme which had been established to promote private sector investment (Department of Trade and Industry 2009).

These incentives consisted of provisions such as improving capital investment. Under this scheme which is expected to run until December 2015, investors in 'greenfield' projects (which use new and unused manufacturing assets) and 'brownfield' projects (expansions or upgrades of existing projects) that involve capital of more than R200 million but less than R1.6 billion, can apply for a tax allowance equal to between 35 and 55 per cent of a project's value (Department of Trade and Industry 2010). The incentive also offers a maximum of R900 million in tax breaks for greenfield projects, and a maximum of R550 million in tax breaks for brownfield projects. Other incentives were in the form of tax deductions for companies which provided training of employees as part of a strategy to upgrade the manufacturing sector and improve productivity. The qualifying criteria for the tax incentives include companies operating in accordance with best practice in terms of business principles and also those in compliance with labour and tax laws.

Trade Policy

Trade policy refers to those measures which target exports and imports with a view to either expanding or contracting them. They are typically used to control the volume of imports into a country and also to promote the growth of exports. South Africa introduced trade policy measures in response to a sharp rise in imports arising from an increase in the exports of China and other Asian countries when in response to a fall in demand for their own exports to Europe, the US and Japan, they increased their exports to South Africa and other countries. The Framework Agreement called for tariffs to be increased beyond prevailing levels (40 per cent) on clothing products to bound levels (around 45 per cent) since under the WTO, countries are allowed to raise them but not above the bound levels. The government also considered the use of WTO Agreement on Safeguards Measures as an alternative strategy. Under WTO rules, safeguards may be applied to a product only if it has been determined that such a product is being imported in such increased quantities as to cause or threaten to cause serious injury to the domestic industry that produces like or directly competitive products. There was also a call for tighter monitoring and control of SACU and SADC trading to prevent abuses such as false labelling to allow trans-shipment of goods from China destined to South Africa.

Industrial Policy

Industrial policy refers to the set of policies and strategies used by a government to promote the growth of industry. It includes a range of instruments which include, but are not limited to the use of incentives to stimulate production, improve efficiency and competitiveness. The government has actually used industrial policy significantly since 1994. For example, from 1995, it implemented the Motor Industry Development Programme (MIDP) which aimed to support the automotive industry in order to boost production, exports and enhance competitiveness.

Measures to Support the Automotive Industry

The government introduced the Manufacturing Investment Programme (MIP) in 2008. The MIP included an Enterprise Investment Programme (EIP) which targeted those investments which will create jobs, advance empowerment and develop rural areas. Clothing and textile companies qualify for this incentive.

Under this scheme, eligible companies can apply for grants towards investment in plant, machinery and equipment (both for new investments or upgrading of existing production capability). The government allocated R750 million for the first year with possible increases subsequently. For investments of less than R5 million, grants up to 30 per cent or R1.5 million will be paid out. For investments of between R5 million and R30 million, grants between 30 per cent and 15 per cent or up to R9 million and R4.5 million will be paid out. For investments up to R200 million, the maximum grant is 15 per cent or R30 million (Department of Trade and Industry 2009).

In 2008, the government approved the new Automotive Production and Development Programme (APDP). The programme is successor to the Motor Industry Development Programme (MIDP) which started in 1994. Although the MIDP was considered to have been successful, the government was concerned that the industry continued to face a number of challenges, a major one being that the country and the sub-region remained a relatively small market in global terms, isolated from larger markets and shipping routes. The APDP aims to stimulate growth in the automotive vehicle production industry to 1.2 million vehicles per annum by 2020, with associated deepening of the components industry. This would provide an opportunity to increase the local content of domestically assembled vehicles. The programme now includes certain locally manufactured heavy industrial vehicles which are both relatively labour-intensive and generate high levels of local value addition. These will benefit from the incentives which are already channelled to the rest of the auto industry.

Although there was support by both business and labour with regard to support to the car industry, there were critics who questioned the use of taxpayers' money to bail out corporates, particularly multinational companies. The funds should instead have been channelled towards supporting component manufacturers that are largely locally owned. These manufacturers offer hope for more indigenous participation in the automotive manufacturing and assembly industry. These are indeed valid arguments. However, I did not have data to show that component manufacturers did not receive the kind of support which they needed. I agree though on the need to review the strategy of bailing out foreign-owned corporations, particularly since they could get the parent companies to support them. Government could still support them in view of the local employment which they are creating but at least the budgetary support would be less.

Measures to Support the Textile and Clothing Industry

These largely took the form of incentive schemes. Some examples are noted below.

Introduction of a Production Incentive for the Textile and Clothing Industry

This entailed the extension to March 2010, of the export incentive to the textile and clothing industry-known as the Textile and Clothing Industry Development Programme (TCIDP) (DCCS). The government entered into negotiations with industry stakeholders with a view to introducing a replacement scheme. An amount of R280 million was allocated in 2007 which was subsequently raised to R550 million in 2009. The purpose of the scheme was to support the industry to deal with the profitability gap in the sector which was aggravated by the global crisis. Under the scheme, companies would receive a subsidy based on their production:
a. A cash grant (80 per cent of total value)
b. A competitiveness cash grant (20 per cent of total value, with 15 per cent being spent on training)
Over the period of the scheme, the cash-grant component would steadily decrease to be replaced by the competitiveness component.

The Clothing and Textile Competitiveness Programme (CTCP)

This programme was introduced in order to assist the industry to upgrade its processes, products and people, as well as to reposition it to compete effectively both domestically and globally. It aims to help the sector restructure itself for long-term sustainability and competitiveness. The CTCP comprises the Capital and Technology Upgrading Programme, the Preferential Financing Scheme, the Competitiveness Improvement Programme, and the core funding mechanism, the Production Incentive. This programme is administered by the Industrial Development Corporation on behalf of the Department of Trade and Industry. The sector was responsive to this incentive. By the end of 2010, the CTCP desk had received over 80 applications to the value of R311.8 million, with applications to the value of R36 million having already been approved. This, however, appears to be a small amount in relation to the urgent need to improve competitiveness of the industry. Unfortunately, there was no up-to-date information with respect to the overall performance of the programme as of 2012. These are information gaps which future research could fill.

Skills Training for the Textile and Clothing Industry

The training was designed to address the chronic shortage of high-end technical skills in the industry and to create opportunities for employment. It aimed to train at least 162 technologists, skills which were crucial for the survival and sustainability of the industry.

Increase in Working Capital to Companies

During the crisis, many companies restricted credit to distressed textile and clothing companies because of the risk of default. Through the state-owned Industrial Development Corporation (IDC), the government increased working capital available to firms in large, labour-intensive sectors such as textiles. The IDC's Clothing and Textile Firms Competitiveness Scheme would provide working capital loans at prime minus five per cent. These loans were earmarked for capital upgrading. The maximum loan period would be five years for working capital. Granting of the loans would be based on stringent criteria such as that applying firms should have active programmes in place and be operating in terms of best practice in business terms and also employment performance or potential.

Competitiveness Improvement Programme

In order to support the clothing and textiles sector, the government introduced the Clothing and Textile Competitiveness Programme under which companies or clusters would apply to the IDC for grants to help fund competitiveness and productivity improvement programmes. Companies can have 65 of their projects funded. The fund was to be geared towards employment retention.

Specific provisions are:

- Five-year funding period
- Approved applicants receive a maximum of R500,000 per year and clusters R5 million per year.

The IDC to Increase Equity in the Textile and Clothing Sector

Government, through the IDC announced that it would increase its equity exposure to those companies which are of strategic importance in terms of the product which it manufactures, its position in a value chain, the geographic area where it operates, the number of people it employs and its technological importance.

Other Support Measures

The government also introduced other support measures such as preferential procurement where it would identify products and sectors including clothing and textiles which could be procured from those industries in distress. Public sector institutions were mandated to procure clothing products such as nurse and police outfits, uniforms for the defence force and navy, protective wear and hats and berets and textile products ranging from bed linen, curtains and blankets to bags and other accessories, At the time of writing this chapter, there was no available evidence to show that the impact of all these public policy interventions had been reviewed.

The government also took steps to protect labour because it was very much aware that in situations of crisis, some companies could flout labour and tax regulations. In order to ensure compliance, the DTI announced that the incentives under the rescue plan would be for those companies which were compliant with labour and tax laws.

Most of the measures described above were essentially short-term in nature, designed to provide urgent support to those industries which were adversely affected by the crisis. The government realized that a more lasting solution actually lay in promoting interventions which could result in structural change. Longer-term interventions would be necessary. This explains the government's introduction of the Industrial Policy Action Plan under the guidance of the DTI. The plan is a detailed policy strategy which seeks to promote the industrialization through value-addition. It focuses on those sectors where the country has abundant resources, for example, agriculture and forestry, mining, automotive manufacturing and tourism, among others. In January 2007, the government adopted the National Industrial Policy Framework (NIPF). The framework aims at diversifying the production and export structure, promoting labour-absorbing industrialization, moving towards a knowledge economy, and contributing to the industrial development of the region. An Industrial Policy Action Plan (IPAP) was subsequently developed to implement the framework. IPAP I was to be implemented over the period 2007/08 whereas the second phase, IPAP II, was adopted in 2009 and was to cover the period 2010/11 to 2012/13. Both plans are quite detailed (DTI 2009). There has not yet been a review of progress with respect to implementation of both plans. Progress in implementation, however, appears to be slow. It is recommended that the government allocates adequate resources for implementation and closely monitors the process. With reference to the three sectors under discussion, a long-term strategy for promoting processing or mineral beneficiation should be developed in order to enable the sector to diversify production towards more processed mineral products. The strategy should also explore ways to increase South Africa's intra-African trade as compared to other export destinations.

Conclusion and Recommendations

The chapter was about assessing the responsiveness of the public sector in South Africa to the global financial and economic crisis with respect to three sectors, the automotive, mining and textile and clothing industries. These sectors were selected as the focus of the study because of their strategic role at a national level in terms of contribution to GDP, opportunities for decent employment, export earnings and also the fact that they are part of the manufacturing sector, an important sector in terms of South Africa's prospects for producing high-value products.

It presented an analytical framework which argues that in order to understand both the impact of the crisis and how the public sector responded to it, one has to analyse the issue within the framework of globalization and how an open economy like South Africa which is now increasingly integrated into the world trading and financial system, is vulnerable through its dependency on primary exports and also through its wholesale opening up to external competition despite its being a higher-cost producer compared to competitors such as China, India and Malaysia.

The evidence from the literature and available data used for the study support the argument that the global financial and economic crisis did have an effect on the automotive, textile and clothing and mining industries. The sectors were affected through declining production, sales, exports, employment and in some instances, company closures.

It was argued that even though, from a technical viewpoint one cannot conclude that because the decline in performance in 2009 coincided with the crisis, the latter was therefore the cause of the decline, based on confirmations from government, industry bodies and associations as well as labour unions, the crisis played a critical role in the declining performance.

The government's response was largely in the form of countercyclical fiscal and monetary policies. Trade and industry policy measures were also taken to deal with the crisis. As indicated in the literature review, these were standard responses which other African countries have implemented as well. Evidence seems to show that responses were timely and successful to some extent in saving some jobs and averting the crisis. This is reflected in the recovery which ensued in 2011 onward. However, the chapter also argued that given the structural nature of the problem, countercyclical measures alone are not enough.

A number of recommendations are made based on the issues raised in the chapter. South Africa, like the rest of Africa, should find it imperative to run an intensive industrialization agenda which aims to diversify its economy, build resilience to shocks, and develop productive capacity for high and sustained economic growth, the creation of employment opportunities and substantial poverty reduction.

The agenda for moving from commodity production to higher-value manufacturing value addition in the textile and clothing as well as the mining industry has to be a central feature of South Africa's long-term development strategy. The National Development Plan has to invent such strategies and the government should engage industry and prospective foreign investors on this. The government could consider opportunities which are offered by joint ventures with companies from emerging economies (BRICS), Japan, and those from the US and Europe which may be willing to invest on the basis of joint ventures or partnerships with the government. Without addressing these long-term structural challenges, and improving productive capacity in mining, the sector will always be vulnerable to the dynamic changes of the world economy. Investing in this kind of long-term development strategy should therefore be a priority.

New competitive advantages should be explored as well through innovations, research and development. Held et al (1999) emphasize that because of global competition, what may have been a country's competitive advantage may change due to stiff competition from other producers or market players. Can developing countries afford such strategies? This is costly.

One of the main reasons why South Africa was vulnerable to the crisis was the concentration of its markets to a few regional destinations, one of which (Asia) has emerged as a major competitor to the country's exports. The country should therefore seriously consider increasing its share of the African market in order to minimize risk of exposure. Investing in African projects to improve trade facilitation and infrastructure development would be worthwhile. COMESA, SADC, the EAC and the Economic Community of West African States (ECOWAS) should be explored as potential destinations for South Africa's auto, textile and clothing industries, as well as mining.

Whereas rescue and stimulus packages can be effective in saving industry from collapse, care must be taken to avoid wasting resources by supporting industries which will or are not likely to recover, important as they may appear to be in terms of their historical role in contributing to GDP and employment. Questions have to be raised about the state of the textile and clothing industry in South Africa and whether it can indeed become internationally competitive given the high labour costs prevailing in the country as compared to the cheap labour used by most of the country's competitors like China, Malaysia and India. A comprehensive review of the competitiveness of the sector and its likely future performance in the light of global competition, should inform the government about the best strategy to adopt for the industry.

A more fundamental issue raised by South Africa's experience with the global crisis, at least in relation to the three industries, is the need to revisit the debate about the role of trade and industry policies in the era of globalization. Whilst the WTO has outlawed their use because they are said to stifle competition and breed inefficiency, it has become clear that liberalization of African industries when they are ill-prepared for external competition can only de-industrialize the continent, and of course South Africa. The need to continue engaging and negotiating with the WTO on the development agenda is now more necessary than ever; South Africa could use its position as a member of the BRICS and G20 and its partnership with other African countries, to lobby for inclusion of the use of trade and industry policies to promote industrial development and growth in Africa.

It is also recommended that South Africa should seriously support African initiatives to build productive capacity and to invest in the relevant technical skills which will make this goal achievable.

References

African Development Bank, 2009a, *Impact of the Financial Crisis on African Economies – An Interim Assessment*. Policy Briefs on the Financial Crisis, No. 1.

African Development Bank and World Bank, 2009b, *Africa and the Global Economic Crisis: Impacts, Policy Responses, and Political Economy*. Paper presented at the AERC Conference on 'Rethinking African Economic Policy in Light of the Global Economic and Financial Crisis' (December).

Alan, R. 1999, 'The Global Financial Crisis and Economic Reform in the Middle East', *Middle East Policy Council Journal* 6 (3).

Avery, C., and Zemsky, P., 1998, 'Multidimensional Uncertainty and Herd Behavior in Financial Markets', *American Economic Review* 88: 724–48.

Baldacci, E. and Gupta, S., 2009, 'Fiscal Expansions: What Works', *Finance and Development* 40 (December): 35–37.
Business Monitor International, 2010, The South African Mining Report (Quarter 2). Chamber of Mines (South Africa), 2009, Various reports.
Chari, V. and Kehoe, P., 2004, 'Financial Crises as Herds: Overturning the Critiques', *Journal of Economic Theory* 119: 128–50.
Chitiga, M., B. Decaluwé, R., Mabugu, H. Maisonnave and Robichaud, V., 'The Impact of the Global Africa'. Available at: www.aerc.org.
Department of Trade and Industry, 1997, *Current Developments in the Automotive industry*, Pretoria: Government Printer. http:/www.the dti.gov.za.
Department of Trade and Industry, 2007, *National Industrial Policy Framework*. Pretoria: Government Printer. Available online at: http:/www.the dti.gov.za
Fosu, A., and Naude, W., 2009, *Africa's Recovery from the Global Economic Crisis*, United Nations University-WIDER Publication, June. Available at: http://www.wider.unu. edu/publications/newsletter/articles/en_GB/09-06-2009/.
Held, D., McGrew, A., Goldblatt, D. and Perraton, J., 1999, *Global Transformations: Politics, Economics and Culture*, Stanford University Press. Stanford.
International Monetary Fund, 2008, 'Fiscal Policy as a Countercyclical Tool', ch. 5 in *The World Economic Outlook*, October, Washington, DC: IMF.
Jacobs, P., 2009, 'Questioning Pro-poor Responses to the Global Economic Slump', *Review of African Political Economy* 122 (36) December.
Jeetah, R., 2007, *Mauritian Textile and Clothing Industry: The Future*. Report by Dr The Honourable Rajesh Jeetah. Minister of Industry, Small Medium Enterprises, Commerce and Cooperatives.
Kaplinsky, R. and Morris, M., 'Trade Policy Reform and Competitive Response in Kwa-Zulu Natal Province of South Africa', *World Development* (27): 717–37.
Kasekende, L., Ndikumana, L. and Rajhi, T., 2009, Impact of the Global Financial and Economic Crisis on Africa', Africa Development Bank Working Paper No. 96.
Kasekende, L., Brixova, Z. and Ndikumana L., 'Africa: Africa's Countercyclical Policy Responses to the Crisis', *Journal of Globalisation and Development* 1(1), Article 16.
Leon, P., 'Whither the South African Mining Industry?', *Journal of Energy and Natural Resources Law* 30 (1): 1–27.
Merz, R., ed., 2012, 'The Future of the Clothing and Textile Industry in Sub Saharan Africa', *politicsweb*, 29 April.
RSA Department of Trade and Industry, 2007, *National Industrial Policy Framework*, Pretoria: Government Printer.
Soludo, C., 2009, *How we have managed the global financial crisis*. Available at: http://www. sunnewsonline.com/webpages/features/money/index.htm.
Statistics South Africa StatsSA, 2011, *Quarterly Employment Statistics (QES)*, December.
Thorton, J., 2008, 'Explaining Pro-cyclical Fiscal Policies in African Countries', *Journal of African Economies* 17 (3): 451–64.
UNECA, 2010, *Economic Report on Africa Promoting High Level Sustainable Growth to Reduce Unemployment in Africa*, United Nations.
United Nations University, 2009a, *Policy Responses to the Global Economic Crisis in Africa*, Policy Brief No. 3, www.unu.edu.

UNECA and African Union Commission (AUC), 2009, *The Global Crisis: Impact, Responses and Way Forward*. African Union, Proceedings of Meeting of the Committee of Experts of the 2nd Joint Annual Meetings of the AU Conference of Ministers of Economy and Finance and ECA Conference of Ministers of Finance, Planning and Economic Development. Cairo, Egypt, 2-5 June.

Van der Westhuizen, C., 2007, 'Trade and Poverty. A Case Study of the South African Clothing Industry', *Studies in Economics and Econometrics*, 31 (2).

Weeks, J., 2009, *The Global Financial and Economic Crisis and Countercyclical Fiscal Policy*, Discussion Paper 26/09, School of Oriental and African Studies, University of London.

Woolfrey, S., 2009, 'Assessment of the Trade Measures Proposed as Part of the Department of Trade and Industry's Draft Rescue Package for the Clothing and Textile Industry', TRALAC Africa, Bonn: FES.

7

Analysis of the Effects of the Global Financial Crisis and Government Measures: The Case of the Timber Industry in Congo, Cameroon and Gabon

Bertrand Mafouta

Introduction

Triggered by the collapse of the US and world financial system since 2007, the global economic crisis deepened during 2008 and continued in 2009. Considered as the most serious and most synchronized for decades, the current crisis has spared no region of the world (ECA 2009; Devarajan 2009). The consequences are felt in all sectors, particularly in terms of international trade, down 11 per cent in 2009, investment and labour market, with an unemployment rate that increases sharply due to the decrease in economic growth (UNDP 2009). Global economic growth is systematically revised downward based on market indicators. With the weak development of the industrial sector, the performances of African economies are highly dependent on market trends in agricultural commodities and minerals. The decline in the demand for raw materials following the recession in developed countries and the slowdown in emerging markets has had a negative impact on African exports.

The timber of the Central African countries faces the effects of the global financial crisis. If the sub-region in 2007 exported 7.9 million m³ of roundwood to Europe (60 per cent) and China (30 per cent), an increase of 6 per cent per year since 2004, exports became lower due to declining demand from buyers. Samuel Nguiffo, Director of the Centre for Environment and Development (CED) points out that Cameroon registered at the end of 2008 about 2,000 lay-offs. Likewise 20,000 direct and indirect jobs were threatened in Cameroon and DRC (Sandouly and Labey 2009).

With regard to Congo-Brazzaville, the timber industry is the second largest economic sector and the second largest employer. Timber is also the second most important export. Similarly, Gabon has an economy characterized by heavy dependence on the oil sector. In 2006, this contributed to the tune of 51.5 per cent of GDP. The country's revenues are also dependent on mining and timber with a contribution respectively of 64 per cent of budget revenues and 82 per cent of export earnings (AfDB 2009). Furthermore, it should be noted that the timber sector represents the second source of employment in Gabon. In Cameroon, the timber sector employs nearly 170,000 persons, including 20,000 direct jobs. Timber is also the second export product of Cameroon.

However, faced with the rise of the effects of the crisis, the activities of the industry were threatened both upstream and downstream. Thus, the overall objective of this chapter is to analyse the impact of the global financial crisis on the timber industry in these countries. Specifically, it is to analyse the potential for production and export of these countries; highlight the effects of the crisis in this sector; and analyse the measures that have been taken by governments to reveal their limitations and suggest alternative solutions.

The research issues guiding the study were as follows: how is the international financial crisis affecting the forestry sector? What are the potentials for production and export of timber in Central Africa, including Congo, Gabon and Cameroon, and the effects of this crisis on the timber industry in these countries? What are the various measures implemented by the governments and the solutions proposed to help stakeholders mitigate the effects of this crisis?

Methodology

The study, which covers eight years from 2001 to 2008, was based mostly on existing documentation. The documentation study was undertaken mainly at the Department of Forestry of the Ministry of Forest Economy in Congo Brazzaville with the analysis of the reports and documents of the International Monetary Fund (IMF), the African Development Bank (AfDB), the World Bank, the Bank of Central African States (BEAC), the documents of various ministries in charge of the forest economy of Cameroon and Gabon and the documents of the International Tropical Timber Organization (ITTO). The effects of the crisis and its increasing complexity today cannot only be viewed as financial. The repercussion on the real economy is getting more and more obvious and it affects developing countries through a number of trade-related channels such as commodity prices, exportations, investment, infrastructure and debt sustainability, macroeconomic imbalances, exchange rate fluctuation, trade finance, and credit for export-oriented production.

One can note that Congo, Cameroon and Gabon are members of the Economic and Monetary Community of Central African States (CEMAC) with a core mission to promote the harmonious development of the member states within the framework of a true common market. Hence our methodology approach was both qualitative and quantitative. The aim was to acquire a general understanding of the logging industry in these countries and analyse the impact of the financial economic crisis on the timber sector through the variation of commodity prices in the international market; the evolution of product; the decline of exportation; the income of states; and job losses; and then analyse the measures undertaken.

Theoretical and Conceptual Framework

The global financial crisis initially affected advanced economies, emerging markets, and low-income countries in very different ways. Advanced economies were first hit mainly by the systemic banking crisis in the United States and Europe. Emerging markets with well-developed financial systems were initially mostly affected by cross-border financial linkages through capital flows, stock market investors, and exchange rates. In financially less-developed countries the growth and trade effects dominated, with lags. Now, however, growth and trade effects are crucial for all countries. The channels through which the global financial turmoil affects developing countries include financial channels and real channels. Financial channels include effects through: stock markets, banking sector (borrowing from advanced economies, foreign ownership of banks, exposure to sub-prime market), and foreign direct investment. Real channels include effects through remittances, exports, imports, terms of trade, and aid (Massa and TeVelde 2008:2).

In Africa, frontier and emerging markets were hit first. By now indirect channels are fully at work in all countries, and risks are mounting that other channels may gain in importance, especially in the financial sector. In all countries, the global slowdown in economic activity has pushed commodity prices down, with negative effects on export earnings and the external current account, fiscal revenues, and household incomes. Commodity exporters face a major term of trade deterioration. IMF research shows that in the past a one percentage point slowdown in global growth has led to an estimated half percentage point slowdown in sub-Saharan African countries. The effects may be more pronounced this time because the tightening of global credit compounds the impact of the slowdown, exacerbating risks for trade finance and their capital flows (IMF 2009).

In fact, the link between African countries and the global market directly affects the production of timber. The exports of all African countries depend largely on the demand of the European, American and Asianmarkets, and in particular China, which is the second largest consumer of timber products in the world. Its growing population and expanding economy are increasing its demand for timber products. So, one can note that a large part of the timber products of these countries is sold on the international market;and many companies in that sector are represented by foreign capital.

Literature Review

The global financial crisis of 2008-09, with its epicenter in the United States, has brought enormous ramifications for the world economy. What started as an asset bubble caused by an array of financial derivatives that, *inter alia*, drove the sub-prime mortgage boom, exploded into housing and banking crises with a cascading effect on consumer and investment demand. The housing crisis quickly grew into a banking crisis with the investment and merchant banks first absorbing the impact before it spread to the commercial banks (Krugman 2009). With the United States' economy contracting sharply, it sent ripples across export-dependent Asian economies, which began to face a contraction as a consequence.

The Impact in African Countries

A number of publications exist on the impacts of the crisis in Africa. These include, but are not limited to, Biekpe (2009) on the impact of the credit crunch on foreign aid in Africa; Myburgh (2009) on correlations between sub-Saharan Africa (SSA) currencies during the 2008 financial crisis; Kiptoo (2009) on the potential impacts of the global financial crisis on African economies; and the International Monetary Fund (IMF) (2009) on the impacts of the global financial crisis on Africa. Many other works exist on country-specific issues on the crisis. The works include, but are not limited to, Ngowi (2009a, 2009b, 2009c, 2009d and 2009e).

According to Balchin (2009), the impact of the global financial crisis is likely to vary across African countries depending on their exposure to the international financial system, their production and export structure, and their capacity to use policy tools to cushion its adverse effects. In general terms, the short-term effects on many African countries are likely to be mitigated by the fact that most countries on the continent are relatively de-linked from the global financial system.

The slowdown in global growth, coupled with a sharp decline in global industrial production, has reduced demand for African exports, reflected most notably in the downward spiral of both prices and demand for commodity exports. This is most alarming given the fact that commodity exports represent the primary source of export receipts for the majority of African countries. Furthermore, the fall in export revenues is likely to have negative spillover effects in terms of reducing government revenues, thereby worsening the already tenuous fiscal position in many African countries.

To analyse the impact on the timber sector, one can note that the decrease of demand affected the price on the world market. Thus, Ngowi (2009) argued that in all African countries, the crisis has pushed commodity prices down with negative effects on export earnings and the external current account, fiscal revenues, and household incomes (IMF 2009; Kiptoo 2009; World Bank 2008). According to Ngowi (2009b), the very few commodities whose price has not declined include gold. This is due to the historical position of gold in international financial and monetary system as detailed in Ngowi (2006). African commodity exporters face major terms of trade deterioration.

Effect on the Timber Industry

The 2008-09 financial and economic crisis has led to a fundamental shift within forestry and the forest industry sectors, the effects of which are being felt through the entire chain from the forest to the markets. Never since the first oil crisis in the 1970s have forest product markets experienced such a downturn.

The UNECE region, which is the largest global producer, exporter, importer and consumer of timber and paper products, and its forest sector, have been badly hit by the economic crisis. The extent to which each country has been affected varies from country to country, depending on different factors such as the fall of forest product prices due to a decrease in demand following the crash of the construction sectors, the decline in both foreign and domestic investment and the fluctuation in currency exchange rates.

The downturn in forest product markets has, of course, impacted the economic situation of the states and private forest owners through reduced demand for raw wood materials. However, the sustained demand for timber energy, buoyed by government polices to promote renewable energy sources, has been the bright spot during the market downturn. Supplying woody biomass maintains harvest levels and income for some forest owners.

In 2008, consumption of forest products in the UNECE region fell by an extraordinary 8.5per cent. This decrease in demand, accompanied by a decrease in production, is expected to be as significant for the current year as indicated by data for the first half of 2009. According to the UNECE/FAO *Forest Products Annual Market Review, 2008-2009* (UNECE/FAO 2009a), most of the 56 UNECE member countries have experienced sharp falls in demand and consumption of timber products.

Throughout the UNECE region the sector suffered from diminished demand for and falling prices of timber and paper products (UNECE/ FAO 2009b). This has led to reduced income for producers, which resulted in mill closures in some countries (e.g. United States, Finland, France), job cuts (Estonia, Cyprus, Finland, France, Sweden, United Kingdom and US), and many companies had reduced profits. The short-term effects have been felt throughout the entire timber and paper processing chain, from primary processing activities to the production of value-added products, as well as the trade in forest products. The employment losses have been tragic, with ripple effects impacting entire communities, often in rural forested areas with low incomes. In just one year, between 2007 and 2008, the consumption of forest products in the UNECE region dramatically decreased by 117 million[3] in roundwood equivalent, of which the biggest proportion (81 million[3]) occurred in North America.

At the same time, in Africa, that sector was also affected. According to Henk-Jan Brinkman and Ali (2010: 2), in Ghana for example timber exports declined. Between January and October 2009, the value (in euros) decreased by 33 per cent and the volume by 25 per cent compared to the same period in 2008. On the other hand, the world market price for timber, as reported by the World Bank's Global Economic Monitor, appears to have been moderately affected by the crisis. Throughout 2008, the price was relatively stable around 150 per cent of its 2000 level. It declined slightly in early 2009 and is reported to have reverted back to 145 per cent of its 2000 level in May 2009 (ILO 2009).

In central Africa, particularly in the Economic and Monetary Community of Central African States (CEMAC), the timber sector has suffered a great loss of activities with subsequent job losses amounting to between 20 and 30 per cent. The direct impact was under-valued. According to Wakeman-Linn and Ali (2009), the overall impact on expected export revenues for 2009 is aggravated by the ongoing contraction in export volumes for timber and other commodities. One can note that timber is a forest product. So in Congo-Brazzaville, for example, forestry companies had considered that a revision of fiscal policy would enable them to cope with the effects of the crisis. Thus, in fear of a permanent cessation and declining revenues, governments have implemented a policy to protect the timber industry at regional and national levels. However, these measures have some shortcomings (Ndzi 2008).

Presentation and Interpretation of Results

The Potential of Republic of Congo

Until 1972, timber was the primary resource of Congo representing more than half of exports. It has been overtaken by oil now contributing approximately 7 per cent of GDP. Moreover, the potential national timber is estimated at over 150 million m^3 in volume sales growth: 130 million in the mountains of northern Congo, 20 million in the massive in South (SANA CONGO 2010: 12). The annual production capacity is currently estimated at 2 million m^3, without compromising natural regeneration (PFBC 2006). At this potential, there is an additional 73,000 hectares of eucalyptus, pines and limba, located in the south, corresponding to a volume of 4,000,000 m^3. FAO estimated an annual levy of 2 million m^3.

The Potential of Cameroon

Cameroon has potential forest and wildlife resources whose exploitation generates substantial revenues for the national economy. Its forest resources are valued at about 22 million hectares of which 17.5 million is exploitable (Ngolle Ngolle 2009). The potential is rich and constituted by diverse flora. It consists of over 300 species of trees. In addition, Thies and Beligné (2007:3) emphasize that with 0.6 per cent of world production of tropical timber, the Cameroonian forestry sector represents 0.5 per cent of world exports of tropical logs, in both volume and turnover. It represents about 3 to 6 per cent of world exports of tropical sawnwood, and about 7 per cent of the export of sawn tropical products in the tropics. While lumber exports are low by world trade levels, they remain the most important in tropical Africa.

The Potential of Gabon

With a dense forest covering some 21.09 million hectares, more than 80 per cent of the country (Mayaux et al 2004), coupled with low population density, Gabon has the highest rate of forest area per capita in Africa (Chevalier 2008:61). Between 1990 and 2005, the recorded loss of forest area remained very limited. This loss represented 0.15 million hectares, or less than one per cent (PNUD 2007: 391). Moreover, the forest has always played an important role in the development of the country. Economically, it has been for a long time the main source of national wealth, before being overtaken by oil in the early 1970s. Currently, the forestry sector ranks second in the export earnings of the country and remains the largest private employer with about 12,868 direct jobs generated (MEFEPPN FORAF 2008).

The Production of Raw Wood

The total production of raw wood in Central Africa (excluding DRC) increased by 18 per cent within 6 years and amounted to 7.9 million m³ in 2007. The situation in the three countries is as follows.

Figure 7.1: Evolution of Raw Wood Product of Congo, Cameroon and Gabon

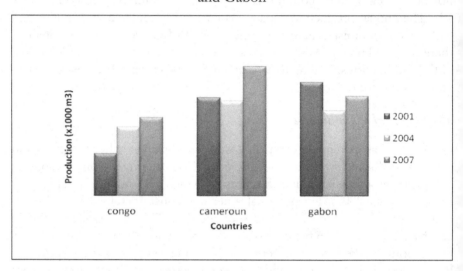

Source: IMF, BEAC, UBIFRANCE 2008

The graph shows that the production of raw wood of Congo and that of Cameroon increased between the years mentioned. These increased from 895,000 m³ in 2001 to 1.65 million m³ in 2007, an increase of almost 84 per cent, and 1.999 million in 2001 to 2,731,000 in 2007, or 32 per cent. One notices also that the production of Gabon declined (25 per cent) between 2001 and 2004 and rose to 16 per cent in 2007. However, one should notice that in terms of timber production, Gabon is the largest lumber producer in Central Africa and the world's largest producer of Okoume.

Evolution of Log Products of Congo, Cameroon and Gabon

The total production of raw wood in Central Africa (excluding DRC) increased by 18 per cent within six years and amounted to 7.9 million m³ in 2007. Moreover, the three countries are major producers of logs in the region (UBIFRANCE 2008: 13). Figure 7.2 shows the evolution of the production of logs from 2000 to 2007.

The graph shows that log production is largely dominated by Gabon, which ranks first, followed by Cameroon and Congo. But this production declined slightly between 2000 and 2004 from 3.8 million m³ to 2.5 million m³. It also grew between 2005 and 2007. Production in Cameroon had some ups and downs over the entire period. However, between 2006 and 2007 it declined by about 225,000 m³.

Figure 7.2: Evolution of Logs Production

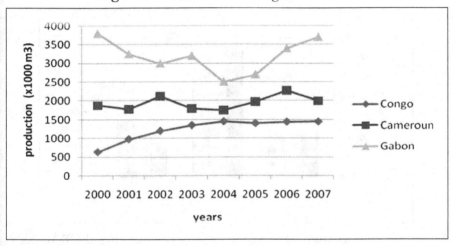

Source: African Forest Observatory (FORAF) 2009

With regard to Congo, its log production witnessed a marked increase between 2000 and 2007. It increased from 630,000 m³ to 1.4 million m³ over a period of seven years, with a rate of increase of 129.3 per cent.

Evolution of Sawn Wood Product

On average, 19 per cent of the countries of Central Africa are exported after having undergone initial processing (UBIFRANCE 2008). For example, Cameroon has thesub-region's most developed processing industry with a total installed capacity of around 2.2 million m³ in 2007. The second transformation that is occuring is provided by industrial companies, SMEs in manufacturing furniture and craft industries. However, the units are mainly focused on the primary level and are usually equipped with hand equipment from Europe. With respect to Gabon, timber processing such as Okoume (peeling, veneer, lumber) that has developed recently is achieved primarily by French companies (Rougier, Leroy, Thebault) that have invested heavily in this activity.

In Congo-Brazzaville, timber processing developed in the northern region where the sawmill industry (downstream activities included) grew at the Congolese Industrial Bois (CIB), Forest Industry of Ouesso (IFO) and Likouala Timber. The graph in Figure 7.3 shows the evolution of the production of lumber from 2005 to 2007.

Figure 7.3: Evolution of Sawn Wood Product of Congo, Cameroon and Gabon

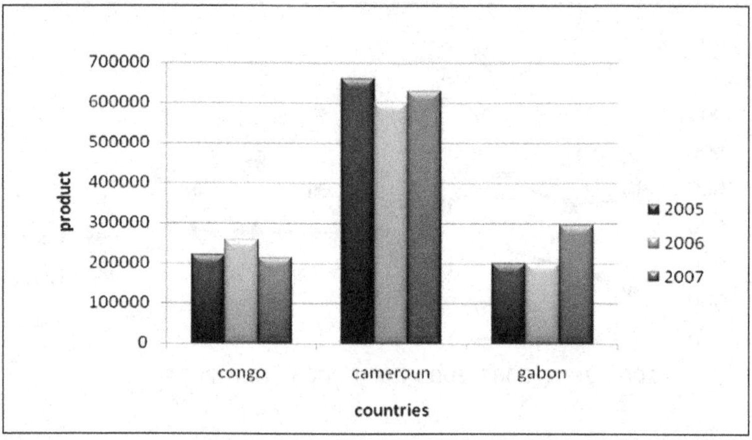

Source: Observatory for the Forests of *Central Africa* (OFAC)/ FORAF 2009

Reading by country shows that the production of sawn wood in Congo-Brazzaville and Gabon remains largely insufficient compared with that of Cameroon. At the level of a country such as Congo-Brazzaville, this production declined between 2006 and 2007. It went down from 235,000 to 210,000 m³, a decrease of -10.64 per cent. Similarly, for Cameroon, this decrease was about of -7.34 per cent. In the case of Gabon, its production increased by 45.5 per cent after stagnating at 200,000 m³ between 2005 and 2006.

Evolution of the Production of Plywood

Plywood production is largely dominated by Gabon, followed by Cameroon and Congo. Yet, it is fitting to note that in the latter two countries, production is relatively low but has seen some increase. However, for Gabon, one observes a sharp drop between 2005 and 2006 and some changes from 2007.

The Potential of Countries in Trade

The potential of these three countries is analysed in terms of exports of logs, sawnwood, veneer and plywood, recorded between 2005 and 2008.

Figure 7.4: Evolution of Plywood Product in Congo,
Cameroon and Gabon

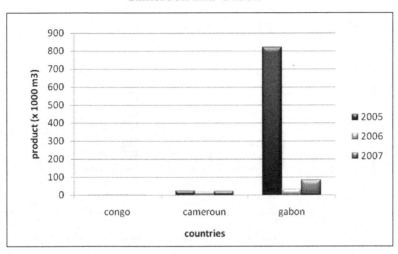

Source: MEFEPPN-FORAF 2008, Timbertrade 2008

Evolution of Log Exports

Gabon is the country which exports most logs in Central Africa. It has performed better than its neighbours as manifested in its exports having increased between 2006 and 2007, an increase of 9.6 per cent. In the other countries, the exports have declined by around 6.7 per cent over a period of three years. Congo's exports recorded a decline between 2006 and 2008. This reduction represents 16 per cent in the same year. Similarly, Cameroon recorded a decline estimated at nearly 18.5 per cent over the same period. The graph (Figure 7.5) below shows the evolution of log exports from these three countries between 2006 and 2008.

The Exports of Sawn Wood

Generally, lumber products are marketed in Central Africa in a raw state and to only a few sawmills in the countries concerned to bring added value by providing dried lumber and then, probably, by providing a specific machine to produce profiles, items of flooring and other materials (Langbour and John Gerard 2007). Thus, unlike the export of logs, lumber exports were dominated by Cameroon over the period 2005-07. These declined between 2005 and 2007 but grew by 2 per cent between 2006 and 2007. Congo's exports grew but exports from Gabon were down slightly. In Gabon, for example, they lost nearly 0.6 per cent during the period 2006-2007.

Figure 7.5: Evolution of Log Exports from 2006 to 2008

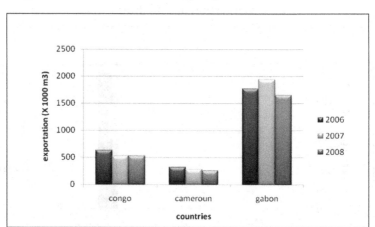

Source: Ministry of Water, Forests, Hunting and Fisheries/Forestry Data Centre (FDC) 2009.

Figure 7.6: Evolution of Sawn Wood Exports

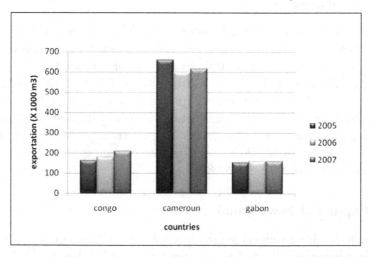

Source: ITTO, AfDB, Ministry of Forest Economy, National Gabon's Wood Company (SNBG), Société d'exploitation des parcs à bois du Gabon (SEPBG) 2009.

Figure 7.7: Evolution of veneer exports from 2006 to 2007

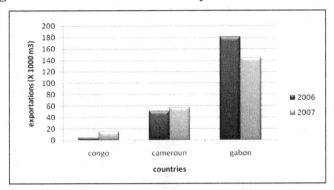

Source: Ministry of Water, Forests, Hunting and Fisheries/Forestry Data Centre (FDC) FORAF.

Plywood Exports

Although log exports may represent much of Gabon's timber exports one can notice that plywood also has a significant part. Thus, in comparison to Congo and Cameroon, Gabon ranks first. However, following the 2006 and 2007 period, we find that these exports were down sharply from 66 per cent. With regard to Congo, its exports declined by 50 per cent contrary to Cameroon that recorded a slight increase of 16 per cent.

Impact of the Crisis on the Timber Industry

Overview

The timber industry has been affected everywhere in Central Africa and on every other continent. According to Valbois (2009) all wood products and trade flows were affected and all stakeholders concerned in the sector have been forced to consider their position.

While global GDP grew sharply (+4 per cent) mainly due to emerging and developing countries (+ 9 per cent), what is seen in this trend is an abrupt decline (- 6 per cent), especially in advanced countries (-7 per cent). In 2008, softwood sawmills in Europe, for example, lost an average worldwide of between US$ 12 and US$ 14/m³ as they earned US$ 8 in 2006. Similarly, European exports, which amounted to some 5.6 million m³ despite a strong euro and high transport costs, had to be reoriented from US (4 million m³ in 2005 against one million m³ in 2008) and Japan (3 million m³ in 2004 against 2 million m³ in 2008) to other destinations like the Middle East, North Africa and Asia.

Figure 7.8: Evolution of Plywood Exports from 2006 to 2007

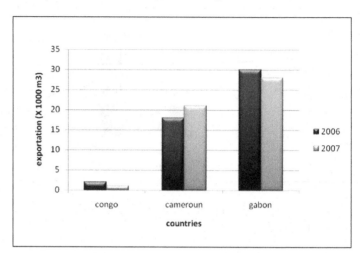

Source: OFAC 2010

Moreover, the crisis was not only limited to softwood lumber. The whole world timber industry was suffering. For instance, tropical plywood prices were severely compressed at the end of 2008 (10 to 20 per cent). Finnish sawn wood prices are another example: the redwoods that were selling for 245 euro/m³ FOB price in October 2007 fell to 160 euro/m³ in April 2009 (Valbois 2009).

Sub-Saharan Africa

In 2007, SSA benefited from the highest growth rate in decades. Real GDP grew by about 6½ per cent, led by progress in the extraction of oil exporting countries as well as rising domestic investment and productivity across the region (IMF 2008). The successes in implementing economic stabilization and structural reforms contributed to this result. Strong global demand for commodities, increased capital inflows in Africa and debt relief increased resources and accelerated expansion. But recently, the external environment became less favourable. The slowing global economy reduced demand for exports from sub-Saharan Africa.

In fact, hit by the collapse in global demand, the sector had to carry out massive layoffs of workers. 'Over 6,000 jobs are destroyed', announced the Ivorian Minister of Water and Forestsin April. In Gabon, Cameroon and Congo, key loggers such as Rougier, Precious Woods or the Company of Gabon timber, were deeply affected (Mouly 2009). Plysorol, a French company, filed for bankruptcy (taken over by a Chinese company), and Rougier stopped the activity of two plants in Congo and Gabontemporarily. Moreover, leaders noted that the group recorded a 26 per cent drop in sales in the fourth quarter of 2008 while it invested 10 billion CFA francs, the equivalent of US$20 million over the previous three years (Mouly 2009).

Central Africa Sub-region

At the state level in Central Africa, forest resources are an important part of international trade. Thus, in most regions, the revenues generated by forest products occupy second rank after those generated by the oil sector. The contribution of the timber sector to GDP is 6 per cent in Cameroon, 2 per cent in Congo, between 3 and 4 per cent in Gabon, 6 per cent in Equatorial Guinea, and 10 to 13 per cent in Central African Republic. It should be remembered that until the 1960s, countries only exported logs (WWF-France 2007). Currently, they sell primary and manufactured products such as planks, plywood, veneer and furniture abroad. Exports of lumber in Central Africa generated an income of more than 1.2 billion euros in 2001. Gabon, Congo and Cameroon accounted for almost 85 per cent of Central African exports. However, the financial crisis affecting the timber industry led to a decline of log exports and sawn wood for countries like the Central African Republic and Democratic Republic of Congo at 16 and 37 per cent, and 14 and 26 per cent respectively with the discontinuation of some mills and closing of some logging camps, particularly in Central African Republic (Eba'aAtyi and al 2009: 21).

Impact in Congo, Cameroon and Gabon

The financial crisis affected the timber industry of these three countriesdifferently. In this sub-section, the impact of the crisis is examined in terms of exports, demand from major customers, business companies, state revenues and jobs.

Impact on the Exports of Congo, Cameroon and Gabon

Congo
Congolese exports were affected by the crisis. One can note that compared to the exports of logs that experienced a small increase (0.19 per cent), sawn wood and logs eucalyptus declined respectively by 16.7 and 17.6 per cent. It is important to notice that the decline in exports of both these products is an enormous loss to the extent that the production of these requires significant investments and provides the industry with products that bring more value added.

Table 7.1: Change in Exports of Some Products between 2007 and 2008

Exports (m³)	2007	2008	Variation
Logs	527 000	528 000	0.19
Sawnwood	209 000	174 000	-16.75
Eucaliptus log	250 000	206 000	-17.60

Source: Author's calculations from Statistics Ministry of Water, Forests, Hunting and Fisheries/Forestry Data Centre (FDC), 2009.

Cameroon

Let us recall that Cameroon has the second largest forest in Africa and among the top five world exporters of tropical timber. Eighty per cent of precious woods are destined for export. The forestry sector has a significant advantage and is even a substantial factor endowment and thus represents a capital in terms of natural resources that should be well exploited. This is especially the case as the sector remains fragile because of the crisis (Republic of Cameroon 2009).

Moreover, the decline in demand for housing was the first consequence of the decline in demand for timber. In 2008, the volume of crude timber exports from Cameroon declined by 4.6 per cent. This decrease was more marked in the second half of the year, when it affected the lumberyard. In relative to the first half, the decline was 9.9 per cent for the raw wood and 10.6 per cent for the sawn wood (GICAM 2009). Provisional data from the first quarter of 2009 confirm this trend with a 35 per cent drop in exports of sawn wood. One can recall that exports of timber and by-products were the second largest export after crude oil (14 per cent in 2008 against 16.3 per cent in 2007). The country recorded a fall of 3.32 per cent in log exports between 2007 and 2008, and 17 per cent for plywood in the same year.

Table 7.2: Variation of Exports by Products between 2007 and 2008

Exportation (m³)	2007	2008	Variation
Logs	266 420	257 578	-3.32
Sawnwood	21 668	17 983	-17.01
Veneer	59 408	64 286	8.21

Source: Author's calculations from Statistics Ministry of Water, Forests, Hunting and Fisheries / Data Center of Forestry (CDF), ATIBT 2008.

Gabon

Log exports from Gabon in November 2008 registered a growth rate of -10.7 per cent against 10 per cent in 2007. Moreover, the quantities exported increased from 1.771 million to 1.582 million m³. The destinations most favoured were India and France, with respective contractions of about 55.8 per cent and 38 per cent (Doumba 2009). Similarly, for the years 2007 and 2008, the growth rate of exports of timber fell from 17 to 3.8 per cent. The growth rate for logs was positive from 10 per cent in 2007 as compared to that in 2008 which amounted to 11per cent.

Moreover, Demarquez Benedict (2008) points out that the relative decline in log exports from Gabon is due to the export quotas imposed by the government, but also to an effective decline of the timber market. There was a decrease of nearly 15 per cent of exports of all log species in 2007 ascompared to 36 per cent in 2000. The decrease of exports of logs from Gabon is more marked by the decrease of the demand in European markets (-63 per cent since 2000); Asian markets (-23 per cent between 2000 and 2008) and in the African market (-32 per cent).

Table 7.3: Change in Exports of some Products between 2007 and 2008

Exports (m³)	2007	2008	Variation
Logs	1 938	1650	-14.86

Source: Author's calculations from Statistics Ministry of Water, Forests, Hunting and Fisheries/Data Centre of Forestry (CDF), ATIBT 2008

Impact from the Demand Change of the Main Recipients

In recent years, China has become the first economic partner of African states. For historical reasons, Europe has long been the main destination for exports of timber from Central Africa. From 1994, China took first place with a market share of between 23 and 30 per cent, closely followed by France (15 to 18 per cent). From Central Africa, China imports not only oil but also timber. As an illustration, China remains the largest buyer of Gabonese timber (all species combined) with a 60 per cent market share, followed by France (only 12.2 per cent). Overall, Asia accounts for 73 per cent of log exports while 22.1 per cent go to Europe (French Economic Mission 2007).

Considering the demand, it must be noted that some buyers of these three countries' timber have reduced their consumption. Thus, the section that follows presents the changes in exports of some products by major destination countries between 2007 and 2008.

The results in Table 7.4 show that Congo's timber exports were down by -8.19 per cent. However, taking into account of the key partners, we notice that Congo's timber exports to China were not affected by the crisis. They showed an increase of 14.23 per cent.

Table 7.4: Evolution of Congo Forestry Exports by Destination

Countries	Volume 2007 (m³)	Volume 2008 (m³)	Variation (per cent)
China	371 255,00	424 070,00	14.23
Portugal	80 885,00	120 382,00	48.83
Morocco	41 059,00	85 206,00	107.52
Spain	88 639,00	79 228,00	-10.62
France	78 744,00	72 484,00	-7.95
Netherlands	64 191,00	37 775,00	-41.15
Belgium	48 757,00	34 082,00	-30.10
Germany	49 502,00	31 961,00	-35.43
Italy	176 705,00	28 818,00	-83.69
UnitedKingdom	36 963,00	26 218,00	-29.07
USA	43 822,00	25 621,00	-41.53
Malaysia	8 150,00	20 672,00	153.64
Switzerland	15 234,00	16 811,00	10.35
Turkey	13 487,00	14 349,00	6.39
Saudi Arabia	7 030,00	12 719,00	80.92
India	9 458,00	10 978,00	16.07
Other	96 335,00	88 105,00	-8.54
Total	1 230 216,00	1 129 479,00	-8.19

Source: Author's calculations from Statistics Atibit 2009

However, other countries such as France and the United States reduced their imports of timber from Congo. This is manifested by a decrease of -7.9 and -41.5 per cent respectively.

Table 7.5: Evolution of Cameroon's Timber by Destination

Country	Volume 2007 (m³)	Volume 2008 (m³)	Variation (per cent)
Italy	114 404,00	111 140,00	-2.85
Spain	104 890,00	88 350,00	-15.77
Netherlands	85 174,00	78 638,00	-7.67
France	67 297,00	62 941,00	-6.47
Belgium	54 856,00	54 963,00	0.20
China+HK+Taiwan	17 043,00	25 127,00	47.43
UK	25 917,00	17 654,00	-31.88
Senegal	17 234,00	16 798,00	-2.53
USA	25 737,00	15 474,00	-39.88
Tunisia	9 128,00	13 347,00	46.22
Portugal	13 653,00	13 015,00	-4.67
Turkey	8 168,00	9 275,00	13.55
Germany	13 367,00	9 235,00	-30.91
Total	556 868,00	515 957,00	-35.24

Source: Author's calculations from Statistics Atibit 2009

In the case of Cameroon, Table 7.5 shows that exports of lumber by this country fell by nearly 35 per cent. However, China including Hong Kong and Taiwan are the countries that imported more timber (47.43 per cent) despite the effects of the crisis. Exports to the United States, however, decreased (-39.88 per cent).

Table 7.6: Evolution of Gabon's Log Exports by Destination,
end of November 2008

Countries	Volume 2007 (m³)	Volume 2008 (m³)	Variation (per cent)
China	992 373,00	1 028 281,10	3.6
France	262 610,00	162 711,60	-38
Morocco	123 872,00	86 739,00	-30
India	165 573,00	73 219,00	-55.8
Turkey	48 396,00	67 686,80	39.9
Germany	32 293,00	28 101,50	-13
Spain	15 791,00	24 393,00	54.5
Taywan	29 722,00	20 131,00	-32.3
Belgium	10 539,00	18 832,20	78.7
Greece	20 738,00	21 355,50	3
Italy	28 085,00	21 377,30	-23.9
South Africa	2 406,00	1 851,00	-23.1
Tunisia	2 571,00	1 333,00	-48.2

Source: VDS/BOLLORE in late November 2008, Doumba 2009

For Gabon, log exports fell to 10 per cent. As in the case of Cameroon's exports to China, one can note an average increase of nearly 4 per cent. However, India, one of the largest importers of timber, cut its imports from Cameroon by more than half, or by -55.8 per cent.

The above three tables tell us that China remains the most important and most reliable partner on which to build support for the three countries to enhance their level of exports. Similarly, although the consumption of European partners is low, recovery in any country of the European Union will also affect the countries of Central Africa including Congo, Cameroon and Gabon. As should be noted, the presence of certain groups such as Rougier (French group) constitutes an important factor to the presence of the old continent in Africa.

Effects on the Revenue Related to Market Prices

State revenue including the admission of foreign exchange for exporters is based on demand but also on the trend in the various markets. Thus, the study undertaken by Eba'aetal (2009) shows a price trend of logs and sawn wood which is as follows:

Figure 7.9: Evolution of Log prices (January 2008-January 2009)

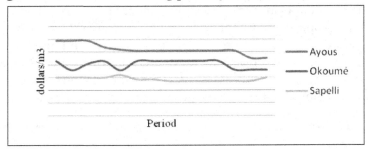

Source: Richard Eba'a et al (2009)

Figure 7.10: Evolution of Sawn Wood Prices
(January 2008 and March 2009)

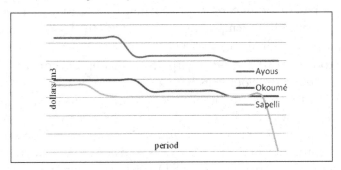

Source: Richard Eba'a et al (2009)

Figures 7.9 and 7.10 show that exports of logs and sawnwood were disrupted. Thus, for the three countries whose exports of timber are based on these main species (Ayous, Okoume, Sapele), falling prices inevitably affected the export earnings of these products. In Gabon, for example, exports of logs represented 1,768,080 m³ so 49 per cent and 51 per cent of Okoume and various timbers. Similarly, for the Congo, Okoume represents nearly 50 per cent of log exports followed by Sapelli (26 per cent) which is the first gasoline exported as sawn (64 per cent).

Impact on Corporate Activities

Key loggers in Central Africa are foreign-owned companies, primarily ofEuropean origin. Since 2000 one notes the arrival of investors from Asia (China, Malaysia) in search of new sources of wood supply following the sharp decline of forest resources in East Asia and a rise in Chinese demand (UBIFRANCE 2008). The group Vicwood (Hong Kong), which operates in Cameroon, Central African Republic and Congo-Brazzaville, has become one of the main operators in terms of export volumes in the area. The German Danzer Group operates in Congo through its subsidiary IFO and in the DRC through Siforco (the leader in forestry in this country). In terms of French actors, the first operator remains the Rougier Group, operating in Cameroon, Gabon and Congo. One also notes the presence of Pasquet Group. Local actors are changing mainly in the category of small and medium enterprises.

Effects of the Crisis on the Major Groups: The Case of Rougier Group

In the Congo, the group stressed that the level of operating profitability achieved in 2007 could not be maintained in 2008; Sapelli was quickly affected by the effects of the housing crisis on the North American and European markets. Also, in the light of the remoteness of production sites and the importance of logistics costs in the cost of production, the group decided to reduce the rate of production approximately by a quarter (Rougier 2009). Activities have since been temporarily stopped with the lay-off of the entire workforce after a hundred jobs were deleted.

In Cameroon, forestry and industrial performance have been deeply affected by the market trend developments with a direct impact on productivity and product quality. Efforts to strengthen the recovery results began in previous years were not sufficient to lower production costs to a level consistent with sales prices. Operating margins were also affected in 2008. The staff level, after rising significantly in the first half, was adjusted at the year end with the further deletion of a team on the site of Djoum. The deteriorating conditions led the group to recognize in its consolidated loss a value of assets amounting to euros 3 million euros. In 2009, the situation will remained tense, with the group focusing on improving resource planning and efficiency of industrial methods so as to reduce costs and control inventory levels.

In Gabon, the Group's operating results held up well and benefited from the good performance of European markets for logs and plywood. The company has not been able to take advantage of the full effect of the liberalization of the marketing of Okoume because of the slowdown in production forest. Moreover, the implementation of export quotas of logs strengthened the development model based on responsible management of the resource and industrialization that led to obtaining FSC certification. Some site of sawn wood in Franceville (Mbouma-Oyali) and Ndjolé (Mévang) were affected by the lumber market of Okoume and decreased their production level. At year-end, the result was improved upon by obtaining a tax credit in connection with the transitional arrangements by the Gabonese government to promote the production competitiveness of plywood on international markets which was burdened due to the non-ratification of EPAs by Gabon.

Effects of the Crisis on Domestic Companies

Congo

Some companies such as the Congolese Industrial of Timber (CIB) have been disrupted, which prompted a dialogue between managers and employees. This consultation resulted in an agreement to stimulate voluntary worker retirement at the company. This policy which was directed towards unskilled labour reduced following the fall of industrial activity. Moreover, other disturbances such as reducing working hours were also recorded within the same company.

Cameroon

Because of the crisis,the Cameroon Forest United (CUF), a logging company based in Douala, took steps to turn off the lights and air-conditioners in offices from 12:30 p.m. In late September 2008,the crisis resulted in the cancellation of nearly 30 per cent of orders (Tassé and Nforgang 2008). Moreover, according to Antoine Darazi, CEO of the company, in early December of the same year this cancellation increased from 50 to 60 per cent. The turnover in October fell to 40 per cent compared to October 2007. Similarly, as with all professionals in the industry, investments were frozen and logging stopped, with the consequent removal of overtime, working weekends, production bonuses, etc.

Gabon

In 2008, the National Gabon Wood Company (SNBG) posted a turnover of over 53.342 billion CFA francs against 47.742 billion CFA francs, an increase of 12 per cent. However, its net profit showed an increase of 3 per cent to 2.616 billion CFA francs (AGP 2009). Yet its export turnover fell from 46.369 billion CFA francs in 2007 to 21.129 billion CFA francs in 2008, a decline of nearly 55.4 per cent. Moreover, the increase in activity appears to have been mainly due to the significant increase in sales value representing 40 per cent of total global exports in 2008 against only 9 per cent in 2007. Eighty-four per cent of company sales were absorbed by China, a leading buyer of Gabonese timber. Conversely, declining exports of Okoume in the European market led to a decline of over 30 per cent. We also note that many timber companies have experienced cancellations of their orders and falling exports.

Impact on State Incomes: The Case of Gabon

State revenues were affected by the crisis through lower export taxes. In Gabon, the decline of log exports led to a decline in tariffs and export taxes from 29.53 billion CFA francs in 2008 against 33.02 billion CFA Francs in 2007, representing a decrease of 10.6 per cent.

Impact on Jobs

Congo

In Congo, the forestry sector, the second largest export and job creation sector (with nearly 9,000 direct and indirect jobs created) was, over a period of about eight months, one of the hardest hit by the global financial crisis. The implications of this were manifested by the collapse of businesses, the significant drop in foreign capital and job losses estimated at nearly 50 per cent of the 9,000 jobs created. In addition, some workers were laid off in all forestry companies (Kitina 2009:4). This situation was much more noticeable in companies located in the northern part of the country. Similarly, one recorded a freezing order in the main markets. Employment deletions and other leave techniques were recorded in the logging companies, such as Mokabi, IFO, LTBI, Likouala Timber, and Thanry Congo. According to Donatien Nzaba, Executive Director of the Forest Economy, 200 jobs within were suspended the Forest Industry of Ouesso (IFO) company.

Cameroon

The downturn resulted in technical unemployment for more than 1,500 people and 762 layoffs. In early 2009, 2,000 job losses were expected. GFBC companies represented 20,000 direct and indirect jobs. Eba'a Atyietal (2009: 25) reported that this crisis laid off 1,000 people and resulted in the sacking of 3,500 people in Cameroon. Similarly, there was a reduction of working time in nearly three certified forestry companies.

Gabon

In Gabon, logging camps of Corawood Gabon drew up a job-cuts plan which saw the departure of 86 employees. With an initial strength of 150 employees, Corawood Gabon today has only 64 workers, an estimated job cut of 26 per cent of all employees. However, the manager promised to rehire 36 people in recovery activities, to work with a reported average of 90 employees (Gaboneco 2009).

Regarding the Forestry Society of Industrial Koulamoutou (SFIK), the drop in demand has also affected the entire chain of production and the company now employs eight workers. In addition, the company conducted a redundancy of nine workers after offloading about 50 workers whose fixed-term contracts had expired. Today nearly 60 workers on permanent contracts are still laid off pending the resumption of activities. Moreover, the operations manager, Jerome Lauhiengiyii, notified that some strategies are not able to improve the situation of the likes of Harvest Bonuscompany and Operations Gabonese Timber (EGG), which have already filed for bankruptcy.

Measures Taken Against the Crisis

Company Responses

Faced with the crisis, forestry companies have taken a number of measures. Moreover, these measures are different from group to group, according to the market share held by these companies. Thus, the Rougier Group (French group) operating in Congo, Cameroon and Gabon advocates for the concentration of activities on sites deemed critical. This strategy is also applied by the Chinese group Vicwood (Eba'a Atyi et al 2009). Locally, the Congolese companies require a reduction of the fiscal taxes.

Policy Implications

According to Uzunidis and Yacoub (2008, 2009), contemporary economic theory justifies the revival of the role of the state. The merits of economic policy based on the existence of the so-called market failures must be the compensated by intervention of the state. Moreover, Yacoub (2008, 2009) points out that institutional inefficiencies, structural, production, distribution, financial, etc, all represent failures of markets that legitimate measures aimed at public administration with a view to ensuring effective functioning of the productive system and promoting its integration into the global economy, according to the challenges of development. In the face of the international financial crisis, the implementation of some measures was deemed urgent in order to mitigate the vulnerability of the key sectors to external shocks. In this regard, the next section presents the measures of the various governments concerned and discusses their scope and limits.

Measures Taken by Each Country

Congo

Some measures were been taken by the government to address the crisis in the timber sector. These measures involved, in particular, temporary increase in log export quota; suspension of completion of collective agreements; the suspension of advance payments of stumpage fees; and a reduction of 5 per cent VAT on imported petroleum products.

Cameroon

We recall that the policy of the forest sector in Cameroon is considered as one of the most advanced in the Congo Basin (Carret 2000; Karsenty 2006). This is the first country that produced and implemented a coherent forest code in the sub-region, immediately after the World Summit on Sustainable Development held in Rio de Janeiro (Brazil) in 1992. Sector policies related to biodiversity conservation and sustainable development in Cameroon mainly include the forests and wildlife regime. Following the crisis, and to protect its industry, the government at a meeting of CEMAC held in Douala in March 2009 (Eba'aAtyietal 2009) took some decisions involving the removal of the bank guarantee; the removal of a tax clearance prior to export; reduction of the FRG by 50 per cent; less than 15 per cent mercurial; and, the revision of the lists of species whose logs are allowed to be exported.

Gabon

Compared to Congo and Cameroon which took a set of measures, Gabon has focused on reducing mercurial. These measures advocated a reduction of almost 30 per cent for all species (Richard et al; Eba'a Atyi et al 2009).

Discussion of These Measures

The various measures taken by governments have a number of limitations. While these measures may be effective in the short term, it should be noted that these will be limited if demand on the international market continues to decline. Similarly, at the level of business activities, these measures do not guarantee financial support from governments.

At the Level of Demand

It is difficult to implement support measures regardless of demand. Indeed, regarding the weakness of domestic demand in these countries, the measures taken at the state level are limited due to the decline in global demand. Moreover, if these measures can produce effects in the short-term, in long term they will not produce conclusive results if major customers are not aware of sustained growth of their economies. However, Congo, Cameroon and Gabon would gain by strengthening relations with China.

Regarding domestic demand, it should be noted that over 90 per cent of total production of industrial round wood in developing countries is used onsite. Yet, neither governments nor corporations that process and market forest products in these countries generally pay this the attention it deserves. One of the major reasons for their lack of interest is that in many countries, the domestic market is dwarfed by the export market. There are several explanations for this, including the fact that in many countries, forest products are an extremely important source of foreign exchange. Furthermore, the largest scale and more concentrated export activities make them more visible, so it is easier for governments to deal with. Often, the value of forest products in the national economy is significantly undervalued, hence the little attention from governments. However, the crisis is a reminder that policies should focus on domestic demand.

The Business Activities

The absence of direct measures to support forestry companies will exacerbate disruption both upstream then downstream. Thus, the entire industry is going to experience disruptions throughout the crisis. Similarly, the expected effects are likely to get worse because the crisis requires deep reforms within enterprises and the pursuit of measures whose performance can adapt to market conditions. Moreover, given the collapse of the banking system, the different groups and companies need to ensure continued funding of their activities. However, for financial institutions, guarantees of these groups can only come from demand in the timber market. But if the demand remains weak, the removal of bank guarantees advocated for example in Cameroon will not benefit all companies, but only a limited number.

Level of Employment

In the three countries, the timber sector represents the second largest provider of jobs. However, it is clear that the intervention levels of these countries do not include measures to mitigate job cuts recorded in the sector since then. Indeed, unemployment is a major handicap for these countries, with nearly half the populations already living below the poverty line. Moreover, lack of employment support is also an impediment to development in areas where commercial activities are supported by employees of forest enterprises (such as the case of the employees of Congolese Industrial Wood in the north of Congo Brazzaville).

Conclusion and Recommendations

Congo, Cameroon and Gabon are oil exporting countries experiencing poor economic performancedue to the effects of the current crisis characterized by falling exports, falling market prices and global demand. Moreover, a weak non-oil sector and the limited diversification of their economies make them more vulnerable to external shocks. Thus, the timber sectors in the three countries experienced the full effects of the crisisas demonstrated in this study.

These countries decreased their exports between 2007 and 2008 which was manifested by lower prices of logs and sawn wood, tax revenue and job losses in companies operating in the sector. Moreover, the measures taken by various governments also face some limitations. Some difficulties exist and governments will implement other measures to mitigate the effects of the crisis. Nevertheless, despite these difficulties, the revival of the Chinese economy would bring an established chain of hope in these countries since Chinaimports nearly half of the timber exports of the Central African countries.

In view of the foregoing discussion, we are making the following recommendations.

At the state level, it is important that governments should promote policies that that will build regional integration within the sub-region to develop a sub-regional market for the timber industry. Similarly, they should stimulate domestic demand through lower prices to stabilize production costs so as to sustain major construction needs. The reduction of forest taxes would also allow domestic enterprises, especially SMEs, to cope with the effects of the crisis. Moreover, the creation of a framework between the government and private companies would contribute to limiting the negative effects of unemployment in the localities in which forestry companies are located.

Thus, in terms of budget surpluses recorded by the Congo, for example, the support given to the timber industry should be through grants to local operators considered most effective; and renewed focus should be more sensitive to the communities whose jobs represent a significant percentage of the national workforce. At this stage, fiscal policy should focus on vulnerable sectors of the economy through a stimulus plan.

References

AfDB, 2009, *Perspectives Economiques en Afrique*, Paris: African Development Bank.

AGP, 2009, *Gabon-économie-bois*: La SNBG *affiche un chiffre d'affaires en hausse en 2008*, Libreville: AGPGABON.

BAfD, 2008, *Etude sur la diversification des sources de la croissance économique*, *Libreville*: African Developement Bank.

Balchin, N., 2009, 'The Impact of the Global Financial Crisis in Africa', *Africa growth Agenda*, Available at: http://www.mthente.co.za/resources/mthente-in-the-news/The%20Impact%20of%20the%20Global%20Financial%20Crisis%20in%20Africa%20-%20Neil%20Balchin.pdf.

Brinkman H.-J., Bauer, J.-M., and Casely-Hayford, L., 2010, *Assessing the Impacts of the Glob- al Economic and Financial Crisis on Vulnerable Households in Ghana: A sequel*, Accra: WFP. Carret, J.-C., 2000, 'La réforme de la fiscalité forestière au Cameroun: Débat, politique Etanalyse économique', Yaoundé: Bois et Forêts des Tropiques, pp. 37–51.

CEA, 2009, *La crise financière mondiale: son impact sur l'Afrique, les mesures et la voie à suivre*, Cairo: ECA.

Chevalier, J., F., 2008, *Les forêts du Gabon*, Libreville: Ambassade de France.

Devarajan, Sh., 2009, *La crise économique mondiale: quels impacts sur l'Afrique subsaharienne?*, Paris: IFRI.

Eba'aAtyi R., Cerutti P. Lescuyer G., Carlos de Wasseige, Bayol N., and Karsenty A., 2009, *Crise financière et secteur forestier en Afrique centrale*, Yaoundé: OFAC/FORAF.

FMI, 2008, *Etudes économiques et financières, perspectives économiques régionales: Afrique subsaharienne*, Washington DC: IMF.

Gaboneco, 2009, *Gabon: la filière bois licencie*, Available at : http://gaboneco.com/show _article.php? IDActu=11953.

Gicam, 2009, *Impact de la crise financière et économique sur le Cameroun, les propositions du Gicam* Available at: http://www.legicam.org/ index2.php?option=com _docman&task= doc_view&gid=168&Itemid=92.

ILO, 2009, *A Rapid Impact Assessment of the Global Economic Crisis on Liberia*, Monrovia: International Labour Organization.

Karsenty, A., 2006, 'L'impact des réformes dans le secteur forestier en Afrique Centrale', Dans Nasi, R., Nguingiri, J. C. and Ezzine de Blas, D., eds, Paris: *L'Harmattan*, pp. 25-60.

Kiptoo, K. C., 2009, 'The Potential Impacts of the Global Financial Crisis on African Economies', *Tygervalle: Africagrowth Agenda*, pp. 14–18.

Kitina, G., G., 2009, 'Secteur forestier congolais: la crise financière cause la pèrte de plus d'un millier d'emplois', Brazzaville: Les Dépêches de Brazzaville. N°726, p.4.

Krugman, P., 2009, *The Return of Depression Economics and the Crisis of 2008*, New York: W.W. Norton & Company.

Langbour, P., Jean Gérard, 2007, *La transformation plus poussée en Afrique centrale*, Yaoundé: CIRAD/OIBT.

Massa I., TeVelde D.W., 2008, 'The Global Financial Crisis: Will Successful African Countries be Affected? Background Note', ODI. Available at http://www.odi. org. uk/sites/odi.org.uk/files/odi-assets/publications-opinion-files/3486.

Mayaux, P., Bartholome, E., Fritz, S., Belward, A., 2004, 'A New Land – Cover Map of Africa for the Year 2000', *Journal of Biogeography*, 33 (6): 861–77.

MEFEPPN - FORAF, 2008, *Fiche de collecte des données pour le suivi de l'état des Forêts d'Afrique Centrale, Niveau national Gabon*, Projet FORAF, Kinshasa, Libreville: MEFEPPN.

Mission économique française, 2007, *La filière bois au Gabon*, Libreville: Ambassade de France.

Mouly B., 2009, Plus de 70 milliards gelés en Afrique. Available at : http://www. jeuneafrique.com/Article/ARTJAJA2532p082-083.xml0/-investissement projet- crise-economique-multinationale-Plus-de-70-milliards-de-dollars-geles-en-Af- rique.html.

Ndzi A., N., 2008, *Le secteur forestier congolais victime de la crise financière internationale*. Available at: http://www.congo-site.com/Le-secteur-forestier-congolais-victime- de-la-crise-financiere-internationale_a2106.html.

NgolleNgolle E., 2009, *Foresterie: les potentialités et opportunités d'investissement dans le secteur forestier*, Yaoundé: Cameroon Investment Forum.

Ngowi, H. P., 2006, *International Trade Finance: A Handbook for Students*, Morogoro: Mzumbe Book Project.

Ngowi, H. P., 2009a, *The Impact of the Crisis on Employment and Official Development Assistance*, Dar es Salaam: ILO.

Ngowi, H. P., 2009b, *The Current Global Financial Crisis: Its Impacts and Solutions in Tanzania*, Dar Es Salaam: IFM.

Ngowi, H. P., 2009c, *The Earth in the World of Global Financial Crisis: Is the Crisis Good or Bad for the Environment? Some Opportunities and Challenges*, Dar es Salaam: US Embassy.

Ngowi, H. P., 2009d, Can the Budget Offer Recovery?, in *The Business Partner*, Issue 3.

Ngowi, H. P., 2009e, *The Global Financial Crisis and its Impacts on Investment in Human Capital*, Arusha: CAPAM.

PNUD/UNDP, 2007, *Rapport mondial sur le développement humain 2007/2008*, New York: Programme des Nations Unies pour le Développement/UNDP.

NUD/UNDP, 2009, 'L'impact de la crise financière et économique sur les économies africaines: le cas du Sénégal', Dakar: Programme des Nations Unies pour le Développement/UNDP.

Rougier, 2009, *Rapport financier annuel 2008*, Available at : http://www.rougier.fr/uploads/media/Communique_du_30_04_2009.pdf.

SANA CONGO, 2010, *Analyse et estimation des besoins et environnement dans le cadre de la mise en œuvre de la déclaration de Libreville*: République du Congo.

Sandouly, P., Labey, A., 2009, 'Panique dans la filière bois', *Jeune Afrique*, Paris, Available: http://www.jeuneafrique.com/Article/ARTJAJA2518p074.xml0/crise- econom-ique-bois-sylviculture-chiffre-d-affairespanique-dans-la-filiere-bois.html.

Tassé E., Nforgang Ch., 2008, *La crise financière abat le bois Africain: cas du Cameroun*, Bruxelles: InfoSud Belgique Agence.

Thies, D. F., Beligné, V., 2007, *Note de synthèse économique du secteur forestier au Cameroun*, Yaoundé: Coopération Française.

UBIFRANCE, 2008, *La filière bois en Afrique centrale, fiche de synthèse*, Yaoundé: Ambassade de France.

UNECE/FAO, 2009a, *Annual Market Review 2008-2009, Geneva Timber and Forest Study*, Geneva: United Nations.

UNECE/FAO, 2009b, *The forest sector in the green economy*, Timber and Forest Discussion Paper N°54, Geneva: United Nations.

Uzunidis, D., Yacoub, L., 2008, Le développement dans la mondialisation: crise de gouvernance mondiale et retour de l'Etat, Paris: Recherches internationales, n°84, octobre-décembre, pp.105–31.

Uzunidis, D., Yacoub, L., 2009, 'La Gouvernance de l'économie mondiale et le renouveau des politiques économiques actives dans les pays en développement, in S. Callens, D. Uzunidis', eds, *Gouvenance, Exercices de pouvoir*, Paris: Marché et Organisations, n°9. pp. 203–43.

Valbois, 2009, *Crise mondiale de la filière bois: bilan et perspectives*, Libramont: Foire Agricole et Forestière de Libramont.

Wakeman-Linn, J., Portillo, R., Iossifov, P., and Milkov, D., 2009, *The International Financial Crisis and Global Recession: Impact on the CEMAC Region and Policy Considerations*, Washington DC: International Monetary Fund.

WWF-France, 2007, *La responsabilité particulière de la France dans l'exploitation et la préservation des forêts tropicales du Bassin du Congo*, Paris: Dossier de presse.

Yacoub, L., 2008, 'Légitimité de la fiscalité de la politique industrielle dans le contexte de la mondialisation: cas de la Tunisie', Thèse de Doctorat en sciences économiques, Tunis: Université de Tunis El Manar.

Yacoub, L., 2009, *La politique économique dans la mondialisation: de la récusation au renouveau*, Tunis: Laboratoire de Recherche sur l'Industrie et l'Innovation.

8

The Impact of the Financial Crisis: Developments in the Mobile Telecommunications Industry in Africa

Maxwell Chanakira

Introduction

The financial crisis began in late 2007 in the sub-prime mortgages market in the United States of America (USA). By 2008, the situation had degenerated into a major crisis in the banking, finance and credit markets resulting in the bankruptcy of several high profile USA international banks and the subsequent bailout of some of these banks by the government. Some commentators have remarked that a financial crisis of this proportion has not been witnessed since the Great Depression of the 1930s. The IMF (2009) observes that the current financial crisis is more global in scope than in any other period of financial turmoil in the past 60 years, lending support to the commentators' views.

The USA is the largest economy in the world, and many foreign countries including advanced economies invest there. The major industrialized economies provide significant investment to emerging markets, accounting for more than 85 per cent of global outward FDI stock (SBG 2010). As a consequence, there are trade and investment linkages between the economies of the USA, advanced countries and emerging markets. Thus, although originating in the USA, the impact affected, first the economies of many developed countries and then spread to countries in the developing world.

At the outset of the crisis, the initial view was that Africa was 'decoupled' from the crisis. Schiere (2010) provides two reasons for this perspective.

Firstly, Africa had limited exposure to the crisis as the continent is not fully integrated into the global financial system. Secondly, the growing relationships with Asian countries, particularly India and China, made African countries less reliant on traditional development partners, which were suffering from a severe economic contraction. However, this perception proved incorrect as the financial crisis did affect Africa, leading to a drop in the rate of GDP growth to 2 per cent for 2008, 4 per cent for 2009 and 5.2 per cent for 2010 (*African Economic Outlook* 2009).

Although its origins are in the financial sector, the negative effects of the financial crisis soon spilled over into other sectors of the general economy, namely: energy and construction, insurance, mining, education, oil, aviation, IT, manufacturing, tourism, logistics, health care, agriculture, real estate, media, telecommunications industries, etc. These industries are being impacted by the crisis in different ways. This is understandable, given that industries have different features and relative importance to national economies. For example, Burger Consultants (2009) identify the energy and construction industries as drivers of national economies and therefore the least affected by the crisis.

The telecommunications sector is not only strategic, but an important contributor to job creation, GDP and the efficient running of businesses worldwide. Research by Frontier Economics on behalf of the Global System for Mobile Association (GSMA) found that the mobile industry in sub-Saharan Africa directly or indirectly employed more than 3.5 million people in 2006; contributed an average of 4 per cent to African countries' GDP; and accounted for 7 per cent of total government revenues in the region (Frontier-GSMA 2008). Since the outbreak of the financial crisis, it is important to step back and reflect on its impact on this critical industry.

This study examines how the financial crisis has impacted the mobile telecommunications industry in Africa. Adopting a single industry approach, the impact of the financial crisis on the industry is examined across key business performance dimensions, namely: robustness of demand on services, revenue, earnings before interest, taxes, depreciation and amortization (EBITDA), Average Revenue Per User (ARPU), operational capital expenditure and operational costs of key telecommunications operators in Africa.

The study is significant in that it analyses how the financial crisis affected a critical industry driving economic growth on the African continent. The insights obtained from the study are required as input by various governments in formulating telecommunications policy which will better support the industry and make it more resilient to future impacts or disruptions of the financial crisis on the industry.

The chapter is organized as follows: the first section provides an overview of the background to the international financial crisis. The second section examines transmission channels and the impact of the crisis on the global economy. An outline of the research focus and method, which is the basis of the empirical investigation, follows in the third section. The fourth section provides the findings of the study, while the fifth section touches briefly on the policy implications of the chapter. The sixth section concludes the chapter.

Overview of the Financial Crisis

Demystifying the Financial Crisis

Mishkin (1991) provides the following definition of a financial crisis: 'a disruption to financial markets in which adverse selection and moral hazard problems become much worse, so that financial markets are unable to efficiently channel funds to those who have the most productive investment opportunities'. Consequently, a financial crisis can steer an economy away from a position of high economic output in which financial markets perform well to a situation in which economic output sharply declines. Hence, the hallmarks of a global financial crisis are considerable economic slowdowns in most countries (Te Velde 2008).

The term financial crisis is a broad term, which, in general, is applied to a variety of situations in which financial institutions or assets rapidly lose a significant portion of their value (Oxbridge Writers 2012). The term also refers to situations in which stock markets crash, there is a steep depreciation of currencies, loan defaults occur and other financial bubbles burst or recession sets in. The effects of a financial crisis fall in the human as well as financial category, causing substantial job losses to the former and drops in foreign investment, export earnings and volumes to the latter.

Channels of Transmission

Although the financial crisis originated in the US, it first spread to industrialized countries before developing countries were rapidly engulfed by the crisis. The crisis spread rapidly from the industrialized countries through multiple transmission channels, including declines in commodity prices, trade volumes, remittances and international credit (Ali, Dadush and Falcao 2009). These transmission channels demonstrate that there are linkages between the developed and undeveloped economies through trade, Foreign Direct Investment (FDI) and aid flows. As a consequence of falling prices and demand for their commodities, many countries have experienced sharp drops in primary commodity exports both in terms of volume and value of earnings.

In Africa, the global financial crisis affected economies in a multiplicity of ways. Ali (2009) argues that the global economic downturn was the major transmission channel of the financial crisis to African economies. Kasekende, Brixovia and Ndikumana (2010) assert this point, explaining that the global financial crisis impacted the continent mostly through real channels: deteriorated terms-of-trade, reduced demand for exports, declines in FDI, remittances, tourism and aid inflows. For relatively well-developed economies, the stock market was another transmission channel for the financial crisis (Soludo 2009; Te Velde 2008).

Impact of the Financial Crisis

The global financial crisis affected all economies, whether advanced, emerging markets or low-income countries, in different ways. The IMF (2009) asserts that, as the crisis developed, growth and trade effects began to affect all countries. Soludo (2009) identified five key areas in which the global financial crisis has affected the global economy: 1. declining real output growth; 2. weakened financial systems; 3. loss of jobs; 4. loss of confidence in financial markets leading to the reduced ability of these institutions to carry out their intermediation role in the economy; and 5. stock market losses. These factors are briefly discussed in the paragraphs that follow.

Declining Real Output Growth

The financial crisis resulted in a global slowdown in economic activity, pushing commodity prices lower. Commodity price drops of over 30 per cent were not uncommon during the height of the financial crisis. A case in point is copper and oil. Oil, a major international commodity, saw its price dip on the international market, inflicting damage on the earnings of oil exporting countries. Figure 8.1 captures the fluctuating prices of oil on the international market from 2006-09. It can be seen that the oil price fell by 35 per cent on its yearly price between 2008 and 2009.

Hence, the decline in export prices and, subsequent export volumes, represented a significant impact on the continent. In effect, the crisis reduced trade, which is the mainstay of economic growth in Africa.

Figure 8.1: OPEC Yearly Basket Oil Price

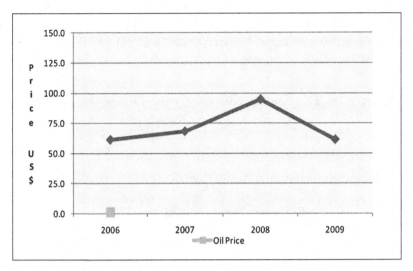

Source: www.opec.org/opec_web/en/data_graphs40.htm

Falling FDI

The financial crisis led to tighter credit conditions as financial institutions became more discreet in their lending approach leading to a situation where credit became scarce and more expensive. Expensive credit came about due to re-evaluation of risks. For transnational corporations (TNCs) in particular, this resulted in lower corporate profits which constrained their ability to carry out investments in both domestic and overseas economies. Correspondingly, private capital flows to developing regions consisting mainly of FDI, significantly slowed, in the process hindering economies that had been relying on these funds for crucial infrastructure projects.

Directly as a result of the global financial crisis, global FDI inflows fell by 14 per cent from a record high of US$1,979 billion in 2007 to US$1,697 billion in 2008 (UNCTAD 2009). There was a further decline of 43 per cent from US$1,979 billion in 2008 to US$1,111 billion in 2009 (see Figure 8.2). This fall is unsurprising, given the severity with which the financial crisis and recession hurt advanced economies.

Weakened Financial Systems

At its height, the financial crisis affected the banking, finance and credit markets resulting in the bankruptcy of some high profile international banks. These banks had to be bailed out by their respective governments in order to prevent their collapse. In contrast to the severe impact of the financial crisis on the financial sector in other regions, the effect on the African financial sector was relatively mild. Very few banks in Africa were directly exposed to off-balance sheet transactions such as securitization or derivatives; so Africa escaped the sub-prime and banking crises, and did not require bank rescue plans (AERC 2009).

Figure 8.2: FDI Flows Before (2007) and During the Financial Crisis (2008, 2009)

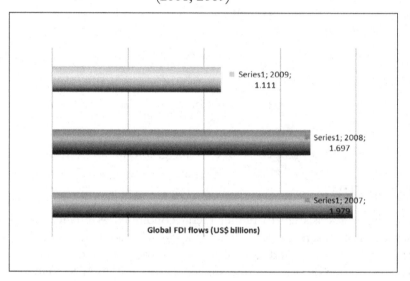

Source: UNCTAD, The World Investment Report 2009

Falling Remittances

As the financial crisis tightened, there were job losses in several countries. This affected many migrant workers who used to send money to their relatives in their home countries, resulting in a drop in remittances. Similarly, most countries are experiencing a slowdown in migrant remittances as a result of the weakening of economies in the West and in African advanced economies. Declining domestic and corporate spending continue to pose significant problems for tourism, affecting tourism revenues. The shrinking world economy meant Official Development Assistance (ODA) as well as voluntary flows were all affected. For example, in Kenya, remittances have been steadily falling since October 2008 from US\$ 61 million to US\$ 39 million in January 2009.

Collapse of Stock Market Prices

The performance of the stock market is one of the principal indicators of the health of an economy. The movement of stock market indices is a pointer to future economic outlook. A falling stock index, for example, reflects the darkening of the investment climate while a rising stock index points to increased investor confidence and soundness of the economy. In his paper, Te Velde (2008) identified the stock market as a transmission channel of the global financial crisis to the economies of less developed countries, noting that the global economic and financial crisis had dragged down stock market values. In some cases, stock markets crashed by as much as 70 per cent.

In summary, the impact of the financial crisis was declining real output growth; weakened financial systems; loss of jobs; loss of confidence in financial markets leading to the reduced ability of financial institutions to carry out their intermediation role in the economy; stock market losses. Was the mobile telecommunications industry affected by the financial crisis? This is most probable in view of the severity of the crisis. What was the nature of the impact? This study provides answers to these questions, by examining how the financial crisis impacted the mobile telecommunications industry in Africa.

The Mobile Telecommunications Industry

The mobile telecommunications industry exerts a positive and significant impact on economic growth. This impact is estimated to be twice as large in developing countries as it is in developed countries (Waverman, Meschi and Fuss 2005). There is now widespread recognition that telecommunications is no longer simply a convenient public service, but an enormously valuable economic resource, and an increasingly important infrastructure for economic growth and development. In their research, Roeller and Waverman (2001) concluded that a good communications network widens markets, creates better information flow, lowers transaction costs and substitutes costly physical transport.

Worldwide, the telecommunications industry is a high-revenue industry that makes a substantial and growing contribution to the world economy. The Telecommunications Industry Association (TIA) estimates that the industry's worldwide revenue was US$3.85 trillion in 2009. Global telecommunications spending will grow at a rate of 6.3 per cent compound annual rate to US$4.9 trillion in 2013 (TIA 2010). According to the GSA, the number of global mobile lines grew from 3.3 billion in 2007 to 4.5 billion in mid-2010. Africa accounts for only 8 per cent of the world's mobile lines.

Africa is now one of the world's fastest growing mobile markets, a long way since the first cellular call was made in Zaire (now DRC) in 1987. Research conducted by Frontier Economics on behalf of the Global System for Mobile Association (GSMA) found that the mobile industry in sub-Saharan Africa employed more than 3.5 million people directly or indirectly in 2006 and the industry contributed an average of 4 per cent to the region's GDP. The same report estimates that the mobile sector accounts for 7 per cent of the region's government revenues.

It is pertinent to examine the impact of the financial crisis on such a strategic industry on the continent. Hence, the focus of this study is on the mobile telecommunications industry in Africa.

Methodological Approach

The contemporary phenomenon under investigation in this study is the impact of the financial crisis, and the context is the mobile telecommunications industry in Africa. In order to assess the impact of the financial crisis on the industry, a trend analysis was carried out on key balance sheet and investment indicators *before* the onset of the financial crisis in the years 2006 and 2007 and *during* the financial crisis in the years 2008 and 2009.

Based on the multiple case study methodology, the trend analysis was constructed from annual reports of five transnational telecommunications operators: Millicom (with operations in seven African countries), MTN with 16, Orascom with seven, Vodacom with five and Zain (now Bharti Airtel) with 16. The five enterprises had a total of 233.1 million mobile subscribers at the end of 2009, representing 61.3 per cent of Africa's mobile customers. Clearly, the results of this study can be generalized to the rest of Africa.

From the databases, tables and graphs that vividly capture trends on the impact of the financial crisis were plotted. These diagrammatic presentations depict growth trends across a number of dimensions: telecommunications growth, revenue, ARPU, EBITDA and operational expenditure. The trend analysis is divided into two phases: before the financial crisis and during the financial crisis. The effect of saturation as a factor in influencing these results is analysed and discounted as a contributory factor.

The case study strategy is particularly valuable in answering the question, 'How did the financial crisis impact the telecommunications industry in Africa?' Multiple, diverse case studies provide greater coverage of the phenomenon and allow a greater amount of testing, elaboration of concepts and comparative analysis between cases (Yin 1994). This is precisely the aim of this study: to investigate the impact of the financial crisis on the telecommunications industry in Africa using several cases.

Impact of the Financial Crisis on Africa

Slackening Telecommunications Growth

The growth of mobile telecommunications services for MTN across its African operations increased by 37 per cent from 36.2 million lines to 49.4 million lines in 2007 (before the financial crisis); 36 per cent from 49.4 million lines to 67 million lines in 2008 (as the effects of the crisis began to be felt in the advanced economies of the world) and only 24 per cent from 67 million lines to 82.8 million lines in 2009 (as the consequences of the financial crisis engulfed Africa). Figure 8.3 below captures this growth trend.

Similarly, telecommunications growth for Millicom rose 65 per cent, from 3.4 million lines to 5.6 million in 2007, 63 per cent from 5.6 million lines to 9.1 million lines in 2008, and 35 per cent from 9.1 million lines to 12.2 million lines in 2009.

A distinct trend of slackening growth in telecommunications numbers is clearly discernible for MTN and Millicom. On aggregate, all the five major operators in Africa showed a similar trend: the rate of subscriber growth fell steeply from 40 per cent in 2007, to 34 per cent in 2008 and 17 per cent in 2009.

A key question to be answered here is: 'What was the cause of this trend?' Could the slackening of growth be due to saturation of the telecommunications markets? No. This phenomenon was not due to saturation. The markets in which these five operators were active during the period under discussion were not saturated.

The average voice penetration for Millicom across all its seven African markets in 2009 was under 25 per cent (Millicom 2009). The average for MTN across its 16 African markets was much higher at 49 per cent in 2009 (MTN 2009). Vodacom's average voice penetration across its five African markets was 40 per cent in 2009 (Vodacom 2009) while the average mobile penetration for Orascom across its seven operations was 51 per cent (Orascom 2009). Therefore, saturation of the markets was not the cause of this trend.

Slowing Revenue Growth

In order to assess the impact of the financial crisis on industry revenues streams, two factors were considered: first, whether revenue was growing or decreasing and second, the rate of change.

Figure 8.3: Customer Growth Trends Across Africa
(as viewed from TNCs)

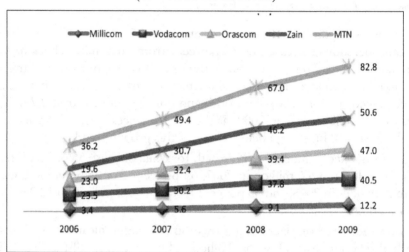

Source: Annual Reports (Millicom, Vodacom, Orascom, Zain and MTN from 2006-2007)

MTN registered revenue growth of 32 per cent in 2007 before the crisis, fell to 21 per cent in 2008 and dropped even further to 4 per cent in 2009 as the financial crisis gripped Africa (see Figure 8.4). Zain displays a similar trend 46 per cent revenue increase in 2007, 27 per cent in 2008 and a drop of -7 per cent in 2009.

These TNCs registered considerable drops in revenue growth rates, with Vodacom and Zain actually registering negative growth. All the firms reported that exchange-rate depreciation was a major contributing factor to the slowing growth rate of revenue. MTN (2009) said of its slowing revenue growth in Ghana, 'Although local currency revenue increased by 25.1 per cent for the period, significantly ahead of subscriber growth, this translated into a 6.3 per cent decline in revenue in rand terms to R5.7 billion at December 2009 due to the combination of rand strength in the second half of the year and weakness in the Ghanaian cedi, particularly in the first half of the year.'

Figure 8.4: Revenue Growth Rates for Telecommunications
TNCs in Africa

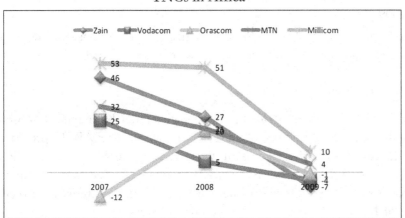

Source: Annual Reports (Millicom, Vodacom, Orascom, Zain and MTN
from 2006-07)

Similarly, Vodacom (2009), commenting on the slowing of its revenue growth said, 'A solid financial performance was achieved in the year ending 31 March 2009; even as the global economic downturn deepened its bite in the Group's operating markets. Higher inflation, driven largely by fuel and food prices, rising cost of debt and currency weakness were features of the operating conditions in South Africa, as was the impact of the commodity price slump on the resources sector. In the DRC, this affected the country's mining-reliant economy severely.' Hence, slowing revenue growth was due to exchange rate depreciation, and as we saw in the commentary, this was induced by the financial crisis.

EBITDA

EBITDA is an important measure of operational profits. It allows one to analyse the performance of a company's operations while eliminating all non-operating and non-recurring items such as depreciation and amortization, interest expense, taxes and one-time charges such as professional fees, or other non-recurring costs.

Millicom posted a 42 per cent rise in EBITDA from US$2.86 billion to US$4.05 billion in 2007 before the crisis, slowed to 20 per cent from US$4.05 billion to US$4.85 billion in 2008 and fell significantly to one per cent from US$4.85 billion to US$4.79 billion in 2009 as the effects of the financial crisis were felt in Africa (see Figure 8.5). Orascom showed a comparable pattern, with revenue growth of 17 per cent from US$1.34 billion to US$1.57 billion in 2007, 22 per cent from US$1.57 billion to US$1.91 billion in 2008 and a spectacular collapse from US$1.91 billion to US$1.72 billion to -10 per cent in 2009.

All the major TNCs operating in Africa registered considerable drops in revenue growth rates, with Orascom even registering a negative growth rate.

Average Revenue Per User (ARPU)

ARPU is an expression of the income generated by a typical subscriber per unit time in a telecommunications network. The ARPU provides an indication of the effectiveness of the revenue-generating potential. ARPU has continued to fall across Africa for the past five years or so as competition forces prices down. However, there are discernible differences between the rate of decrease before and after the financial crisis.

Orascom recorded a drop in ARPU of 5.19 per cent from US$12.13 to US$11.50 in 2007, worsening to 6.96 per cent from US$11.50 to US$10.70 in 2008 and plummeting 12.80 per cent from US$10.70 to US$9.33 in 2009 as the financial crisis hit hard (Table 8.6).

Figure 8.5: EBITDA Growth Patterns for Telecommunications TNCs in Africa

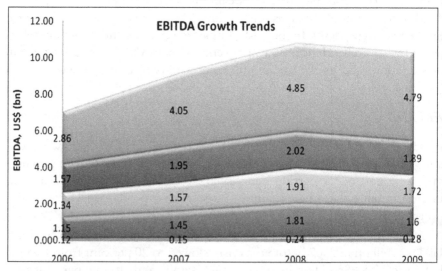

Source: Annual Reports (Millicom, Vodacom, Orascom, Zain and MTN from 2006-07)

Millicom registered a fall in ARPU of 9.6 per cent from US$9.20 to US$8.31 in 2008, accelerating to 20.5 per cent from US$8.31 to US$6.60 in 2009 as the financial crisis began to bite harder.

Table 8.1: ARPU Trends Across Africa

Mobile Operator	ARPU (US dollars)			
	2006	2007	2008	2009
MTN	n/a	17.40	12.44	10.00
Millicom	n/a	9.20	8.31	6.60
Orascom	12.13	11.50	10.70	9.33
Vodacom	n/a	9.26	9.17	8.84

Source: Annual Reports (Millicom, Vodacom, Orascom, Zain and MTN from 2006-07)

Commenting on the causes of the weakening of its ARPU, Millicom (2009) said, 'Africa was by no means immune from the effects of the global economic crisis in 2009. Overall, weaker economies have led to lower ARPUs and steadier penetration growth, and we have suffered from significant currency depreciation in Ghana and to a lesser extent in DRC and Tanzania.'

The resultant economic weaknesses evident in different countries emanating from the effect of the financial crisis have led to lower ARPUs. As a result, the trend of falling ARPU has intensified as operators offered several promotions, cut prices in order to retain customer numbers in a tough operating environment.

Operational Capital Expenditure

In 2006, the total operational capex between the five TNCs rose 26 per cent from US$4.58 billion to US$5.79 billion before the financial crisis began, grew 18 per cent to US$6.83 billion as the crisis began to bite and grew at an even slower rate of -2 per cent to US$6.70 billion as the effects of the financial crisis were felt across Africa (see Figure 8.7). On average, operators actually cut operational capex by a significant 20 per cent between 2008 and 2009.

Figure 8.6: Capital Expenditure Trends in Africa

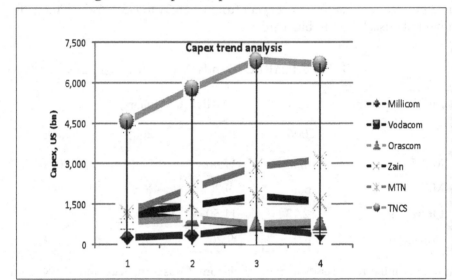

Source: Annual Reports (Millicom, Vodacom, Orascom, Zain and MTN from 2006-07)

UNCTAD (2009) argues that tighter credit conditions, expensive loans, plummeting stock prices and shrinking corporate profits have greatly diminished the value of, and scope for, crossborder mergers and acquisitions (M&As). In addition, slackening demand for goods and services has caused companies to cut back on their investment plans in general. Operational costs have also risen because the financial crisis has boosted the cost of capital for the mobile industry, a capital-intensive industry.

Millicom (2009), in its annual report says of its capital expenditure programmes,

> Inward investment programmes have been put on hold, and the fall in commodity prices has seen the mothballing of some mining projects and put pressure on GDP. In markets like Tanzania, the impact on the important tourism trade has also been felt.

Policy Implications

The effect of the financial crisis on Africa led to a drop in the growth rate of GDP to 2 per cent for 2008, 4.1 per cent for 2009 and 5.2 per cent for 2010 (*African Economic Outlook* 2009). On the other hand, although the telecommunications industry was affected by the global telecommunications industry, registering much slower growth than previously, growth in the sector was still higher than the growth of the overall economy on the continent, demonstrating its resilience. This resilience is partly explained by the fact that the telecommunications services are deemed an essential item in household budgets.

In fact, because of this resilience, the telecommunications industry played a major role in supporting accelerated growth, through a partnership between private investment and supportive regulation. Companies from other industrial sectors were able to use telecommunications solutions in deploying value-added interventions to improve their performance, such as real-time inventory and procurement management or video and teleconferencing. The companies also focused more closely on efficiently controlling their operating expenses, executing transformation programmes and precisely managing commercial costs.

The results in this study show that the telecommunications industry is a bellwether industry in times of economic and financial crisis, resilient in itself and shielding other industries. So what is the policy implication for this position? As a consequence, policy makers must continue to recognize the critical role that the telecommunications industry plays, and increase competition in the industry to make it more efficient. Firstly, independent regulation in the industry must be strengthened so that the competitive playing field is evenly balanced. As much as possible, regulators must be financially independent and be shielded from political interference. Fair regulation motivates industry players and increases investment in a given country.

Secondly, governments must encourage investments in the telecommunications sector so that the service reaches wider populations of the country. Investments in both voice and data technologies are necessary in order to expand the services offered. Policy makers must come up with incentives to attract investors in this critical industry. This may entail making it easier to do business in the country and the elimination of corrupt business tendencies.

Finally, policy makers must adopt the use of telecommunications services for both individuals and companies. Companies must be encouraged to embrace telecommunications services in order to reduce costs and save time. The increasing use of e-recruitment, video and teleconferencing, e-procurement, a paperless office will not only save time and money but in the event of a financial crisis, prepare companies to respond better.

Conclusion and Recommendations

The conclusions and recommendations of this study are briefly discussed in the paragraphs that follow.

Conclusion

The global economic crisis created unfavourable foreign currency fluctuations in many African countries. Consequently, the telecommunications market was characterized by reduced interest and investment income and higher financing costs, profoundly affecting TNCs' top and bottom lines. Across all mobile operators, a distinctive trend of slowing growth, slackening revenue growth, falling ARPU and EBITDA is consistent. This is because the global financial crisis has exerted pressure on consumers to restrain telecommunications spending.

This study shows that the effect of the global economic crisis on the mobile telecommunications industry was felt in 2008 and 2009. The effect for 2009 was worse than the effect of 2008, suggesting that there was a time lag between the effects of the global crisis being felt in the advanced economies and Africa. This is understandable, given that it takes time for the transmission channels of trade and remittances to reach the continent.

Recommendations

Governments should bolster telecommunications regulation so that it becomes independent in the true sense of the word. In addition, governments should encourage companies from other industrial sectors to deploy telecommunications solutions to improve their efficiency. Value-added services such as real-time inventory and procurement management or tele- and videoconferencing improve business performance. This will go a long way to making companies more efficient and better prepared to survive in a financial crisis.

Hence, although the telecommunications sector was itself affected by the global financial crisis, albeit on a smaller scale, the industry actually played a role in helping countries weather the effects of the global financial crisis. Governments could look to this critical industry in future financial crises to help other industries to weather the storm better.

References

AERC, 2010, 'Implications for Growth and Development of Africa's Financial System', *Policy Brief*, Number 4, March.

African Economic Outlook, 2009, 'Future Growth Projection in October 2009', African Development Bank Group.

African Economic Outlook, 2010, *Governance and Political Issues (www.africaneco-nomicoutlook.org), Accessed 20 July 2010*.

Ali, S., 2009, 'Impact of the Financial Crisis on Africa', *International Economic Bulletin*, April.

Ali, S., Dadush, U. and Falcao, L., 2009, 'Financial Transmission of the Crisis: What's the Lesson?', *International Economic Bulletin*, June.

IMF, 2009, *Impact of the Global Financial Crisis on Sub-Saharan Africa*, Washington, DC: IMF.

Kasekende, L. Brixova, Z. and Ndikumana, L., 2010, 'Africa: Africa's Counter-Cyclical Policy Response to the Crisis', *Journal of Globalization and Development* 1 (1), Article 16.

MTN, 2009, MTN *Annual Report 2009*, Johannesburg: MTN Group.

Millicom, 2009, *Annual Report and Accounts 2009*, Millicom International Cellular S.A., Luxembourg.

Mishkin, F. S., 1991, *Anatomy of a Financial Crisis*, NBER Working Paper No. W3934, 1991, Available at: http://ssrn.com/abstract=227370.

Ojo, T., 2004, 'Old Paradigm and Information & Communication Technologies for Development Agenda in Africa: Modernisation as Context', *Journal of Information Technology Impact* 4 (3): 139–50.

Oxbridge Writers, 2012. Available: www.oxbridgewriters.com/essays/business/the-term-financial-crisis.php.

Roeller, L. and Waverman, L., 2001, Telecommunications Infrastructure and Economic Development: A Simultaneous Approach, *American Economic Review* 91 (4): 909–23.

Roland Berger Consultants, 2009, *Different Industries Are Being Impacted In Various Ways by the Financial Crisis and the RMB 20 Trillion Economic Stimulus Plan in China*, Think: Act Content.

SBG, 2010, 'BRIC and Africa: New Sources of Foreign Capital Mobilising for Africa Complementing and Competing with Traditional Investors', *Economics*, August.

Schiere, R., 2010, 'Building Complementarities in Africa between Different Development Cooperation, Modalities of traditional development partners and China', Paper pre- sent-ed at the AfDB's Seminar on policy on China's Increasing Engagement in Africa in the Aftermath of the Financial Crisis, Tunis, Tunisia, on 25-26 March.

Soludo, C.C., 2009, *Global Financial and Economic Crisis: How Vulnerable is Nigeria?*, Central Bank of Nigeria, January.

Te Velde, W., 2008, 'The Global Financial Crisis and Developing Countries', *Overseas Development Institute*, Background Note, October.

TIA, 2010, 'ICT Is Key Driver for Global Economy', TIA's 2010 ICT *Market Review & Forecast*, Presented by A. Gruen and N. Fetchko, April 28.

UNCTAD, 2009, The World Investment Report 2009: *Transnational Corporations, Agricultural Production and Development*, New York and Geneva: United Nations.

Vodacom, 2009, *Vodacom Annual Report 2009*, Johannesburg, South Africa: Vodacom Group.

Waverman, L., Meschi, M. and Fuss, M., 2005, 'The Impact of Telecoms on Economic Growth in Developing Countries', *Vodafone Policy Series*, Number 3, March.

Yin, R.K., 1994, *Case Study Research: Design and Methods* (2nd Edition), Thousand Oaks, CA: Sage Publishing.

PART IV

PERSPECTIVES AND EXPERIENCES FROM ASIA

9

Shoot Yourself in the Foot: Philippine State and Society in the 1997 and 2008 Financial Crises

Rolando Talampas

Introduction

In 1997, the Philippines had foreign borrowings of US$44.81 billion from multilateral lending and corporate creditors (Intal and Llanto 1998: 64) and in 2008 some of its biggest banks lost less than US$400 million to foreign entities. Both incidents plunged the country into crisis, the first time due to internal problems, the second time round by seeming recklessness. Nowadays, a Philippine tourism campaign slogan says 'It's more fun in the Philippines'; one may ask what country on earth then would be more exciting? Like a roller-coaster ride for about two decades, the ups and downs of the national output have coincided very well with domestic political challenges and externally-induced financial disasters. In the span of this period, political leaderships which have always been expected to address the impoverishment of huge sections of the working population have changed over time and their abilities to implement mitigating measures have never ceased to be tested.

What has caused the continuing failure of state efforts to stay away from the effects of the financial and economic crises? What should have been done by government in the light of the character of the said crises? Why does it seem – with the reported poverty incidence reaching an all-time high of nearly a quarter of all households (SWS 2012) – that the consequences for the poor people have been more serious than before? Rhetorically, one might ask: Would state interventions then not amount to shooting oneself in the foot?

This chapter argues that the 1997 and 2008 financial and economic crises undermined the capacity of the Philippine state to intervene, that the lessons from these crises have remained unlearned, and that crises of similar nature and greater magnitude would consequently be more likely to occur. Continuously beset by leadership changes since 1986, the Philippines has addressed crisis after crisis ineffectively. The state apparatus has been captured by different profit-motivated rent-seekers that are compliant and subservient to the neo-liberal order. This political fact has also triggered events that have charted the roller-coaster ride of both country and people, such as shown in Figure 9.1 below.

What distinguishes the Philippines case is that other Southeast Asian countries such as Thailand and Indonesia that had also faced the same shocks have already bounced back to even greater heights. The Philippines, instead, has been consigned to the bottom despite worldwide-acclaimed 'people-powered. democratic restoration in 1986 and subsequent subscription to neo-liberal regime. While such authors as Bello et al (2004) or Abinales and Amoroso (2005) blame the 'anti-development state' for succeeding in frustrating genuine change, it is also important to find out what else contributed to this state of affairs.

As the country prides itself on a hospitable, young and English-literate population, together with a liberal economy that has been working to increase national output from the agricultural, industrial and service sectors, it has also been unable to reduce poverty incidence in regions and social groups that have heretofore been mired in daily survival struggles and frustrations. State efforts to help the poor seem dissipated in widespread, persistent, and deep-seated corruption. At best, politicians continue to ride on the old cliché of fighting both corruption and poverty with very few observable outcomes. Indeed, the country has shown spurts and spikes of aggregate growth, but the poor are seldom to be found among its beneficiaries.

To support the contentions herein, this chapter presents a brief narrative of post-1986 Philippine leaderships and the state of the economy. Then, it proceeds to describe and compare the two episodes of crises (1997 and 2008) and the lessons that should have been learned, and identifies factors that may determine the recurrence of the same in the future. In the first episode, I argue that the early post-Marcos years marked by the troubled return to elite democracy and subsequent gross subscription to neoliberal world order weakened the country's immunity to the crisis contagion that began with the collapse of the Thai currency and worsened with capital flight. In the second instance, the crisis struck at the heart of the financial system but this has been dismissed by key players as having little impact in the country's economic performance. It thus leads to the main argument that recurring crises will haunt the Philippine economy for its failure to give relief to the poor people who need more help than anybody else.

Figure 9.1: Annual Growth Rates of Real GDP and Real GNP, 1989-2009

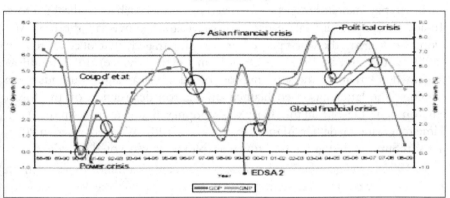

Source: HGC 2009: 2

The Philippines after the 1986 EDSA 'Revolution'

In 1986 Corazon 'Cory' Aquino, widow of assassinated exiled opposition leader ex-Senator Benigno 'Ninoy' Aquino, Jr., succeeded ousted President Ferdinand Marcos, who had ruled the country since 1965. In 1992 she anointed and was succeeded by Fidel Ramos (1992-98), then by Joseph Estrada (1998-2001). The longest post-Marcos term as president was held by Gloria Macapagal Arroyo (2001-10). Quite by surprise, when 'Cory' died, her nonpolitical son Simeon Benigno Aquino III ('Noynoy'/'PNoy') became president in 2010.

'Cory'came to power in the heady days of February 1986, in the aftermath of the 1986 EDSA Revolution, named after the major thoroughfare in the national capital region.[1] She presided over a tumultuous transition with rightist coups and leftist and Muslim insurgencies and was able to finish her term of six years under a constitution that still bears her name (the 1987 'Cory Constitution'). Under pressure from big businessmen and their patrons, she committed to honouring foreign loans, allegedly largely pocketed by Ferdinand Marcos and his cronies. Anyhow she set into motion the unfinished health care (through a generic medicines law), agrarian reform, and local government reforms[2] that promised democratic and empowering changes. With her religious background, she appointed a health secretary with strong negative attitude towards artificial family planning methods that had been supported largely by foreign donors. Her family-owned Hacienda Luisita continued to hold an agricultural estate that was very much at the heart of agrarian revolt in the Central Luzon region.

The new local government code sought to decentralize decision-making but many low-income municipalities complained that their finances were unable to pay standard wages to devolved personnel such as medical doctors. To add to the presidential headaches, Cory years also oversaw the 1987 MV Doña Paz tragedy, the worst peacetime maritime tragedy that killed more than 4,000 people, and in 1991 the Ormoc (in Leyte province) flood/mudflow tragedy that left about the same number of people dead and thousands more missing. The latter has been blamed on wanton destruction of the forest environment. Despite all this, Cory was a popular figure, more so in the West. Time magazine made her 'Man of the Year' for 1987. When she died in 2010, her son Simeon Benigno (also known as 'Noynoy') was voted president.

In 1992, army general Fidel Ramos was elected as a minority president in an eight-party contest. He signed a peace agreement with the Moro National Liberation Front (MNLF), then a major Muslim separatist movement in southern Philippines, whose negotiations he headed during the Cory years. The MNLF guns were silenced as generous aid poured into southern Philippine projects as guerrillas were demobilized or integrated into the regular armed forces. Ramos sought to transform the Philippines into the latest Asian tiger cub under the banner 'Philippines 2000' with targets on job generation, employment, income, and per capita GDP growth, among others. He took bold steps to end the power outage problem. He immediately implemented a 'leapfrogging strategy' by large-scale state asset privatization (former army military camp Fort Bonifacio was sold to private developers), telecommunication, banking, transport liberalization, tax reforms and the like that endeared him to many leaders abroad. Reportedly seeking to continue his reform programme, he favoured – some sectors suspected he even promoted – charter change ('cha-cha') that would lift constitutional restrictions on property ownership. His health secretary Juan Flavier strongly promoted the use, among other things, of condoms to address the unabated population growth rate especially among the poor families. As Ramos was about to step down, the Asian financial crisis hit the Philippines in 1997. But that was not his problem anymore.

Popular actor-turned politician Joseph Ejercito (better known as 'Joseph Estrada,' his screen name, or 'Erap'), succeeded Ramos in 1998 with the most number of votes received by any presidential aspirant before and hence. His popularity drew from his movie roles as a crusading man of the underdog, the rough uneducated funnyman who speaks broken English that endeared him to most people who, despite the education that they have had, could understand but could hardly express themselves well in (American) English. He was a close ally of the deposed President Marcos. This plus his well-known weaknesses for women, wine, and gambling strengthened, rather than undermined, his political support from across the social divides. 'Erap''s political career began from being mayor of a town (with its sections of commercial establishments from poor communities to gated communities) to being elected senator. Elected later as vice president, he headed a presidential anti-crime task force that drew both admiration and flak from different quarters at a time that bank robberies and kidnapping of Chinese-Filipinos became daily news. As president, self-exiled first lady Imelda Marcos and Ferdinand Marcos' cronies returned to the country to recover their assets and status, not to mention privilege.

Estrada blamed Ramos for the growth of Muslim secessionist military capabilities and launched an all-out attack on many physical camps of the Moro Islamic Liberation Front (MILF) in the central Mindanao. MILF was able to set up many physical camps and tunnels Central Mindanao allegedly from government funds meant for irrigation projects. Estrada's fallout from friendship with a known gambling provincial lord triggered a Senate impeachment proceeding that investigated his alleged ownership of multi-million peso bank accounts (suspected to be hidden under the name of a fictitious 'Jose Velarde' which was later admitted by one of his own cronies) that contained his share from local illicit lottery operations. A walkout towards the end of the impeachment proceedings triggered an early evening version of the 1986 EDSA Revolution. The 'Resign-Impeach-Oust' (called RIO) design to unseat 'Erap' catapulted Vice President Gloria Macapagal Arroyo (daughter of 1960s president DiosdadoMacapagal) to power, blessed by a Supreme Court decision on the legality of her assumption of power in January 2001.

On the basis of the unfinished impeachment process, 'Erap' was arrested, prosecuted and imprisoned in large measure in comfortable confinement. His well-known associates were also jailed and/or indicted for complicity in pseudo-foundations created to conceal other allegedly ill-gotten funds. Erap's supporters, reportedly drawn from urban poor communities and nearby rural areas, staged EDSA in the very early morning of 1 May to storm the presidential palace called Malacañang. Gloria Arroyo quelled this street disorder and other later similar planned uprisings of a group of junior military officials called the Magdalo. Seemingly politically isolated, she was nevertheless able to unite the sundry forces (legal opposition, church, business, Left) to oppose her as they sought to impeach and overthrow her via popular street marches.

Arroyo sought to endear herself to the poor by using excess extended value added tax (EVAT) collections to subsidize electricity bills, gasoline and rice prices. Like 'Erap' though, Arroyo would face charges of 'stealing the 2007 election' in her bid to be a duly elected president and not just one who simply finished the remainder of the six-year term of the ousted 'Erap'. It was on account of an audio recording of her telephone conversation with an election official that became public. This infamous call now remembered as 'Hello, Garci…'[3] became viral as it became both joke and spite and cellphone ringtone. Reportedly that was evidence that she personally made sure that her strong rival, popular movie actor Fernando Poe Jr., old friend of Erap would lose, earlier survey results nothwithstanding. Recently elected as representative of her hometown in Congress, Arroyo was arrested in November 2011 and criminally charged but has been under hospital/house arrest while still under medical care.

The 1997 Crisis: Did the Sick Man of Asia Really Escape from the Pneumonia?

After long years of service to then President Gloria Macapagal Arroyo (2001-04; 2007-10), two leading erstwhile palace insiders (Velasco and Saludo 2010: 251) look back to the 1990s and the 1997 crisis in these words:

> In the early to mid-1990s, there was a dramatic reduction in tariffs across the board, which many believed was the right thing to do at that time. The government sent the signal to the international community that its economic policies were flexible. The tariff reductions were well intended and the government expected to harvest the fruits of what it planted. But nobody had anticipated the 1997 financial crisis.

Was anything really 'planted' at all, one might ask. Was it pure luck? Quite frankly, being least considered for growth seemed to be better, in hindsight of course. Noland (2000) credits the 1980s management of policy interventions in the crises that hit the Philippines, but also the stars for keeping threats and risks to the economy and financial system at bay.[4]

But that was long before the crisis. Former Marcos economic planning minister, Gerardo Sicat (1998: 290–91), paints the Philippine picture as a little rosier closer to 1997. He says that GNP was between 4–5 and 7 per cent in 1994/5-1996; exports grew to about 25 per cent and that US$25 billion in export earnings may have announced the birth of a new 'Asian tiger'. Sicat also said that the 'large current account deficit of about 5 per cent of GNP during 1993 to 1997 was viewed as an indication of rising investment and therefore not a cause for alarm.'

Noland, citing the Goldstein estimate of country crisis probability due to external exposure, has indicated that the Philippines was least likely to suffer the fate of the more exposed Indonesia and Malaysia. These latter two countries and a few others had been directly affected by falling foreign direct investments and so-called 'hot money' from mutual funds. The Philippine crisis in 1997, smaller as it was relative to other countries, was 'home grown', concludes Noland. As will be seen below, 1997 was less critical than 1998 for the Philippines. The crisis concealed its virulence behind early indications of affliction.

So who or what planted and secured its growth at home? Was it a Marcos behest problem? The term 'recession' was introduced by economists who debated whether it was a 'technical' one or not. It might seem to be hair-splitting the issue but it seems they were just looking at the numbers and the graph. As Alburo differentiates the relative tardiness of Philippine involvement with 'footloose/casino' capital, he is also quick to say that the Philippines likewise was hit by the contagion. He adds that what eventually happened was a 'technical recession' (1999: 454) as 'growth nosedived' and 'all the other social conditions deteriorated.' Looking back later, Alburo adds that 'although technically the country suffered a recession following the Asian crisis, its full year (1998) drop in GDP was only -0.6 percent.' (Alburo 2002: 10) As Philippines secured US$ 4 billion assistance from the International Monetary Fund, banks were not asked to close shop due to bad loan losses estimated at 3 per cent. Grabe (n.d.) writes that 'banking distress began to emerge in mid-1998 as the peso's depreciation increased the cost of foreign loan obligations.'

What the country received was supposed to cushion the impact of the crisis; but it only made the economy more dependent on foreign sources. It postponed the more severe and more widespread repercussions; higher inflation rates set in and credit became less accessible. The import-dependent economy began exchanging more pesos for each US dollar needed to procure its many survival requirements.

When this writer recently sought clarification from the Bangko Sentral ng Pilipinas (BSP), the country's monetary agency, Racquel Claveria and Diwa Guinigundo, BSP Deputy-Governor, said that the BSP detailed how it intervened during the 1997 crisis, taking pride in what it had done within its authority. They rejected Alburo's claim of 'technical recession' by saying:

The Philippines did not slip into a technical recession because of the 1997 Asian financial crisis. While real GDP contracted by 1 percent in Q3 1997 and 13 percent in Q1 1998 on a quarter-on-quarter basis, the Philippine economy rebounded in between as real GDP expanded by 14 percent in Q4 1997.

The non-consecutive character of the said GDP contractions may be explained by heavy last quarter – Christmas – spending but BSP did not mention this. Alburo maintains his position though. Could there have been a recession – technical or otherwise – due to some reason or another? He says that there was so much foreign money coming in as bank loans, on top of what Sicat (1998) mentions as FDIs and portfolio investments on the eve of the 1997 crisis. Forex inflows rose from US$156 million in 1990 to almost US$7 billion, but it was only in 1995 that bank borrowings surged and continued to do so until 1997 (Alburo 2002: 6).

Sicat (1999:293) says that when the Bureau of Treasury held interest rates, it resulted in the depreciation of the peso. Even given that, forex-denominated loans that had to be paid certainly helped increasingly to wipe out the peso, including the few pieces in the hands of the poor. The poor paid severely for the indiscretions of the rich. For that matter, not only did the Philippines suffer severely in 1997 but in the following years; such that one can see that no matter what people did to earn a living, their incomes could not meet their daily needs. Poor people who were still recovering from the 16 July 1990 intensity 7.8 earthquake and the June 1991 Mt. Pinatubo eruption, especially those whose farms and homes went under tonnes of volcanic ash, were the hardest hit. These were years that poor people were being driven to desperation and despondency.

But 1998 seemed to be just the beginning. That year, the Philippine economy and society seemed to be more threatened by the elections. Montinola (1999), a close watcher of Philippine politics, writes that assuring the 1998 election to the presidency of Ramos' anointed, House Speaker Jose de Venecia, would be attended by fraud and violence. If Ramos could not have his second term to continue his programme, his anointed choice would secure his continuing role as advisor or statesman. Pitting De Venecia against the very popular 'Erap' was a huge gamble. Likewise, president 'wannabe' Gloria Arroyo had to be threatened with withdrawal of election finance support should she join the race. She became the eventual winning vice president.

Years later, Alburo (2002:2) was not just talking about technical recessions, but that a mixed blessing came along the way of the crisis. Economic decline, he says, prevented further environmental degradation. But economic decline certainly has other results. Alburo opines: 'Without a sufficient buffer in terms of natural resources, income, and social infrastructure not to mention economic fundamentals, the lower income deciles bore the brunt of the crisis, unemployment worsened, and poverty incidence deteriorated.'

As for the banks, they have and still are protected by the concept of 'limited liability', as described by Sinn (2010: xiv) as being spared blame for 'gambling with their customers' money in the international financial markets'. Who then can people turn to? The state fails to regulate business practices, the banks' hands will always be clean, and lenders will always win. Therewith and thereby, only the poor will lose.

So, just as the 1997 crisis that wiped out in so short a time the value of the Philippine currency vis-à-vis the US dollar, the national debt continued to increase as a percentage of the GDP. As Figure 2 shows, GDP reportedly rose from 2002, and so did the national debt as percentage of the GDP. Some may argue indebtedness may be consequential but little to the performance of the economy in general, but it could perhaps be acceptable as long as trade and other receipts showed signs of improvements over time.

The other compelling evidence against the utility of GDP as an argument to say that people should not worry as long as the economy grows (as measured by GDP) has to do with employment. Figure 9,3 shows that even as the GDP grew modestly between 1998 and 2004 (except for 2001), many people were still left without jobs as unemployment made them scarce from the active labour force. In fact, if business was unable to provide jobs, government spending could still add up to positive GDP growth, no matter where public funds really went. Countries borrow to improve the people's well-being usually by expanding employment and enhancing purchasing power. The question in the light of increasing indebtedness – to insignificant percentages of gross international receipts – is: where did all that money go? Certainly it was not spent so much in creating new jobs, as the unemployment rate simply went hand-in-hand with the limited GDP rise.

Table 9.1 below shows that in the period 1998-2009, the GDP growth rate tapered as unemployment rose, while the employment growth rate generally treaded a downward direction even as GDP supposedly improved. Those who could not find full-time jobs were, and still are, resorting to alternative (part-time) employment. This implies a shift of income source from regular jobs to occasional low-paying and generally service-oriented ones, or those relating to petty trades.

Figure 9.2: Debt as Per cent of GDP, 2000-11

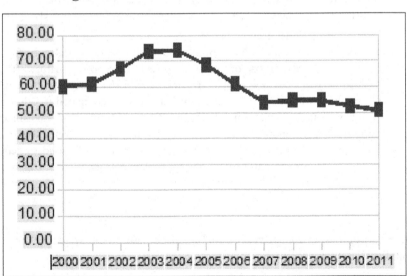

Source: NSCB

Figure 9.3: GDP Growth and Unemployment Rate, 1998-2008

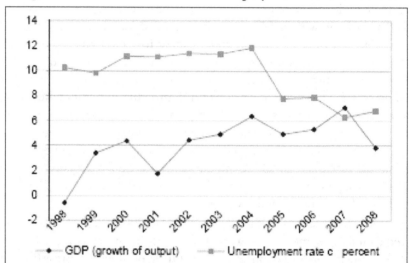

Source: ADB, cited in Balboa and Mantaring 2011: 9

If bank loans were not helping people via employment, who then typically benefited from the said loans? The Philippines was not alien to the unproductive use of capital underlined by Foster and Magdoff (2009:45) in the world economy. Filipinos can easily find resonance with these words in their conditions but financial institutions exert little effort at transparency:

> Financial institutions of all types now accumulate huge quantities of debt as they attempt to make money with borrowed money. This debt undertaken by financial institutions for the purpose of speculation has little to no stimulatory effect on production. Relatively few people are employed in the process of speculation (say, per billion dollars borrowed and speculated with) compared to other more productive uses for that capital. Profits resulting from these debt-financed transactions rarely are turned into investment in factories of service sector firms that create jobs. Rather, such speculative profits are normally used to generate even more profits through various other speculation schemes, or for high living by the rich. As a result, stagnation in employment in recent years has gone hand in hand with a new opulence among the beneficiaries of the financial expansion.

The Philippine specific story is that banks had just been made to improve capitalization, reduce non-performing loans, and to limit exposure to the real estate sector:

> No Philippine commercial bank has gotten into serious financial trouble. Banks have become timid in lending, partly owing to uncertainty about the movement of exchange rates and, consequently, interest rates. Domestic credit has tightened as

a consequence. Public sector credit remained stable, so that the squeeze was felt mainly by the private sector. The banking sector remained relatively strong despite the squeeze on its profits (Sicat 1998: 293).

Meanwhile, Alburo also definitely points an accusing finger at government, as no other entity would be in a position to address questions of natural resources, social infrastructure and economic fundamentals. Thus, the burden of the crisis fell neither on banks or state agencies but directly upon the working people who have relied simply on meagre daily earnings. Sabarwal, Sinha and Buvinic (2009, cited in UNIFEM 2009:10) argue:

> In the Philippines, housewives responded to the 1997 Asian Financial Crisis by reducing consumption, eating only two meals a day in order to feed their children three meals. Poor households pulled out children from school and reduced their utilization of health care services, resorting instead to herbal remedies, indigenous health practitioners, or self-medication. Previous crises affecting low income countries have also shown that girls in poor countries with low preexisting female schooling are highly vulnerable to being withdrawn from school to cope with declining.

A battle cry of the 1997-98 period was for a new financial architecture, whatever that may have really meant, or whether it is really achievable. What seems clear is that people most severely affected by financial crisis would not have any say in drawing any new architecture. Even in the initial discussions on the new architecture, it has not been clarified as to the role of the people. But in this kind of scenario, there are those who insist there remains such a need:

> (T)his macro-vision of a new international financial architecture has not materialized, as economists today admit that there still exists a real need for an international financial architecture to design the rules of the financial system in ways that enhance global stability and promote economic growth (Muchhala 2007: 8).

Thailand, Indonesia, South Korea and Malaysia learned their lessons from this episode. However, the Philippine government was too preoccupied with other matters. In early 2001, a middle-class uprising shortened the term of actor-turned-politician Joseph Estrada. This led to the rise of the vice president, economist Gloria Arroyo, to complete the remaining term of the presidency. In about four years, Arroyo herself was confronted by allegations of 'electoral sabotage' and a united front of opposition members, some of whom were promptly sent to jail, courtesy of a declaration of a state of national emergency in early 2005.

Table 9.1: Labour Market Trends, 1998-2009

	1998	1999	2000	2001	2002	2003	2004	2005	2006	2007	2008	2009
GDP Growth Rate	-0.6	3.4	6	1.8	4.4	4.9	6.4	5	5.3	7.1	3.7	1.1
Unemployment Rate	10.3	9.8	11.2	11.1	11.4	11.4	11.8	Break in Data Series	8	7.3	7.4	7.5
Employment Growth Rate (Total)	1	4.2	-1	6.2	3.1	1.9	3.2	2.2	2	2.8	1.6	2.9
Full-time Employment Growth Rate	-2.1	3.8	1.9	-2.1	2.5	3.8	2.8	4.2	-0.6	0.7	3.9	-0.5
Part-time Employment Growth Rate	6.1	5.5	-5.8	21.2	3.4	0.2	2.7	0.8	6.3	2.3	-2.6	8.4

Note: A break in the data series occurred in 2005 due to the adoption of a new official definition of unemployment in conformity with the international standard definition.

Source: Bureau of Labour and Employment Statistics, cited in Alegado (2010)

While government may have indeed relied upon the revitalized and independent central bank (Bangko Sentral) to address problems with the financial system, chiefly by compelling banks to compete with foreign ones under a liberalized environment and to merge with and acquire smaller banks in order to achieve scale and cost-efficiency in interest rate terms, it was either not empowered to look into the bank labour cost of reforming the banking sector, which in itself poses another kind of problem faced by many small bank employees left at the mercy of their employers. Dacanay (2007: 3) writes:

> In an efficiency study involving seven countries, Kwan found that the Philippines labor cost ratio to total operating cost is highly statistically significant and has a negative sign. Kwan interprets the negative coefficient of labor price as evidence that Philippine banks use relatively more labor because it is cheap. From the database used in the study, the unit price of labor, defined as the personnel and fringe benefit expenses of the banks divided by the number of employees, has been steadily declining from as high as US$ 13,813 in 1995 to US$7,000 in 2004 in real terms.

The 1997 crisis happened more in 1998 as it was occasioned by a period of continuing transition attended by more liberalization and privatization and the expansion of opportunities for those who had access to power and resources. Although the Philippine case was due to contagion, political conditions bordering on leadership crisis contributed to the unsettling economic scenario as when Erap was ousted and when Arroyo sought a new term as president in a manner that spiked popular protest.

The 2008 Crisis: Was the Philippines Ready for it?

Velasco and Saludo cite attempts by the Arroyo government to liberalize trade, consistent with her belief in the power of globalization to solve poverty, but foreign exchange rate appreciation, among other effects, dampened exports and threw many workers out of the workplace. Quite paradoxically, the devalued Philippine peso in the aftermath of the crisis increased exports. It could be one reason why, as Velasco and Saludo claim, 'the Philippines never went into recession as some of our neighboring countries did' (Velasco and Saludo 2010: 270).

In 2003, the Bangko Sentral corrected the 'overstated' figures in the first Arroyo years of the presidency. It said that the Philippines had a surplus ofUS$660 million for 2002, compared to a US$192 million deficit for 2001'. The correction was reportedly due to adjustments in trade data which were not released soon. The positive position was attributed to migrant worker dollar remittances and increased exports. However, by the middle of 2003, the picture began to sour as Fitch Ratings lowered both long-term foreign and local currency ratings of the Philippines.

The ensuing calls for Mrs. Arroyo's resignation easily transformed into a crisis as described in the brief narrative above. As Salazar (2006: 230) recounts:

> The market reacted immediately to these developments. The peso neared its record low of 56.45 to the U.S. dollar while the stock market suffered. The top three rating agencies, Fitch, Standard and Poor, and Moody's, changed their outlook for the Philippines from stable to negative. In addition to the raging political crisis, the rating agencies pointed to the Supreme Court's suspension of the expanded value added tax (EVAT), a key component of the government's fiscal reform agenda (Salazar 2006:230).

Velasco and Saludo (2010: 264-69) opine that the years between 2005 and 2008 scored significant victory for Arroyo via taxation and service delivery. If it were not for the 2008 global crisis, they say, everything would have turned out right. Positive ratings for the Philippines as a consequence of the Arroyo victory in EVAT, did not insulate the Philippines from the crisis. Tax collection issues owing to corruption, the 'irrational tax system,' and general 'institutional capacity,' claims Doraisami (2011), caused the tax-GDP ratio to drop from 17 per cent in 1997 to about 12 per cent in 2002, [5] made the Arroyo government seek new tax measures including the EVAT that sought to fund efforts at cushioning the impact of the crisis on the poor.

In September 2008, seven Philippine banks told a Senate inquiry that they had a combined exposure of US$ 386 million to Lehman Brothers. They included: Banco de Oro Unibank (US$ 134 million); Development Bank of the Philippines (DBP) (US$ 90 million); Metropolitan Bank and Trust Co. (US$ 71 million); Rizal Commercial Banking Corp. (US$ 40 million); Standard Chartered Bank (Manila branch) (US$ 26 million); Bank of Commerce (US$ 15 million); and United Coconut Planters Bank (US$ 10 million). The question is whether the monetary leaders had prior knowledge of this or not, considering that a government bank (namely, the DBP) had a part in it.

As for the central bank, a shadow of doubt has been cast by such authors as Sek (2009: 27–28, my emphasis) and Armenter (2011):

> With the exception of Thailand, the policy reaction functions in Korea and Philippines do not react significantly to the exchange rate movements in the two (post-crisis) sub-periods. *The results imply that central banks in these countries do not follow as what they have claimed.* Although these countries have implemented the inflation targeting after the financial crisis, only Thailand shows a significance reaction of monetary policy to the inflation variable. The policy maker in Philippines pays higher concerns on output gap stability after the crisis.

There seem to be more questions than answers in the light of this scenario. Did or do these banks have so much money to loan out to other financial institutions? Was the said total exposure of the seven banks really no 'cause for concern' simply because other countries had much higher exposures? Did the said exposures expect more returns than if they were loaned out to local entrepreneurs? Which would have been riskier? Or which of these were more acceptable risks?

What is clear is that, as can be seen in Figure 9.3, the inflation rate spiked to record high in 2008 owing, reportedly, to 'continuing higher annual price increases in the heavily weighted food, beverages and tobacco index' (NSO 2008).

Writer Arroyo (2009) and economist Valdepeñas (2011), both of the state economic planning agency National Economic and Development Authority, seem positive about the economic situation and monetary policy after the crisis, respectively. It is important to note that migrant workers' remittances are key ingredients in their stated outlooks.

Figure 9.4: Inflation Rate, 1999-2009

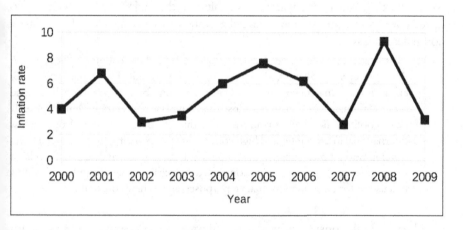

Lessons Unlearned

Yap (2009: 10) summarizes the two crises in the Philippines in these terms:

> What is common in both crises is the deterioration in the fiscal situation. A major cause for concern is that reforms were introduced in response to the 'fiscal crisis' that emerged in the latter part of 2000-2004. While these reforms bore fruit as gleaned from the improvement in the fiscal deficit in 2005-2008, it is clear from the projected 2009 deficit that the gains have not been sustained. Given political economy constraints, it is uncertain whether a new round of revenue-generating measures can be implemented in the near future. Perhaps emphasis can be shifted towards reforms in tax administration.

If the Philippines escaped the 1997 crisis but suffered in its aftermath, could it have maintained distance from the source of the external turmoil in 2008? Why did state leaders think that the adverse conditions from 1998 onwards would not impact more negatively on the people at large? Were these leaders in any way ready to do so, one might ask too. If the causes of the crisis in this episode were 'home grown', were they addressed well?

Writers and analysts have simply insisted on differentiating between the two main causes of the 1997 crisis, only to admit later on that the contagion did it, at least for the Southeast Asian countries, the Philippines included. The 1997 crisis was said to be regional, the 2008 global. Is a national crisis different from these two? Sheng (2009: 9–10) states: 'National crisis is about the failure of domestic markets, policies or institutions, but global crisis is about the breakdown transmitted through the interdependence of economies in a networked world.'

Jomo K.S. (in Muchhala 2007: 35) argues that financial globalization, not totally weak governance, was responsible for the Asian crisis. He has also opted for a new international financial architecture. Speaking of the crisis-hit countries, he says in sum:

> First, macroeconomic and financial policies should be counter-cyclical, rather than pro-cyclical. Second, developing countries should have policy space for expansionary macroeconomic policies. Existing policy conditionalities and other circumstances conspire against that. The last few years have undoubtedly been good for developing countries, but this has been exceptional due to low international interest rates and high commodity prices. Third, there is a need to re-develop development finance institutions at both national and regional levels, as many of these institutions have contracted and changed significantly, or become less useful for development finance purposes due to new constraints.

The World Bank considers the role of migrant workers and the concomitant policy as counter-cyclical. It notes the remarkable record of remittance flows from 2007 but it has warned that 'as the economy recovers, the strength of these remittances is projected to wane in 2010'. Large remittance flows in recent years, not to mention the continuing US crisis, strengthened the peso vis-à-vis the US dollar. But as more Filipinos become migrant workers and more families depend on remittances, it has become a delicate balancing game of the monetary authorities as to how to keep different interests satisfied: migrant workers and their families hate the strong peso, importers the strong dollar. So, the monetary authorities have kept watch on migrant family savings, investment and consumption patterns and promoted 'financial literacy' that sees more growth in terms of basically the same input.

Garten (1999) reserves a place for the IMF, despite its mistakes and mishandling, in the financial world that is bound to experience more crises ahead. But he stresses that cooperation should help smaller economies and that bigger stakeholders take more responsibility for their actions.

In the Philippines, government has not been remiss in handling the situation but it has placed a great deal of the burden upon incomes of the expatriate labour force, thus gearing the migration constituency to earn precious foreign exchange (Asis 2010).

Figure 9.5: Remittances have been Strongly Countercyclical in Real Peso Terms Index, constant prices (October 2008 = 100)

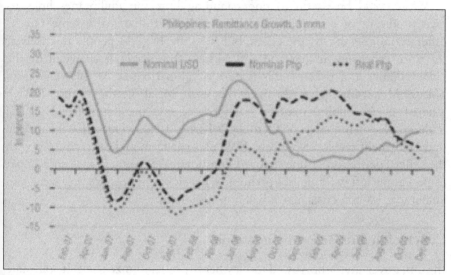

Source: World Bank 2010

Recurring Crisis?

While those with no fixed jobs and income sources weathered their new predicaments by a number of adjustments, the truly impoverished ones have grown in number (Reyes et al 1999), especially in areas where government and its service agencies have heretofore been inaccessible.

It is therefore hard to accept that both crises have not really slid into recession, contrary to consistent claims by the Department of Finance (DoF 2008, 2009, 2019 *Annual Reports*), the World Bank (2009) and the IMF (2010). Employment and incomes have not really increased, indebtedness has risen, credit has been restricted, prices continue to rise, stock market has been lacklustre, the impact of cash transfer to the poor has yet to be ascertained as politicians have sought to take credit for making monthly pay-outs to bolster campaign bids for the May 2013 local elections and as truly indigent beneficiaries have sought alternative uses of received state subsidies to health and education. Business and observers have already indicated that the tell-tale signs of de facto recession have been around since 2008.

Blaming government for all the troubles that the poor face might be too easy but who else should take the fall? Short of accepting responsibility for the growing concerns over fiscal and other matters, finance managers have drawn not exactly rosy pictures of the financial situation that mask the true state of the nation as it joined the bandwagon of neoliberal globalization, anf of financialized capitalism (Foster and Magdoff 2009).

What could be useful to understanding how the Philippines links its own predicament is not just by showing how it shares the same fate as other economies hit by the crises, but how the Filipino people themselves, the poor especially, understand and address the problems spawned by the vulnerabilities and risks of this feature of global crises. At this stage, says pollster Mahar Mangahas (2013) of the outfit Social Weather Station (SWS), 'one of every Filipino wants a real job.' He says the unpublished official underemployment rate as of October 2012 was 19 per cent, while the official unemployment rate is 6.8 per cent. SWS uses the term jobless to contrast with the official definition of unemployed. It estimates joblessness at almost 25 per cent. People left without jobs go hungry, get sick, and become very weak and vulnerable. When crisis hits, it will not miss them.

Conclusion and Recommendations

In sum, government borrowed money heavily to legitimize itself. It sold state assets to finance development projects even as some pocketed more than was actually spent for the people at large. Its strength relied on minority mandate, populist acclaim, or on the enduring belief in the reliance of the people, the poor especially, on the elites for their deliverance. Strength, in short, derives from weakness.

The banking sector risked other people's money. The central bank became party to the crisis in a manner that helped some and forgot about the others. It helped monitor and promote growth that has been confined to select sections of population that participate in the money economy. Growth in the macro sense must have taken into consideration the real impact on more people with less means, without jobs or with small incomes.

When the state is captured by vested interests and the society at large is vulnerable to continuing crisis, both are able to frustrate real development, assuring recurring crisis with even greater toll on the poor.

In 1997 and 2008, the Philippines suffered severe outcomes from exposure to foreign borrowing and foreign lending, respectively. It is important to understand how this came about and do the utmost to prevent its repeat.

Since 1986, political changes and reforms have seemed unable to deliver thorough changes that would secure the lot of the poor. The poor have seemed to be more and more reliant on state moves and subsidies that promoted populism entrenched patronage and dynastic rule. The financial crises have made their choices even weaker, more unpredictable and particularly disempowering.

No doubt, crisis after crisis will hit the Philippines despite its well-publicized growth performance among the Asian economies. The said crisis will impact on the poorest people in the poorest places in the country – those without jobs, unable to work abroad and to remit money back home, without access to basic social services, and those powerless to meaningfully participate in making decisions about how they would survive the onslaughts not only of natural calamities but also the impacts of financial and economic crises and government neglect.

People's organizations will have to continuously and vigorously take to task every state decision and action that compromises poor people's ability to live decently and to ensure that health, education, and livelihood opportunities lift them up from the squalid conditions they inhabit. Policy reform advocacy must go hand-in-hand with people's own initiatives in building their own infrastructures for self-help, though sympathetic local government actors can also be partnered with to maximize effect.

Relevant education and information programmes on the roots of the crisis and what can be done cutting across sectors and classes should broaden the constituencies for the fight for effective pro-people governance, political and electoral reforms, and justice and human rights. These are assurances of continuing counter-hegemonic battle against apathy, loss of identity, and gross injustice.

Migrant workers, being significant sources of the country's economic and financial stability, should leverage themselves by organizing and committing to broad and specific programmes that address poverty and the root socio-economic causes of their exodus. Their diasporic networks and foreign counterpart organizations and other development agencies can be built into the global campaigns for genuine migration and development programmes.

Scholars and the intelligentsia should join these movements and provide the needed knowledge and understanding that no one escapes the crisis and no one should believe that anyone really could without hurting themselves.

Notes

1. In early February 1986, a 'snap' election was held to choose between Marcos and Cory Aquino. Allegedly, Marcos cheated the very popular Aquino widow. Soon, street protests were mounted but Marcos did not budge. The Left that boycotted the election would be almost vindicated in its claim that Marcos would not step down without a bloody fight. A rebel faction of the Armed Forces of the Philippines (AFP) tried to stage a coup by the third week of February but was nipped in the bud. What followed was the 1986 EDSA Revolution that toppled the Marcos dictatorship.The military rebellion consisting of junior officers had the blessings of Defence Secretary Juan Ponce Enrile and Army Gen. Fidel Ramos. Enrile and Ramos held a press conference at Camp Crame as the very sick Marcos thumbed down a proposed military attack on the military rebels. Then Church leader Jaime Cardinal Sin called on the people to protect the Enrile-Ramos group by encircling the camp with civilian supporters. Millions turned out on the EDSA in what has been dubbed the 'People Power Revolution'. Some few people had misgivings about this type of regime change. It was also during this time that the long-struggling forces of the Communist Party of the Philippines-New People's Army-National Democratic Front (CPP-NPA-NDF) were marginalized in the transition period and became the object of Cory's 'total war' policy after the peace talk collapsed in early 1987. Nevertheless, Cory too became the target of ten unsuccessful coup attempts between 1986 and 1990.

2. D. Crone (1993) claims that social welfare worsened during the Cory Aquino years.

3. 'Garci' is short for (Virgilio) Garcillano, an official of the Commission on Elections, who assured Arroyo in the remainder of the audio recording that she getting the needed votes all right. Garci went into hiding and later resurfaced but only to run for public office – he lost, of course.

4. Historically, Philippine borrowing levels were within seemingly acceptable (legal) ceilings, relative to GNP. Falling foreign investment levels, deteriorating trade balance and two oil shocks occasioned the rise of Philippine public indebtedness despite efforts by the Central Bank to arrest the rise of current account deficit through the early 1980s. Dohner (1989: 174) completes the picture:

   > By 1982 the share of short-term debt, including monetary sector debt, in total debt rose to 47 percent, a much higher share than in other LDC debtors. The Philippines first considered declaring a moratorium in late 1982. When it finally did so in October 1983, its foreign exchange reserves were nearly exhausted.

   > Countries borrow to improve the people's well-being usually by expanding employment and enhancing purchasing power. The question in the light of increasing indebtedness is: where did all that money go? Certainly it was not spent so much in creating new jobs, as the unemployment rate simply went hand in hand with the limited GDP rise.

5. Yap (2009: 9) adds: 'The tax to GDP ratio has stalled in the range of 12-13 per cent of GDP compared to 14 per cent in 2008 and a peak of 17 per cent in 1997. As a result, the fiscal deficit already reached P111.8 billion (US$1=PHP49) in the first four months of 2009 compared to P25.8 billion (US$1=PHP44.6) in the same period last year.'

References

Abinales, P.N. and Amoroso, D., 2005, *State and Society in the Philippines*, Pasig City: Anvil.

Alburo, F., 1999, 'The Asian Financial Crisis and Philippine Responses: Long-Run Considerations', *The Developing Economies* 37: 439–59. Available online at: http://202.244.105.132/English/Publish/Periodicals/De/pdf/99_04_04.pdf.

Alburo, F., 2002, 'Crisis, Recovery, and Growth in the Philippines Institutional and Coping Mechanisms', Paper at the 'International Seminar: Promoting Growth And Welfare: Structural Changes And The Role Of Institutions In Asia'. Available online at: http://www.eclac. cl/brasil/noticias/noticias/4/9794/alburo.pdf.

Alegado, A.S., 2010, 'Rise in Part-time Jobs Tied to Economic Downturn Episodes', *Business World*. Available online at: http://www.bworldonline.com/Research/economicindicators.php?id=0391.

Armenter, R., 2011, 'Output Gaps: Uses and Limitations', *Business Review* Q1 2011. Available online at: http://www.philadelphiafed.org/research-and-data/publications/business-review/2011/q1/brq111_output-gaps-uses-and-limitations.pdf.

Arroyo, D., 2009, 'The Global Economic Crisis and the Philippine Economy'. Available at: http://philexport.ph/events/NEDA%20on%20the%20crisis%20 contingency%20plan.pdf.

Asian Policy Forum, 2009,'Recommendations of Policy Responses to the Global Financial and Economic Crisis for East Asian Leaders'.

Asis, M.B., 2010, 'The Global Financial Crisis and International Labor Migration in the Philippines', Paper prepared for MISA Project Phase 2 and presented at the ILO/SMC Conference on Assessing the Impact of the Global Economic Crisis on International Migration in Asia: Findings from the MISA Project . http://smc.org.ph/misa/uploads/country_reports/1285920115.pdf.

Balboa, J.D. and Mantaring, M., 2011, 'The Impact of the Global Financial Crisis on the Labour Market: The Case of the Philippines', PIDS Discussion Paper Series 2011-22.

Balisacan, A. et al, 2010, 'Tackling Poverty and Social Impacts: Philippine Response to the Global Economic Crisis', http://www.undp.org/content/dam/undp/library/Poverty%20Reduction/Poverty%20assessment%20and%20monitoring/PSIA/The%20Philippines-Full%20Report.pdf.

Bello, W., 2007, 'All Fall Down: Ten Years after the Asian Financial crisis', http://www.tni.org/article/all-fall-down-ten-years-after-asian-financial-crisis.

Bello, W. et al., 2005, *The Anti-Development State-The Political Economy of Permanent Crisis in the Philippines*. 2nd ed, Quezon City: Department of Sociology, University of the Philippines Diliman and Bangkok: Focus on the Global South.

Berg, A. and Pattillo C., 2000, 'The Challenges of Predicting Economic Crises', International Monetary Fund. Available online at: http://www.imf.org/external/pubs/ft/issues/issues22/ index.htm.

Caucus of Development NGO Networks, 2010, *Survey on the Impact of the Global Financial Crisis on Philippine NGOs*, http://www.code-ngo.org/home/images/stories/pdf/Eco_Crisis_Survey_Report_FINAL.pdf.

Chang, H.J. et al, eds, 2001, *Financial Liberalization and the Asian Crisis: Financial Liberalization and the Asian Crisis*, Palgrave.

Claveria, R. and Guinigundo, D., 2012, Email responses to questionnaire.

Crone, D., 1993, 'States, Elites and Social Welfare in Southeast Asia', *World Development*. Vol. 21, No. 1, 55–66.

Dacanay, S.J., 2007, *The Business Review, Cambridge*, Vol. 7, No. 2, Summer 2007, pp. 315–22. Paper presented at The International Business & Economics Research Conference, Beverly Hilton, Los Angeles, California, USA, 15 June 2007. Department of Finance, 2008, 2009, 2010, Annual Reports.

Dohner. R. and Intal, P. Jr., 1989, 'Debt Crisis and Adjustment in the Philippines'. in J. Sachs, *Developing Country Debt and the World Economy*, University of Chicago Press. Available online at: http://www.nber.org/chapters/c7525.

Doraisami, A., 2011, 'The Global Financial Crisis: Countercyclical Fiscal Policy Issues and Challenges in Malaysia, Indonesia, the Philippines, and Singapore.' Working Pa- per No: 288, 8 June. http://www.adbi.org/working-paper/2011/06/08/4581. gfc.countercyclical.fiscal.policy.issues.challenges/case.studies/.

Dullien, S. et al, eds, 2010, *The Financial and Economic Crisis of 2008-2009 and Developing Countries*, UNCTAD.

Dumlao, D., '7 Philippine banks hold Lehman instruments worth $386M', *Philippine Daily Inquirer*. http://business.inquirer.net/money/breakingnews/view/20080918-161468/7-Philippine-banks-hold-Lehman-instruments-worth-386M.

Engelen, E. et al, 2011, *After the Great Complacence: Financial Crisis and the Politics of Reform*, New York: Oxford University Press.

Focus on the Global South and Save the Children – UK, 2001, *The Asian Financial Crisis and Filipino Households: Impact on Women and Children*, Focus on the Global South. http://www.focusweb.org/publications/Books/women%20and%20children.pdf

Foster, J.B. and Magdoff, F., 2009, *The Great Financial Crisis: Causes and Consequences*, New York: Monthly Review Press.

Grabel, I., n.d., 'Rejecting Exceptionalism: Reinterpreting the Asian Financial Cri- ses', https://www.mtholyoke.edu/courses/sgabriel/ilene_grabel.htm.

Garten, J., 1999, 'Lessons for the Next Financial Crisis', *Foreign Affairs* 78 (2) (Mar.-Apr.): 76–92.

Goldstein, M., 1998, *The Asian Financial Crisis: Causes, Cures and Systemic Implications*, Institute for International Economics.

Guinigundo, D., 2009, 'The Impact of the Global Financial Crisis on the Philippine financial system – an assessment', BIS Papers No 54, http://www.bis.org/publ/bppdf/ bispap54s.pdf.

_____ and Claveria, R., 2012, Email to R. Talampas re Philippine crises of 1997 and 1998 (Private communication).

Haggard, S., 2000. *The Political Economy of the Asian Financial Crisis*, Institute for International Economics.

Hamilton-Hart, N., 2002, *Asian States, Asian Bankers: Central Banking in Southeast Asia*, Ithaca: Cornell University Press.

Home Guaranty Corporation, 2009, *MacroEconomic Report: 2009 First Quarter*, Available online at http://www.hgc.gov.ph/downloadable/MER_2009Q1-final-B.pdf.

Intal Jr., P.S. and Llanto, G.M., 1998, 'Financial Reform and Development in the Philippines, 1980-1997: Imperatives, Performance and Challenges', PIDS Discussion Paper 98-02, available at: http://www3.pids.gov.ph/ris/pdf/pidsdps9802.PDF.

International Monetary Fund, 2010, 'Philippines: Financial System Stability Assessment Update', IMF Country Report No. 10/90. Available online at: http://www.imf.org/external/pubs/ft/ scr/2010/cr1090.pdf.

Kanaoka, M., 2012, 'Have The Lessons Learned from The Asian Financial Crisis Been Applied Effectively in Asian Economies?' *International Journal of Economics and Finance* 4 (2): 10–115.

Kang, I.S., 2004, 'A Study on the Early Warning Indicators of Currency Crisis: A Regional Perspective', http://wwwsoc.nii.ac.jp/jsie/Tohoku_Univ/211_2.html.

Kant, C., n.d., 'East Asian Crisis and Capital Flight', http://www.apeaweb.org/confer/hito05/papers/kant_c.pdf.

Knowles, J., Pernia, E. and Racelis, M., 1999, 'Social Consequences of the Financial Crisis in Asia', ADB Economic Staff Paper Number 60. Manila: ADB.

Llanto, G. and Badiola, J.A., 2009, 'The Impact of the Global Financial Crisis on Rural and Microfinance in Asia', PIDS Discussion Paper Series No. 2009-24, http://www.ruralfinance.org/fileadmin/templates/rflc/documents/1267399334345_The_Impact_of_the_Global.pdf.

Mah-hui, L. and Chin, L., 2010, *Nowhere to Hide: The Great Financial Crisis and Challenges for Asia*, Singapore: ISEAS.

Mangahas, M., 2013, 'Joblessness and Underemployment', *Philippine Daily Inquirer*, 22 Feb- ruary. Available online at: http://opinion.inquirer.net/47439/joblessness-and-underemployment.

Mohapatra, S. and Ratha, D., 2011, 'The Impact of the Global Financial Crisis on Migration and Remittances', http://siteresources.worldbank.org/EXTPREMNET/Resources/C17TDAT_297-320.pdf.

Montinola, G., 1999, 'The Philippines in 1998: Opportunity amid Crisis', Asian Survey 39 (1) (Jan.-Feb.): 64–71.

Muchhala, B., 2007, *Ten Years After : Revisiting the Asian Financial Crisis*, Woodrow Wilson International Center for Scholars.

Nanto, D., 2009, *The Global Financial Crisis: Analysis and Policy Implications*, US Congressional Research Service.

National Economic and Development Authority-Republic of the Philippines, 2009, 'Global Economic Crisis and the Philippine Economy', http://www.neda.gov.ph/erp/downloads_/Global%20crisis%20and%20RP%20economy.pdf.

National Statistics Office, 2008, Cited in 'Philippine Inflation Hits Nine-year High in May 2008'. Available online at: http://articles.economictimes.indiatimes.com/2008-06-05/news/27699068_1_core-inflation-higher-inflation-philippine-inflation-hits.

Noland, M., 2000, 'The Philippines in the Asian Financial Crisis: How the Sick Man Avoided Pneumonia', *Asian Survey* 40 (3) (May- Jun.): 401–12.

Putra, F., 2011, 'Economic Development and Crisis Policies in Southeast Asia (Comparative Study of Asian Crisis 1997 and Global Financial Crisis 2008 in Malaysia, Thailand and the Philippines)', http://www.ipedr.com/vol28/31-ICEMM2012-T20016. pdf.

Sabarwal, S. Sinha, N. and Buvinic, M. 2009, *The Global Financial Crisis: Assessing Vulnerability for Women and Children*, World Bank Policy Brief. Washington DC: World Bank.

Salazar, L., 2006, 'The Philippines: Crisis, Controversies, and Economic Resilience', *Southeast Asian Affairs*, pp. 227–46.

Sek, S.K., 2009, 'Interactions between Monetary Policy and Exchange Rate in Inflation Targeting Emerging Countries: The Case of Three East Asian Countries', *International Journal of Economics and Finance* 1 (2): 27–44.

Sheng, H., 2009, *From Asian to Global Financial Crisis: An Asian Regulator's View of Unfettered Finance in the 1990s and 2000s*, Cambridge University Press.

Sicat, G., 1998, 'The Philippine Economy in the Asian Crisis', ASEAN *Economic Bulletin*, 15 (3) (December): 290–96.

Sinn, H., 2010, *Casino Capitalism: How The Financial Crisis Came about and What Needs to be Done Now*, Oxford University Press.

Social Weather Stations – SWS, 2012, 'First Quarter 2012 Social Weather Survey: Hunger at record-high 23.8% of families; Moderate Hunger at 18.0%, Severe Hunger at 5.8%'. Available at: http://www.sws.org.ph/pr20120508.htm.

Tellis, A. et al, eds, 2009, *Economic Meltdown and Geopolitical Stability* (The Executive Brief of Strategic Asia 2009-10), Washington DC: National Bureau of Economic Research. Available: http://www.nbr.org/publications/strategic_asia/pdf/SA09-10_ExecBrief.pdf pdf.

Tetangco, A., Jr., 2007, 'The Philippine Economy Ten Years after the Asian Crisis',Presentation file in PDF available at: http://www.bis.org/review/r070511f.pdf ?frames=0.

Tuaño, P.A., 2002, 'The Effects of the Asian Financial Crisis on the Philippines Labour Markets. EADN Regional Project on the Social Impact of the Asian Financial Crisis. UNIFEM, 2009, 'Making Economic Stimulus Packages Work For Women and Gender Equality, UNIFEM Working Paper, http://www.unifem.org/attachments/ events/ UNIFEM_Working_Paper_Making_Economic_Stimulus_Packages_Work_ for_Women.pdf.

United Nations, 2009, *The Global Economic and Financial Crisis: Regional Impacts, Responses and Solutions*, New York: United Nations.

Valdepeñas, V. Jr., 2011,'Monetary Policy in the Philippines after the Crisis.' Presentation file in PDF.

Velasco, R. and Saludo, R., 2010, *Beating the Odds: The Philippines Stands up to Terror, Drugs, Dreadful Disease, Coup d'etat, Economic Storms and Intractable Conflict at the Gates of the 21st Century*, Future Templates Enterprises.

World Bank, 2011, *Navigating Turbulence, Sustaining Growth*, World Bank East Asia and Pacific Economic Update, Volume 2.

World Bank, 2010, 'The Philippines: Site Pages', http://siteresources.worldbank.org/ INTEAPHALFYEARLYUPDATE/Resources/550192-1270538603148/eap_ april2010_philippines.pdf.

Yap, J., 2009, 'The 2008 Global Financial and Economic Crisis: Impact on the Philippines and Policy Responses at the National and Regional Levels', PIDS *Policy Notes* No. 2009-03. http://dirp4.pids.gov.ph/ris/pn/pidspn0903_fnl.pdf .

Yap, J. et al., 2010, 'Impact of the Global Financial and Economic Crisis on the Philippines, PIDS Discussion Paper Series 2009–30.

10

Global Economic Crisis and Insecurity in Afghanistan, Pakistan and Tajikistan

Hidayet Siddikoglu

Introduction

There is one truth that is not open to denial. The global financial crisis initially emerged from the United States (US) and quickly spread in the global financial institutions. In the context of an integrated global economy, the consequences of disaster became clear to all. However, the global financial crisis had diverging impacts upon countries with different forms of governing institutions and geopolitical locations. Moreover, damage in terms of economic deficit, social welfare and human development were extremely different among the developed, developing, and special condition and post-conflict countries.

People-centric democratic states and state-centric authoritarian countries implemented policy responses in order to reduce the impacts of the global economic crisis and strengthen their economies, whereas the least developed, special condition and post-conflict countries mostly failed to take effective measures to tackle the financial crisis. These countries were mostly concerned with internal and external problems such as corruption, weak governance, political instability and geostrategic issues. Usually these kinds of countries are heavily dependent on multilateral and bilateral foreign aid and remittances from the developed world.

In the contemporary integrated global economy, particularly the presence of a strong interdependent economic structure within the orbit of developed world led the developed countries to be the prime target of the global financial crisis. Due to their dependency on remittances and financial aid assistance from the developed world, the economic recession negatively impacted on security and political stability of special condition and post-conflict states. Research from the Human Development and Public Services Team of the World Bank (2009) indicated that aid flow following the crisis fell an average of 20 to 25 per cent.

In the globalized society, borders of states no longer create barriers for social activities penetrating distinct societies of different countries. Thus, events in one society profoundly impact other societies across the borders. The intra-state conflicts, radical extremism, terrorism in the global South, particularly in the developing, special condition and post-conflict states, are spreading across the borders. The main factors inducing such a phenomenon are economic underdevelopment and the failure of weak and poor states to protect their citizens and provide them with social services.

The 11 September 2001 (9/11) terrorist attacks in the US led to a paradigm shift, which entirely changed the world order. The attacks led to the start of new international war 'the global war on terror'. The terrorist attacks were considered as masterminded in the Al-Qaeda bases stationed in Afghanistan. In October 2001 the US and its allies started invading Afghanistan. Under the umbrella of the global war on terror, Pakistan and Tajikistan, which share their longest borders with Afghanistan (see Map 10.1) became very important countries to facilitate the route and turned out to be frontline countries in the so-called Operation Enduring Freedom in Afghanistan. Thus, in the current era of global war on terror, this region plays a central role in global security related to international terrorism.

According to the United Nations' geographical region classification, Afghanistan and Pakistan are located in South Asia and Tajikistan is part of Central Asia. From the onset of 'great game' politics in the contemporary global war on terror, Afghanistan and Pakistan played significant role in the global political arena. After the dissolution of Soviet Union, Tajikistan became a conduit for the expansion of terrorism and drug-trafficking to Central Asia and beyond.

The history of drug-trafficking and opium production in Afghanistan goes back to the late 1970s. After the Soviet invasion of Afghanistan, under auspices of the Central Intelligence Agency (CIA) and Pakistan's Inter-Services Intelligence (ISI) opium economy became the backbone of the war economy in Afghanistan. Opium production flourished in the regions where Afghan *Mujahidins* (Afghan guerilla fighters) backed by the West had their strongholds. According to Goodhand (2005), CIA and ISI developed the narcotic trade in Afghanistan and Pakistan. Today, there are a series of reasons for opium production in Afghanistan. Lack of economic opportunities, insecurity, corrupt state actors, and high demand of opium lead poor marginalized farmers in conflict-torn regions (south and southwest) to produce opium for household incomes.

Map 10.1: Geographical Location of Afghanistan,
Pakistan and Tajikistan

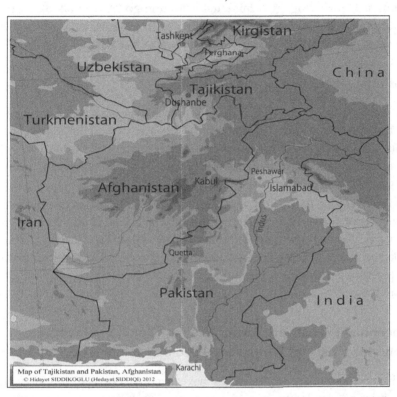

Source: Author's own elaboration

The first section of this chapter deals with elaborating the impacts of global economic crisis on security and political stability of Afghanistan. In the second section it examines how the global economic crisis burdened government of Pakistan's capability in providing adequate social services for its citizens in order to halt the rapid expansion of radical extremism and terrorism in the country. The third section deals with the negative impacts of the global financial crisis on the degraded economy of Tajikistan. Extreme dependency on foreign economies left Tajikistan vulnerable to the global financial crisis. This is particularly so, considering the fact that Tajikistan shares the longest mountainous border with conflict-torn Afghanistan.

Lastly the section deals with policy implications and evaluates the importance of building collaborative and sustainable bilateral, economic and political relations between these three countries. Such a relationship will play a central role in eradicating terrorism and solidifying economic and political stability in these three states. Accordingly, this chapter rationalizes the inevitable role of regional cooperation empowered by the international community, including governmental and non-governmental development organizations in eradicating terrorism and extremism and strengthening economic and political stability in Afghanistan, Pakistan and Tajikistan.

Methodology

The importance of the region covered in this chapter for the international political arena enabled this research to engage with unlimited qualitative resources. This research was based on secondary data collection. A qualitative evaluation of data under a substantive method of selecting relevant qualitative bibliography was utilized in this study.

Moreover, due to the importance of region for the global security relevant to extremism and terrorism, daily news from the local and international media was a special point of interest for this study. Additionally, journals, e- journals, published articles, official documents, official reports and newspapers provided an opportunity to work at the cutting edge of the descriptive method of this research.

Conceptual Framework for Impacts of Global Financial and Economic Crisis on Political and Security Instabilities

In the contemporary world, states have become crucially interdependent. The role of non-state organizations and multinational corporations is overwhelmingly prominent in the global multipolar society. Accordingly, states have become extensively embedded in the international system.

The relationship between the international financial crisis and political instability associated with the insecurity emanating from radical extremism and terrorism is quite complicated. Each phenomenon has a different structure and characteristics. It is important to note that global economic recession is not a direct cause of the political instability and insecurity of a given state. Moreover, the impacts of global financial and economic crisis can be distinctively seen in developing countries (Fukuda-Parr 2008). The main goal of this study is to analyse the specific impacts of global economic recession on security and political stability of developing countries, particularly on special condition and post-conflict states.

According to Acharya (2011), poverty and the lack of economic opportunities can cause insurgency and terrorism. The impact of a global financial crisis on the least developed countries can be devastating, but its impacts in terms of political instabilities associated with insecurity emanating from terrorism and extremism are relevant to geostrategic and political situations of a state. According to Kiras (2011), the link between terrorism and poverty vary between the regions – for example, despite being a very poor region, sub-Saharan Africa does not favour terrorism.

The impact of the global financial crisis on developing countries, particularly the special condition and post-conflict states such as Afghanistan, Pakistan and Tajikistan is key for studying the relation between the crisis and instability. Throughout history, Afghanistan and Pakistan played a pivotal role in the global political arena. The political stalemate over border issues between Afghanistan–Pakistan (Afghan–Pak) fostered the cold war politics in South Asia. The involvement of the East and West blocs in Afghan–Pak border disputes internationalized the bilateral conflict. In the context of cold war politics, both the US and the Soviet Union indiscriminately exploited every single opportunity in thwarting the expansion of rival ideologies. Accordingly, the concept of exploiting religion for the interest of cold war led to a paradigm shift. This shift empowered and militarized religious extremists and led to the formation of non-state terrorist and extremist organizations in Afghanistan, Pakistan and Tajikistan.

After the dissolution of the Soviet Union in 1991, each of Central Asian States (CAS) was born as an independent entity entangled with a set of socioeconomic and political problems. Russian isolation of CAS further intensified economic distress and exacerbated unemployment ratios in each state. Tajikistan, having a long mountainous border with a conflict-torn country, Afghanistan (see Map 10.1) lurched into a civil war in 1992. A joint military operation by Russian, Uzbek and Tajik forces ended the civil war in 1997. However, Tajikistan as a post-conflict state remains as a fragile state under serious threats of radical extremism, terrorism and drug-trafficking.

With the end of the cold war era, the international community led by the US disengaged from this region. This kind of phenomenon facilitated the expansion and empowerment of non-state terrorist organizations. This development resulted in cross-border terrorist activities, which led to a new era of global war on terror. On the other hand, regional states, crippled by precarious political and economic situations, failed to curb the expansion of terrorist networks.

Non-state terrorist organizations and radical extremists are profoundly active in underdeveloped marginalized remote regions. A weak economy is one of the main factors hindering regional states in providing social and economic security in these regions. In such a precarious situation, these states faced contagion impacts of the global financial crisis. The negative impacts of global economic recession on these states have been harsh in terms of Foreign Direct Investment (FDI), migrants' remittances and Official

Development Assistance (ODA). All these factors contribute to government incompetence in handling issues of political stability and security, particularly in countries where the risk of post-conflict relapse is high. The causal path of impacts of global economic recession on political instability and insecurity associated with extremism and non-state terrorism in post-conflict states can be traced in Figure 10.1.

Figure 10.1: Impacts of the Global Financial and Economic Crisis on Developing, Special Condition and Post-conflict States

Related Literature

There is vast literature available on the global financial and economic crisis and its impacts on both developing and developed countries. However, empirical studies elaborating on the impacts of financial crises on developing, special condition and post-conflict countries particularly in relation to state security and political stability, are scantly available.

Fukuda-Parr (2008), emphasises the contagion impacts of global financial crisis on developing countries, stating that the impacts of global economic crisis on developing countries are several such as domestic economic downturn, constraints in exports, decline in ODA and a decrease in remittance. Most of the authors like Rashid (2012), Felbab-Brown (2010) Muzalevsky (2009) and Majidov (2011), emphasize that state failure in providing adequate social services due to economic backwardness is one of the main reasons of insecurity associated with terrorism and political instability in a country.

Bakken (2007) states that terrorist acts bring social status and economic prosperity for perpetrators; and suicide bombings benefit families economically. The author mentions findings by Shaked (2000) that the 'family usually receives a cash payment of between US$1,000 and US$2,500'. However, according to Paizza (2006) poverty and underdevelopment cannot be a direct cause of terrorism, but can exacerbate it.

There is a shortage of empirical studies on the impacts of the global financial crisis on political instability and insecurity of a state associated with radical extremism and terrorism. Thus, this chapter will analyse the role of the global financial and economic crisis in exacerbating political instability and state insecurity particularly in relation to terrorism and radical extremism. In this perspective, this chapter examines the impacts of the global financial and economic crisis on political instability and insecurity of Afghanistan, Pakistan and Tajikistan. Each state has diverse political institutions and different socioeconomic developments; however, they share concerns over insecurity associated with radical extremism, terrorism and drug-trafficking.

Afghanistan: Emerging out of Ashes

Afghanistan is a multi-ethnic landlocked country located in South Asia (see Map 10.1). It is bordered to the north by Turkmenistan, Uzbekistan, and Tajikistan, to the southeast by Pakistan, and to the west by Iran. It has a population of about 31 million people. The multi-ethnic society of Afghanistan comprises 42 per cent Pashtun, 25 per cent Tajik, 10 per cent Hazara, 10 per cent Uzbek, and remaining other minorities such as Turkmen, Baloch and Aymaq (Katzman 2013).

The enduring contemporary conflict in Afghanistan has its roots back in the Soviet invasion of Afghanistan in 1979. Decades of protracted war in Afghanistan destroyed almost all of the civil service institutions in the country. As a result of man-made and natural disasters, Afghanistan remains one of the world's poorest countries. According to the World Bank, Afghanistan is one of the least developed countries, with more than a third of its population living below the poverty line and more than half on the brink of falling into poverty (World Bank 2012).

Despite the installation of a new government after the collapse of Taliban regime in 2001, after more than a decade Afghanistan has to tackle a series of acute challenges regarding security, economic downturn, corruption and absence of the rule of law. In terms of economic growth, Afghanistan remains the poorest country in South Asia in comparison to its all neighbours in the region, including the post-conflict state of Tajikistan (see Table 10.1).

Table 10.1: Regional Comparison of Gross Domestic Product (GDP) per capita

	Afgha-nistan	Pakis-tan	Tajikis-tan	Uzbe-kistan	Turkme-nistan	Iran
GDP per capita (2011 current US$)	542.9	1.189.4	934.8	1,545.9	5,496.6	4,526.9

Source: World Bank 2009

Note: All data is for 2011 except Iran, which is for 2009

Foreign aid and agriculture, the pillars of the Afghan economy, shape an economy in perennial crisis. Worse still, there are the effects of unstable, undependable climate change and natural disasters like floods and drought. Consequently, the agriculture sector alone cannot support the country's economic prosperity. The driving force behind the development programmes relevant to the construction of mega projects, such as highways and airports to support public and private sectors, is foreign aid. These two sources of funding form the leading labour-producing sectors in Afghanistan. As can be seen in Figure 10.2, the evolution of Afghan GDP is highly linked to the evolution of GDP growth.

Figure 10.2: Volatile GDP Growth of Afghanistan

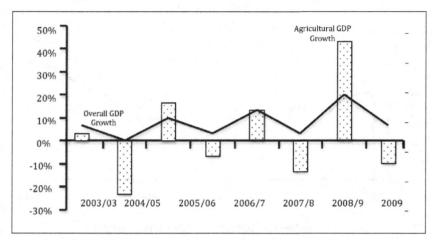

Source: World Bank 2011

Due to its political and strategic problems, Afghanistan remains almost totally dependent on foreign aid. According to the World Bank (2012) almost 90 per cent of the Afghan budget comes from foreign aid. Most of the donors were hit by the global financial crisis, and had to reduce expenditures. Such measures had a deleterious impact on their commitments on ODA. According to the Organisation of Economic Cooperation and Development (OECD 2012), major donors' aid to developing countries fell by 3 per cent in 2011.

In long-term policy, these cuts have negative impacts on developing countries like Afghanistan. The World Bank (2012) estimated that the impacts of a decline in foreign aid on Afghanistan would be devastating, as they would impinge upon security and the political stability of the country. According to the development report issued by Ministry of Finance Afghanistan (2010) there is an increasing gap between the commitments and disbursements of ODA to Afghanistan (see Figure 10.3).

Figure 10.3: Afghanistan, Gap between Commitment and Disbursement
of ODA, 2007-2010

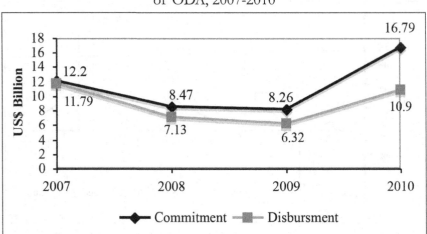

Source: Ministry of Finance Afghanistan (2010)

There are several reasons why Afghanistan remains nearly exclusively dependent on foreign aid. After a decade of the presence of Western troops led by the US, security in Afghanistan remains highly volatile. The enduring Taliban insurgencies against the Afghan government negatively impacted on economic activities such as investments and industrialization. Thus, insecurity is the key factor for economic downturn in the country. Some of the other factors strengthening Afghanistan's dependency on foreign aid are weak governance and the prevalence of corruption in governmental institutions, including international non-governmental organizations.

The absence of security and the rule of law left most of the rural areas in Afghanistan untouched by the reconstruction and development programmes. Underdevelopment and lack of economic opportunities, particularly in volatile regions led people to rely on poppy cultivation for their household needs. According to the United Nations Office on Drugs and Crimes (UNODC 2010), Afghanistan produces about 85 per cent of global opiate. As Table 10.4 shows, the main incentive for Afghans' poppy cultivation is a better source of livelihood. As Narayan et al (2009:446) observe, 'farmers regarded poppy as an important source of income in the absence of alternative livelihood, as no other crop could command such a high price.'

Figure 10.4: Reason for Poppy Cultivation 2012

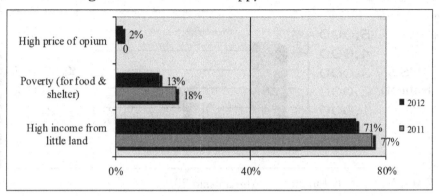

Source: UNODC 2012

Historically, there were no traces of high poppy cultivation in Afghanistan prior to the Soviet invasion in 1979. Poppy cultivation flourished as the Afghan Jihad thrived in Afghanistan. Currently, poppy cultivation is prevailing mostly in regions where Taliban have their strongholds. Southeast Afghanistan is the most volatile region in the country. The United States Institute of Peace (2009) stated that the Taliban received about US$50 million in 2008 as tax revenue (10 per cent of raw output) from the southern regions of the country. According to a news report by the British Broadcasting Corporation (November 2012), the Taliban profits greatly from the drug business in Afghanistan.

Incompetence of the government to provide economic and social security for its citizens favours the role of extremists, drug traffickers and criminals in the country. Inadequate wages for governmental employees is one of the main causes of the prevailing corruption in governmental institutions, especially in the security sectors. Both the Ministry of Finance of Afghanistan and the World Bank predict further decline in ODA disbursements to Afghanistan (see Figure 10.5) due to the financial and economic crisis. If this scenario materializes, insecurity and political instability of the country will bloom.

Figure 10.5: Forecast of Aid to Afghanistan for 2011-13

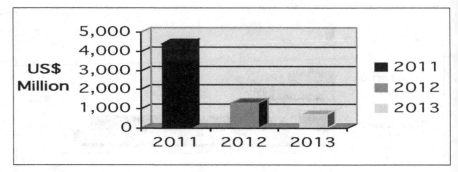

Source: Ministry of Finance of Afghanistan 2010

Afghanistan is heavily dependent on foreign aid to function. The presence of the North Atlantic Treaty Organization (NATO) and US forces in Afghanistan directly or indirectly contributes to the household incomes of many Afghans. However, international forces were scheduled to leave Afghanistan by the end of 2014. There are deep concerns about socioeconomic and political stability of Afghanistan in the post-2014 period.

Pakistan: Dwindling Economy with Rising Radical Extremism

Pakistan is a multi-ethnic country located in South Asia. It is bordered to the east by India, to the west by Iran and Afghanistan, to the north by China and to the south by the Arabia Sean (see Map 10.1). The government-estimated population as of 2004 was about 152.8 million people. The multi-ethnic society of Pakistan comprises 44.2 per cent Punjabi, 15.4 per cent Pashtun, 14.1 per cent Sindi, 10.5 per cent Saraiki, 7.8 per cent of Muhajirs, 3.6 per cent of Baloch. Six per cent are other minorities such as Brahui, Hindo and Persian-speaking Hazara (Library of Congress 2005).

On 14 August 1947 the British Raj over the Indian sub-continent was ended. The Indian sub-continent was partitioned into two distinct and hostile states: the Islamic Republic of Pakistan and the Republic of India. Pakistan was born as a conflict state. In the wake of its creation, it was crippled by a set of border and ethnic disputes with both of its main neighbours, respectively India and Afghanistan (see Map 10.1).

The precarious political, strategic and security environment in South Asia after the British withdrawal from the Indian sub-continent forced Pakistan to look for allies. According to Rizvi (2004), security concerns regarding India and Afghanistan were the catalyst for Pakistan's alignment stance with US. In the context of cold war politics, Pakistan played a very important role in American foreign policy on South Asia. The geographic and strategic location of Pakistan connecting the Indian sub-continent with the Middle East and Central Asia best suited the American interest in this region. According to McMahon (1994), the British and American politicians and strategists considered the Middle East a very important region for their economic and political stability. To protect this region from Soviet influence, they considered Pakistan as an important ally in South Asia.

Pakistan received massive aid from the US on two important occasions: first during the cold war period when the Soviet Union invaded Afghanistan and second, after the 9/11 atrocities when the US led the global war on terror. On the one hand, this aid played a pivotal role in the country's economic growth and military expansion. On the other hand, it catapulted the country into a set of challenges associated with sectarian violence, radical extremism and terrorism. According to Malik (2008) in the context of the global war on terror, the US provided Pakistan US$10.5 billion in aid between 2002 and 2007.

Upon the outbreak of the Soviet invasion of Afghanistan in 1979, Pakistan welcomed the influx of millions of Afghans to Pakistan. Most of the Afghan refugee men were trained and sent back to fight against the Soviet forces in Afghanistan. On observing the strong faith of Afghans in Islam and their fearless fight for the sake religion, the CIA of the US and the ISI of Pakistan fabricated the notion of international Islamic Jihad against Soviet 'infidels' in Afghanistan. This kind development attracted hundreds of thousands of militants and radical extremists from all around the world. Consequently, Pakistan became a global nest for religious radicalism and extremist militancy.

Most of the training camps in Pakistan were located in the Federally Administered Tribal Areas (FATA) and on the periphery of Peshawar city (see Map 10.2). FATA is controlled under the inherited British regulatory law known as the Frontier Crime Regulation (FCR).

Map 10.2: Pakistan, Federally Administered Tribal Areas (FATA)

Source: Author's own elaboration

The political impasse over the border and Pashtun tribal issues between Afghanistan and Pakistan fostered the geostrategic and political interests of the United States and the Soviet Union during cold war era. Particularly, the belligerent tribal rivalries in FATA society in Pakistan went through grandiose changes under the Afghan Jihad. The absence of state law, the presence of tribal skirmishes among distinct Pashtun tribes and, moreover, the accumulation of thousands of international militants in the context of Afghan Jihad shifted this region from being a federation of neglected, marginalized tribal areas to the one of the most dangerous region in the world. Economic and political marginalization, heavy involvement in Afghan Jihad left FATA severely underdeveloped and highly vulnerable to extremist exploitation (see Table 10.2).

Most of the economic revenue from the US and other bilateral aid has been mainly used in military expenditures (see Figure 10.6), depriving development programmes in the country. According to the World Bank (2013) Pakistan is the poorest South Asian country. Pakistan allocates the lowest budget for child nutrition and education remains a serious challenge for the country. Rashid (2012) states that between 2001 and 2010 Pakistan received about US$44 billion including military aid (US$14.4 billion) from the US, Germany, Japan, the World Bank and other donors. Government officials and the Pakistan army sucked out most of the aid and there was little allocation to human development programmes.

Table 10.2: Development Indicators of Pakistan, Khayber Pakhtunkhwa (KP) & FATA

Indicators	Pakistan	KP	FATA
Literacy rate	54.4%	50%	17.4%
Literacy rate (female)	44.7%	31.1%	3.0%
Literacy rate (rural)	33.4%	27.4%	NA
Access to clean drinking water	86%	56%	41.5%
Population to doctor ratio	1,341	1,594	2,179
Roads per km²	0.26	0.13	0.17

Source: Government of Pakistan 2008, 2011

Figure 10.6: Comparison of Pakistan Government Expenditure on Different Sectors

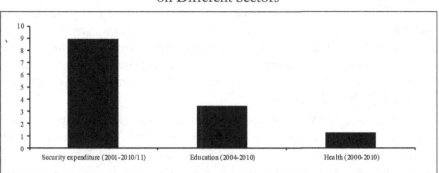

Source: Shahbaz et al 2012

The Federally Administered Tribal Areas (FATA), historically involved in militancy and extremism, is turning into a still more dangerous region. Religious leaders and tribal elders control the region in the absence of state law. Widespread illiteracy, unemployment and a wrong understanding of Islam made the region into a source of extremism, terrorism and drug-trafficking. With the onset of the global war on terror, this region became predominantly under the control of extremist groups, hence leaving the youth population highly prone to extremist exploitation. According to Qazi (2011) most of the local recruitment by extremists in the FATA was not because of ideological radicalization, but because of economic and political marginalization.

In the last ten years, Pakistan was hit by heavy natural and manmade disasters such as the Kashmir earthquake in 2005. As a result of such an earthquake 73,000 people died and 3.5 million people were left homeless (UNICEF 2008). Additionally, in 2010 a flood exacerbated this situation; 20 million people were affected, 1.6 million homes were destroyed and over 14 million people became highly vulnerable (Oxfam 2011).

This is worrisome as the flood destroyed most of the country's arable land. Agriculture is a strong pillar of the national economy in Pakistan. According to the Food and Agriculture Organization (FAO) of the United Nations (UN), agriculture accounts for 24 per cent of the GDP and employs 48.4 per cent of total the labour force in Pakistan (FAO 2004). These two massive natural disasters profoundly exacerbated a high level of poverty and underdevelopment in the country. Already beleaguered by these natural disasters, Pakistan was severely hit by the global financial and economic crisis in 2008.

Due to the global financial crisis, the high cost of imported oil brought new calamities into the country. Oil and food prices increased, unemployment soared, daily public protests started, and extreme power shortage devastated the limited industrial output in the country. The textile industry plays a vital role in the manufacturing sector. It employs 38 per cent of workforce in the industrial sector. Severe shortage of power and decreasing demands from the international market due to the global financial and economic crisis negatively impacted on the industrial sector.

According to the World Bank (2011), in 2009-10 Pakistan's exports stood at US$19.7 billion mainly contributed by the textile and the agriculture sectors. Its imports stood at US$31.2 billion mainly due to oil purchases. Thus, the trade deficit was recorded at US$ 11.5 billion. Additionally, Table 10.3 shows that foreign direct investments and remittances also declined. However, due to recurrent aid from the international community some improvements have been seen in economic growth. Conversely, the decline in FDI due to insecurity, shortage of power and the reduction of remittances due to the global financial crisis heightened tension in Pakistan's economy.

Table 10.3: Pakistan External Sector (2009/10-2010/11)

	US$ billion	
	2009/10	2010/11
Export	19.7	13.2
Import	31.2	19.6
FDI	2.1	0.9
Remittances	8.9	6.1

Source: State Bank of Pakistan 2010, 2011

The IMF (2010) reported that the percentage of people living in poverty was 22 per cent in 2005/06; however, the global financial crisis in 2007/08 further exacerbated the level of poverty in the country.

The 9/11 terrorist attacks once again made Pakistan an important frontline country in the contemporary global war on terror. However, the US-led invasion of Afghanistan forced the non-state terrorist organizations stationed in Afghanistan to move their camps outside the country. Under the Afghan Jihad, FATA, which had earlier served geostrategic and political interests of the cold war, once again became an important region for the non-state extremist and terrorist organizations to shelter in. With the onset of the global war on terror, operations of distinct extremist groups from Kashmir, Afghanistan and Central Asia overlapped and formed a united front against Western troops in Afghanistan.

The US started operating drone attacks in 2004 in order to demolish terrorist bases in FATA. Pakistan, a strong US ally in the global war on terror, also started military operations against its formerly trained militants. All those who once fought for the strategic and political interest of Pakistan and the US now reversed as a strong enemy, creating insecurity not only for Pakistan, but also for the entire world. Collateral damage caused by Pakistan military operations and US drones has resulted in thousands of civilian casualties. Continuation of military operations in this region has aroused people's resentment against the government of Pakistan and the US. This development fostered the extremists' role in FATA.

For terrorist and radical extremist militants to keep the flame of war going, it is essential to have ample economic revenues. The economic income from drug-trafficking, arm deals and associated crimes, including human trafficking, give an upper hand to terrorists and extremists to offer the iilliterate, unemployed population in such places as FATA high wages for high and respectful posts to recruits into their ranks. Hence, in the public perception, the recruiters became godlike saviours.

There are two main reasons for the rapid expansion of radical extremism in Pakistan, particularly in FATA: first, Jihadi rhetoric is prevailing in the religious educational institutions (*madrasas*) of Pakistan, and second, due to socioeconomic distress. Bakken (2007) states that after suicide attacks, both the perpetrators' and their families' social and economic statuses rise. According to Paizza (2006) terrorism is the expression of socioeconomic desperation. Local gangs and drug traffickers became religious leaders and radical militants and formed organized groups linked with bigger international terrorist groups such as Al-Qaeda and Islamic Movement of Uzbekistan (IMU) (Kronstadt and Katzman 2008).

The day-to-day increase in terrorist and radical extremist activities, economic downturn and social unrest are leading Pakistan into political instability. From the onset of its formation, Pakistan was concerned about security challenges emanating from Afghanistan and India; thus, the Pakistan Army and ISI (Pakistan's spy agency) have dominated the foreign affairs of Pakistan. Here it is important to note that the urgency of defeating the Soviet Union in the context of cold war politics led the international community to overlook the importance of growing radical extremism in the region.

Pakistan's bad political relations with its two main neighbours and the failure of civil government to tackle these issues have been responsible for frequent military coups. General Ayub Khan was the first general who came to power in 1958. Khan served as a military officer in the British Empire and was the first native Chief of Army Staff of Pakistan prior to becoming the President of Pakistan. Khan's good relations with Britain, and later with the US, led Pakistan to be a strong ally to the US during cold war era. As a result, Pakistan and the US signed a series of bilateral agreements including the South East Asian Treaty Organization (SEATO) and the Mutual Defense Assistance Agreement in 1954.

Another military coup was carried out led by General Zia-ul-Haq in 1978. From the onset of General Zia's presidency, Pakistan was placed under economic embargo. However, the Soviet invasion of Afghanistan in 1979 entirely altered Pakistan's fortunes overnight. In the context of cold war politics, Zia received billions of dollars of aid from the international community led by the US. According to Rashid (2000), Zia received about US$ 5 billion as aid from the US during the Afghan Jihad. After Zia's death in a mysterious plane crash, the civilian government led by the Pakistan People's Party (PPP) and the Muslim League (later the Muslim League Nawaz) could not fulfil their terms due to series of mismanagement and corruption charges.

Such a political situation invited another important military coup in 1999 led by General Pervez Musharraf. Musharraf's era was as important as Zia's period. The September 11 terrorist attack on the US once again fueled American interest in Pakistan. This time, Pakistan, with good experience of American conditional aid, demanded plenty of economic and military assistance in comparison to the cold war era. With such political background, Pakistan is under dire thread of fast expanding militarization and radical extremism. Since Pakistan is a massively populated nuclear power, its destabilization would lead to chaos in the region, which in turn would endanger international security.

Tajikistan: A Gateway of Drug-trafficking, Extremism and Terrorism

Tajikistan is a small landlocked country located in Central Asia. It is bordered to the south by Afghanistan, to the north by Kyrgyzstan, to the east by China, to the west by Uzbekistan. In 2006, Tajikistan's population was estimated to be about 7.3 million people. The ethnic composition of population is 79.9 per cent Tajik, 15.3 per cent Uzbek, 1.1 per cent Russian, and 1.1 per cent Kyrgyz (Library of Congress 2007).

At the time of their independence, each Central Asian State was entangled in a series of socioeconomic and political problems. Soviet isolation of CAS and their poor economies under authoritarian communist rulers became one of the main causes for the growth of the mass of unemployed youths, particularly in the densely populated Ferghana Valley (shared among Uzbekistan, Tajikistan and Kyrgyzstan), where these youths are widely exploited by the extremist groups (see Map 10.1). The World Bank (2000) has estimated that about 33 per cent of the Tajik population is unemployed. The extremists had been previously infiltrated in this region during the Afghan war. Through the activities of the fast-expanding madrassas in Ferghana Valley, the breadth of extremist power grew larger every day. The background of this was the tremendous support from the Deobandi and Wahhabi schools of thought, which were centred in the Arabian Gulf States, Pakistan and Afghanistan.

The Republic of Uzbekistan, a densely populated dominant country among the CAS, became the prime and the main target of extremism in Central Asia. However, the passing of the repressive Act by the Uzbek parliament against the freedom of religion gave a free hand to the President of Uzbekistan, Islam Karimov, to suppress Islamic movements. As a result of strict counter measures, radical leaders such as Tohir Yoldashib and Jumma Namangani fled to Tajikistan and later to Afghanistan.

On the other hand, Islamic movement gained power in Tajikistan. Uzbek militants joined the Islamic Renaissance Party of Tajikistan and participated in armed conflicts against the Tajik communist regime. Thus, a civil war erupted in Tajikistan in 1992. Protracted civil war in Tajikistan threatened Central Asian security and increased tensions in Moscow and Tashkent. Consequently, a joint military operation by Russian, Uzbek and Tajik forces ended the civil war in 1997. However, Tajikistan remains entangled with small-scale insurgencies led by the radical religious groups that are strongly active in the Ferghana Valley and in the regions adjacent to the Afghan border.

The Ferghana Valley is located in one of the worst enclaves of the world. Demarcation of borders between Uzbekistan, Tajikistan and Kyrgyzstan by the Soviet Union in the early twentieth century became one of the causes of regional political conflict among the CAS. Thus, Tajikistan suffers a series of challenges in terms of economy, social services, political instability and volatile relations with its neighbours. One of the main challenges the country faces is insecurity emanating from radical extremism and drug-trafficking, which is rooted in Afghanistan. Tajikistan's unstable economy and weak governing institutions face serious obstacles in securing its long mountainous border with Afghanistan.

Tajikistan is the main route for Afghan narcotics trafficking. Almost all of the Russian and the main portion of the European drug supply can be tracked through this route. According to the UNOCD (2010), 25 per cent of total heroin manufactured in Afghanistan is smuggled through Tajikistan to CAS, Russia, China and Europe. Drug-trafficking in Tajikistan has become a prominent problem for the government. A weak economy and widespread corruption are the main obstacles in fighting against drug-trafficking. Excessive dependency on foreign economies, particularly on Russia, causes the country to be fragile in terms of the global financial crisis.

The decline in national revenue, mainly due to the global financial and economic crisis, trimmed government expenditure on security sectors. Low wages are incentives for widespread bribery among security personnel, thus leaving the long porous border with Afghanistan as an easy passage for extremists, narcotic traffickers and other criminals to cross in and out the country.

On the one hand, the government is stricken by an economic crisis, and unable to create a robust economy, jobs or provide sufficient wages for government employees. On the other hand, drug lords offer lucrative jobs with high-income salaries to the young unemployed population. Consequently, a substantial part of the unemployed workforce is left exposed to either criminal exploitation or migration abroad.

The high level of unemployment has led Tajikistan to become one of the top labour-exporting countries in the world. The Tajik economy mainly relies on two sectors; first remittances, second exports (see Figure 10.7). Almost half of the country's GDP relies on remittance flows from workers abroad mainly in Russia (Danzer and Ivaschenko 2010). According to the World Bank Remittance Fact Book (2012) in 2011 remittance inflow to Tajikistan was equivalent to 47 per cent of Tajik GDP. Tajikistan's exports are mainly aluminum and cotton. A fall in price for commodities on the global market undermined the country's main export output. The United Nations Development Programme (UNDP 2010) reports that Tajikistan's trade deficit stood at US$1.6 billion in 2011; that is 38 per cent higher than the deficit level recorded in 2010. The gap was covered by remittances from Russia.

Figure 10.7: Tajikistan, Merchandise Exports and Remittances (2007-10)

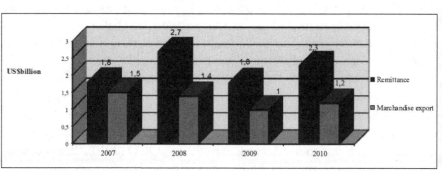

Source: UNDP 2010

The Tajikistan economy is inextricably linked to the Russian economy. The global financial crisis that hit Russia in 2008 provoked a 31 per cent decrease in Tajik remittances. This trend created serious economic problems in the country. Continuous mass labour migration from Tajikistan led Russia to gain political leverage and exploited the Tajik labour force. A weak economy, high unemployment level and excessive dependence on foreign aid impacted negatively on political stability, human security and human development programmes in the country.

Labour migration is essential to keep the Tajikistan economy on track, especially to cover up the economic shortfalls. However, extreme migration abroad causes deleterious side effects on the social life of Tajiks who are left behind in the country. Particularly, those labour migrants who settle down to a new life in Russia usually leave thousands of women and children deprived, psychologically ill and poor in Tajikistan. According to a news report by the BBC in October 2012 there were several negative impacts on children of Tajik migrants. They became depressed, psychologically ill, dropped out schools and started working at very early ages.

As in the case of Afghanistan and Pakistan, the unemployed young population inside the country is vulnerable to exploitation by the radical extremists and drug traffickers. To expand their recruitment, the extremists and drug traffickers have two strong weapons; one is religion; the second is the economy. Despite having been under Soviet communist rule for decades, Tajikistan remained a Muslim nation. However, people have very limited knowledge of Islam, particularly in rural areas with higher unemployment levels and strong faith in Islam which has made them prone to recruitment by religious extremists and exploitation by drug cartels.

During a meeting of Tajikistan's Security Council on 10 February 2011, President Emomali Rahmon, expressed concerns about 'the growth of religious extremist feelings in the society'. According to the President, these 'feelings threaten national security and stability in Tajikistan' (Majidov 2011).

The extremists, who collect high revenues from drug-trafficking, offer high wages to recruits. As mentioned above, the Tajik government, lumbering under loads of economic problems, particularly after the global financial and economic crisis, failed to tackle security challenges. These challenges not only threaten the national security of Tajikistan, but also endanger the security of the whole of CAS. Hence, rising unemployment levels in the country due to the economic crisis strengthened the role of religious extremists and drug traffickers.

The Islamic Movement of Uzbekistan (IMU) is the most powerful extremist organization in CAS and is very active in Tajikistan. Other than IMU, there are also smaller associate groups of IMU such as Hezb-ut-tahrir and Islamic Jihad

Union that are mostly active in Tajikistan and the Ferghana Valley. According to Rashid (2002), weak government and an unstable economy are providing a safe nest to extremists in Tajikistan. The government of Tajikistan has taken strong steps against religious groups, banning several religious schools that were active around the country. Yet large numbers of the young unemployed population are highly prone to recruitment by extremists.

For the government of Tajikistan, it is far more difficult to strengthen the economy and create jobs while their primary concern is to fight against radical extremism and drug-trafficking without meaningful support of the international community. The problem Tajikistan faces today is not just national or regional. Rather it is international; therefore, Tajikistan should not be alone in the responsibility for tackling these problems. While there is some active participation by international and regional aid organizations, Tajikistan still needs strong support from the international community to break away from the global economic recession in order to sustain economic and political stability, which would promote peace and socioeconomic prosperity in the region.

Conclusion and Policy Implications

The impact of the global financial and economic crisis is severe in developing countries with weak governance and unsteady economies. The developing countries, and more particularly the special condition and post-conflict countries, are prone to becoming politically destabilized.

For countries such as Afghanistan, Pakistan and Tajikistan, getting economic assistance will not be an absolute remedy to overcome economic and political problems. However, regional cooperation and collaborative economic and political relations with the neighbouring states can play a vital role in sustaining political and economic prosperity. The uneasy relations of Afghanistan, Pakistan and Tajikistan with their neighbouring countries and the absence of cordial relations among them are some of the main obstacles to economic and political stability. In particular, Pakistan's geostrategic and political disputes with India and Afghanistan force it to allocate a big portion of its revenues to the security sector.

Tajikistan has a territorial dispute over its border with both of its neighbours, to the north with Kyrgyzstan and to the west with Uzbekistan. This political milieu has intensified Tajikistan's political and economic challenges. A weak economy, lack of resources, excessive dependency on foreign cooperation and geographic proximity with conflict-torn Afghanistan has made the country highly vulnerable. In order to tackle these problems, it is in Tajikistan's vital interest to effect reforms in its domestic and foreign policies.

The failure of governments in Afghanistan, Pakistan and Tajikistan to provide basic social services for their citizens gives the upper hand to the radical extremists and terrorist groups. They provoke continuous instability against the states and expand their radical ideology and recruitment. One of the reasons behind focusing on these three countries in the context of this topic is their shared concern over the spread of extremism, drug-trafficking and government incapacity to create jobs and provide adequate social services for their citizens, especially for those who are affected by the global financial and economic crisis, natural disasters and internal conflicts.

Problems emanating from insecurity such as direct violence and structural violence are correlated to the economic backwardness of a country. The negative impacts of the global financial and economic crisis due to the integrated international economy and their dependency on foreign aid have made these three states unable to sustain political and economic stability, which has in turn undermined their ability to eradicate the root causes of extremism and terrorism from the region. Regional and international cooperation is fundamental to eradicate radical extremism, terrorism and drug-trafficking from this region.

References

Acharya, A., 2011, *Human Security: The Globalization of World Politics and Introduction to International Relations Fifth Edition*, New York: Oxford University Press.

Bakken, N. W., 2007, 'The Anatomy of Suicide Terrorism: A Durkheimian Analysis', Available at http://www.ifpo.org/articlebank/Bakken_Suicide_Terrorism.pdf

BBC News, 2012, http://www.bbc.co.uk/news/world- asia-20407511, 20 November.

BBC News, 2012, http://www.bbc.co.uk/news/world- asia-19920528, 13 October.

Danzer, A. M. and Ivaschenko, O., 2010, *Migrations Patterns in a Remittances Dependent Economy: Evidence from Tajikistan during the Global Financial Crisis*. Available at http://siteresources. worldbank.org/INTPROSPECTS/Resources/334934-1110315015165/Danz- erIvaschenko.pdf

Goodhand, J., 2005, 'Frontier and Wars: The Opium Economy in Afghanistan', *Journal of Agrar- ian Change 5* (2): 198, Available at http://www.giz.de/Themen/de/dokumente/en-opium-economy-2005-afg.pdf.

FAO, 2004, Fertilizer *Use by Crop in Pakistan: Land and plant Nutrition Management Service Land and Water Development Division*, Rome: FAO.

Felbab-Brown, V., ed., 2010, *The Drug Conflict Nexus in South Asia: Beyond Taliban Profits and Afghanistan. The Afghanistan-Pakistan Theatre Militant Islam, Security & Stability*, US: FDD Press.

Fukuda-Parr, S., 2008, *The Human Impact of the Financial Crisis on Poor and Disempowered People and Countries*, New York: The New School, available at http://www.un.org/ga/president/63/interactive/gfc/sakiko_p.pdf

IMF, 2010, 'Pakistan: Poverty Reduction Strategy Paper-Joint Staff Advisory Note', available at http://www.imf.org/external/pubs/ft/scr/2010/cr10182.pdf

IMF, 2011, 'World Bank Afghanistan Economic Update', October, http://siteresources.worldbank.org/AFGHANISTANEXTN/Resoures/305984-1297184305854/AFGEconUpdate2011.pdf

Katzman, K., 2013, *Afghanistan: Politics, Elections, and Government Performance*, available at http://www.fas.org/sgp/crs/row/RS21922.pdf

Kronstadt, K. A. and Katzman, K., 2008, November, *Islamist Militancy in the Pakistan-Afghanistan Border Region and U.S. Policy* (Order Code RL34763) CRS Report for Congress. Available at http://www.fas.org/sgp/crs/row/RL34763.pdf

Kiras, J. D., 2011, *Terrorism and Globalization: The Globalization of World Politics and Introduction to International Relations*, Fifth Edition, New York: Oxford University Press.

Library of Congress, 2005, Country Profile: Pakistan, Available at http://lcweb2.loc.gov/frd/cs/profiles/Pakistan.pdf

Library of Congress, 2007, Country Profile: Tajikistan. Available at http://lcweb2.loc.gov/frd/cs/profiles/Tajikistan.pdf

Malik, H., 2008, US *Relations with Afghanistan and Pakistan, The Emperial Dimension*, New-York: Oxford University Press.

Majidov, S. 2011, *Russia Pressures Tajikistan on Military Cooperation*, Johns Hopkins University, Central Asia-Caucasus Institute Silk Road Studies Program. Available at http://www.cacianalyst.org.

McMahon, R.J., 1994, *The Cold War On The Periphery: The United States, India, And Paksitan*, New York: Columbia University Press.

Muzalevsky, R., 2009, *Kyrgyz Operations against IMU Reveals Growing Terrorist Threat*, Johns Hopkins University, Central Asia-Caucasus Institute Silk Road Studies Program. Available at: http://www.cacianalyst.org/?q=node/5144.

Narayan, D., 2009, 'Post-Taliban Recovery and the Promise of Community-Driven Development in Afghanistan', in D. Narayan & P. Petesch, eds, *Moving out of Poverty*, UK World Bank, pp. 418–72.

OECD, 2011, *Development: Aid to Developing Countries Falls Because of Global Recession.* http://www.oecd.org/newsroom/developmentaidtodevelopingcountriesfallsbecauseof-globalrecession.htm.

Oxfam, 2011, 'Pakistan Floods Progress Report July 2010/July 2011'. Available at: http://policy-practice.oxfam.org.uk/publications/pakistan-floods-progress-report-july-2010-july-2011-137665.

Paizza, J. A., 2006, *Rooted in Poverty?: Terrorism, Poor Economic Development and Social Cleavage*. Available at: http://www.tandfonline.com/doi/abs/10.1080/095465590944578.

Qazi, S. H., 2011, *An Extended Profile of the Pakistani Taliban*. Available at: http://www.ispu.org/pdfs/ISPU%20Policy%20Brief%20Extended%20Profile%20of%20Pakistani%20Taliban.pdf.

Rashid, A., 2012, *Pakistan in Brink: The Future of America, Pakistan, and Afghanistan*, United States: Viking Penguin Group.

Rizvi, H.A., 2004, 'Pakistan's Foreign Policy: An Overview 1947-2004', Briefing Paper for Pakistani Parlimentarians, Retrieved from Pakistan Institute of Legislative Development and Transparency-PILDAT website: http://www.pildat.org.

Shahbaz, et al., 2012, *Livelihoods, Basic Services and Social Protection in North Western Pakistan,* London: Sustainable Development Policy Institute. Available at: http://www.odi. org.uk/sites/odi.org.uk/files/odi-assets/publications-opinion-files/7782.pdf.

UNDP, 2010, 'Fourth Inter-Agency Conference on Improving Regional Coordination in Managing Compound Risks in Central Asia'. Available at: http://europeandcis.undp. org/ourwork/cpr/show/E28DBC86-F203-1EE9-B5B8FFAFDE170966.

UNDP, 2012, 'Tajikistan-Fast Facts from the November Data (4 January 2011)'. Available at: http://europeandcis.undp.org/senioreconomist/show/52D4B5D0-F203-1EE9-B81E67CB6439232F.

UNICEF, 2008, 'UNICEF Pakistan's Earthquake Response Overview', Pakistan. Available at: http://www.unicef.org/pakistan/Overview-Updated-September-2007-1_(2). Pdf.

UNODC, 2010, 'World Drug Report'. Available at: http://www.unodc.org/unodc/en/data-and-analysis/WDR-2010.html.

UNODC, 2012, 'Opiate Flows Through Northern Afghanistan and Central Asia, A threat Assessment'. Available at: http://www.unodc.org/documents/data-and-analysis/studies/Afghanistan_northern_route2012_web.pdf.

World Bank, 2000, *Republic of Tajikistan Poverty Assessment,* June. Available at: http://www-wds.worldbank.org/servlet/WDSContentServer/WDSP/IB/2000/08/14/0000949 46_00080105305244/Rendered/INDEX/multi_page.txt.

World Bank, 2011, *Pakistan's Economic Update: Poverty Reduction Economic Management Finance and Private sector Development,* SAR. Available at: http://www-wds.worldbank. org/ex- ternal/default/WDSContentServer/WDSP/IB/2012/08/14/000333037_2 0120814000342/Rendered/PDF/718430WP00PUBL0onomicupdateJune2011.pdf.

World Bank, 2012, Migration and Development Brief 19. Available at: http://siteresources.worldbank.org/INTPROSPECTS/Resources/334934-1288990760745/MigrationDevelopmentBrief19.pdf.

World Bank, 2013, *Pakistan Overview,* available at http://www.worldbank.org/en/country/pakistan/overview.

11

Accountability in Public-Private Partnerships: The Emerging Development Paradigm in India amidst Financial Crisis

Tanvir Aeijaz

Introduction

The contemporary global economic crisis, including the financial collapse of September 2008, has become systemic in its manifestations. The crisis no longer restricts itself to be tackled and tamed by monetary and fiscal policies; rather its spill-over effects can be seen as afflicting what Gramsci called the sphere of complex super structure: political, legal, cultural. The crisis has raised certain fundamental questions about the foundational functioning of free-market capitalism, and therefore, there has been a shift in focus from the analysis and critique of one form of capitalism to any and all forms of capitalism, even also when and where it is putatively working well. Samir Amin reminds us of three contemporary crises at the global level (a) the crisis of accumulation in the real productive economy, (b) the energy crisis and the depletion of natural resources, and (c) the crisis of peasant societies including the agro-alimentary crisis (Amin 2011), to which one more may be added that undergirds the three – the crisis of development policy paradigm. Nation states grappling with the economic and its associated crises are responding with varying development policy options. Most of them have returned to the idea of mixed economy – a mix and match formula of the association of public and private sectors – accompanied by strong social policies.

One of the ways in which the governments, including both the majority of developed and developing nations, are responding to the development policy crisis is by resorting to a newly-designed phenomenon called public-private partnerships (PPPs). The use of these methods to augment development is largely seen as a means to avoid the opprobrium that has come to be associated with both contracting out and privatization in some quarters (Savas 2000). Governments have generally been able to sustain them, unlike the politically incorrect and unpopular idea of privatization, without large-scale opposition but also without much justification. However, the moot question that emerges in their usage has to do with the question of accountability in the backdrop of the emerging development paradigm, post-financial crisis.

The Indian government has also embarked on the much sought-after development paradigm of PPPs as a means of strengthening the economic reforms launched in 1991. The major push to such response by the Indian government has been seen more in the last decade, particularly during the visibility of global economic crisis, as privatization – the key reform of the agenda in 1991 – became a somewhat politically risky proposition for political parties. In the health care sector, the Indian government roped in the private sector to deliver health care facilities and services to poor and marginalized sections of society. In its 12th five-year plan (2012-17) a steering committee on health has been constituted to review and assess the role of the private sector and PPPs in health care and delivery and medical education. This chapter has three parts, the first dealing with some theoretical debates on intervention in the development process and PPPs as one of the modes of such intervention; the second with the exploration of meaning and various dimensions of accountability and its linkage with PPPs; and the final one about the Indian experience of PPPs specially in the health care sector.

State Intervention, Development and PPPs

State intervention in social planning and programmes gained credence in the post-depression and post-war period in the US and European nations. Liberal governments were keen to put an alternative to class conflict in the depression era, by shaping up a cooperative effort of social planning and regulation of the economy. Planning, either direct or indirect, was necessary because of the collapse of supposedly free, self-regulating markets and social coordination of corporations, unions and interest groups. Karl Mannheim (1950) argued that new, democratic forms of planning had to be found involving government control over the growing monopoly power of the corporations, centralization in most areas of decision-making, strong legislative oversight and governmental initiatives to foster citizen access and group competition. Most of the liberal democratic nations sought indirect planning through Keynesian economics.

As the state gradually increased its role in underpinning citizen welfare, higher living standards were accompanied by the growth of major public enterprises, often in place of failed embryonic markets. Governance meant state intervention, perhaps greater control, in the economy fiscal (e.g. taxes, deficits) and monetary (e.g. interest rates, money supply) policies or through economic commands quotas and control. The burgeoning growth of public enterprise brought together elements of state (public) and market (largely private in traditional view). The dominant idea, moreover, around the mid-twentieth century remained nationalization with the state largely substituting public enterprises in the provision of public goods and services for private market policies. Ramanadham (1984) postulates that public enterprises have two faces: one, governmental as they are owned by the state and need to serve public goals, and the other, enterprise oriented in as much they are expected to be business-like in their operations. For him, public enterprise can be organized as a department or part of it, as a statutory corporation, as a state-owned company, or as a local government activity.

The modern privatizing bug gained hold in the 1980s when the reformers started questioning the very raison dêtre of public enterprise. The so-called government failure was seen as justifying the removal of public enterprise and much else from the public realm. The dominant market oriented and government limiting ideas came from the proponents of public choice theory (Tullock 1965; Niskanen 1971; Ostrom 1973; Breton 1974). The agenda of reform concentrated on the reduction of inflation, lower taxation, privatization, deregulation, use of market forces in the public sector and institutional and constitutional reform to reduce the role of the state in social transactions and to limit it vis-à-vis the market.

From the 1980s, however, financial engineering meant, in most developed countries, refinancing existing properties or financing new projects, through leases or sale-and-buy-back arrangements (effectively purchases on credit from private firms). For instance, the Conservative government in Britain in 1992 introduced the Private Finance Initiative (PFI) which was continued by New Labour later in a friendlier-sounding public-private-partnership label. The very notion of PPPs in contemporary times has come to be associated with collaboration, cooperation, communicative governance and co-management (Kooiman 2003).

The Indian Context

The political economy of the Indian state, including its economic policies, their rationale and consequences has been extensively documented (Chakravorty 1988; Jalan 1991; Bhagwati 1993; Dreze and Sen 2002; Panagariya 2008). The first Prime Minister of India, Jawaharlal Nehru, emphasized rapid industrialization, economic independence and socialistic pattern of society and therefore opted for the import substituting industrialization model (ISI). In the early years, ISI led to improvement in literacy rates, mass communication and urbanization in the context of political democracy. However, ISI also generated classic conditions of low productivity. The twin ISI-driven dynamics of slow economic growth and social mobilization played an important role in generating the fiscal crisis of the Indian government (Krueger 1997).

By the mid-1980s, the Indian state development paradigm made a shift from ISI to trade-led growth (TLG) and reduced direct government intervention in the economy (Shastri 1995). However, it was the fiscal and balance of payment crisis (foreign exchange crisis) in 1991 that led to an agreement between the government and the International Monetary Fund to open up the possibility of exploiting the crisis to liberate the economy by a pro-trade and private sector-oriented government. Interestingly, globalization and global competition catalysed the coming together of business and state in many ways. Government started seeking policy inputs from industry firms, both during the formulation and implementation of policy-making. Liberalization, privatization and globalization demanded a 'policy paradigm' shift, including a greater role for private capital, and a new development issue linkage in a two-level game between the IMF, the government, and Indian industry. Public private partnerships emerged as somewhat of a consensus development paradigm in the Indian policy regime.

Public Private Partnerships (PPPs)

There are multiple grammars as to the meanings of PPP (Linder 1999). According to Foster (2005), there is a consensus among scholars on PPP, though writing from different perspectives that the term PPP must be seen in relation to previous more pejorative terms such as contracting-out and privatization. The collaborative advantage of a win-win-win or trifecta situation in PPP presents an attractive alternative to the market, quasi-market and contractualized relationships that have dominated the public management reform movement in the past decade and a new form of organization created from the bodies that come together (Linder 1999).

PPPs have become some sort of institutionalized co-operative arrangements between public-sector and private-sector actors. It is the co-operation of some sort of durability between public and private actors in which they jointly develop products and services and share risks, costs and resources which are connected with these products. Since the mid-1990s, PPP has generally eferred to long-term infrastructural-contractual-type PPPs, including schools, hospitals, security services, waste water treatment and so on. It is also seen as an important part of governmental reform in most OECD countries as well as in developing countries such as India, Brazil and South Africa.

PPP is unique, in a sense that the proponents of this partnership (Linder 1999; Savas 2000; Teisman and Klign 2000; Foster 2005; Stuart and Newman 1997) have distinguished it from outsourcing, privatizing and contracting. They also argue that ideologically, the private sector is superior to the public sector in producing and delivering goods and services and pragmatically government leaders can bring in special technical expertise, funding, innovation or management know-how from the private sector to address complex public policy problems. The uniqueness of PPPs seems to be more pronounced in its central characteristics such as (a) the partnership is usually a long-term rather than a one-time relationship as in a conventional contract for a good or service; (b) the private party cooperates in both the decision making and the production and delivery of that good and service which normally has been the domain of the government, and (c) the relationship involves a negotiated allocation of risk between the public and private sectors, instead of government bearing most of the risk. The partnerships, therefore, are seen as the shared procedural activities of productivity involving human skills and resources.

PPPs Vis-à-Vis Privatization, Outsourcing and Contracting

One of the most sought-after ways in which government reforms, involving the private sector, are initiated is through PPPs. Transferring government functions to non-profit organizations or the private sector to achieve greater fiscal control and more efficient delivery systems is preferably called outsourcing. In fact, government outsourcing is an application of the make-or-buy decision to government operations, even functions that have been the traditional domain of governments. The presumption is that private vendors can provide some public services more cheaply than government agencies (Savas 2000). There is nothing intrinsic to outsourcing that requires a partnership is the core argument of distinction.

Privatization involves the transfer of some activity and its assets that in the past was operated by the public sector to the private sector, through a sale concession or some other mechanism. Either the government eliminates direct control and ownership of the function and the delivery of services (full privatization), or it retains some influence by holding stock in the privatized firm. The idea is, in such cases, that the day-to-day production and delivery of the goods and services is left to private operators, i.e. the market and the government's involvement is primarily regulatory. As in outsourcing, there is nothing intrinsic to privatization that requires a partnership.

The contracting out approach is a method by which government dictates the terms and conditions for service production and delivery. The government agency (the purchaser) defines what it needs, specifies the desired product or service, and then issues a request for proposal to allow those in the private (or non-profit) sector – vendors – to bid on the good or service being sought. The government, therefore, may contract out for the design and construction of an infrastructure project without a bidder's involvement in the design specifications, financing or operations of the project. After awarding the contract, the public sector serves as the project manager or overseer, making sure the vendor supplies the goods and services promised in a timely and effective manner.

PPPs are often justified on one fundamental assumption and one fundamental presumption. The assumption is that governments often do not have the in-house knowledge of the most cost-effective ways to deliver public goods and services. In a globalizing world that is more integrated, complex and volatile, government simply may not possess the prerequisite knowledge, capacity or managerial skills due to the absence of effective incentive and motivation structure systems in the public sector. In such cases, governments need to engage partners that have the necessary expertise and managerial adeptness needed to carry out government responsibilities. The presumption is that governments can partner with private firms in a common goal where both of their fortunes are linked to the success of the overall project, providing the incentives for both sides to cooperate, innovate and work collaboratively towards the success of the enterprise. Accountability in PPPs, therefore, is linked to the specific relationship created and the obligations and requirement accepted by both the government and the private firm. However, understanding what constitutes the best design to ensure accountability is case specific and public managers are supposed to sort out, assess, and address various dimensions of accountability when considering a PPP.

Contextualizing Accountability

Government is the accountability holder and the holdee. It has to perform within its ability to manage its tools and hold its tool users accountable. Governments, both in the developing and developed world, are experiencing fiscal deficits and resorting to PPPs as an alternative way to finance and deliver public services to ensure efficiency and economy. With the increased use of PPPs, the issue of accountability at all levels has become the core question raised in public policy and development discourse.

Accountability is an important aspect of democratic polity. The substance of accountability requires government to make laws work as intended in their content, to exercise lawful and reasonable administrative discretion, to recommend new public policies and enhance citizens' confidence in the governmental institutions. Above all, government's prime responsibility is to function in the public interest and to respond to the politics of the governed.

Traditionally, government accountability was seen in terms of principal–agent relations. In this sense, there is the delegation of sovereign authority to public officials empowered to act in the name of the people and their representatives, resulting in the necessity to maintain control over those officials' action. In recent times, governments have been asked to conform to legitimate and popular accountability expectations, both at informal and formal levels. They are asked to be accountable to other governmental and state agencies, to impersonal standards, to hierarchical accountability and to finances, fairness and performance.

Accountability: Various Dimensions

Accountability as the key concept and central concern of both the study and practice of governance remains rather elusive and controversial. The word continues to excite a great deal of academic debate and practical application and is commonly used in close association with other ideas, particularly responsiveness, answerability, representation, efficiency, equity and legitimacy. The term may be used to describe a general, subjective sense of responsibility, the upholding of professional values and standards even in the absence of external scrutiny, a demonstrated responsiveness to particular clients or to the community at large, and the requirement for transparency, a democratic discourse and public participation in governance areas.

Accountability may also mean as the ineluctable quest for control that governmental policy-making is often more devoted to while avoiding the worst outcomes. This attitude reflects the synonymity of control, as in Klitgaards (1997) formulaic $C=M+D-A$ (Corruption equals Monopoly plus Discretion minus Accountability). The purpose of accountability has been put into clear perspective by Thomas (2001) who has pointed out that: '...preventing the potential abuse of power is the ultimate goal of numerous accountability arrangements and procedures adopted by contemporary governments'.

Though used interchangeably in popular parlance, accountability and responsibility are not synonymous. Accountability is a matter of political and organizational house-keeping, whereas responsibility is often about moral conflicts and dilemmas about goals and procedures of an individual action. Mosher (1968) has made a conceptual distinction between objective responsibility and subjective responsibility. Objective rationality essentially means that someone is answerable to someone else for the carrying out of specified tasks with commensurate authority and resources. It requires agents (politicians or bureaucrats) to give an account of their actions to specific others, who have the right and capacity to monitor performance and to invoke sanctions and rewards, and to be answerable to those with an account of how and why decisions were made, discretion exercised and actions taken. Subjective rationality is a psychologically-oriented idea, focusing on moral conflict and choice among the subjectively felt duties of obligation confronting politicians and administrators.

In the complex world of public policy-making it is often extremely difficult to trace cause and effect; all sorts of endogenous and extraneous factors combine to produce outcomes that are seldom finite and change over time and therefore the contributions of particular individuals to policy 'success' and 'failure' can seldom be demonstrated conclusively. Hannah Arendt (1963) described bureaucracy as the rule of nobody, implying that bureaucratic organizations are, by definition, collective not individualist systems.

The combination of various control and responsibility factors makes accountability anything but straightforward for public managers. As Behn (2001) points out, the result is an overlapping set of independent and competing mechanisms – and a variety of independently operating accountability holders. If politics is who gets what, when and how, then accountability is a forum of stewardship and/or responsibility involving account giving, both procedural and substantive, for who gets, what, when and how. Therefore, accountability serves as a useful analytical tool, both for civil society and government, to manage and enhance the perceptions of key stakeholders in the political process.

Accountability in PPPs

PPP actors are positioned within an already existing set of complicated and often competing chains of authority. Accountability in PPPs demands attention to the existing constraints and requires new approaches to management. The existing literature addresses many contemporary challenges of managing horizontal relationships, unlike vertical hierarchy as the principal method of controlling the acts of those within an organization, within indirect and networked government (Kettl 2002; Milward and Provan 2006; Posner 2002) or managing multi-sector responsibilities through service contracts (Cooper 2003; Guttman 2002; Savas 2000). These approaches emphasize the changing demands on accountability when government responsibilities are shared with private and non-profit entities. Many PPPs, especially infrastructure projects, involve public sector organizations getting access to private capital and construction expertise and private sector organizations getting new orders and securing new customers (Hodge and Greve 2005). A key to ensuring accountability, taking a long-term view of partnership relations, is the recognition that the public entity needs to be aware that its responsibility for contract management does not end once the contract has been awarded.

In fact, PPPs require controls and oversight both *ex-ante* and *ex-post* contract formation. Ex-post involvement needs to be taken as ongoing negotiation between the public and private partners.

Exercising accountability in PPPs ultimately depends on clarifying responsibilities in relationships. The manner of interaction between public and private partners affects the overall ability of an agency to monitor compliance and reward and punish success or failure by the contractor. Both parties, i.e. the public and the private, require mechanisms to demonstrate their commitments to the partnership in both short-term and long-term contracts. According to Milward and Provan (2006) accountability in this sense is seen as two-sided, implying both a willingness to take responsibility for one's action and an expectation that these actions will be recognized. Both partners develop interdependence under the stewardship of the government so that accountability is ensured and, therefore, public managers must take care of two very important dimensions, *inter alia*, of public sector accountability. These dimensions are socio-political impact and partnership collaboration. The other dimension such as understanding and allocating risk among the partners, costs and benefits, expertise and performance measurement also play an important role in the assessment of accountability. The nature of partnership collaboration and its outcomes are intrinsically connected with the social and political impact. These two dimensions, therefore, explain the potential for the effective exercise of accountability.

Socio-Political Impact

PPPs may affect different social systems, for instance, health-related, legal, educational and environmental systems. However, in assessing impact of social equity outcomes and effects, the differential impacts on socio-economic segments (caste in India) of the society need to be considered. The distribution of social impacts may have implications for the political system, potentially affecting electoral outcomes.

The perception of a partnership's success or failure can determine its ability to carry on the public service delivery. The failure in a public sector network has all kinds of political ramifications such as negative influence on the future re-election of the politician who supported the partnership, and so, undermines the politician's support for future funding of the partnership. For any partnership to continue, even when elections bring change in the government regime, sufficient political backing is essential. There is always a risk that political support will not be maintained if the programme's elected sponsors are voted out.

In such a situation a few questions regarding social and political factors and public accountability become important. Particularly, what is the strategy of each partner in identifying social, economic and environmental impacts and which partner will address those impacts? And, what is the involvement of the affected stake-holders, both potential and current, in the decision-making process?

Partnership Collaboration

The clarity in expectations for coordination as well as flexibility to facilitate collaboration and also the networked relationships within a PPP are what need to be specified in PPP contracts. This would enable a government agency's ability to monitor compliance and reward success or punish failure by the private partner. There are many potential inter-personal challenges that need to be considered, such as communication with stakeholders, effective leadership, project management and trust. Consistent and clear communication with all stakeholders involved in the PPP is essential to ensuring success in a partnering effort. Effective communication builds trust and encourages transparency which may increase engagement and translate into increased buy-in from those whose support is needed for success.

Policy entrepreneurship and effective leadership empowered throughout the organization is required to ensure accountability from all involved. 'It is important to recognize the differences and to understand which roles are needed at what stage and for what purpose. It is equally important to ensure that the best person is allocated to a particular role.' Therefore, it is the effective leaders who can maintain the momentum of the partnership and ensure that goals are met in the agreed upon time frame and hold those accountable for missteps and missed deadlines.

Another key to success is effective project management. The project manager's role is to guide the project through its course to ensure that goals, deadlines and benchmarks are met appropriately along the way.

Most importantly, and finally, the component of trust within the partnership is vital to success. Open and candid communication and transparency both with internal and external stakeholders that compose the partnerships is essential to engender trust. Trust typically does not exist on day one of the partnership and needs to be cultivated over time. The way the two organizations regard each other is crucial and above all else there must be mutual trust or the relationship may break down. There are two important questions that come immediately to mind in the aspects of trust, collaboration and accountability:

I. Are the terms of contract useful in creating an innovative climate for the stakeholders involved in the PPP?

II. What is the strategy for developing and sustaining open collaboration among the PPP stakeholders?

However, the processes and the outcomes in PPP are fraught with several challenges to governance structures and mechanisms. Government engages itself at various levels during the partnership deals as they are complex, non-transparent and expertise-oriented. These deals are rarely open to public scrutiny. At times, there is a host of organizations – both private and public – involved in the partnership. So the question of government's role in policy advocacy concerning PPPs and its actions as resolving multiple conflicts of interest – as economic developer and steward for public funds, as elected representative for decision-making and regulator over the contract life, and finally as a commercial signatory to the contract and planner – are of utmost importance. Government also has to decide when to choose a PPP over an alternative governance form. The most daunting challenge for government is to manage partners from the private sector that follow their own strategic agenda. The long-term nature of the contract makes it almost by definition impossible to foresee which factors can influence the governance environment in the long run. PPPs, therefore, present challenges to the various forms of public administration and posit different accountability and governance arrangements.

Trajectory of PPPs in India

Interestingly, neoliberal ideology tried to sustain itself by highlighting the conflict between the state and private actors and promising a better investment climate with minimal state intervention during the last couple of decades of the twentieth century. It also attacked the idea of public interest, or public good and argued that government or public service that is able to serve the public good is myth. The neoliberal crisis that culminated into the 2008 crisis exposed the fallacy of neoliberal development paradigm, that of self-regulating market in both economic theory and public policy. There has emerged widespread consensus that the unfettered privatization agenda of economic reforms is flawed and, therefore, the state's role as provider, regulator and a partner in the decision making at all levels in partnerships is called for. The fanning out of the state, the spanning out of the state, the privatization of state and para-state institutions, and the sub-contracting of state functions is what governance is about in contemporary times (Chandhoke 2003). This is down to the effect of a new concern which can be called as the governance of globalization.

It would be naïve to state that the 2008 crisis did not affect the Indian economy and policy paradigms. However, India proved to be a little more resilient to the crisis when compared to the other G-20 countries. The down drift from the global crisis that reached Indian shores, came to an economy that was expanding with a great deal of momentum (2003-08 had been exceptionally dynamic for India, averaging nearly 9 per cent growth). India had followed an incrementalist approach to both domestic regulation of banks and other financial intermediaries and to capital account convertibility. The financial system could not be exposed to the clawing-up institutions of the West. Also, in the 2008-09 budget, India had gone for extraordinary fiscal profligacy – due to the general elections of spring 2009 – and also to store up fiscal and inflationary problems for the future, which had the major effect of countering the deflationary shock from the global financial and economic crisis.

As the RBIs Annual Report for 2008-09 observes, '…despite India being one of the least affected countries in relation to other G-20 countries in terms of scale of growth deceleration, the fiscal stimulus used by India has been one of the largest as a percentage of GDP. The government and RBI tried to ramp up both monetary and fiscal stimuli to counter the deflationary effects of the global financial turbulence and the Great Recession' (Shankaracharya 2012).

In the wake of such developments, India has pressed hard to push PPP as the new face of development. The Eleventh Five Year Plan (2007-12) explains the state's agenda for furthering PPP as follows:

> The approach to PPPs must remain firmly grounded in principles which ensure that PPPs are formulated and executed in public interest with a view to achieving additional capacity and delivery of public services at reasonable costs. These partnerships must ensure the supplementing of scarce public resources for investment in infrastructure sectors, while improving efficiencies and reducing costs… Public private partnerships must aim at bringing private resources into public projects and not public resources into private projects.

That the Indian government has intensified the pace of PPPization in both infrastructure and social sectors is evident from the fact that a PPP cell has been created by the Ministry of Finance a viability gap funding (VGP) scheme is being initiated for the projects which are economically justifiable but not commercially viable; and a government company India Infrastructure Finance Company Ltd (IIFCL) has been established to provide long-term finance to infrastructure projects and intensive capacity building at the state and central level.

Table 11.1: Growth in health infrastructure in India

Indicator	1951-52	2005-06	Remarks
Population	361 mn	127 bn	Census data
Primary health centres	725	22,669	
Allopathic hospitals	2,694	15,393	Both public & private sectors
Allopathic beds	--	683,545	Both public & private sectors
All beds	117,178	914,543	
Doctors (allopathic)	61,800	660,801	Registered at MCI*
Doctors (Indian systems)	--	724,823	Ayurveda, Unani & homeopathy
Nurses	16,550	908,962	General nursing, midwives only
Five Year Plan Budgets (Rs mn)	653 (I Plan)	589,203 (X Plan)	Includes health, family welfare, Indian systems plus homeopathy
Medical Colleges	30	262	

Source: Medical Council of India

Lessons from the Indian experience of PPPs in healthcare

There is near unanimity that the Indian state has failed to provide even a minimal level of healthcare, according to global standards, to its vast population, especially the poor. As a public policy intervention across the world in 1990, PPPs are being increasingly adopted for critical health care, where loss of control and outright privatization are considered unacceptable. This kind of health care reform policy is grounded in Amartya Sen's capabilities approach to development as a response to rising inequality and stunted growth. In a review of health sector reform initiatives in Peru, Guatemala, Costa Rica, Columbia and Dominican Republic, Abramson (1994) identifies that public sector contracts with NGOs to deliver primary health services have led to (a) extending coverage in the scope of services as well as geographic area for underserved populations; (b) increasing the availability of medicine and medical supplies (c) improving the quality of care; and (d) improving efficiecy, cost control and optimal use of resources.

India has one of the world's largest networks of health centres and hospitals under a public health system. Since independence, the social infrastructure for India's public delivery of health services grew substantially and the health of its population improved. The achievements, however, have not been uniform across all sections of society or across different regions of the country. For instance, Kerala and Tamil Nadu are comparable to middle-income countries while the BIMARU states (Bihar, Madhya Pradesh, Rajasthan, Uttar Pradesh) resemble the least developed countries.

Despite significant progress in health status and the creation of a vast network of institutions, the public health system has been unable to deliver healthcare services at desirable levels of quality and efficiency. The financial crisis of 2008 has alerted the state to focus on the social sector which can act as a foundation for its capacity building leading to growth in the long run. The Indian state has also focused on strengthening its PPP capacity by involving private players in primary health centres, social franchising and demand-led financing of the health industry and therefore, resurrecting health care services. The investor-friendly approach to PPP in health care services is to make healthcare accessible to the rural and urban poor. However, studies have documented the extent of economic stress on the poor and have also indicated that the average utilization level of government health institutions in rural areas is less than 25 per cent. The critical problems afflicting public sector health systems are (a) inadequate financial resource commitments, including budgetary allocation; (b) inability to address emerging diseases and the epidemiological transmission; (c) structural and managerial inefficiencies, including administration of health personnel; (d) unregulated growth of the private health sector and its consequences; and (e) poor mobilization of the community, including local bodies, NGOs and the private sector, as critical stakeholders in the health sector. Inequities in the private health sector and malfunctioning in the public health system exacerbate the impoverishment of India's poor as they seek healthcare. Governments and policy-makers are exploring alternative policy options and strategies not only to improve efficiency, performance and quality of the public health system but also to enhance the equity, accountability and affordability of the private health sector. Health reforms in the developing countries may be done at three levels. According to Thomason (2002), these levels are: (a) changes in financing methods that includes user-charges, community financing, insurance, stimulating private sector growth and increased resources to health sector; (b) changes in health system organization and management through decentralization, contracting out services and reviewing the public-private mix ; and (c) public service reforms per se by rightsizing public sector, productivity improvement, improving geographic coverage and increasing the role of local government. While there is consensus that the health sector requires radical reforms, perspectives on the contents of reforms range from marketization to complete government provision of health services.

Hospitals entering PPPs

Governments, both at the centre and state levels, have already begun to involve the private sector in delivering healthcare services to the poor sections of society. The central government is expected by the World Health Organization and other donor countries in the area of health, and also by the people, to play a catalytic role by developing standards and mechanisms for PPPs. Since India is a federation, with both centre and states responsible for healthcare, the states are supposed to identify specific programmatic needs to map the private, to design the specific partnership details, to develop standards for interim accreditation, to improve capacities of government to monitor and regulate the private sector, and to build capacity at district level. During the past decade, both central and state governments have initiated PPP arrangements. While most of these initiatives involve collaboration between the public and the private sectors, several could be bracketed under government grant-in-aid schemes.

Based on the study by Venkatraman and Björkman (2009) on public private partnership in healthcare in India, it is interesting to note the challenges of implementing public-private partnerships and to explore whether partnership with the private sector can be designed to deliver healthcare services to the poor as well as the consequences for beneficiaries. From the above-mentioned study, the following aspects of policy implications are observed for the processes of PPP:

- It is difficult to ascertain the initiator of the policy option for PPP. However, states that experimented with partnership ideas before formalizing a policy seem to be more successful than states that promulgated a formal policy well before experimenting with it.
- There is no uniform pattern to indicate which services are best provided through partnerships and which services are strictly off-limits for private partners.
- It seems contracting is the predominant form of partnership; most successful hassle-free partnerships have been with private non-profit organizations.
- It is not clear whether the PPP policy option was guided by multi-lateral development funding agencies, compulsory resource constraints, competitive bureaucracy or state intentions to innovate in healthcare delivery.
- It is also relevant that policy pronouncements by government alone are not sufficient to initiate partnership. The major stakeholders, such as social policy entrepreneurs, visionary leaders, bureaucracy and private sector initiative at times are essential prerequisites for successful partnerships.
- Pre-negotiated partnership agreements based on detailed dialogue are more effective than competitive bidding in the choice of partners. Partnership initiatives by the bureaucracy have less success than partnerships initiated by private partners.
- The private non-profit sector is more likely to undertake partnerships at the primary care level than the for-profit sector which is more likely to provide secondary and tertiary clinical care.
- The capacity of private partners and the bureaucracy to manage partnerships is underdeveloped. Known for their informal and flexible systems in organizational processes, private partners are uncomfortable with the rigid organizational and managerial processes and procedures of the public sector bureaucracy. Successful PPPs require a proactive and enterprising bureaucracy; therefore, administrative systems and procedures must be modified or reformed.
- Contract agreements and MoUs must include performance indicators, supervision and monitoring, documentation and information system, incentives or penalties, dispute settlement mechanisms, exit options and quality standards to be followed.
- Policy innovations like PPPs are contextual. They cannot be uniform across all the regions or suitable under all political and administrative dispensations. PPPs are no substitutes for the provision of health services by the public sector through better governance.

- Though the initiation of PPP can be an administrative decision, political support and community perception are critical. In states where the private sector is prevalent, partnership initiatives are an alternative, not necessarily because of competitive efficiency but to prevent further pauperization of the under-served and the poor.

- Engaging the private sector is fraught with political risk. Given the government trend to transfer its responsibilities to the private sector, any collaboration with the private sector is perceived suspiciously. It is imperative to create sufficient political consensus as well as appropriate legal systems in order to delineate the scope for partnership. Likewise, a policy shift towards PPPs requires institutional systems within bureaucracy including trained personnel, procedural guidelines for resource management and financial systems, management information systems, supervision and monitoring.

- Given limited evidence, it is too early to judge whether it is more effective to subsidize inputs or to provide direct subsidies to the poor by purchasing the services from the private sector. Likewise, it may be inappropriate to conclude that partnerships with the private sector have a catalytic effect on public sector health services, which is quality of care, accessibility, service utilization level and human resource performance.

Policy Practice

Engendering PPP as an alternative to ward off deficiencies in healthcare delivery systems may not be a panacea for the major ills of public sector health systems in developing countries. To make PPPs successful, in developing nations in particular, it is important to synergize the strengths of government, community, NGOs and the private- for-profit sector. Local politics and experiences need to be considered – a bottom-up approach – to make PPP area-specific, demand-driven, needs-based and people- centred while designing the projects and programmes. Also, implementation and sustainability must be explored through pilot projects in health services in terms of quality of care, accessibility, service utilization level and human resource performance.

It is also important to note that decentralized partnership initiatives are more likely to be useful. However, these require capacity building at local-level institutions to get the contract right, an accountability framework of checks and balances to ward off corruption, proper definition of standards in terms of resource allocation, safety nets, health package, modes of payment and communication patterns. Since government is the prime mover, it has to play a decisive role in steering and monitoring of PPPs. It has to facilitate the regular exchange of communication, joint planning of activities as well as problem-solving, training and stability of key personnel. However, a government that fails to deliver quality services due to lack of administrative capacity would not be able to contract either clinical or non-clinical services. It is imperative, therefore, that for development concerns to be met, administrative development and reforms must take place simultaneously.

Conclusion

The development policy crisis may have led different nation states to embark on PPPs but the road ahead seems perilous as far as addressing the questions of socio-economic equity and who benefits in the collaboration is concerned. Private capital, in search of greater accumulation, has a high degree of penetrative capacity to fuse public capital and adapt it to its own image. PPPs applied in various contexts and by various governments are still in a process of locating accountability for larger public legitimacy.

The private sector, for any of its activity looks for private-profit maximization, and the public sector essentially functions to serve public interest by not rendering worse-off those who are on the margins of development. In such a situation, PPP adopted by developing countries is an attempt to find a zone of consensus and collaboration between the two. No doubt it is a difficult task.

Privatization has led to market failures; and in the context of public services, it has led to the exclusion of the poor with serious ramifications for equity and access. Though the Indian economy was a little resilient during the financial crisis, the lesson learnt from unfettered privatization, à la neoliberal recipe, is to bring the state back in with the ideation of partnership, particularly in the soft social sectors such as health and education. Also, privatization post-financial crisis is not a politically viable agenda for political parties. At the same time, accountability issues vis-à-vis access, equity and finances remain crucial. The time is ripe to debate the sudden arrival and pertinence of PPPs in India's development strategies and explore real alternatives for social change (Data 2009). Nonetheless, the challenge remains.

References

ADBI, 2000, *Public Private Partnerships in Health:* Executive Summary Series No. S34/01, Executive Summary of Proceedings, 30 October-3 November, Ayutthaya, Thailand, Tokyo, Asian Development Bank Institute.

Amin, S., 2011, *Ending the Crisis of Capitalism or Ending Capitalism?*, Oxford: Pambazuka Press.

Arendt, H., 1963, *Eichmann in Jerusalem: A Report on the banality of Evil,* Harmondsworth: Penguin Books.

Avery, G., 2000, 'Outsourcing Public Health Laboratory Services: A Blueprint for Determining whether to Privatize and How?',*Public Administration Review* 60.

Baru, R., 1998, *Private Healthcare in India: Social Characteristics and Trends,* New Delhi: Sage Publications.

Behn, Robert D., 2001, *Rethinking Democratic Accountability,* Washington, DC: Brookings Institution Press.

Berman, P. and Dave P., 1994 'Experiences in Paying for Healthcare in Indias Voluntary Sector', in S. Pachauri, ed., *Reaching India's Poor : Non-Governmental Approach to Community Health,* New Delhi: Sage Publications.

Bhagwati, J., 1993, *India in Transition: Freeing the Economy,* New York: Oxford University Press.

Chakravarty, S., 1988, *Development Planning: The Indian Experience,* New Delhi: Oxford University Press.

Chandhoke, N., 2003, *Governance and the Pluralization of the State: Implications for Democratic Citizenship,* EPW, July 12.

CII-McKinsey Report, 2004, *Healthcare in India: The Road Ahead,* New Delhi: Indian Healthcare Federation and Confederation of Indian Industries.

Datta, A., 2009, 'Public-Private Partnerships in India: A Case for Reform?' *Economic and Political Weekly,* 15 August, 73–78.

DFID, 2000, *Making the Most of the Private Sector,* Workshop Organized on Behalf of the Department for International Development, London, Health Systems Resource Centre.

Donahue, J.D., and Nye, J.S. Jr. eds, 2002, *Market Based Governance: Supply side, Demand side, Upside and Downside,* Washington DC: Brookings Institution Press.

Dreze, J. and Sen, A., 2002, *India: Development and Participation,* New York: Oxford University Press.

Edwards, P. and Shaoul J., 2003, 'Partnerships: For Better, For Worse', *Accounting, Auditing and Accountability Journal,*16: 397–421.

Escobar, A., 1995, *Encountering Development: The Making and Unmaking of the Third World,* Princeton: Princeton University Press.

Flinders, M., 2005, 'The Politics of Public Private Partnerships', *British Journal of Politics and International Relations* 7: 215–39.

Foster, D., 2005, 'Practical Partnering: Making the most Complex Relationships', *PPP Bulletin,* Aug/Sept, Issue 2.

Goldsmith, S. and Eggers, W.D., 2004, *Governing by Network: The New Shape of the Public Sector,* Washington DC: Brookings Institution Press.

Government of India, 2005, *Concept Note on Public Private Partnerships,* New Delhi: Department of Family Welfare, Ministry of Health and Family Welfare.

Grimsey, D. and Lewis, M.K. 2004, *Public Private Partnerships: The Worldwide Revolution in Infrastructure Provision and Project Finance,* Cheltenham, UK: Edward Elgar. Heinrich, C. and Laurence, L., eds, 2001, *Governance and Performance,* Washington, DC: George Town University Press.

Hodge, G. and Carsten, G., eds, 2005, *The Challenge of Public-Private Partnership: Learning from International Experience,* Cheltenham (UK): Edward Elgar.

Jalan, B., 1991, *India's Economic Crisis: The Way Ahead,* New Delhi: Oxford University Press. Kearns, K.P., 1996, *Managing for Accountability: reserving the Public Trust in Public and Non- Profit Organizations,* San Fransisco: Jossey-Bass.

Kettel, D.F., 2002, *Managing Indirect Government, in* L.M. Salamon, ed., *The Tools of Government: A Guide to the New Governance,* New York: Oxford University Press.

Kettel, D.F., 1993, *Sharing Power,* Washington, DC: The Brookings Institution.

Klitgaard, R., 1997, 'Cleaning up and Invigorating the Civil Service', *Public Administration and Development* 17.

Kooiman, J. 2003, *Governing as Governance,* London: Sage.

Kreuger, A., 1993, *Political Economy of Policy Reform in Developing Countries,* Cambridge, MA: MIT Press.

Kulkarni, S., 2003, *India Sector Paper : Health Overview and Prospects,* New Delhi: Centre for Media Studies (submitted to ADB).

Light, P. C., 1993, *Monitoring Government: Inspectors General and the Search for Accountability,* Washington, DC: Brookings Institution Press.

Linder, S.H. 1999, 'Coming to Terms with Public Private Partnerships: A Grammar of Multiple Meanings', *The American Behavioural Scientist* 43 (1).

Lynn, Lawrence E., Jr, 2006, *Public Management: Old and New,* New York: Routledge. Mannheim, K., 1950, *Freedom, Power and Democratic Planning,* New York: Oxford University Press.

Mosher, F.C., 1968, *Democracy and the Public Service,* New York: Oxford University Press.

Mukhopadhyaya, A., 2000, 'Public Private Partnership in the Health Sector in India', in Y. Wang, ed., *Public Private Partnership in the Social Sector : Issues and Country Experiences in Asia and the Pacific,* Paper No.1, Tokyo: ADBI, pp 343-56.

Nellis, J., 1994, *Is Privatization Necessary: Public Policy for the Private Sector, Washington,* DC: World Bank.

Osborne, S., ed., 2001, *Public-Private Partnerships: Theory and Practice in International Perspective,* London: Routledge.

Panagariya, A., 2008, *India: The Emerging Giant,* New York: Oxford University Press. Posner, Paul L., 2002, 'Accountability Challenges of Third Party Government', in Lester M. Salamon, ed., *The Tools of Government: A Guide to the New Governance,* New York: Oxford University Press.

Przeworski, A., Stokes, S.C. and Manin, B., 1999, *Democracy, Accountability and Repre- sentation,* Cambridge: Cambridge University Press.

Ramanadham, V.V., 1984, *The Nature of Public Enterprise,* London: Croomhelm.

Rosenau, P.V.C., ed., 2000, *Public Private Policy Partnerships,* Cambridge, MA: MIT Press.

Savas, E.S., 2000, *Privatization and Public-Private Partnerships,* London: Chatham House. Sel varaju, V. and Annigeri, V.B., 2001, *Trends in Public Spending on Health in India,* New Delhi, NIPFP, Background Paper for the Commission on Macroeconomics and Health. Shankaracharya, G., 2012, *India After the Global Crisis,* India: Orient Blackswan.

Shastri, V., 1995, 'The Political Economy of Policy Formation in India', PhD Thesis, Cornell University, Ithaca.

Stinson, J., Pollak, N. and Cohen, M. 2005, *The Pains of Privatization: How Contracting Out Hurts Support Workers, Their Families and Healthcare,* Vancouver: Canadian Centre for Policy Alternative.

Thomas, P.G., 2001, 'The Institutional Context and the Search for Accountability in Manitoba Health', The Report of the Review and Implementation Committee for the Report of the Manitoba Pediatric Cardiac Surgery Inquest, Winnipeg, Government of Manitoba, ch 2.

Thomason, J.A., 2002, *Health Sector Reform in Developing Countries: A Reality Check,* Available online at: www.sph.uq.edu.au/acithn/conf97/papers97/thomason.htm

Venkatraman, A., 2002, *Institutional Reforms in Health Sector : A Study of Personnel and Organizational Issues in Health Sector Reforms,* Robert MacNamara Research Fellowship Report, World Bank, Faculty of Management Studies, University of Delhi.

Venkatraman, A. and Björkman, J.W., 2006, *Public Private Partnership in in the Provision of Healthcare Services to the Poor,* Indo-Dutch Programme for Alternatives in Development Research Report, Faculty of Management Studies, University of Delhi.

Venkatraman, A. and Björkman, J.W. 2009, *Public Private Partnership in Healthcare in India,* New York: Routledge.

Walsch, K., 1995, *Public Services and Market Mechanisms: Competition, Contracting and the New Public Management,* London: Macmillan.

World Bank, 2001, *India: Raising the Sights: Better Health Systems for Indias Poor,* Washington DC, HNP Unit-India, Report # 22304.

World Bank, 2004, *India: Private Health Services for the Poor,* Draft Policy Note.

Wetten, R., 2003, 'The Rhetoric and Reality of *Public-Private Partnerships',* *Public Organization Review* 3 (1): 77–107.

WHO, 1997, *Public Private Sector Partnership for Health: Role of Governments,* New Delhi: WHO Regional Office.

WHO, 2000, *Health Systems Improving Performance,* The World Health Report.

Yescombe, E.R., 2007, *Principles of Policy and Finance,* Burlington MA: Butterworth- Heinemann/Elsevier.

PART V

BUILDING POLITICAL AND ECONOMIC
ALTERNATIVES TO THE ECONOMIC CRISIS

12

Chinese Social Transformation and its Implications for the Future of Afro-Asian Solidarity

Horace G. Campbell

Introduction

On 25 December 2011, China and Japan unveiled plans to promote direct exchange of their currencies. This agreement will allow firms to convert the Chinese and Japanese currencies directly into ech other, thus negating the need to buy dollars (*BBC News* 2011). This deal between China and Japan followed agreements between China and fourteen other countries to trade outside the sphere of the US dollar. A few weeks earlier, China had also announced a 70 billion Yuan ($11 billion) currency swap agreement with Thailand. These reports were carried in the financial papers and the organs that understood the response of the Chinese to the continued devaluation of the US dollar. The disguising of these devaluations as 'quantitative easing' did not fundamentally deceive societies of the African and Asian blocs that wanted protection against a future financial collapse in the Western capitalist states (Johnson and Kwak 2010). As recently as March 2012, one expert speaking at the Board of Governors of the Asian Development Bank stated that, 'It may only be a matter of time before the US dollar gets replaced as the main currency in international trade.' The Western media and financial papers have been careful in reporting on this seismic shift in the international financial system. There are major implications that will emanate from this direct exchange of currencies between the first and second largest holder of US Treasury Securities.[1] Prior to this agreement between China and Japan, the Japanese formed a core partner in the post-World War II international financial architecture that maintained the dollar as the currency of world trade and supported the hegemonic position of the United States in the international political economy.

This currency swap agreement was deepened by a later investment agreement between China, Japan and the Republic of Korea. Hence, while the corporate media has focused on the battle by the US and EU to 'bully' China into allowing its currency to significantly appreciate (i.e. be determined by market forces) and ultimately fully internationalized so that its currency could be traded by global financial institutions, China has been truly doing its own thing (like establishing the current swap trade settlement arrangements with neighbours) based on its strategic calculations and economic interests. The ability of China to chart its own path is in itself a dimension of a new international economic order. This aspect of Chinese economic relations has been accompanied by rapid and fundamental changes in the nature of the world economy.[2]

This chapter will seek to lay out an African perspective on the changes in the global political economy, delving into the implications of the 'Rise of China' and the debates on the nature of China in the global economy. Vijay Prashad in his study of the relationships between the Darker Nations and the imperial powers had spelt out how anti-colonial nationalism within the non-aligned movement had been the foundation of an alternative world order based on peace, self-determination and international cooperation (Prashad 2008). This book, *The Darker Nations: A People's History of the Third World,* was written before the collapse of the neo-liberal financial system in 2007-08. Since the emergence of the BRICS formation as a centre of alternative financial resources, there has been a growing realization from all continents that new forms of economic arrangements will be necessary to bypass the Breton Woods system. In the face of this realization and the aggressive deployment of financial and economic resources by China, there has been a spate of anti-Chinese ideas that China has emerged as the new imperialist hegemon. One of the many challenges will be whether the access to Africa's natural resources and energy resources will follow the path of plunder and brutality that emerged from Western colonial domination. Like Africa and the rest of the other countries of the Afro-Asian bloc, China has been through periods of brutal imperial domination and wars, and therefore shares the aspirations of moving to new forms of relations. The Chinese aspiration for alternative social relationships within the context of socialist transformation has been fought for in a revolution. Under the political leadership of the Communist Party of China, it was recognized that independence and economic growth had to be defended so that the defence of the Chinese revolution has taken many twists and turns. Many scholars and policy makers in the West credit the present spectacular growth to the opening up of China to the West. But as

Samir Amin has argued, even if China's opening is within the capitalist mode of production, the future result of this 'evolution' would be a multi-polar world organized around the newly emerging powers.

One of the fundamental questions posed by the present conjuncture is whether the challenge of the Afro-Asian bloc can continue without even greater militarism and militarization from the United States and its allies. Will the current depression end up in open global warfare?

This chapter seeks to grasp the implications of the call by the people of the Afro-Asian bloc who want a new mode of organization and whose campaigns for environmental justice seek to build on the struggles for independence. Will the rise of China reproduce the barbaric exploitation of workers that has been the history of capitalism as well as the ecological disaster? The reality of the environmental crisis is sharpening the debate and discussions on transformation. Transformations and climate debt (reparations) are interrelated and the challenge is how to move the Afro-Asian solidarity bloc in a direction away from the 'development models' that devalued their humanity. How can our work as intellectuals and activists assist in the transformation of society, to develop human potential for self-emancipation from all forms of bondage and restrictions, mental, racial, economic, gender, social and cultural?

This is the essence of an understanding of transformation, a tremendous change in social organization, modes of thinking, cultural and gendered practices. In this sense, transformation involves far more than legal changes, such as political independence or simply the transition from one mode of production to the next. Transformation involves a thorough change in society from top to bottom. Throughout the world, the new vigor of Chinese investment in the infrastructure of societies in Africa, Asia and Latin America has opened new possibilities for reconstruction away from the old forms of relations with Western Europe. Reconstruction after wars of devastation offers opportunities for societies to make a break with old forms of economic and social relations. I argue in this chapter that it is the social struggles of the working peoples in the Afro-Asian world that can lay the basis for a new transition beyond capitalism. This argument is not new in Africa since during the period of the anti-colonial and anti-apartheid struggles, progressive intellectuals from centres of study and reflection had been writing about the challenges of the transition to socialism (Thomas 1976). This author benefited from the theoretical insights of the Dar es Salaam School that had grappled with the challenges of the transition beyond capitalism. Tanzania in both theory and practice was one of the anchors of the spirit of South-South cooperation.

After examining the trajectory of Afro-Asian solidarity up to the current changed world situation, the chapter will lay out some of the debates on the nature of the social transformation in China. We will then conclude with the call by Samir Amin for the progressives of the North and South to be bold in formulating a political alternative to the existing system. Amin proposed three main directions (a) socialize the ownership of monopolies, (b) definancialize the management of the economy and (c) deglobalize international relations. These audacious proposals require new forms of struggles and new networks globally. The revolts against neoliberalism throughout the world provide a firm basis for building social relations between the classes in China and the other countries of the Afro-Asian Bloc to chart a new course for humanity. It is this break that brings the peoples of Africa and China together. This break involves a rethinking of the basic ideas of linear thinking and the view that associates development with European stages of growth, as modernity and enlightenment thinking are now being interrogated. Finally, we will make the case for *ubuntu* and the shared sense of humanity as the basis for twenty-first century relations. The theoretical base for this chapter rests on a South-South perspective that is nested within the conceptual framework of *ubuntu*. Five years ago, in another conceptual analysis of the relationships between Angola and China, Sreeram Chaulia and I mapped out the theoretical framework for a South-South analysis. Then, it was articulated that the relations between Africa and China emerged out of struggles, common interests and transformation (Campbell and Chaulia 2009). Julius Nyerere had developed the formulation of Unequal Equals to characterize the incubation stages of the relationship between Tanzania and China in the period of the Cold War. The transformation of the economic basis of twentieth century international relations was being forced on to the international stage by the emergence of new international players in the twenty-first century (Prashad 2013). Realist conceptions of power and might predispose academics, even within China, to think of world politics in terms of the dynamic of great power rivalry. What this chapter will seek to do from the analysis of the ideas of Bandung, is show that there was a search for a multipolar world, and that this process is occurring so rapidly that it is eroding old ideas of economic alignments.

The ideas and practices of the anti-colonial leadership period were not adequate for the movement to make a quantum leap outside of the orbit of international capitalism. The social and economic conditions in this period of capitalist depression require new ideas, new alliances, and a new politics for the twenty-first century. This will be one of the surest paths to transcend this obsolete capitalist system (Amin 2010).

The Spirit of Bandung and the Peoples of the World

'Let a New Asia and a New Africa be Born'

These words of President Sukarno of Indonesia were delivered at the opening session of the Asian-African Conference that was held in Bandung, Indonesia from 18 to 24 April 1955. After the independence of India in 1947 and the accelerated decolonization process, Jawaharlal Nehru committed India to support independence and decolonization in all parts of the world. Nehru was the host for the Asian Relations Conference held from 22 March to 3 April 1947 in Delhi in which 250 representatives from twenty-five Asian countries participated as well as those from Australia and New Zealand as observers. India, then, had not yet gained its independence officially. Jawaharlal Nehru was the Prime Minister of the interim government and he outlined his vision of peace and independence when he said in his address:

> We have laid a strong foundation for our work. I hope that this endeavor will continue that this towering tree of Asian unity that has brought us together will culminate into something wonderful... universal peace based on freedom. For we, at present, cannot separate the destiny of one people from the destiny of other peoples because they interact together. Any sane person can understand that it is impossible to disassociate the problems confronting us today. It is impossible - as has been said a long time ago - there cannot be a world which is half free and half under the yoke of slavery, nor part of the world torn by war and another part enjoying peace. Freedom is for all, peace is for the entire world (Afro-Asian People's Solidarity Organization 2013).

In his quest for unity in Asia, Nehru worked with the new leaders of China to articulate a clear expression of solidarity with the peoples of Indo-China who were fighting for freedom. In June 1954, during the Geneva conference on the future of Indo-China, the Chinese premier Chou En-Lai accepted an invitation to visit India. The invitation had been extended to him by V. K. Krishna Menon, India's representative at the conference. The ensuing talks between Chou En-Lai and Nehru ended on 28 June 1954 in the signing of a joint statement on the principles on which relations between India and China were to be based. These principles, which were subsequently known as the Five Principles of Peaceful Co-Existence or Panchsheel, were: (1) mutual respect for each other's territorial integrity and sovereignty; (2) non-aggression; (3) non-interference in each other's internal affairs; (4) equality and mutual benefit; and (5) peaceful coexistence (Mohanty 2005). Parallel to this meeting of minds between Nehru and Chou En-lai, there had been a new assertiveness by the peoples of Indonesia who were maturing out of the struggles against Dutch Colonialism.

In April 1954, the Indonesian government proposed the convocation of an Asian-African conference. In December of the same year, the five prime ministers of Burma, Ceylon (Sri Lanka), India, Indonesia and Pakistan held a conference in Bogor, Indonesia, reached an agreement on convening an Asian-African conference and decided that the conference would be jointly proposed by the five countries. When the conference did meet, it captured the energies of the ongoing struggles for independence and the conference was attended by twenty-nine Asian and African countries besides the five countries mentioned above, namely, Afghanistan, Cambodia, China, Egypt, Ethiopia, the Gold Coast (Ghana), Iran, Iraq, Japan, Jordan, Laos, Lebanon, Liberia, Libya, Nepal, the Philippines, Saudi Arabia, Sudan, Syria, Thailand, Turkey, the Vietnam Democratic Republic, South Vietnam (later reunified with the Democratic Republic of Vietnam) and Yemen (Republic of Yemen).

The conference was chaired by Indonesian Prime Minister Ali Sastroamidjojo and the Indonesian President Sukarno made an opening address entitled, 'Let a New Asia and a New Africa be Born'. Recalling the anti-imperialist and militant formations that had been alive during the capitalist depression from the time of the Conference of the League against Imperialism, Sukarno declared, 'our nations and countries are colonies no more. Now we are free, sovereign and independent.... We are again masters in our own house. We do not need to go to other continents to confer.' Sukarno also warned that 'colonialism is not yet dead, so long as vast areas of Asia and Africa are unfree'. Sukarno also called for unity beyond religious differences.

There were strong pressures by Western states to seek to isolate China but the leader of the Chinese delegation, Zhou En-lai refused to be drawn into a bruising debate with China's neighbours and instead offered a conciliatory approach to the relations with the neighbors of China based on 'peaceful coexistence.'[3] In tracing the history of colonialism, Chou En-lai said that, 'the rule of colonialism in this region has not yet come to an end, and new colonialism are attempting to take the place of the old ones... He continued by noting that, 'they are clamoring openly that atomic weapons are conventional arms and are making precautions for atomic war. The people of Asia shall never forget that the first atomic bomb exploded on Asian soil and that the first man to die from experimental explosion of a hydrogen bomb was an Asian.' The Chinese prime minister directed his comments especially to the leaders of Thailand and the Philippines in declaring that the Chinese delegation came to Bandung to 'seek unity and not to quarrel... to seek common ground, not to create divergence.'

The conference had been divided into three committees, namely, political, economic and cultural; and the final communiqué outlined basic principles which included economic cooperation, cultural cooperation, human rights and self-determination, the issue of people in dependent countries, other issues, promotion of world peace and cooperation as well as the adoption of the Declaration on Promotion of World Peace and Cooperation, and listed ten principles in handling international relations. The conference reached consensus on the crucial question of independence and support for all peoples under colonial rule. It was noted that at that time, the question of colonialism in Puerto Rico was high on the agenda of Bandung and Nehru of India was firm that the movement must support decolonization everywhere. There were six African societies represented: Egypt, Ethiopia, Gold Coast (Ghana), Liberia, Libya and the Sudan. These countries formed the backbone of a new alignment which was envisaged as a counterweight to the United States and the Soviet Union.

The spirit of unity of the Asian and African people, opposing imperialism and colonialism, struggling for the defence of national independence and world peace and the promotion of friendship among the peoples as demonstrated at the conference is known as the 'Bandung Spirit'. Since that conference African activists have held on to the ideals of solidarity and cooperation that echoed from this meeting.[4]

This idea of solidarity was carried forward leading to the support for the rapid decolonization process in Africa and the nationalization of the Suez Canal in 1956. President Sukarno of Indonesia had been emboldened by the spirit of Bandung and he carried these ideas to the United Nations in 1960. He noted,

> It has been said that we live in the midst of a revolution of rising expectations. It is not so. We live in the midst of a world of rising demands. Those who were previously without freedom now demand freedom. Those who were previously without a voice now demand that their voices be heard. Those who were previously hungry now demand rice, plentifully every day. Those who were previously unlettered demand education. The whole world is a vast powerhouse of revolution, a vast revolutionary ammunition dump. No less than three-quarter of humanity is involved in this revolution of rising demands, and this is the greatest revolution since man first walked erect in a virgin and pleasant world. The success or failure of this organization will be judged by its relationship to that revolution of rising demands. Future generations will praise us or condemn us in the light of our responses to these challenges (Surkano 1960).

Sukarno did not live to see the realization of the spirit of Bandung; he was overthrown in a violent counter-revolutionary and anti-communist putsch which killed more than half a million Indonesians (Scot 1985). This military coup in Indonesia, the war against the Vietnamese people and the assassination of Patrice Lumumba in the Congo were all part of the efforts of Western Europe and the United States to destroy the national liberation project and diminish Afro-Asian solidarity. Despite these measures, after the revolution in Cuba and the expansion of the Tricontinental conference, the efforts to create the nonaligned bloc created a new force with calls during the seventies for a New International Economic Order (Prashad 2007: 214–10).

Prior to the convening of the first nonaligned meeting in Belgrade in September 1961, there emerged a new force called the OSPAA (Organization for Solidarity for the People of Africa and Asia). After the Anglo-French, Israeli war against Egypt in 1956 there had been a meeting of solidarity that had gathered in Cairo, Egypt in 1957. There were 500 delegates from thirty-five countries that met for the convening of the Afro-Asian Peoples Solidarity Organization (AAPSO). AAPSO was officially launched on 1 January 1958 with Cairo as the headquarters of this organization. One of the more overlooked outcomes of the meeting of the Afro-Asian Peoples Solidarity Conference in Egypt was the prominent role played by women, especially the sterling leadership of Egyptian women. The formation of the Afro-Asian Federation for Women was the forerunner of numerous areas of collaboration between women from the Third World that later took on a massive presence in the UN work relating to women (Prashad 2007: 57).

After this effort the Cubans extended this solidarity to include the peoples of Latin America and in 1966 called the Organization of Solidarity with the People of Asia, Africa and Latin America (Organización de Solidaridad con los Pueblos de Asia, África y América Latina), abbreviated as OSPAAAL, meeting in Havana. It was here that Amilcar Cabral delivered his important speech on liberation in Africa, 'The Weapon of Theory'.

The crucial issue for the peoples of this moment was a better quality of life. As Cabral maintained, 'Always bear in mind that people are not fighting for ideas, for the things in anyone's head. They are fighting to win material benefits, to live better and in peace, to see their lives go forward, to guarantee the future of their children.'

The NIEO and the Future of our Children

Prime Minister Nehru of India was one of the most committed of the leaders of the Third World that had come to be loosely organized in the formation called the non-aligned movement. From the outset, the non-aligned movement was conceived as a loose formation that would be based on international solidarity and building a new base for international economic relations.[5] Mahatmas Gandhi had inspired freedom fighters in many parts of the world and Nehru had worked closely with Gandhi to expel the British from India. As early as 1946, even before the full independence of India in 1947, Nehru had called for a separate identity of the former oppressed peoples. He did not envisage a new bloc and wanted the non-aligned movement to be a force for peace, decolonization and anti-racism. In his presentation at the Belgrade summit in 1961, Nehru said,

It is a strange thing that a few year ago-six, seven or eight if you like – this business of non-alignment was a rare phenomenon. A few countries here and there talked about it and other countries made fun of it, or at any rate did not take it seriously. Non-alignment? What is this? You must be on this side or that side. This was the argument. Well that argument is dead today; nobody dare say that, because the whole world of history of the last few years has shown the growing opinion, the spread of this concept of non-alignment.[6]

Nehru envisaged a strategy of cooperation that would support total independence. Gamal Abdel Nasser of Egypt echoed the same philosophical position in 1961 when he stated that, 'non-alignment means that we ought to decide what we believe in and not according to what might satisfy any particular country. It means that our policy is not attached to the policy of any other country or any big powers.'

In the spirit of Bandung there was renewed confidence among the colonized and in the early sixties the massive decolonization process was accompanied by high expectations about economic cooperation among the non-aligned countries. During the era of Nehru, Indian scholars and diplomats were very active in support of liberation, but Western planners scheming through universities and the Bretton Woods institutions worked hard to wean India from the ranks of militant anti-colonial fighters so that by the year 2012, India was the largest recipient of World Bank aid.

Although China was not a member of the non-aligned movement, the foreign ministry in China followed the deliberations of the non-aligned movement very closely and Chou En-lai strengthened the capabilities of the Chinese state to support liberation. As a leader who understood the impact of colonial domination, Chou En-lai undertook visits to the countries of Africa and Asia, including one visit of seven weeks to Africa. This was the period when China was still seeking the support of the members of the non-aligned movement to regain its seat at the United Nations as the official representative of the Chinese people, a position that had been usurped by Taiwan with the support of conservatives in the United States. The visit of President Richard Nixon to China in 1972 after secret negotiations between Henry Kissinger and the Chinese leaders provided new room for US legitimacy at a moment when the forces of liberation in Africa, Asia and Latin America were calling for the isolation of the United States. One year after the Nixon visit to China, this same administration was involved in the murderous overthrow of the leadership of the Chilean people on 11 September 1973 (Qureshi 2008). Kissinger and Nixon had feared the implications of the redistribution of wealth in Chile and the positive lessons that may have been learnt. The assassination of Salvador Allende followed the trajectory of the opposition to democratic participation and expression in the Third World. This opposition to democracy, while loudly proclaiming support for democracy and human rights, was consistent with the needs of US capital to repress working peoples throughout the world.

When the United States devalued the dollar in 1971 there was an even greater impetus among the non-aligned states as they worked to strengthen institutions within the United Nations system that would work for a New International Economic Order (Addo 1984). However, the United States and her allies within Western Europe were bent on rolling back the gains of independence and popular representation in trade unions and other forums for democracy. A. M. Babu, Samir Amin, Vijay Prashad, Archie Singham and numerous others have written extensively on the massive campaign by the United States to reverse this anti-colonial front and undermine solidarity (Singham 1977). US cultural institutions, universities and media houses were mobilized to diminish the importance of non-alignment and penetrate those classes in the non-aligned world that had ideological proclivities with US imperialism (Schiller 1992).[7] India was one target of this penetration with sustained support for the emerging capitalists in India who turned away from the social democratic ideas of Nehru (Srikant 1984). This was most manifest in many areas of military, cultural and economic relations and it is important to highlight one, in relation to India. This was the dropping of the claim that the question of the independence of Puerto Rico should be placed on the agenda of the decolonization committee of the United Nations.

The total onslaught on the ideas of independence, economic cooperation and non-alignment took many forms but was most destructive in the elimination of the leaders who wanted to make a break with the colonial order. 'The western powers were not going to accept the spirit of Bandung and non-alignment on their own free will, neither on the political level, nor on that of the economic battle. The true hatred that they kept for the Third World radical leaders of the 1960s (Nasser, Soekarno, Nkrumah, Modibo Keita…), almost all overthrown at the same time, during the years 1965–1968 – a time in which the Israeli aggression of June 1967 against Egypt, Syria, and Jordan happened – shows that the political vision of non-alignment was not accepted by the Atlantic alliance.'[8]

The 2011 invasion of Libya and the execution of Muamar Gadhafi exposed the devastating continuities of the policies of the United States to halt the move towards economic independence and economic cooperation (Campbell 2013). Yet every act of military oppression instigated even new forms of solidarity. This solidarity was at its peak in the twenty-year period 1955-75 and it was in the same moment that societies such as the Vietnamese were able to repulse the US military aggression and inspired the mobilization of millions in the global peace movement. This solidarity was also inspired by the anti-apartheid struggles in South Africa to the point that even those who were cooperating with the imperial supporters of apartheid had to pay lip service to the call for the release of Nelson Mandela and the unbanning of the African National Congress.

In every part of the non-aligned world, whether in Vietnam, Palestine, South Africa or Western Sahara, Afro-Asian solidarity was able to survive when the states of the non-aligned movement succumbed to pressures from the international financial institutions. Julius Nyerere of Tanzania had distinguished the peoples of Tanzania in their forthright support for the decolonization of Southern Africa and attempt to develop a self-reliant economic path. Elsewhere in my scholarship on the IMF and Tanzania, I have documented extensively the assault of the Western financial institutions on the experiment in Tanzania which was based on an African conception of socialism, *ujamaa* (Campbell and Stein 1989). It was Nyerere who was forthright in calling the IMF and World Bank institutions of oppression as he called for the cancellation of the Third World debt. The statement of Nyerere became legend as he intoned, 'Must we starve our children to pay our debts?' (quoted in Booker 2004).

Julius Nyerere joined with leaders of the non-aligned movement such as Fidel Castro of Cuba and Michael Manley of Jamaica to mobilize many societies in the South and in the Afro-Asian community to oppose the IMF and called for the cancellation of the odious debt. This form of Afro-Asian solidarity took deep roots in Latin America and grew into one branch of the anti-globalization campaign. Scholarly work by African intellectuals at the Economic Commission for Africa exposed the levels of capital flight from Africa under the guise of aid, while explaining that 'debt sucks the natural resources out of a country, forcing countries to become dependent on international creditors for more aid and new loans' (Jubilee USA n.d).

This theme of the future of the Children of the Afro-Asian bloc was honed by scholars such as Dr. Adebayo Adedeji, who wrote that 'Debt is tearing down schools, clinics and hospitals and the effects are no less devastating than war'(Jubilee USA n.d).

In noting that the relations between the West and Africa were a manifestation of a new kind of slavery, this international campaign outlined how the IMF and World Bank took away the sovereignty and freedom that had been won at independence. When countries are enslaved by debt they cannot improve the lives of their citizens nor gain control over their own futures. 'Every child in Africa is born with a financial burden which a lifetime's work cannot repay. The debt is a new form of slavery as vicious as the slave trade' (Jubilee USA n.d).

It is the nature of the total assault on African self-development which has led many African scholars to be cautious in using the term 'Cold War' to refer to the all-out attack against independence. In all parts of the Third World, from Vietnam to Guatemala and from Angola to Nicaragua, the poor experienced the brutal unleashing of the Cold War's anti-communist machinery. Whether it was in the wars against the peoples of Angola or the support for the racist apartheid regime in South Africa, the United States became politically and diplomatically energized as they carried out crimes of war against the peoples of the world. Mahmood Mamdani has documented the ways in which one can chart the militarization of the planet from the wars against the Vietnamese people to the current militarization that carries the label, 'War on Terror'. Mamdani wrote: '1975 was the year of American defeat in Indochina. 1975 was also the year the Portuguese empire collapsed in Africa. It was the year the center of gravity of the Cold War shifted from Southeast Asia to Southern Africa. The question was: who would pick up the pieces of the Portuguese empire, the US or the Soviet Union?' (Mamdani 2002).

As the centre of gravity of the 'Cold War' shifted, from Southeast Asia to Southern Africa, there was also a shift in US strategy. The Nixon Doctrine had been forged towards the closing years of the Vietnam War but could not be implemented at that late stage – the doctrine that 'Asian boys must fight Asian wars' – was really put into practice in Southern Africa. In practice, it translated into a US decision to harness, or even to cultivate, terrorism in the struggle against regimes it considered pro-Soviet. In Southern Africa, the immediate result was a partnership between the US and apartheid South Africa, accused by the UN of perpetrating 'a crime against humanity'. Reagan termed this new partnership 'constructive engagement'.

It is this interconnection between multiple wars in Africa and Asia that should encourage a newer generation to interrogate the scholarship from Realist scholars in China and India about new superpowers in the twenty- first century. As the United States carries out its present campaign to launch its Africa Command, it is an opportune moment for business and political leaders in Africa to reflect on the conjuncture where the militarism of the United States is no longer capable of maintaining the dominance of the IMF and US capitalism. In all parts of the Afro-Asian world, the lessons of the military and economic assault of the Triad (North America, Western Europe and Japan) are being absorbed as new relations are being fashioned. It was in East Asia where these new relationships blossomed in response to the Asian financial crisis (Chang 2002, 2010). These relationships within Asia have now placed the Asian societies at the centre of the world economy. More importantly, has been the intellectual assertiveness of these societies to reject the neoliberal approach to economic relations. Vijay Prashad in *his book Poorer Nations: A Possible History of the Global South* has been able to document the tenacity of social movements from the Third World. In the intellectual fora sponsored by the imperial states there has been the inclination to diminish the intellectual assertiveness of the societies that reject the neoliberal approach to economic relations.

ASEAN States Oppose Neoliberalism

After the spectacular cohesion of the non-aligned group in the 1970, there was a counter-offensive from the Eestern states on economic, military and cultural fronts. Culturally, the Western media and intellectuals denigrated the idea of Afro-Asian solidarity; militarily, these states attempted to halt the processes of decolonization (highlighted by the Western alliance to preserve apartheid); and, economically, assaulting autonomous economic initiatives through the International Monetary Fund (IMF) structural adjustment programmes. Scholars have subsumed these assaults as one component of neoliberalism which is essentially the reconstitution of class power by the global economic elite. David Harvey, in particular, argued that neoliberalism in its practice has not been a 'utopian project to realize a theoretical design for the reorganization of international capitalism' but a practical political project meant to restore the power of economic elites. This power has been concentrated in the financial sector in the West and it is now legend how this financial sector reproduced a form of political legitimacy by its corruption of the intellectual enterprise. In his book, *Predator Nation: Corporate Criminals, Political Corruption and the Hijacking of America,* Charles Ferguson (2012) detailed the complicity of the top intellectuals in the USA in purveying neoliberal ideas when they were compromised by their association with the banking and financial sector.

This conflict of interest between the top academics in the United States and the society as a whole had been discussed by many authors and commentators who have linked the corporate criminality to the collapse of the Western financial system. During the period after the Wall Street collapse in 2008, the political leaders of the United States were willing and ready to throw out the very same free market neoliberal principles which they promoted globally, when these principles threatened the power of the financial oligarchy. State intervention came in the form of massive bailouts for the banks. One of the intellectual proponents of the principles of neoliberalism, Alan Greenspan, had to admit that there was a 'flaw' in the free market philosophy when he testified before a Congressional Committee in the United States in October 2008 after the fall of the Lehman Brothers financial firm and the US government bailed out the financial industry (Leonhardt 2008).[9]

The societies of East Asia had learnt the lesson that neoliberalism was a practical political project meant to restore the power of economic elites during the late 1990s when the Asian financial crisis was engineered for the expansion of US imperial power in Asia. After the devastating results of the 'shock therapy' imposed on Russia and the countries of Eastern Europe, the societies of East Asia searched for levers that would release them from the former position where their currencies were tied to imperial currencies. This led to the strengthening of the Association of Southeast Asian Nations.

Malaysia, a key member of the non-aligned movement had been vigorous in the proposing of an East Asia Economic Caucus comprising the members of ASEAN as well as the People's Republic of China, Japan, and South Korea. Based on their experience with the Wall Street financiers, the political leaders of Malaysia wanted to counterbalance the growing influence of the United States in the Asia-Pacific Economic Cooperation (APEC) and in the Asian region as a whole. The ASEAN plus three proposal was also frowned upon by China which wanted to develop bilateral relations instead of multilateral relations. However, after the start of the new century with the clear decline of the United States, the importance of the ASEAN states grew and these states grasped the new role of China in the world economy. The Chinese also moved to develop multilateral relations after the financial crisis and on both sides there were moves to work for further integration under ASEAN Plus Three.

These societies sought to change the nature of how they were integrated into the global economy on terms that better supported the quality of life of their populations. These states had embarked on economic management projects that generated a rising rate of GDP growth (or exports) over a long period of time (more than a decade). Simultaneously these societies were able to obtain a higher level of GDP per capita than in other parts of the Afro-Asian World. Simultaneously, these East Asian societies strengthened local economic capabilities and deepened initiatives which could be categorized as schemes which fostered greater cooperation among Asian nations. These schemes also fostered the integration of the economies of Asian nations. In an effort to escape the Dollar Wall Street Regime (DWSR), these countries were seeking to deepen ways to strengthen their firewall to protect their economies from the continued devaluation of the US dollar. In the year of the 'Eurozone crisis' when the future of the EURO as a viable currency was fraught with uncertainty, many states were reconsidering holding their reserves in the US dollar.

The primary initiative that Asian societies used to build a firewall is that each nation took steps to build up large amounts of hard currency reserves so that they would have the financial resources to avoid ever having to be dependent on (at the mercy of) the IMF. The second initiative that the ten ASEAN nations plus Japan, China and South Korea agreed on was to deepen their cooperation with each other by pooling their financial resources into a regional pool of money which all of them could have access to if they ever faced a financial crisis again. This was the Chaing Mai Initiative (CMI). Initially when the CMI was launched, the government of the People's Republic of China (PRC) had been lukewarm its goals; but over a decade, especially after the 2007-08 Wall Street crash, the preliminary partnership that was called ASEAN plus three (viz ASEAN countries plus China, Japan and Korea) matured to the point where the ASEAN Swap Agreements have now been expanded to the Chiang Mai Initiative Multilateralization (CMIM) agreement. The CMIM set of rules with structured mechanisms for financial regionalism to work for the development of Asian bond markets. These three pillars of the new Asian economic cooperation – CMIM, Asian Bond Markets and bilateral swap agreements – mark a new stage in the international political order. In March 2012, the CMIM leaders agreed to double the size of a regional fund that aims to defend their economies against currency volatility. Though modest in international terms (from US$120 billion to $302 billion) it was one indication that countries were seeking an exit the dollar. At the Asian Development Bank (ADB) meeting on 3 May this cooperation continued to evolve to a deeper level on a wide range of fronts, all of which in total reflect the efforts by Asian societies to develop a regional financial architecture with their own institutions which again helps to create better development opportunities from the ways in which Asian nations are integrated into the global economy. In October 2013, the Chinese President Xi Jinping mooted the idea of the Asian Infrastructure Investment Bank (AIIB) as an international financial institution to provide finance to infrastructure projects in the Asia Pacific region. One year later in November 2014, the AIIB was launched in Beijing at the time of the meeting of Asian Pacific Economic Cooperation (APEC).

These measures in Asia to escape the volatility of the US financial system and the devaluations that came in the crisis management of this international financial architecture were hastening the discussion of new financial agreements in all regions of the world. From Latin America, a process of democratization broke the old political alliances with the United States and democratic governments come together to establish the Latin American Reserve Fund. The same central banks that form the kernel of the Latin American Reserve Fund have been working towards the establishment of the Bank of the South. Pushed by leaders who are claiming their voices, Latin American societies are breaking with the orthodox approaches and this was most manifest by the boldness of the leaders of Argentina in relation to the mandate of the Central Bank. The Central Bank was mandated 'to promote, to the extent of its ability and in the framework of policies established by the national government, monetary stability, financial stability, jobs and economic growth with social fairness'. When the President of Argentina, Cristina Fernández, followed by nationalizing foreign oil companies, Western commentators were worried about the demonstration effect for the other sections of the Afro-Asian world. Apart from the initiatives of President Cristina Fernández' government, the peoples of Latin America are slowly laying the groundwork for a new currency, the SUCRE. As in Asia, the Bank of the South will be one of the fundamental institutions of the Union of South American Nations that has been launched in Latin America in order to guarantee the independence of the societies of Latin America.

We have already made reference to the most coherent formation that resulted in the cooperation in the ASEAN nations. At the same time, it is worth repeating what is known: that in the face of the orientation towards socialism in China, the US and the West fought the 'Cold War' differently in the Asian countries than they did in Africa.

In order to create a counterweight to the influence of Cuba in the non-aligned movement, the United States supported governments such as Singapore, Saudi Arabia and Morocco in order to limit the influence of the ideas of socialist transformation. To counter 'communism', the US invested in countries that are now referred to as the Asian Tigers – Singapore, Taiwan, Hong Kong and South Korea. This anti-communist strategy meant that the West supported the breaking up of large landholdings and supported land redistribution programmes. At the same time, the West adopted policies which allowed Asian capitalists to copy patents, and for governments to support local industries and opened their markets to imports to help build indigenous capitalists linked to global markets. But in Africa and the Middle East, they supported killers and dictators and the likes of Jonas Savimbi; they overthrew Kwame Nkrumah; joined in the killing of Patrice Lumumba; orchestrated military coups; supported apartheid; and fuelled wars and conflicts that are to date the bane of the continent's destabilization. In short, after Vietnam, the West fought Africans militarily and economically by (a) using armed forces/violence to defeat 'nationalist' forces labelled as 'communists', and (b) using neoliberal policies, tied to foreign assistance programmes which prevented indigenous economic transformation and perpetuated colonial-based economic relationships to global markets.

China and Kissinger in the Midst of the War Against Vietnam

Even while the war against Vietnam was being waged, the United States under Richard Nixon and Henry Kissinger moved decisively to wean a section of the political leadership of the People's Republic of China into a de facto political alliance with the United States. Henry Kissinger, who described himself as an 'interlocutor' in the relations between the United States and China perfected a form of duplicity that is now called, 'strategic ambiguity'. In this process, Henry Kissinger has now written for posterity the tremendous investment that was made by the political and financial leaders in the United States to support a brand of anti-communism inside a state that was committed to socialist reconstruction (Kissinger 2011). In the ambiguous relations that ensued over the next period, both the United States and the People's Republic of China could claim to resolve a contentious issue on which the parties remain far apart, and to do so in a manner that enables each to claim obtaining some concession on it. The West claimed that this period set China on the course of 'reform' while for the Chinese, it was fulfilling the axiom of Deng Xiaoping that the Chinese should, 'Hide your capabilities, bide your time.'

From the African point of view, the Kissinger diplomatic overtures to China were being carried out at the same time as he oversaw the National Security Study Memorandum 39, which stated that the white racists were there to stay in Southern Africa and that the US should support the white minority regimes (Lockwood 1974). Kissinger and the United States was opposed to the independence of Africa and his diplomatic overtures were followed by successive US policy makers who worked with the Chinese political leadership to oppose the African National Congress in South Africa and the MPLA in Angola. There was no ambiguity when Chinese assistance was organized against African liberation in the name of weakening the Soviet Union. Western Europeans confused the questions of independence and liberation in Africa with the goals of the United States to 'constrain Soviet expansionism' (Coker 1979).

In pursuit of his goal of 'containing Soviet expansionism', Kissinger has recounted in great detail how China was enlisted in a quasi-alliance or a de facto alliance against the socialist camp, which not only contributed to the dissolution of the existing socialism in Eastern Europe but, as well, inflicted a devastating blow against national liberation and progressive movements in Angola, Afghanistan, Nicaragua, Vietnam (and Indochina generally). Boasting of this alliance between China and the USA after China had invaded Vietnam 'to teach it a lesson', Kissinger exalted,

> The war had been extremely costly to the Chinese armed forces, not yet fully recovered from the depredation of the Cultural Revolution. But the invasion served the fundamental objective: when the Soviet Union failed to respond it demonstrated the limitation of its strategic reach. From that point of view, it can be considered a turning point for the Cold war, though it was not fully understood as such at the time. The Third Vietnam war was also the high-point of Sino-American strategic cooperation during the Cold War (Kissinger 2011: 340).

Kissinger's open acknowledgment of the deceptions and subterfuge that led the US and China to become allies in support of a genocidal government in Cambodia is still not yet interrogated by international scholars. However, this military assault was only one component of the overall attempt to weaken

Afro-Asian solidarity. While the US acted militarily with China, Japan acted in the context of investments to undermine socialist transformation in Vietnam. Immediately after the Vietnamese victory over the US in 1975, the Japanese worked closely with international organizations to penetrate Vietnam to purse the strategy of depoliticaization which had been the guiding principle of foreign policy after the start of the Cold War. The Asia desired by Japan after World War II was one drawn together by economic aspirations; in other words, what Japan wanted and what the west supported was for Asia to become depoliticized through the myth of development and economic growth.[10] In the twenty-year period after the collapse of the Soviet Union, the societies of Asia moved decisively to strengthen economic cooperation. This move was intensified after the Asian financial crisis in 1997 and by the start of the twenty-first century China had begun to be integrated into a new axis of the world economy in East Asia.

While the peoples of Asia were consolidating economic cooperation, in Latin America, the rise of democratic governments led to the articulation of a new path to socialism based on Latin American history of independence. At the head of this initiative, called the Bolivarian Alternative for Latin America was the political leadership of Venezuela. With the retreat of US capital from Latin America there was intensified attention to holding on to Africa as the base for accumulation for Western capital. Professor Adebayo Adedeji (former head of the UN Economic Commission For Africa) noted that all of the home-grown plans of the Africans from the period of the Lagos Plan of Action in 1980, through to the Africa's Priority Programme for Economic Recovery 1986-90, including the African Alternative Framework For Structural Adjustment (1989), the African Charter for Participation and Development, as well as the African Union were opposed. In many instances, they were sabotaged directly by the international financial institutions and, to a great extent by the leaders of the USA and the European Union. Adedeji drew attention to the fact that 'all of the plans for self-reliant development in Africa had been opposed, undermined, and dismissed by the Bretton Woods institutions and Africans were thus impeded from exercising the basic and fundamental right to making decisions about their future.'

The challenges of Africans vis-à-vis the Bretton Woods Institutions were supported by the new energy of China that became vigorous in its strengthening of relations with Africa. This new turn in international politics challenged Africans and Asian activists to reconceptualize the ideas and forms of politics that had guided the thinking at Bandung. These challenges required even more understanding of what was going on inside of China.

The Economic Transformation of China

It is now possible in the midst of the worst depression since 1929 to re-evaluate the ideas and policies of capitalist development and socialist transformation of the last century. Conceptions of reconstruction from the International Monetary Fund (IMF) and the International Bank for Reconstruction and Development (IBRD) have reinforced the underdevelopment and exploitation of the peoples of Africa, Asia and Latin America. Slowly, the peoples of Asia have been making a break with the neoliberal ideas of the US and the rapid growth of the ASEAN economies now points to the reality that state intervention for economic planning is a superior form of economic management. In Africa, where the structural adjustment policies of the IMF rolled back the gains of independence, the conditions of the peoples have deteriorated by every index of quality of life. This deterioration can be compared to the qualitative transformations inside of China.

Since the successful socialist revolution of 1949 and the coming to power of the Chinese Communist Party (CCP), the Chinese peoples have escaped the worst ravages of the capitalist depression. The impressive economic growth rates in China have prompted differing interpretations on the foundations for the doubling of the size of the Chinese economy every eight years. Between 1978 and 2005, China's economic output, as measured by real gross domestic product GDP, grew 9.6 per cent per year.

Between 1981 and 2005, an estimated 600 million Chinese people moved out of poverty. This growth has led to a substantial increase in real living standards and a marked decline in poverty. Between 1981 and 2005, the proportion of China's population living on less than $1.25/day is estimated to have fallen from 85 to 15 per cent, meaning that roughly 600 million people were taken out of poverty (Shah 2011).

In 1949, 89 per cent of China's population lived in the countryside, with agriculture accounting for about 60 per cent of total economic output. The backbone of China's economy, agriculture and industry, together employ more than 70 per cent of China's labour force and account for over 60 per cent of the country's GDP. Beyond these empirical facts of the impressive growth there is a great difference in scholary analysis on the foundations of this economic transformation. One Canadian publication summed up the economic dynamism of China in this way,

> Chinese firms have positioned themselves to exploit China's comparative advantage as the final stage in sophisticated global value chains producing computers, sports equipment, clothing, household fixtures and a wide range of other products. Understanding China's role in these global production networks is critical to understanding China's emergence as an economic power. The popular image of China as the manufacturing center of the world is thus misleading.

Instead, China has become an integral part of a much more complicated reality that involves leading firms in North America, Europe, and Japan, resource firms all over the world, manufacturers of components in the more advanced economies of East Asia such as Korea, Taiwan, and Malaysia, and final assembly in China, Vietnam, and other countries in East Asia. Chinese leaders have now concluded that their success in positioning China as the point of final assembly in an integrated East and Southeast Asian manufacturing system is no longer the key to future development. They are now trying to reposition the country so that it can create a capacity for indigenous innovation, pursue scientific development, develop its own technologies and industries, and bring further inland the benefits of industrialization. If the past thirty years are anything to go by, these goals are likely to be reached sooner rather than later (Hart 2012).

By the end of 2011, the foreign-exchange reserves of China reached US$ 3.2 trillion. This was an unprecedented turn of events in the annals of the international economic rebalancing (Chinability 2011). This impressive economic transformation has been met with hostility in many parts of the Western world with increased commentaries of the nature of the international system.

When China Rules the World

Martin Jacques (2009), author of *When China Rules the World* argued to the European readers of his work that, 'History is passing our country and our continent by. Once we were the centre of the world, the place from where power, ideas and the future emanated. If we drew a map of the world, Europe was at its centre. That was how it was for 200 years. No more. The world is tilting on its axis in even more dramatic style than when Europe was on the rise. We are witnessing the greatest changes the world has seen for more than two centuries. We are barely aware of the fact. And therein lies the problem' (Jacques 2012). From the point of view of Martin Jacques, the problem for Europeans was their view that economic development was associated with stages of human history that Europe had passed through to arrive at what was called in Europe, 'the Enlightenment'. The intellectual orientation of the European scholarship from both the right and the left has been to associate development with European stages of growth.

Martin Jacques' admonition for Europeans to take a fresh look at China is more positive than the more hostile economists who argue that China is manipulating its currency and that pressures should be mounted so that the Chinese currency is revalued (Bergsten et al 2008). This chorus of the currency manipulation of the Chinese is echoed by other hostile writers who write on 'How China is colonizing Africa and threatening the American way of life' (Leeb 2011; Navarro and Autry 2011). These hostile books and articles focus on corruption, environmental degradation, inequalities, uncertainty, and other social ills that are placed on the shoulders of a 'totalitarian' communist party. In the most recent political skirmishes inside the Communist Party of China, Western commentators have been quite ready to diminish the achievements of the transformation by pointing to 'The Secret World of China's Communist Rulers' (McGregor 2010). Within China itself, the generation of leaders who had been trained under Chou En-lai has given over to a new class that looks to the West for intellectual leadership and has internalized the ideas of Realism in international relations. Henry Kissinger has written approvingly of this new stratum within China, and these forces reproduce themselves by sending their children to institutions of higher learning in North America and Western Europe.[11]

The fact that these students have the requisite disposable income to be able to pay fees in the United States was one indication of the growing inequalities inside of China. In 2011, China was home to the second largest number of billionaires and in November counted one million millionaires (Balfour 2011). Though negligible in numbers, in relation to the rest of the 1.3 billion persons, this new class of millionaires was becoming a pole of wealth and conspicuous consumption, belying the socialist heritage of China. One writer commented, 'Between these top party functionaries along with the new rich noveau riche people and the rest, the gap has continuously widened: the richest families (i.e., the top 10%) had 65 times the income of the poorest (the lowest 10%)' (Wu 2010). In 2011, China leapfrogged Japan to become the world's second-largest economy, a title Japan had held for more than 40 years.

The interpretation of this rapid transformation has drawn differing ideas about the real meaning of this economic development and change. From within China itself, the present leadership has opted for a political platform of 'harmony' with recourse to Confucian principles as the basis of state legitimation (Dotson 2011). As reported by US officials who were studying the deployment of the principles of 'harmonious' development, The newfound praise for Confucius is tied closely to the Party's official narrative of a 'Harmonious Society'. This propaganda theme emphasizes: the Party's benevolent concern for the welfare of the common man; an (at least nominal) effort to balance growth more evenly between China's haves and have-nots; and, above all, the clearly implied responsibility of China's citizens not to challenge CCP rule. In this political environment, the Confucian emphasis on ethical behavior and loyalty to the existing political order has made the Chinese government a belated convert to Confucian philosophy – or at least, it would very much like for its citizens to internalize selected aspects of Confucian philosophy. As stated by Dr. Cheng Li, a scholar of Chinese politics at the Brookings Institution, '[Confucianism is] such a big basket you can select whatever you want. They will ask people to behave appropriately, not too aggressive, not use violence and don't pursue revolution' (Dotson 2011: 6).

Even while the political leadership was proposing 'harmonious development' and the establishment of Confucius Institutes, there was one section of the Chinese intelligentsia who were calling for a more confrontational foreign policy. One book in particular, *Unhappy China – The Great Time, Grand Vision and Our Challenges*, argued that China has no choice but to become a superpower. This call for China to be a superpower meant that there are some Chinese intellectuals who are not making the distinction between imperial states and oppressed nations. In the past, the position of the leaders of China was that China represented a core section of the South and was a 'developing country'. This is especially the case in the negotiations of international meetings. In 2011 during the United Nations Climate Change Conference (COP17) meeting in Durban, South Africa, and the context of international negotiations of global warming, China's political leaders positioned it as a developing country and sought alliances with societies from the global South to resist the pressures from Europe and the USA that because of its impressive economic growth, China should be classified as a developed country. In the same week that the government of China issued its White Paper on Climate Change, Martin Khor, Executive Director of the South Centre in Geneva wrote an op-ed in the main English language newspaper, *China Daily*, under the heading, 'Is China still a developing nation?' Khor answered in the affirmative (Khor 2011).

Here was another case of ambiguity. For certain international negotiations, the Chinese political leadership would draw from its political capital with the anti-globalization centres such as the South Centre in Geneva while in its universities the Realist views of military strength and superpower dominate. The language in the books by sections of the intelligentsia is very different from the official position articulated at the meetings between China and other societies of the Afro-Asian bloc.

It was in Latin America where the legacies of Afro-Asian solidarity had proclaimed for socialism. In Latin America and other parts of the world that had been in the past dominated by Western imperialism, there is an expectation that the planet will be moving from a uni-polar world to one of cooperation. The Cuban Revolution continues to hold out the promise of an alternative to the North American form of capitalism and has been one source of support for the radical wing of the Afro-Asian Bloc. Latin American societies that have declared their opposition to imperialism of all forms are taking the lead to establish institutions such as the Bank of the South to de-link from the imperialist financial institutions. Bolivia and Venezuela established very robust relations with China based on mutual respect and cooperation. Brazil stands out in this region as a state on the rise but for millions of African descendants and indigenous peoples, the fact that Brazil has overtaken the United Kingdom as the sixth largest economy has not been of any comfort in relation to their quality of life. The anti-racist struggles of Latin America were heightened at the World Conference against Racism in Durban in 2001 where the spirit of Bandung brought back the issues of racism, xenophobia and intolerance to the forefront of international politics. This area of the Bandung period has been resisted by many governments in the South and societies such as India opposed the UN conference against racism in their rush to hold on to the obsolete caste system in the twenty-first century.

The Indian bourgeoisie and its intellectual defenders continue to look to the United States and Western Europe at a moment when the current deep and multi-faceted capitalist crisis is being exploited by extreme right-wing and neoliberal forces. These intellectuals from the BRICS societies who aspire to reproduce the European stages of development do not grasp the interconnections between the xenophobic sentiments in Europe and old conceptions of white supremacy. Acts of discrimination and racist violence are multiplying throughout Europe and questions about economic growth cannot be separated from issues of free movement of peoples and the strengthening of the International Labour Organization to protect workers everywhere. Thus far, the traditional left has supported the anti-racist struggles but in this era of the depression this international solidarity requires a more vigorous expression.

Because of the long traditions of socialist and social democratic scholarship in Western Europe, there has been robust discussion on the meaning of the political directions in the emerging nations, especially China. Inside Europe, the changes in China are being followed by the officials of the European Union. Leaders such as the former President of France called upon China to bail out Europe. As the *New York Times* commented during the period of financial uncertainty in the Eurozone countries, 'Why China Should Bail Out Europe'.

> Indeed, the call by President Nicolas Sarkozy of France this week to President Hu Jintao of China, seeking support for the European Financial Stability Facility, could represent a major change in the global landscape: the consolidation of China's economic dominance at the expense of the status quo powers – the United States and Europe (Subramanian 2011b).

The same commentators from institutes such the Petersen Institute urge the Chinese to support the IMF without a real change in the voting power and direction of the IMF.

In Western Europe where the centre of Anglo-American media gives Western intellectuals a privileged voice in shaping international opinions, there is a constant stream of books highlighting the weaknesses of the

socialist foundations of Chinese society. Jonathan Fenby's book, *Tiger Head,
Snake Tails: China today, how it got there and where it is heading,* reproduced the
liberal views on the limits of Chinese transformation (Fenby 2012). Other
British writers who believe that Chinese citizens should forget their 300
years of history and internalize the ideas of the European Enlightenment
arrogate the right to educate the Chinese on the need for 'liberal democracy'.
Will Hutton in his book, *The Writing on the Wall: China and the West in the 21st
Century,* warned the Chinese that it the next century is going to be Chinese,
it will be only because China embraces the economic and political pluralism
of the West in general, and our Enlightenment institutions in particular. 'The
rule of law, the independence of the judiciary, the freedom of the press, the
scientific and research processes in independent universities, or the very idea
of representative, accountable, checked and balanced government – all these
flowed from the great intellectual, philosophic and political wellspring that we
call the Enlightenment' (Hutton 2007).

One of the most challenging questions for scholars in the twenty-first
century is to be able to grasp the reality that the two wings of the European
Enlightenment (Adam Smith and Jean Jacques Rousseau) internalized the
Newtonian ideas of separation and compartmentalization. This Newtonian
paradigm of lower and higher stages was reproduced in versions of Marxism
that sought to denude Marxism of its revolutionary content. Hence, within
these wings of liberal thought there is very little understanding of the
possibility of a leap that transcends the stages that Europe went through.
These sterile renditions of Marxism can be found among sections of the
Latin American left and the last remnants of the European Marxists. Perry
Anderson one of the holdovers from Europe and of the *New Left Review*
argued, 'If the twentieth century was dominated, more than by any other
single event, by the trajectory of the Russian Revolution, the twenty-first will
be shaped by the outcome of the Chinese Revolution.' Marxists and non-
Marxists have weighed in on this debate on the meaning of the Chinese
revolution noting that Anderson did not distinguish between transformation
within socialism and the modernization project of international capitalism.
Other writers within the New Left were not as ambivalent on the content of
'The Chinese Road: Cities on the Transition to Capitalism'. Richard Walker
and Daniel Buck stated clearly that the revolution in China was a revolution
on the road to capitalism or 'capitalism with Chinese characteristics'. These
authors examined the commodification of land in China, the growth of an
internal market along with the strength of the capitalist classes within the
Chinese Communist Party.

From Africa, Samir Amin more than fifteen years ago pointed out the
reality by asking whether China was evolving toward a stabilized form of

capitalism. This is itself a contradiction in so far as there has never been a stabilized form of capitalism. Capitalism is prone to crisis and this current crisis is creating the conditions for polarization of social classes within China and the political choices being made in Chinese foreign policy beyond the charade of 'strategic ambiguity'. It is here where the Chinese are faced with the choice between socialist transformations of deepening integration into the world capitalist system. Amin had argued that,

> The Chinese ruling class has chosen to take a capitalist approach, if not since Deng, at least after him. Yet it does not acknowledge this. The reason is that its legitimacy is rooted in the revolution, which it cannot renounce without committing suicide. The real plan of the Chinese ruling class is capitalist in nature and "market socialism" becomes a shortcut whereby it is possible to gradually put in place the basic structures and institutions of capitalism while minimizing friction and difficulties during the course of the transition to capitalism...

> My central question is this: is China evolving toward a stabilized form of capitalism? Or is China's perspective still one of a possible transition to socialism? I am not asking this question in terms of the most likely "prediction." I am asking it in altogether different terms: what inconsistencies and struggles have emerged in China today? What are the strengths and weaknesses of the approach adapted (to a large extent capitalist in fact)? What advantages do the (at least potentially socialist) anticapitalist forces have? Under what conditions can the capitalist approach triumph and what form of more or less stabilized capitalism could it produce? Under what conditions could the current moment be deflected in directions that would become a (long) stage in the (even longer) transition to socialism? (Amin 2005).

Seven years after writing this, Samir Amin was even more explicit on the path of peripheral capitalism which implied, 'a barbaric exploitation of workers that recalls the nineteenth century; an ecological disaster' and those features of industrialization which emanated from the focus on 'the development of the productive forces'. This author will agree with the assessment which argued that,

> The future of China remains uncertain. The battle of socialism in this respect has not yet been won. But neither has it been yet lost. In my opinion, as I have already tried to show above, it will not be lost until the day when the Chinese system renounces the right to land for all its peasants. Until then, the political and social struggles can sway the course of evolution. The ruling political class directs its efforts to controlling these struggles solely through wielding its bureaucratic dictatorship. Fragments of this class also consider circumventing the emergence of the bourgeoisie by the same means. The bourgeoisie and middle classes as a whole have not decided to fight for an 'American style' democracy. With the exception of a few ideologists, these classes accept the 'Asian style' autocratic model without difficulty, provided that it allows the deployment of their consumer appetites. The popular classes fight on the grounds of defense of their economic

and social rights. Will they manage to unite their fights, devise suitable forms of organization, produce a positive alternative approach and define the contents and means of a democracy capable of serving it? (Amin 2011c).

The one area that was excluded by Amin was the possibility of the strengthened solidarity between the popular classes in Africa and the popular classes in China. In the final section we will draw out how the imminent challenges to US financial dominance is creating conditions for greater solidarity between countries of the Afro-Asian Bloc.

Spirit of Bandung and the BRICS Bank

Since the financial crisis in 2008 and the deepening depression, it has become clearer every day that it may only be a matter of time before the US dollar gets replaced as the main currency in international trade. This reality is so evident that in all parts of the world there are pressures for different governments to find an alternative to the US dollar as a reserve currency. In this chapter, we started out with the implications of the currency swap agreements that have been initiated among the countries of Asia. In 2012 the countries of Brazil, Russia, India, China and South Africa agreed to establish a Development Bank (Campbell 2012).

At the end of the fourth BRICS summit where the leaders met in New Delhi, India, on 29 March 2012 under the theme, 'BRICS Partnership for Global Stability, Security and Prosperity', the leaders signed two pacts to stimulate trade in their local currencies and agreed on a joint working group to set up a South-South Development Bank that will raise their economic weight globally. The five leaders issued the 50-point Delhi Declaration declaring their intention to further strengthen 'our partnership for common development and take our cooperation forward on the basis of openness, solidarity, mutual understanding and trust.'

The decision by these societies to establish a 'development bank' was one more indication of the erosion of the power of the Bretton Woods Institutions. Throughout the countries of Africa, Asia and Latin America the vigour of Chinese investments has had a fundamental impact in relation to infrastructures (roads, rail, ports, information and telecommunications, air transport, energy and power generation, canals and water management). Already, the Export Import Bank of China and the China Development Bank spend more money in the developing world than the World Bank. The *Financial Times* reported that in 2009 China spent over US $108 billion while the World Bank spent US $100.3 billion. This shift in the source of development funds is most explicit in Africa where according to information from the Exim bank of China, in 2011 China invested more than US $35 billion. According to He

Wenping of the Chinese Academy of Social Sciences, 'China overtook the United States as Africa's largest trade partner in 2009, and the bilateral trade volume surged from $10 billion in 2000 to more than $160 billion in 2011' (Wenping 2011).

Slowly, this economic clout of China has served to break the dominance of Western European capital but the deformed patterns of extraction of resources have not changed. It is in Africa where the recent histories of the anti-apartheid struggles enthuse new forms of organizing which is inspiring a new revolutionary era. It is significant it was the home of the Afro-Asian solidarity movement where the Egyptian revolution of February 2011 has pointed to another possibility in the forms of solidarity for the nations that were once dominated by imperialism. The challenges and opportunities of the new revolutionary moment as well as the possibilities of economic cooperation in the Afro-Asian world are similar to the challenges of the 1970s when OPEC first appeared on the international stage. Then, Perez Alfonzo, the Venezuelan diplomat who was one of the founding members of OPEC wrote two years before his death,

> I am an ecologist first of all. I have always been an ecologist first of all. Now, I am not interested in oil anymore. I live for my flowers. Still OPEC is a good instrument for the Third World. It just has not been used properly (quoted in Prashad 2007: 190).

Here Alfonzo was confronting the realities of where states in the Third World found themselves at a particular stage of human history. These challenges are also present in Africa as the new explorations for hydrocarbons bring African societies and peoples into the orbit of the oil exploration countries, especially those from Third World societies such as Brazil, India, Malaysia, and China. In a recent book, *To Cook a Continent,* African scholars have been warning about the dangers and consequences of the destructive forms of extraction of resources from Africa. The proposed BRICS Bank will be put on notice that Africans will be vigilant to see that other 'emerging nations' operate in ways that respect Africans as humans. African workers are organizing against capitalists from BRICS that seek to reproduce low wage environments with the absence of the rights of workers. Africans will not replace plunder from Western capitalists by new extractive capitalists from the East and from Brazil. Importantly, African progressives will not support another financial institution that facilitates capital flight from Africa. BRICS can move decisively to ensure that it is committed to the principle of the return of stolen assets and reparations.

Afro-Asian Solidarity in the Era of the Bio-economy

The very success of China as an industrialized state and an economy which registered the fastest transformation holds the seeds of the catastrophic conditions of environmental degradation. Environmental degradation is now so severe that suffocating smog blocks traffic on major highways and transportation arteries routinely in the major urban areas of China. The right to breathe in China is now as important as the right to live in the cities. It is widely known that emissions of sulphur dioxide from coal and fuel oil, which can cause respiratory and cardiovascular diseases as well as acid rain, are increasing even faster than China's economic growth. Major publications of environmental groups can reel off the figures of environmental destruction in China: over 500 million without access to clean drinking water, rampant deforestation, sixteen of the world's most polluted lakes, acid rain over two-thirds of the Chinese territory, 58 per cent of the land arid and semi-arid, the massive use of coal in Chinese industry, and so on and on. This information on environmental degradation is now reinforced by the reality that China is the top greenhouse gas emitting country, wish is not only a health problem for the Chinese people but also for its neighbours. Non-governmental organs and grassroots movements in China are at the forefront of challenging the mantra of economic growth that is at the base of this deepening destruction of the earth.

It is in the context of the environmental challenges where the Chinese popular classes are being called upon to join the environmental justice movements of the global South which are calling for a fundamental change in the priorities of the international system.[12] In the past year, prior to the COP 17 meeting in South Africa, the government of China attempted to preempt major struggles over climate change by coming out with a White paper on Climate Change in November 2011 (Peoples Republic of China White Paper 2011). The White Paper advanced legally binding targets for the next five years. These included a 17 per cent cut in carbon emissions, a 16 per cent decrease in energy use per unit of GDP, and a goal of lifting non-fossil-fuel energy usage from its current level of 8.6 per cent, to 11.4 per cent of total energy consumption.

If the relationship between Henry Kissinger and the Chinese leaders were a reflection of 'strategic ambiguity' this White Paper exposed even further the extent to which this 'ambiguity' has trapped the political leadership into an ideological cul de sac. The White Paper on Climate Change reflected the real contradictions within Chinese society with its neoliberal discourse on carbon trading and other ideas on 'Clean Development Mechanism' and carbon offsetting. The neoliberal discourse on clean development mechanisms will provide opportunities for vested interests to control the pace and nature of the projects that are supposed to be designed to tackle climate change.

This requirement for clarity on the paths of environmental transformation in the twenty-first century has also been highlighted by the militarization of the competition for fossil fuels. By 2012, the Chinese oil company, Petro China, overtook Exxon Mobil as the biggest producer of oil and gas. For years, Exxon Mobil was the largest publicly traded company in the US and the biggest producer of oil and natural gas in the world. This competition from a state-owned entity in China is intensifying anti-Chinese sentiments in the West at a historic moment when new forms of energy production were on the horizon. Leading think tanks and foreign policy centres such as the Council on Foreign Relations in the United States have been speculating on the global push for more oil resources and the logic behind Chinese engagement with Africa. Alessi and Hansen (2012) argue,

> China's booming economy, which has averaged an annual growth rate of 9 percent for the last two decades, requires massive levels of energy to sustain that growth. Though China relies on coal for most of its energy needs, it is the second-largest consumer of oil in the world behind the United States. Once the largest oil exporter in Asia, China became a net importer of oil in 1993. The International Energy Agency's World Energy Outlook 2011 projects that China will become the world's largest net importer of oil by 2020. The report estimates the country's net imports for 2011 at nearly five million barrels per day, a number it says will climb to around thirteen million by 2035.

The militaristic planning that flows from these forecasts perpetuates the ideas of the international system as a conflict zone well into the twenty-first century. This author is arguing here that it is a fool's paradise to consider militarizing control and access to energy resources in the twenty-first century because the promise of fusion and twenty-first century technologies will fundamentally alter the modes of production and consumption.

All energy that can be effectively harvested and used by living organisms comes in the form of light, heat, or chemical energy. Of these, the primary sources are light, originating exclusively from the sun, and heat, primarily resulting from accumulated absorption of sunlight by the atmosphere on earth. These primary energies nourish and sustain the planet's creatures, and all fundamental organic processes were derived from them (Bradford 2008: 24).

China has invested heavily in solar energy and other forms of alternative energy resources and since 2009, the top leadership of China has shown a clear commitment towards building a Green Economy. In his book on the *Solar Revolution*, Travis Bradford deepened the analysis of the quantum changes that will be generated by a return to renewable energy sources. There are two organisms that have stored solar energy and these are plants and animals. Plants absorb their energy directly from the sun through a process of photosynthesis and animals absorb their energy from eating a combination of plants or other animals. Because plants and animals adapt to specific local conditions over millions of years, these conditions provided the conditions for a wide variety of robust and complex ecological systems.

Most of the countries of the non-aligned movement and of the Bandung spirit are located in the South where the future of solar energy has tremendous potential for transforming the future of economic relations. This solar resource is amplified by the fact that biomass resources are plentiful along the equatorial region. Biomass refers to 'materials that are biological in origin, including organic material (both living and dead) from above and below ground, for example, trees, crops, grasses, tree litter, roots, and animals and animal waste'. Biologists are now grasping the real meaning of 'power plants' as the genetic materials of Africa are being viewed as an unlimited source to feed the energy sources of the planet in the twenty-first century. These power plants form the foundation of what is called biomass resources. Biomass contains stored energy from the sun, and because of the abundance of this energy source there is a new thrust to harness the biomass resources in what is termed the bioeconomy.

In all parts of the formerly colonial societies the states and peoples are developing the technological expertise that will break the dominance of the former imperial states in the era of the bioeconomy. There is an understanding that the pace of urbanization and the coal-driven industrialization cannot continue much longer in China. More importantly, the triple disaster in Japan in March 2011, in which the Fukushima Daiichi nuclear plant was struck by huge earthquake and tsunami, sharpened the urgency of developing new energy resources beyond fossil fuels, nuclear power and conventional sources. For a long time the Japanese held the view that nuclear power was an alternative to fossil fuel but this triple disaster has confirmed the position of Hermann Scheer who wrote that, 'Nuclear energy technology has created limitless potential for destruction; it is increasingly clear that keeping this potential under control is beyond the power of governments' (Scheer 2006: 37). In the face of this limitless potential for destruction from nuclear power and the realization of the contribution of fossil fuels to global warming, there is research and development into renewable energy sources such as solar energy, wind energy, biomass energy, geothermal energy, tidal energy and hydro power.

To this end one can see the massive investments in research into renewable energy resources in all parts of the world, especially China. This investment and the ambitious plans to achieve energy efficiency in China come at a moment when it was announced that China has been able to develop one of the fastest computers in the world. China now boasts more than seventy-four of the fastest super computers and the technology will enable China to move in the direction of putting on stream clean energy technologies. However, this chapter argues that the question of cleaning up the environment cannot be resolved as a technical question, but one linked to political struggles. It is here where the progressive forces must take courage from the new alliances that were built between the least developed countries, the Africa group, the peoples of West Asia and the Latin American societies that are grouped in the Bolivarian Alternative for Latin America. It is in the midst of these major social and economic changes where the ideas of 'peaceful coexistence' and 'peaceful development' will be tested. Samir Amin has inspired the future of this alliance with his appeal for audacity to remove the power of the Western states and monopolies in international politics. It is from Africa where there is clarity on the tasks ahead. Reflecting on the challenges and opportunities, Samir Amin called for 'Audacity and more audacity' His essay was the theoretical guide to support mobilization of the youths in the streets of Cairo, Madrid, Athens and Wisconsin. In calling for the socialization of the 'ownership of the monopolies', Amin spelt out how 'the historical circumstances created by the implosion of contemporary capitalism requires the radical left, in the North as well as the South, to be bold in formulating its political alternative to the existing system'. While economists in North America continuously complain that the barons of Wall Street socialize losses while privatizing profits, Samir Amin spelt out in great details for citizens of all continents,

> the alternative social project should be to reverse the direction of the current social order (social disorder) produced by the strategies of monopolies, in order to ensure maximum and stabilized employment, and to ensure decent wages growing in parallel with the productivity of social labor. This objective is simply impossible without the expropriation of the power of monopolies (Amin 2011c).

If one reads an economist such as Samir Amin and others who are progressive (in the US context) such as Robert Reich, one can see that Amin is drawing from the depth of the spirits of Afro-Asian solidarity and the traditions of Bandung. The challenge of the left is to understand the outline of the alternative social project and translate this into practical day-to-day programmes so that wherever one lives and works one should not succumb to the Afro-pessimism that calls for more 'aid' and 'assistance' to Africa. Chou En-lai fought against Han chauvinism and supported liberation and independence with equality for all. The people of China will decide whether they are moving towards modernization and catching up and surpassing the major capitalist powers or building an alternative economic system that can reclaim the earth and start the long road to human emancipation.

Conclusion

When President Sukarno of Indonesia called for a 'New Asia and a New Africa' to be reborn, he was anticipating the new energies of the emancipation movement that was then sweeping the world. In that historic moment of Bandung 1955, Sukarno had said,

Irresistible forces have swept two continents. The mental, spiritual and political face of the whole world has been changed and the process is still not complete. There are new conditions, new concepts, new problems and new ideals abroad in the world. Hurricanes of national awakening and reawakening have swept over land, shaking it, changing it, changing it for the better (quoted in Prashad 2007: 33).

Western Europe and North America had invested in a mode of economic organization that did not want a new Asia and a new Africa. Under the leadership of US capitalists, there was an effort to stop this awakening. Sukarno was overthrown, Patrice Lumumba was assassinated and the wars in Asia held back the capability of the new birth. Despite the intense military, cultural, economic and ideological wars, the peoples of the South resisted, fought and have surged in the twenty-first century. In this new surge, the peoples of East Asia, especially China, Japan and Korea have created a new axis for the international economic order. This new axis has opened new tensions in the international system. In this axis, there are a number of possible openings but Western capital has zeroed in on what is called the Singapore model as the basis for the future survival of Western capitalism in Asia.

Lee Kuan Yew (former prime minister of Singapore) symbolizes the link between the model of authoritarian accumulation built on an intellectual infrastructure that inspires coercion and fear. From this well of thinking there are scholars who now write on the need for closer US-Chinese relations. One author proposed a new term Chinmerica to highlight the interdependence of the United States and China, especially the reality that it is the Chinese government that is the principal holder of US Treasury bonds. China has emerged as the largest creditor to the United States when the world economy was on the brink of collapse. In reality, when one stripped away the language of 'complex cooperation' it could be said that the Chinese Communist Party was the safety valve for the US capitalist classes. This new changed situation was most evident in 2009 when Lee Kuan Yew visited Washington and praised China for moving in the direction of Singapore in relation to the model of economic development. Singapore now sits at the crossroads between the US military projections in Asia and the nationalism of overseas Chinese which is now being harnessed by the social classes in China who admire the Singapore model.

Despite the dependence of the US on Chinese purchases of US bonds, the jingoistic impulses in the US ensured that there was a steady stream of anti-Chinese statements from politicians who declared that the undervalued Chinese currency had a negative impact on US jobs. Anti-communism, chauvinism and racist sentiments provided a combustible situation that required clear and sensible leadership in the USA and China. For the working peoples of the US, opposition to racism and militarism was necessary in order to challenge the militarization of the society in the midst of a capitalist depression.

The tensions associated with the new military postures have been intensified by the crisis of Western capitalism with the deployment of NATO as the principal force for the projection of the power of Western capitalism. The limits of this projection have been revealed in Afghanistan and in Iraq. From Africa there is the clear evidence of the military engagement of Western capital; the recent 'humanitarian' deployment in Libya sharpened the need for unity and clarity inside Africa on future engagement with the international centres of power. African activists and thinkers have drawn from the rich history of struggles and are now inspired by the revolutionary openings in Africa where there is a new *African awakening*. In this awakening, this scholar has commented on the implications for new forms of politics and the ideas that can hasten the transformation of Africa. I have advanced the ideas of *Ubuntu* and sharing as elements of a twenty-first century ethos that arose directly out of the struggles against apartheid.

The former prime minister of India, J. Nehru, was an opponent of apartheid and colonialism. His vision was clear that there cannot be peace in the world when half of the world is free and half is enslaved. Nehru was emphatic that 'freedom is for all, peace is for the entire world'. Since the era of Nehru and Chou En-lai, there has come a new generation of leaders and thinkers who have turned their backs on the spirit of Bandung and yearn for recognition as superpowers.

Throughout the era of the expansion of neoliberal capitalism, the peoples of Latin America carried forward the ideas and principles of Bandung and came out with the call for 'another world'. This call was nurtured by numerous social movements that benefited from the radical traditions of the non-aligned movement and the tenacity of the Cuban Revolution in resisting US blockades and mischief-making. After fifty years of seeking to isolate Cuba, it is the US that is now isolated in the Americas with the rise of states such as Bolivia, Ecuador and Venezuela calling for the building of twenty-first century socialism.

These new calls for socialist transformation are occurring at moments of dynamic technological change when it is now possible to conceptualize new forms of organizing economic and social life. Within the progressive social justice movements there is a network that is associated with *The Right to the City: Social Justice and the Fight for Public Space* (Mitchell 2003). However, some of the activists within this movement have not paid equal attention to the conditions of more than five billion citizens who continue to make their livelihood from agricultural production (Amin 2004). The future of agriculture and the forms of ownership in the agricultural sector are issues that demand urgent attention so that the promise of the twenty-first century is not one of a new scramble for land and resources and the deepening of capitalism in the Third World. He Wenping of the Chinese Academy of Social Sciences (CASS) has called for a new research agenda and the deployment of Chinese 'soft power'. Her scholarship in now leaning in a direction where there is engagement between Chinese scholars and African scholars and this call is an important direction that can be supported with concrete relations between scholars and thinkers who want to escape the dominance of the European conceptions of development. Thus far, Chinese social scientists have stood aloof from the platforms of the South-South solidarity that has been refined in the context of the anti-globalization movements. After years of building peoples movements on many fronts from Port Alegre in Brazil there is now a clear platform for Afro-Asian Solidarity. New networks for peace, environmental justice, labour rights and the rights of women have converged into the South South Peoples Solidarity Forum. In their self-description they maintained,

> South South Peoples Solidarity is a platform of progressive social organizations, movements and individuals from Africa, Asia, the Caribbean and Latin America striving for a world of peace, security, equality, dignity and human-centered sustainable development. It aims at furthering exchanges of information and experience among its members, promoting joint researches on people's alternatives to neo-liberal globalization and facilitating networking for joint actions and progress on alternatives. The platform is open to all progressive organizations, movements and individuals from Africa, Asia, the Caribbean and Latin America for strengthening South-South people's solidarity in the common struggle for justice, peace, security, national independence and peoples' sovereignty, democracy and social progress, for a better world for all.[13]

> Samir Amin has not only called for audacity in conceptualizing new paths forward but he has also outlined a clear understanding of solidarity in the twenty-first century based on democratization. He maintained that:

> > Democratization is a process which could not be reduced to a static and definitive formula, like the one evoked by 'representative democracy' (multiparty-ism, election, human rights). Democratization – synonym of people's power – concerns all aspects of social life, and not exclusively the management of its politics. It concerns all relations between individuals, within the family, in places of work, in their relations with the economic, administrative and

political decision-makers. These relations are both individual and collective (class relations which are by nature unequal in the capitalist society, founded on the private appropriation of the means of production by a minority, excluding the people). Those limits are limits of democracy – whenever it exists – in capitalism. Democratization implies that one surpasses those limits, and thereby going beyond capitalism along the road of building the socialist alternative (Amin, n.d).

I agree with the proposition that democracy-building at all levels of social reality constitutes the objective of democratic and progressive people's movements concerned and associated with the new forms of solidarity of the twenty-first century. Throughout this chapter, this author has drawn attention to the fundamental changes that have occurred in the past thirty years. Within the corridors of power in the West there is the raging discourse that China is the new exploiter in Africa and the Third World. In a discussion on whether China is the new imperialist in Africa, Stephen Marks stated in *Pambazuka News*,

> It would be wrong to suggest that China's impact only raises problems, or is merely a re-run of past imperialisms. The fact that Western corporations and government now face competition can give African states more room for manoeuvre, and an alternative to accepting the dictates of the IMF. Naturally, NGOs, human rights campaigners and trade unionists have concentrated on cases where this room for manoeuvre has been exploited by repressive regimes seeking to avoid pressure exerted on Western governments to impose some minimal human rights or environmental conditions. But that does not mean that the 'Chinese option' could not also be exploited to widen the room for all African states, not only those abusing human rights (Marks 2006).[14]

Our chapter started from the proposition that transformations take millennia. This is a different starting point from those who would want to make definitive statements on the basis of the relationships between China and the rest of the Third World in the last twenty years. When asked in the 1960s what he thought of the French Revolution, the former Chinese prime pinister, Chou En-lai, replied: 'It is far too early to say', in recognition that social revolution and transformation from one mode of production to the next is a process.

This process of democratization dictates that initiatives for new financial relations in the form of currency swaps or new financial arrangements cannot build solidarity within the framework of the Bretton Woods thinking about depoliticization. While supporting the new initiatives of the ASEAN financial arrangements, I would like to underline the argument that

> Development cannot be reduced to its apparently major economic dimension – the growth of GNP and the expansion of markets (both exports and internal markets) – even when it takes into consideration the 'social' dimensions (degrees

of inequality in the distribution of income, access to public services like education and health). 'Development' is an overall process that involves the definition of political objectives and how they are articulated: democratization of society and emancipation of individuals, affirmation of the power and autonomy of the nation in the world system (Amin 2011b: 131).

It was this conception of solidarity and development that was articulated at Bandung. One can now see that after fifty years of dictatorship, societies such as Indonesia have been recovering their nerve and have associated themselves with the need for national control over resources. Many societies in Asia such as Malaysia, Korea and Vietnam have worked hard to transform (through education of the people) their human capital base during the past decades. These societies are now positioning themselves to utilize greater amounts of technology as reflected in recent investments by multinational corporations in such areas of microchips (Intel) and the aerospace sector. In a sense, state-led education for transformation is now viewed by global capital as 'high tech/ skilled' in the same way Cuba's society in areas like biotechnology is viewed by global capital. China is now teetering between the building of the internal capacity to end the low wage economy and the Confucius type ethos that seeks to entrench old hierarchies.

The multidimensional crisis in Western Europe has clarified to the peoples of the world that even when countries prompt sufficient domestic transformation processes which attract the attention of global capital, the process of transformation is endangered if there is dependence on the financial oligarchs of the West. This has been the concrete experience of Ireland. This was a country that implemented processes of structural transformation and attracted the attention of global capital. Yet, because this process was left to the vagaries of the 'financial markets', the processes of domestic transformation have now come to haunt the Irish as they are faced with the same austerity measures that are being deployed against European workers. The failure of Ireland's society to learn the lessons which Asia learned from their 1997 crisis is proving to be very costly for the people of Ireland and other societies that believed that European capitalism could grow forever.

From the experiences and lessons of the past fifty years it can now be understood that the initial engagement of Nehru and Chou En-lai offered lessons in cooperation that need to be revisited in order to study how to end the militarism that makes a mockery of the Bandung plans for peaceful co-existence. From these contexts, one can ask and answer the question about what forms of Afro-Asian, Latin American and African cooperation can be created which would help societies to navigate global capital forces in ways which would enable processes of domestic structural transformation. The same boldness and audacity that was associated with the call for the

New International Economic Order can now be engaged with the concrete experience of the new boldness with the currency swaps and the BRICS banks. Africans will be forced to engage in new discussions of an African Monetary Union as the collapse of the dollar and the euro force alternatives on the world. Some answers to the alternatives have been generated since the period of the Lagos Plan of Action in 1980. Now it is possible to frame the future paths of the unity of the peoples of Africa in response to the question: what should not be done?

The peoples of Egypt have given one answer and the present revolutionary process in Africa will impact transformations in all parts of the world.

Notes

1. For the amounts held by the major holders of US Treasury Securities see 'Major Foreign Holders of Treasury Securities', Department of the Treasury/Federal Reserve Board, April 2012, http://www.treasury.gov/resource-center/data-chart-center/tic/Documents/mfh.txt. China's foreign exchange reserves increased by US$197.4 billion in the first three months of 2012 to US$ 3.04 trillion by the end of March.
2. Essentially, a currency swap is a transaction between two nations to exchange the interest and principal payments on loans issued by two different nations. The two countries gain access to foreign exchange reserves. This limits the nations exposure to exchange rate fluctuations because they can pay back the liability associated with its currency instead of in dollars.
3. For an account of the anti-communist speeches that preceded the speech by Chou En-lai, see Jack (1955).
4. See Samir Amin's interview with Herrera (2005).
5. For a bibliographic essay on the writings on the New International Economic Order see Hoskins (1981)
6. See J. Nehru's speech in, *The Conference of Heads of States or Government of Non-Aligned Countries: Belgrade September 1-6, 1961*, Belgrade, pp. 107-17.
7. For one study of the non-aligned movement from the point of view of the US establishment see Jackson (1987).
8. See Samir Amin's interview with Herrera (2005).
9. For an analysis of the thinking behind Greenspan and the neoliberal doctrines see Johnson and Kwak (2010).
10. For an analysis of the Japanese project of depoliticaization see Miyagi (2008).
11. According to the *Washington Post*, there were 157,558 Chinese students in the United States in the academic year 2010-11. The number of students from China makes up 22 per cent of all international students. (This group grew 23 per cent in one year for all Chinese students and 43 per cent for undergraduates.) Other popular countries of origin are: India with 103,895 students, South Korea with 73,351 and Canada with 27,546. See Johnson (2011).
12. According to Prashad (2013), the global South is a term that properly refers not to geographical space but to a concatenation of protests against neoliberalism.

13. See the homepage of the South South Peoples Solidarity Forum: http://www.south-solidarity.org/. Also available is the final declaration of this South South Solidar-ity Forum, http://www.southsolidarityforum.org/documents/homepage/publication01.pdf.
14. See also Brautigam (2009) and Horace Campbell (2008).

References

Addo, H., ed.,1984, *Transforming the World Economy?: Nine Critical Essays on the New In-terna- tional Economic Order,* Kent (UK): United Nations University and Hodder and Stoughton. Afro-Asian Peoples' Solidarity Organisation, 2013, 'The 40th Anniver-sary of the Found- ing'. Available at: http://aapsorg.org/ar/archive-en/68-information/documents/390-the-40th-anniversary-of-the-founding-of-the-aapso-experiences-and-future-perspectives.
Alessi, C. and Hanson, S., 2012, 'Expanding China-Africa Oil Ties', Council on Foreign Relations'. Available at: http://www.cfr.org/china/expanding-china-africa-oil-ties/p9557.
Amin, S. n.d. 'Creating Another World: Agenda for Action'. Available at: http://www.southsolidarityforum.org/index.php?option=com_content&view=article&id=63:cr eating-an- other-world-agendas-for-action.
Amin, S., 2004, *The Liberal Virus: Permanent War and the Americanization of the World,* New York: Monthly Review Press.
Amin, S., 2005, 'China, Market Socialism, and U.S. Hegemony', *Review* (Fernand Braudel Center) 28 (3): 259–79.
Amin, S., 2010, 'Capitalism in Crisis: An Obsolete System', *Pambazuka* News. http:// pam- bazuka.org/en/category/features/69276.
Amin, S., 2011a, 'Audacity, More Audacity', *Pambazuka News.* http://pambazuka.org/en/category/features/78392.
Amin, S., 2011b, *Ending the Crisis of Capitalism or Ending Capitalism?,* Oxford: Pambazuka Press.
Amin, S., 2011c, 'The South Challenges Globalization', *Pambazuka News.* http://www.pambazuka.org/en/category/features/81307.
Balfour, F., 2011, 'China's Millionaires Leap Past 1 Million on Growth, Savings', *Bloomb-erg News.* http://www.bloomberg.com/news/2011-05-31/china-s-millionaires-jump-past-one-million-on-savings-growth.html.
BBC *News,* 2011, 'China and Japan plan Direct Currency Exchange Agreement'. http://www.bbc.co.uk/news/business-16330574. .
Bergsten, C. F., et al., 2008, *China's Rise: Challenges and Opportunities,* Washington, DC: Pe-terson Institute for International Economics.
Booker, S., 'Africa's Debt: Who Owes Whom?', Foreign Policy Forum. http://www. ip-oaa.com/africas_debt_who_owes_whom.htm.
Bradford, T., 2008, *The Solar Revolution: The Economic Transformation of the Global Energy Industry,* Cambridge, MA: MIT Press.
Brautigam, D., 2009, *The Dragon's Gift: The Real Story of China in Africa,* New York: Oxford University Press.

Campbell, H. and Chaulia, S., 2009, 'Unequal Equals: Angola and China', *World Affairs* 13 (1): 44–83.

Campbell, H. and Stein, H., 1989, *Tanzania and the IMF: The Dynamics of Liberalization*, Boulder, Colorado: Westview Press.

Campbell, H., 2008, 'China in Africa: Challenging US Global Hegemony', *Third World Quarterly* 29 (1): 89–105.

Campbell, H., 2012, 'Africa and the BRICS Formation: What Kind of Development?', *Pambazuka News*. http://pambazuka.org/en/category/features/81471 .

Campbell, H., 2013, *Global NATO and the Catastrophic Failure in Libya: Lessons in the Forging of African Unity*, New York: Monthly Review Press.

Chang, H., 2002, *Kicking Away the Ladder : Development Strategy in Historical Perspective*, London: Anthem Press.

Chang, H., 2010, 23 *Things They Don't Tell You About Capitalism*, New York: Bloomsbury Press.

Chinability, 2011, 'China's Foreign Exchange Reserves, 1977-2011'. Available at: http://www.china- bility.com/Reserves.htm.

Coker, C., 1979, 'The United States and National Liberation in Southern Africa', *African Affairs* 78 (312): 319–30.

Dotson, J., 'The Confucian Revival in the Propaganda Narratives of the Chinese Government', *U.S.-China Economic and Security Review Commission Staff Research Report*. http://origin.www.uscc.gov/sites/default/files/Research/Confucian_Revival_Paper.pdf.

Fenby, J., 2012, *Tiger Head, Snake Tails: China Today, How it Got There and Where it is Heading*, New York: Simon and Schuster.

Ferguson, C., 2012, *Predator Nation: Corporate Criminals. Political Corruption and the Hijacking of America*, New York: Random House.

Hart, M., 2012, 'Ambiguity and Illusion in China's Economic Transformation: Issues for Canadian Policy Makers and Business Leaders', *Canadian Council of Chief Executives*. http://www.ceocouncil.ca/wp-content/uploads/2012/02/Ambiguity-and-Illusion-in-China-Michael-Hart-February-2012.pdf.

Herrera, Rémy, 2005, 'Fifty Years After the Bandung Conference: Towards A Revival of the Solidarity Between the Peoples of the South', *Inter-Asia Cultural Studies* 6 (4).

Hoskins, L. A., 1981, 'The New International Economic Order: A Bibliographic Essay', *Third World Quarterly* 3 (3): 506–27.

Hutton, W.H., 2007, *The Writing on the Wall: China and the West in the 21st Century*, London: Little Brown.

Jack, H., 1955, *Bandung: An on the Spot Description of the Asia –African Conference, Bandung, Indonesia*, 1955, Chicago: Towards Freedom Pamphlet.

Jackson, R. L., 1987, *The Non-aligned Movement, the UN and the Superpowers*, Westport, Connecticut: Praeger.

Jacques, M., 2012, 'Why Do We Continue to Ignore China's Rise? Arrogance', *The Guardian*. http://www.guardian.co.uk/world/2012/mar/25/china-rise-ignorance .

Jacques, M., 2009, *When China Rules the World: The Rise of the Middle Kingdom and the End of the Western World*, New York: Penguin Press.

Johnson, Jenna, 2011, 'Chinese Students Enroll in Record Numbers at U.S. Colleges', *Wash- ington Post*, 14 November 14.

Johnson, S. and Kwak, J., 2010, 13 Bankers: The Wall Street Takeover and the Next Financial Meltdown, New York: Pantheon Books.

Jubilee USA, n.d 'Why Drop the Debt?'. http://www.jubileeusa.org/truth-about-debt/why-drop-the-debt.html.

Khor, M., 2011, 'China Still A Developing Country' China Daily. http://www.chinadaily.com.cn/opinion/2011-11/25/content_14159547.htm.

Kissinger, H., 2011, On China, New York: Penguin Press.

Leeb, S., 2011, Red Alert: How China's Growing Prosperity Threatens the American Way of Life, New York: Business Plus.

Leonhardt, D., 2008, 'Greenspan's Mea Culpa', New York Times. http://economix.blogs.nytimes.com/2008/10/23/greenspans-mea-culpa/, 23 October.

Lockwood, E., 1974, 'National Security Study Memorandum 39 and the Future of United States Policy toward Southern Africa', Issue: A Journal of Opinion 4 (3): 63–72.

Mamdani, M., 2002, 'Good Muslims, Bad Muslim, An African Perspective', American Anthropologist,104 (3): 766–75.

Manji, F. and Ekine, S., 2011, African Awakening: Emerging Revolutions, Oxford: Pambazuka Press.

Marks, S., 2006, 'China in Africa: The New Imperialism?', Pambazuka News. http://www.pambazuka.org/en/category/courses/32432.

McGregor, R., 2010, The Party: The Secret World of China's Communist Rulers, New York: Harper Collins.

Mitchell, Don, 2003, The Right to the City: Social Justice and the Fight for Public Space, The New York: Guilford Press.

Miyagi, T., 2008, 'Looking Beyond Cold War History in Asia', The Tokyo Foundation. Available at: http://www.tokyofoundation.org/en/articles/2008/foreign-and-security-policy/ looking-beyond-cold-war-history-in-asia.

Mohanty, M., 2005, 'Asian Cooperation and Visions of Panchsheel and Bandung', En: Seminaro Internacional REG GEN: Alternativas Globalizacao (8-13 October), Rio de Janeiro, Brazil. http://bibliotecavirtual.clacso.org.ar/ar/libros/reggen/pp04.pdf.

Navarro, P. and Autry, G., 2011, Death by China: Confronting the Dragon – A Global Call to Action, Upper Saddle River, New Jersey: Pearson Prentice Hall.

Peoples Republic of China White Paper, 2011, 'China's Policies and Actions for Address- ing Climate Change,' Information Office of the State Council, The People's Repub- lic of China. Available at: http://www.gov.cn/english/official/2011-11/22/content_2000272. htm.

Prashad, V., 2007, The Darker Nations: A Peoples History of the Third World, New York: Free Press.

Prashad, V., 2013, The Poorer Nations: A Possible History of the Global South, New York: Verso Books.

Qureshi, L., 2008, Nixon, Kissinger, and Allende: U.S. Involvement in the 1973 Coup in Chile, New York: Lexington Books.

Scheer, H., 2006, Solar Manifesto, New York: Routledge.

Schiller, H. M., 1992, Mass Communication and the US Empire, Boulder Colorado: Westview Press.

Scott, P. D., 1985, 'The United States and the Overthrow of Sukarno, 1965-1967', Pacific Affairs, 58 (2): 239–64.

Shah, A., 2010, 'Poverty Around the World', *Global Issues*. http://www.globalissues. org/ article/4/poverty-around-the-world#WorldBanksPovertyEstimatesRevised.

Singham, A.W., ed., 1977, *The Nonaligned Movement in World Politics*, Westport, Connecticut: Lawrence Hill & Co.

Srikant, D., 1984, *India and the Third World: Altruism or Hegemony*, London: Zed Books. Subramanian, A., 2011a, *Eclipse: Living in the Shadow of China's Economic Dominance*, Washington, DC: Institute of International Economics.

Subramanian, A., 2011b, 'Why China Should Bail out Europe', New York Times. http:// www.nytimes.com/2011/10/28/opinion/europe-should-look-to-china-for-financial-help.html.

Surkano, A., 1960, 'To Build the World Anew: An Address by President Sukarno of the Republic of Indonesia at the Fifteenth General Assembly of the United Nations, Friday Afternoon, September 30, 1960'. http://kemlu.go.id/Books/Buku%20 kompilasi%20statement%20UNGA%201951%20-%2012010%20minus%20 cover. pdf.

Thomas, C., 1976, *Dependence and Transformation: The Economics of the Transition to Socialism*, New York: Monthly Review Press.

Wenping, H., 2011, 'More Soft Power Needed in Africa', China Daily. http://www.chinadaily.com.cn/cndy/2012-02/27/content_14696733.htm. 27 February.

Wu, G., 2010, 'Dilemmas of Scientific Development', *Asian Survey* 51 (1):.18–32.

13

The Global Financial
and Economic Crisis and the South:
What Have We Learned and Where Do We
Go from Here?

Theresa Moyo

Introduction

When the Council for the Development of Social Science Research in Africa (CODESRIA) convened an international conference in order to debate and analyse the impact of the global financial and economic crisis on the countries of the South, its purpose was to open some space for scholars from that region to share real experiences from their respective countries. The main objective of the conference was to discuss the nature of the crisis, its fundamental causes, its effects and impact of the different countries of the South. Critically, it was to analyse the ideological, policy and strategic implications of the crisis with respect to how these countries could and should approach their own development in the era of globalization which has accentuated their vulnerabilities to external shocks and crises. In terms of coverage, the studies looked at regional, national and sectoral perspectives. The experiences of Latin America and the Caribbean as a region and also in some specific countries were examined. A comparative study on Mexico and South Korea attempted to contrast the impact of the crisis on two countries with some similar characteristic features but coming from two different regions. Specific country experiences were presented, for example, the case of the Phillipines, Tajikistan, Afghanistan and Pakistan. From Africa, case studies were presented on specific sectors which had been worst affected by the crisis, for example, the analysis of African stock markets, the impact of the crisis on the timber industry in Gabon, Cameroon and Congo-Brazzaville and also the case of the automotive, textile and clothing, and mining sectors in South Africa. The other studies explored alternative approaches which could assist countries of the South to reduce their vulnerabilities in the future. The detailed study on China emphasized the opportunity offered by South-South cooperation as a strategy to reduce dependence on primary commodities and on Northern markets. The chapter on Public-Private Partnerships (PPPs) in India was an attempt to demonstrate that markets alone or governments alone are not adequate to deal with the complexity of development. Rather, it called for strengthening of the role of both institutions in advancing a win-win situation because of the relative attributes of both.

Methodologically, with the exception of the empirical study of African stock markets, presented by Terfa Abraham, most of the studies were theoretical papers which were based on secondary data from the respective regions, countries or sectors.

The purpose of this chapter therefore is to summarize the key issues and debates emerging from the various studies. These include: the nature of and the root causes of the crisis and its effects on the different regions and economies of the South; the transmission channels and mechanisms by which the crisis affected them and, finally, the implications in terms of strategies and policies which the South should pursue in future in order to substantially reduce their risk and vulnerability to external shocks.

Conclusion

The overwhelming evidence from all the regional and country-level studies presented in this volume shows that the global and financial crisis definitely had an effect on the economies of Latin America and the Caribbean, Africa and Asia. However, most of the authors indicated that the crisis was less severe as compared to previous crises. This is confirmed by Ocampo (2009:1) who also argues that although the crisis hit the region hard, it was less severe compared to previous episodes.

There is clear agreement that the crisis was sparked off by the collapse of the housing bond market in the United States and Europe and that, subsequently, the contagion effect then spread out to countries of the South particularly in the case of those that were more integrated in the economies of the North. The ultimate result of the crisis was a global recession marked by declining import demand from the world's leading economies where the crisis originated. In Africa, Latin America and the Caribbean, there was a slowdown in economic activity as commodity prices declined, particularly primary commodities. All this had negative effects on terms of trade for commodity exporters, export earnings and the external current account, fiscal revenues and household incomes. Whereas the popular view perceives the collapse of the US bond market as the root cause of the crisis which then affected the rest of the world through various channels, more critical perspectives in this volume attribute the crisis to structural factors. As argued by Bértrain and Campbell, for example, the crisis was a manifestation of the instability of the capitalist system, a reminder that in fact, this may not be last of such phenomena as long as the capitalist mode of accumulation continues to be the dominant ideological and political paradigm which dictates how economies should operate. Although there is general agreement that it was a global crisis, questions are raised about the 'wholesale' labelling of what occured, as a 'global' crisis. Labelling the crisis as 'global' seems to make it a problem which originated globally and in which all countries are equally to blame whereas in fact, the United States was actually solely responsible. In the quest for lasting solutions, correct identification of the origins of the crisis is crucial. Other authors focus more on the effects of the crisis rather than on the debate on its globality or non-globality.

A running thread across most of the studies is a serious critique of neo-liberal policies which for decades have pushed for policies for the state to roll back its intervention in the economy. This was responsible for the deterioration in the regulation and supervision of the financial system which ultimately led to the crisis in the US bond market.

The volume also emphasizes the structural problems faced by some developing countries in Africa, arguing that the dominance of commodities in their exports and the continued dependence on Northern markets exacerbated their risks and vulnerability to external shocks.

The evidence presented also examines the transmission processes by which the crisis affected economies across the world. The channels were both financial as well as real. Financial channels included effects on banking and financial systems, stock markets, foreign direct investment flows, interest rates and exchange rates. It also includes changes in commodity prices, fiscal revenues and household incomes. Real channels included impact on production of goods and services, export and imports or trade, decline in commodity prices, terms of trade deterioration, job losses or retrenchments. Emerging markets with well-developed financial systems were initially mostly affected by cross-border financial linkages through capital flows, stock market investors, and exchange rates. In financially less-developed countries the growth and trade effects dominated, with lags. Transmission through real channels was clearly demonstrated in the studies on the timber industry in Cameroon, Gabon and Congo-Brazzaville and also the automotive, textile and clothing, and mining industries of South Africa. In all these countries, production, exports, and export earnings were negatively affected due to the collapse of demand in the North. Job losses were also recorded in these countries. In some Latin American countries, Africa and the Philippines, the crisis adversely affected financial and capital markets. Equity prices fell in many parts of Latin America as hedge funds and other institutional investors cashed out of investments in emerging markets. In parts of Africa, stock markets became volatile, although impact varied among countries. In Tajikistan, Afghanistan and Pakistan, the crisis further destabilized a region which was already stressed with conflict. In South Africa, the impact was more pronounced in the real than financial sector. This is shown in the study of the automobile, textile and clothing, and mining sectors in South Africa. Production volumes, sales, exports volumes and earnings, government revenues and employment levels were in all cases negatively affected. In the study on Central Africa, it was shown how the impact was greater in the real sector, specifically, the timber industry in Congo-Brazzaville, Cameroon and Gabon, all of which are major timber producers and exporters. As a result of falling commodity prices in the face of falling consumer demand in Europe and the US (their main export destination), there was a decline in exports, tax revenues and rising job losses. Some sectors, however, proved to be resilient. The study on the mobile telecommunications sector in Zimbabwe showed that the sector was not significantly affected. On the contrary, it actually played an important role in assisting other sectors to weather the effects of the crisis. That study demonstrated how the use of telecommunication technology to deploy value-adding solutions contributed to improved performance in other sectors and thus enabled them to cope with the shocks.

Evidence presented in this volume suggests that the magnitude or extent of impact varied from country to country and from region to region. A number of factors explain those variations: the degree or extent of integration of a country's economy with the economies of the US and Europe. Countries with a relatively larger share of exports to the Northern countries, where the crisis started, were more adversely affected than those with a smaller share or those whose export markets were predominantly in East Asia. Those countries which had more diversified destinations (such as Republic of Korea (ROK), for example, whose export base largely consisted of economies in East Asia and China, regions which were less directly affected by the crisis), were less adversely affected than, for example, Mexico and other Latin American and Caribbean economies whose export markets were predominantly the United States of America. The decline in the production and export performance of the automobile and mining sectors in South Africa was also due to the fall in consumer demand in the Northern countries since South Africa is more integrated into European markets than the rest of Africa.

The composition of exports was another key factor. Those economies which had a relatively larger share of manufactured exports as compared to commodities were also less affected. This explains why the ROK was less affected than Mexico. It also explains variations in impact among the economies of Latin America and the Caribbean. It was also shown in the case of South Africa's textile clothing and mining sectors, where commodity sectors were more adversely affected as demand in Europe and the US declined. Major oil exporters like Venezuela and Mexico were buffered as prices rose through the early part of 2008. The oil price slump during the second half of the year had the reverse effect. Brazil, Argentina, and Ecuador were beset, to a lesser degree, by similar problems.

As demonstrated by the empirical study on the crisis and African stock exchanges, exposure to the international financial system was a key determining factor of vulnerability. Thus, those exchanges which were more integrated into the US and UK financial systems were more adversely affected than the less integrated.

The state's capacity to use appropriate policy tools to cushion itself against external shocks also explained variations in impact among regions and countries. The comparative study of Mexico and the Republic of Korea demonstrated that while in Mexico, the pace of the response was slow with more limited resources allocated for that purpose, the state in the ROK was swifter in response, using both fiscal and monetary measures and also it allocated more financial resources into that effort. Consequently, the ROK was less negatively affected than Mexico. Other experiences from Latin America and the Caribbean were also used to show the importance of state capacity to respond. A related factor was the strength of institutions and regulatory framework whereby those countries with more regulated and prudentially managed economies were less vulnerable than those where controls were less.

The state of the economy prior to the onset of the crisis also played a role in determining the extent of vulnerability. It was shown that in Latin America, some of the countries were able to reduce the effects because of improvements in their external balance sheets in the period preceeding the event. Their absorption of large capital inflows when they experienced booms contributed to a healthier foreign reserve situation. This enhanced their capacity to manouvre. However, in other instances, the magnitude of trade shocks outweighed those advantages. In the case of Africa, according to the African Development Bank (2010:1), due to prudent macroeconomic policies and reforms, Africa entered the global crisis on a stronger footing than during past recessions. Some countries were therefore able to implement stimulus packages. However, many low-income and especially fragile and post-conflict countries were not in a position to adopt counter-cyclical measures when the crisis hit.

The nature of the policy responses that were implemented by states were critical in reducing the damage caused by the shocks. Evidence showed that in the case of Latin America, states such as Brazil, Argentina and Venezuela which had more interventionist approaches, were able to move more swiftly to implement countercyclical policies to offset the effects of the crisis. This was also the case with South Africa. On the contrary, Mexico's policy response in the form of pro-cyclical fiscal policies tended to worsen rather than ameliorate the effects. The ROK implemented countercyclical fiscal and monetary policies more rapidly and managed to offset some of the damage.

With respect to actual responses to the crisis, these also differed from country to country depending on their capacity, their resource base and economic policy orientation. Typical responses to counter the crisis included, but were not limited to: (i) fiscal stimulus packages; (ii) expansionary monetary policies; (iii) targeted sectoral assistance; (iv) new regulations in the banking sector; and in some instances social measures such as wage increases, to stimulate aggregate demand. Other measures aimed at improving the business environment and alleviating supply-side bottlenecks.

An important message emerging from the entire book is that, in the era of globalization, integration into the world economy still has many risks for economies of the South. That is more so for those which continue to depend heavily on commodity exports and also those whose export destinations are concentrated in the economies of the North. There are inherent dangers in globalization and, as has been emphasized in various other fora, it is urgent that states in the South develop and implement more comprehensive strategies which seek to reduce the vulnerability of their economies to external shocks or crises.

Recommendations

In making our recommendations, we recognize that the debate around causes and effects of the global financial and economic crisis is actually not a new one. For years now, serious questions have been raised about the fallacy of the notion of 'self-regulating markets'. Scholars such as Amin (2009) have repeatedly questioned the model of capitalist accumulation and emphasized how countries of the South are at risk when they integrate themselves to the global trading and financial system despite the asymmetrical power relations between them and countries of the North.

In response to the issues raised in the volume, therefore, we make a number of recommendations, more to emphasize the urgency for countries of the South to implement the many proposed strategies which have been made, and some of which they have already committed themselves to over the years. We make the following key recommendations:

Recognizing that many economies in Latin America, the Caribbean, Africa and Asia are still vulnerable to external shocks, it will be critical for them to intensify their efforts to challenge an asymmetrical global trading and financial system in which they have little voice in decision-making and control. They need to pursue the agenda for a more equitable and fairer international trading and financial architecture. Some of the policy frameworks which they have adopted over the years, policies have been dictated by dominant institutions such as the Bretton Woods institutions which have been instrumental in promoting the fallacy of 'self-regulating markets' and called for a reduction of state intervention in the form of regulation of economies. It is significant to quote Jean Feyder, president of the board of the United Nations Commission on Trade and Development (UNCTAD) who raised some of the contradictions between the North and South and then recommended as follows:

> In the North, the state has played a major role in overcoming the financial crisis.
>
> In the South, it should be a key player in the financing of productive capacities, starting with industrialisation and the protection of infant industries (Agazzi 2010).

The crisis has demonstrated clearly that the state has an important role in regulating markets. It has also highlighted the relevance of Keynesian-type countercyclical macroeconomic policies and that, during recessions, governments should use them and do so adequately and timeously. It has also been demonstrated, though, that important as they are, countercyclical policy interventions at best are short-term measures which unfortunately will not resolve the root causes behind the vulnerabilities to external crisis of countries of the South. Samir Amin (2009: 8) considers such strategies as tantamount to efforts to 're-establish capitalism'. He is also critical of the reforms which have been touted by international institutions calling for 'reform of the financial sector' as 'grand words to evade the real questions…. He adds that 'the restoration of the system, which is not impossible, will solve no problems, but rather aggravate them'.

It is also out of the realization of the short-term nature of countercyclical policies that this volume also calls for countries of the South to carry out more fundamental structural reforms of their economies. Countries of the South have to increase their resilience through implementing structural reforms to diversify their economies. They should pursue with greater vigour, strategies to promote industrialization and development of their manufacturing sectors. Thus, the agenda for industrialization should be implemented in order to transform the structure of their economies from primary commodity production and exports towards manufactured exports. Transformation also calls for prioritization of creating and broadening of domestic markets so that even in the face of volatile external markets, domestic demand helps to protect the economies from externally-induced crises. The African Development Bank (2010:6) calls on African economies, for example, to diversify risks and achieve broad-based growth, by supplementing their export orientation with strategies to promote domestic markets through public investment, promotion of SMEs catering to local markets, and regional integration.

The crisis has also demonstrated the vulnerability which arises due to the politics of inequality and exclusion of a large segment of the population from participation in the economy of the country. The experience of South Africa which is still today a highly unequal society, where millions of black people do not have access to economic resources because land reform has been very slow, unemployment is very high and the economy continues to be dominated by a minority class of local and foreign capital. While acknowledging the efforts that the government has made to address these challenges, much more has to be done in order to redistribute wealth.

Diversification of export markets will enable economies of the South to cope with any external crises. Increasing cooperation with other economies of the South such as Asia will contribute to diversification and better risk management.

The role of China in Latin America, Africa and the Caribbean has come under closer scrutiny once again. While some countries have definitely benefited from trade and other cooperation with China, serious questions have been raised with respect to the political agenda of China and in particular, with regard to the nature of the cooperation which it is promoting. This has been most clearly articulated in the studies from Latin America and the Caribbean where China's role appears to be widely perceived as 'an exploitative, dependency neo-extractive model' (Pablo Nacht) which may perpetuate or replicate the traditional North-South model which many countries of the South have strongly criticized. The controversy around the role of China in relation to countries of the South calls for more serious debates and engagement in order to define the kind of model which leads to a win-win situation for both parties. This must be on the development agenda of South-South cooperation.

The capacity of states to respond both timeously and adequately to changes in global market conditions has to be strengthened through deliberate actions. Part of that capacity includes a shift in mindset from more conservative or orthodox approaches to economic management towards more acceptance of a much wider role for the state on matters such as the regulation and supervision of financial markets, use of countercyclical monetary and fiscal policies in line with the Keynesian macroeconomic framework.

Adequate provision for social protection should be an integral part of countercyclical policies. In many countries, part of the effects of the crisis was realised through job losses as companies cut down production and export volumes and sales. Rescue packages were not always adequate to meet those needs.

Deepening regional integration can also contribute towards reducing risks and vulnerability.

Governments in Latin America, the Caribbean, Asia and Africa, should also consider pursuing more seriously, the agenda of South-South cooperation in the context of trade, foreign direct investment, technology transfers, among others. This is not a call necessarily for them to shift from trading with countries in the North but to pursue a trading strategy which diversifies their risk profiles and vulnerability. Writing about harnessing new partnerships and natural resources, the African Development Bank (2010) argues that:

> As China has been increasing sophistication of its production and moving up the technology ladder, it has created space for other countries in the lower value-added manufacturing. It has been recognized that this trend has created an opportunity for Africa to develop its underperforming manufacturing sector.

Thus it encourages economies to pursue labour-intensive industrialization strategies in order to increase employment and household incomes. The ADB, however, points out that in order to attract investment in labour-intensive manufacturing, African economies need to pursue structural reforms to make their economies more attractive to investors, including those from China and other new trading partners.

References

Agazzi, I., 2010, 'Markets Can't Self-regulate: State Should Step-In', in UNCTAD-Inter Press Service, May 12.

African Development Bank, 2009a, *Impact of the Financial Crisis on African Economies – An Interim Assessment*, Policy Briefs on the Financial Crisis, No. 1.

African Development Bank, 2010, 'Containing the Impact of the Global Crisis and Paving the Way To Recovery in Africa', Meeting of the Committee of Finance Ministers and Central Bank Governors. Cape Town, 21 February.

Amin, S., 2009, 'Emerging from the Crisis of Capitalism'. http://www.e-joussour.net/en/node/3244.

Greenberg, S., 2004, 'Post-apartheid Development, Landlessness and the Reproduction of Exclusion in South Africa', *Centre for Civil Society Research Report No. 17*.

International Monetary Fund (IMF), 2009, *Impact of the Global Financial Crisis on Sub-Saharan-Africa*. http://www.imf.org/external/pubs/ft/books/2009/afrglobfin/ssaglobal fin.pdf.

International Monetary Fund, 2010, *Impact of the Global Financial Crisis on Sub-Saharan Africa*, IMF.

Ocampo, J.A., 2009, 'Latin America and the Global Financial Crisis', in *The Global Financial Crisis* (special issue), Cambridge Journal of Economics 33 (4): 703–24.

Third World Network, 2009, 'The Global Financial Crisis and Growing Discontent in Africa', No. 231/232.

United Nations (UN) ECA and African Union Commission, 2009b, *The Global Crisis: Impact, Responses and Way Forward*, Proceedings of Meeting of the Committee of Experts of the 2nd Joint Annual Meetings of the AU Conference of Ministers of Economy and Finance and ECA Conference of Ministers of Finance, Planning and Economic Development. Cairo, Egypt, 2-5 June.

United Nations University, 2009a, *Policy Responses to the GlobalEconomic Crisis in Africa*, Policy Brief No. 3. Available at: www.unu.edu.

Weeks, J., 2009, The Global Financial and Economic Crisis and Countercyclical Fiscal Policy, Dis- cussion Paper 26/09, School of Oriental and African Studies, University of London.

Printed in the United States
By Bookmasters

Printed in the United States
By Bookmasters